Dagmar

P9-DVE-564

FEB, 2000

Solomon Islands

Mark Honan
David Harcombe

◁◯▷ ◁◯▷ ◁◯▷ ◁◯▷ ◁◯▷ ◁◯▷ ◁◯▷ ◁◯▷ ◁◯▷

Solomon Islands

3rd edition

Published by
Lonely Planet Publications
Head Office: PO Box 617, Hawthorn, Vic 3122, Australia
Branches: 155 Filbert St, Suite 251, Oakland, CA 94607, USA
10 Barley Mow Passage, Chiswick, London W4 4PH, UK
71 bis rue du Cardinal Lemoine, 75005 Paris, France

Printed by
Colorcraft Ltd, Hong Kong

Photographs by
Simon Foale, Mark Honan, Holger Leue

Front cover: Children fishing off Sandfly Island, Nggela Islands (Simon Foale)

First Published
November 1988

This Edition
August 1997

Although the authors and publisher have tried to make the information as accurate as possible, they accept no responsibility for any loss, injury or inconvenience sustained by any person using this book.

National Library of Australia Cataloguing in Publication Data

Honan, Mark.
Solomon Islands.

3rd. ed.
Includes index.
ISBN 0 86442 405 1.

1. Solomon Islands – Guidebooks. I. Harcombe, David.
Solomon Islands, a travel survival kit. 2nd ed. II.Title.
III. Title: Solomon Islands, a travel survival kit. 2nd ed.

919.59304

text & maps © Lonely Planet 1997
photos © photographers as indicated 1997

All rights reserved. No part of this publication may be reproduced, stored in a retrieval system or transmitted in any form by any means, electronic, mechanical, photocopying, recording or otherwise, except brief extracts for the purpose of review, without the written permission of the publisher and copyright owner.

Mark Honan

After a university degree in philosophy opened up a glittering career as an office clerk, Mark soon decided that there was more to life than form-filling and data-entry. He set off on a two-year trip around the world, armed with a backpack and a vague intent to sell travel stories and pictures upon his return to England. Astonishingly, this inchoate plan succeeded and Mark became the travel correspondent for a London-based magazine. He toured Europe in a campervan, mailing back articles to the magazine and gathering the experience that would later enable him to contribute to the 1st edition of Lonely Planet's *Western Europe*.

He has written LP's *Switzerland*, *Austria* and *Vienna* guides as well as contributing to *Central America* and two more editions of *Western Europe*. Although more than happy not to be a clerk any more, he finds, curiously, that life as a travel writer still entails a good deal of form-filling and data-entry.

David Harcombe

Born in England, David spent much of his early years reading about faraway places and peoples. This led him, after a politics and economics degree from Oxford, to work as a fundraiser for Oxfam, a large British-based overseas aid organisation. After brief visits to Eastern Europe and West Africa, he was lured eastwards through Asia to Australia. By now an avid fan of freedom and travel, he returned to Australia, after a spell in the Caribbean, Latin America and southern Africa, to live in the remote northwest, working among Aboriginal Australians. While there he became a sometime gold prospector and an amateur disc jockey on a community radio station. David is the author of the first two editions of *Solomon Islands* and author of the 1st edition of *Vanuatu*.

From Mark Honan

A volley of curses should be directed at the hit-and-run driver who hospitalised me five days before I was due to depart for my research trip. I managed to make my flight, and am indebted to Kate for her chauffeuring and tea-making while I recuperated during a stopover in Texas.

In Honiara, many US Peace Corps volunteers gave me useful insights and updates at the outset of my trip. Various Lata-based expats helped me get to grips with Temotu, but especially David and Sarah Arathoon, who also provided updates on Rennell and Bellona. Sean Dooley from Melbourne gave me information (via Indra Kilfoyle in LP's Melbourne office) on Malaita and the Russell Islands. Fiona and Stirling told me about volcano-climbing on Kolombangara.

Numerous Solomon Islanders were friendly, helpful and informative. Owen showed me round Kirakira. Moses and his family allowed me to experience village life at Kmagha, southern Isabel. Philip (of Solomons Village Stay) proved a solicitous host in Malaita. Hillary, the customs man at Tulagi, canoed me to Honiara when I was in danger of being stranded and missing my flight to Choiseul. Cedric, No 2 chief on Tikopia, provided me space in his home. The list could go on.

Thanks to Justine at GTS for her tips, assistance and sympathetic ear. Other people involved in the tourism industry who provided help beyond the call of their business interests include Keith and Denis at Tavanipupu Resort, Mia and Duane at the Gizo Hotel, and Danny and Kerrie at Adventure Sports in Gizo. Staff from Solomon Airlines were helpful, especially Steve Langhorn in the UK and Floyd Smith in Honiara. Sacha Pearson of LP's San Francisco office tracked down some US travel info for me, and Elspeth Wingham of World Heritage provided useful accommodation details.

Finally, thanks to all the LP readers who took the trouble to write in after reading the 2nd edition.

This Book

The 1st and 2nd editions of the *Solomon Islands* were researched and written by David Harcombe. Mark Honan updated this edition.

From the Publisher

This book was edited at the Lonely Planet office in Melbourne by Katie Cody, Brigitte Barta, Paul Harding and Liz Filleul. Katie and Brigitte proofread the text. Jenny Jones designed the book and drew the maps with help from Matt King, Jacqui Saunders and Tony Fankhauser. Jane Hart and Rachel Black drew the illustrations. Layout of the book was by Andrew Tudor. The cover was designed by Adam McCrow. This is the first LP Melbourne book produced using Quark Xpress, and the result of many hours of preparation, planning and troubleshooting by Andrew Tudor and Dan Levin. Any hiccups the guinea-pig production team experienced are valued for what they will teach future generations of LP editors and designers.

Thanks

Many thanks to the travellers who used the last edition and wrote to us with helpful hints, useful advice and interesting anecdotes:

Tonas Artzi, Maggie Bowes, Prof Stan Ford, Robert Garing, John & Jean Glenister, Ronald Grant, Vincent Hefter, Susan Hills, Craig & Jenny Jarrett, Kimberlee Lenander, Cyril Manning, Lin Padgham, Peter & Jeanne Pockel, Wendy Rayner, Dave & Jane Santos, Susan Sjoberg, John Small, Graham Walker

Warning & Request

Things change – prices go up, schedules change, good places go bad and bad places go bankrupt – nothing stays the same. So, if you find things better or worse, recently opened or long since closed, please tell us and help make the next edition even more accurate and useful.

We value all of the feedback we receive from travellers. Julie Young coordinates a small team who read and acknowledge every letter, postcard and email and ensure that every morsel of information finds its way to the appropriate authors, editors and publishers.

Everyone who writes to us will find their name in the next edition of the appropriate guide and will also receive a free subscription to our quarterly newsletter, *Planet Talk*. The very best contributions will be rewarded with a free Lonely Planet guide.

Excerpts from your correspondence may appear in updates (which we add to the end pages of reprints); new editions of this guide; in our newsletter, *Planet Talk*; or in the Postcards section of our web site – so please let us know if you don't want your letter published or your name acknowledged.

Contents

GLOSSARY

BOXED ASIDES

Map Index

Solomon Islands Provincial Boundaries p12
Air Routes - West of Honiara p81
Air Routes - East of Honiara p82
Index of all maps p269

Solomons Provinces:
Map Index

0   200   400 km

PAPUA NEW
GUINEA

Choiseul Island &
Province p175

Western Province p131

Isabel Province p182

Malaita Province p202

Central Province p119

Guadalcanal pp90-1

Makira/Ulawa Province p230

Rennell & Bellona
Province p192

Temotu Province p242

Map Legend

BOUNDARIES

International Boundary
Province Boundary

ROUTES

Walking Track
Cable Car or Chairlift
Ferry Route
Walking Tour

Major Road
Major Road - Unsealed
Minor Road
Minor Road - Unsealed
City Road
City Street

AREA FEATURES

Park, Gardens
Building
Pedestrian Mall
Market
Cemetery
Built-Up Area
Beach
Forest
Reef

HYDROGRAPHIC FEATURES

River, Creek
Intermittent River or Creek
Rapids, Waterfalls
Lake, Intermittent Lake

SYMBOLS

✪ CAPITAL	National Capital	✈	Airfield	❄ Lookout
◉ Capital	Provincial Capital	✈ Airport	♠ Monument
● City	City	⚓ Anchorage	▲ Mountain or Hill
● Town	Town	❸ Bank	)(Pass
● Village	Village	✕ Battle Site	➈ Petrol Station
		⚲ Beach	Planewreck
▪	Place to Stay	⬤ Bus Station	★ Police
⚲	Camping Ground	Canoeing	✉ Post Office
⚏	Caravan Park	Cave	Shipwreck
⌂	Hut or Chalet	⊞ Church	❖ Shopping Centre
⌂	Youth Hostel	Dive Site	◎ Spring
▼	Place to Eat	Embassy	☎ Telephone
▱	Cafe	✿ Gardens	❶ Tourist Information
⛾	Pub or Bar	⌐ Golf Course	Trail Head

Note: not all symbols displayed above appear in this book

Introduction

The Solomons is the third-largest archipelago in the South Pacific, comprising 992 islands. These range from large landmasses with rugged mountains and virgin forests, to tiny, low-lying coral atolls encircling stunning lagoons.

Yet the country is much more than its landscapes, though these are impressive enough. Snorkellers and divers can enjoy a peerless combination of copious fish life, colourful coral, and hundreds of war wrecks – remnants of some of the fiercest fighting in the Pacific in WWII.

One of the slogans used to market the country is 'islands adrift in time'. That's not some flight of fantasy – it really is like that. Most people live in small villages, clinging to a lifestyle that has barely changed for centuries. Traditional practices such as calling sharks and exchanging unwieldy *kastom* money can still be seen – as can sacred skull shrines, reminders of the days of cannibalism and head-hunting. Visiting these settlements is like peering back into the past.

The Solomons gets little more than 4000 tourists per year. If you ever wanted to get off the beaten track, this is the place. You could have a dozen beaches all to yourself. In places like Choiseul, Isabel and Makira you could find you're the only tourist in the whole province!

Of course, all this means that there isn't the tourism infrastructure of some other destinations. There are few restaurants and high-class hotels, and getting anywhere outside the main air and shipping routes can be a challenge. But the Solomon Islands offers a rare chance to uncover a pristine archipelago in its raw and natural state.

The people of a place make a trip and Solomon Islanders are some of the nicest you'll meet anywhere. People are always smiling and solicitous in the country they call the Happy Isles. You'll find a warm and genuine welcome wherever you go.

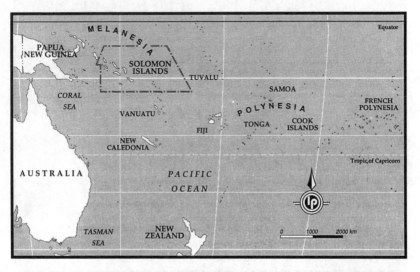

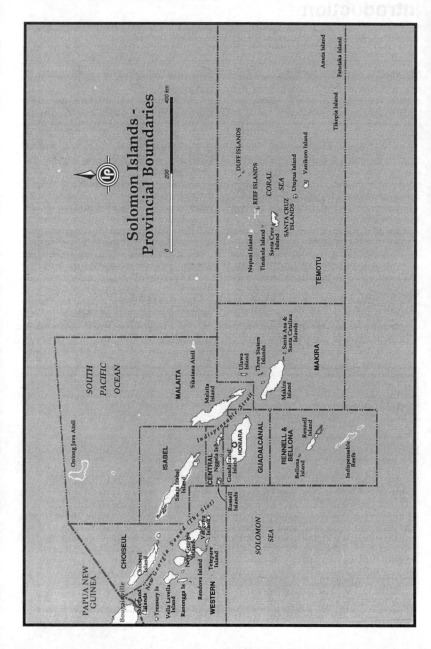

Solomon Islands –
Provincial Boundaries

Facts about the Country

HISTORY

About 25 million years ago, the first islands of the present-day Solomons began emerging from the ocean depths. Once this seismic activity ceased, coral growth began accumulating around these newly emerged volcanic shores.

Most historians believe human settlement in the Pacific originated in South-East Asia. At least 60,000 years ago, and perhaps much earlier, island people began to migrate through Indonesia and New Guinea towards Australia and the South Pacific. This movement was facilitated by the lower sea level during the Pleistocene period, or Great Ice Age.

By about 30,000 BC, Papuan-speaking hunter-gatherers in New Guinea were settling on the nearby islands to the south and east of what is now modern Papua New Guinea, possibly reaching as far as the eastern Solomons before the sea level began to rise with the end of the Ice Age in 10,000 BC.

Agriculture developed in South-East Asia from around 7000 to 5000 BC, and Austronesian-speaking proto-Melanesian migrants from there began to arrive in the archipelago around 4000 BC, bringing with them new techniques in crop husbandry, pig breeding, canoe building and sailing. The global warming and rising sea level which accompanied the end of the Ice Age restricted the Papuan speakers to the few islands they had already reached in the Solomons. Meanwhile, the Austronesians, who were much more skilled with canoes, settled throughout the remainder of the area, except for a few marginally fertile atolls.

Between 2000 and 1600 BC, people of the Lapita culture appeared. (They are named after an archaeological site at Lapita in New Caledonia.) In a remarkable millennium of long-range canoe voyages, they left their distinctive pottery at a string of sites from the Bismarck Archipelago in eastern Papua New Guinea all the way to Samoa. Some have suggested that the Lapita people were ancestors of modern-day Polynesians. However, it's more likely that they were absorbed by pre-existing peoples, as remains of their ceramics show clear signs of cultural change from the 2nd century AD onwards.

Meanwhile, most Melanesians in the Solomons lived in small villages on well-established tribal lands. They practised shifting cultivation and engaged in fishing, hunting, carving, weaving and canoe building. Feasting and dancing were regular activities.

Each settlement was composed of related family groups and captives from other places, and inhabitants kept to themselves except when they raided their neighbours' settlements. Rule was by *kastom* or tradition as recalled by clan elders. Ancestors were worshipped and blood feuds, head-hunting and cannibalism were frequent.

Polynesian Settlers

Between 1200 and 1600 AD, random westward migrations of small groups of Polynesians reached the outer edges of the Solomons, where they found the main mass of the country already settled by Melanesians. Voyaging in small canoes from Polynesian islands some 800 to 3000 km east of the Solomons, they found only small, isolated landmasses and atolls available. Their legends tell of small pre-existing populations which they usually eliminated or absorbed shortly after settlement.

Once established, Polynesian settlements in the Solomons suffered intermittent raids from Tonga and Tokelau during the period from the 14th to the 18th century, as eastern Polynesian rulers tried unsuccessfully to exact tribute from their western counterparts. Long-range Polynesian canoe

Polynesian Ocean Voyaging

Polynesian canoe trips today pale in comparison to the epic voyages of the past, but many islanders are still conversant with the ancient methods of navigation. The principal navigational aid is *kavenga*, or 'star paths', where certain stars indicate the presence of an island. For example, the star Rigel, used in conjunction with prevailing winds, can indicate the position of Tikopia and Anuta islands.

When night skies are overcast, ocean-going canoeists navigate by means of *te lapa*, or 'underwater lightning'. Small flashes of light two metres below the waterline indicate the direction of an island. This natural feature, best observed 150 to 180 km out, disappears once land is close.

The presence of foraging birds will indicate that land isn't far, though terns and gulls can fly up to 30 or 40 km from home, and boobies may venture as far as 60 km.

The strangest navigational method involves taking a dip in the ocean to feel and assess the pulse of waves reflected back from land formations. Apparently a man's most sensitive body part for picking up these rebounds is the bare testicles! ■

journeys in search of new land became a rarity in the 19th century, as the fear of Tongan violence led to a growing suspicion of all foreigners. This in turn produced the widespread habit of attacking strangers on sight, further discouraging such voyages.

Spanish Exploration

Meanwhile, in the early 1560s, rumours swept Spanish-occupied Peru of the existence of a group of islands, or even a great continent, far to the west in the Pacific. Inca legends told of a sea journey made in the mid-15th century to these legendary islands by one of their kings, Tupac Yupanqui.

Legends claimed he found two islands – Nina Chumbi, or Fire Island, and Ava Chumbi, or Outer Island – and brought back with him gold, dark-skinned slaves and the head of a horse-like animal. Some also believed that a larger southern continent was likely to exist just to balance the northern hemisphere's huge mass.

Don Alvaro de Mendaña y Neyra, the 25-year-old nephew of Peru's Spanish viceroy, was chosen to find the legendary islands or continent. He left Peru with two ships in November 1567, sighting land twice – first in Tuvalu, and later what was probably the Roncador Reef near Ontong Java in the north-eastern Solomons. Then,

on 7 February 1568, his expedition saw a large island, naming it Santa Isabel.

Mendaña and his men sailed around the neighbouring landforms, giving them Spanish names, some of which have survived to this day. Much of the explorers' time was spent searching for gold or fighting with islanders over food. Finally, on 11 August 1568, after six months of constant conflict, the expedition set sail for Peru, where Mendaña described the islands in glowing terms. Initially, he and his crew simply called the archipelago the Western Islands, but by 1570 the name Yslas de Salomon – the Solomon Islands – was in common use.

Mendaña was keen to return, but wasn't able to raise enough money for another fleet until 1595. This time he sailed with four ships and 450 men and women – would-be colonists. No doubt the promise of riches implied by the name Solomon (recalling the fabulously wealthy biblical king) helped Mendaña get the venture under way.

But the expedition was ill-fated. At first Mendaña, by now an admiral, couldn't find the way, losing a ship in the process. Finally, he discovered and named Santa Cruz, and settled there. Sickness, internal squabbles and islander resistance disrupted the project, and Mendaña himself died of malaria. After only two months, the expedition abandoned its small settlement, limping back to Peru via the Philippines.

By the beginning of the 17th century Spain was in decline, with no money for unproductive ventures. However, Mendaña's chief pilot from 1595, a Portuguese named Pedro Fernandez de Quiros, was still in the employ of the Spanish Crown. He shared his former admiral's zeal to discover and colonise the fabled great southern continent, or Terra Australis as it was also called.

It took Quiros 10 years of pleading to raise the cash for a third and final expedition. He left Peru with three small ships on 21 December 1605, with a crew scoured from Spanish America.

Quiros missed Santa Cruz Island and reached the Duff Islands early in 1606. Islanders told him of 72 other islands they knew of, including a great country less than 700 km away which Quiros fervently believed would be the legendary southern continent.

He found instead Espiritu Santo Island in northern Vanuatu. His ill-assorted fellow expedition members soon made the colonisation of Santo a similar disaster to the two previous Spanish ventures in the area. Quiros returned in disgrace, thereby signalling the end of Spanish interest in the western Pacific.

Further Exploration & Early Trading

The first map-makers who charted the Solomons placed it far to the east of its correct position. Consequently, except for two Dutch expeditions which are believed to have glimpsed Ontong Java, there was no further recorded contact until the late 18th century. By then, several European governments were financing official expeditions to discover new lands in the name of scientific research.

Captain Philip Cartaret, a Briton, blundered into Santa Cruz in 1767 and then passed on to Malaita, at first refusing to believe that he had rediscovered the Solomons. A stream of British, French and American explorers followed, including

Jean de Surville, who sighted the large islands of Makira, Malaita, Santa Isabel and Choiseul and called them La Terre des Arcasides, meaning 'the land of rustic-living, people'.

Many whalers visited the archipelago from 1798 onwards. Sandalwood traders followed between the 1840s and late 1860s, buying pigs, turtle shell and pearl shell in the Solomons to sell to islanders in Vanuatu (then called the New Hebrides) in exchange for sandalwood logs, which they then sold in China. Bêche-de-mer was another highly valuable commodity in China, even though it was fairly plentiful on reefs.

Prior to the large-scale trading contacts of the 19th century, relationships between neighbouring islands in the Solomons had been reasonably peaceful. This period, known to islanders as the Great Peace, had prevailed for several generations at least. The conduct of the traders quickly changed this; some persuaded villagers to collect huge loads of sandalwood but then refused to pay for it, shooting the villagers if they objected.

Shortly after a ship visit, island populations were often decimated by illnesses. Lack of immunity to common European sicknesses like influenza, measles, chickenpox and scarlet fever caused islanders to die in their hundreds.

Soon the sandalwooders came to be hated by many of the local people, who would kill any white person they saw. Although the trade was worked out by the late 1860s, resentment towards European treachery and diseases led to the murder of a number of missionaries at the time.

The Solomons quickly gained the reputation of being the most dangerous place in the Pacific – an island group inhabited by an often fierce, warlike and cannibalistic population. While there were many peaceful contacts, there were a number of unpredictable attacks on foreigners, and savage massacres. Churches moved cautiously in the Solomons even though this was a period of intense mission activity elsewhere in the Pacific.

Despite this violent situation, by the 1860s there were many places in the archipelago where sailors knew they would be welcome. Iron and steel tools were in great demand, as were calico, tobacco, beads, fish-hooks and, later, guns. The newly acquired firearms soon produced an explosive growth in head-hunting and slave raids.

As head-hunting by islanders increased, so also did labour recruiting (blackbirding) by Europeans. During the last 35 years of the 19th century, 29,000 Solomon Islanders were taken to work on sugarcane plantations in Queensland (Australia) and Fiji.

Some islanders were keen to go, but many were taken by force, especially in the early days of blackbirding. Islanders would be invited aboard to trade and then seized as the ship sailed away with them. Some blackbirders even dressed in priestly white, held a shoreside service and then kidnapped everyone. However, official controls over blackbirding and improved conditions in the Australian and Fijian canefields had eliminated most of the trade's abuses by the mid-1880s.

The Protectorate

During the 1890s, about 50 British traders and missionaries (all males) were resident in the Solomons. At the same time, Germany was active in much of what is now Papua New Guinea, as well as in the Shortlands, Choiseul, Santa Isabel and Ontong Java.

On 6 October 1893, Britain proclaimed a protectorate over the southern part of the group. This claim was extended in 1897 and again in 1898. In 1899, Britain relinquished all claims to Western Samoa, and in return Germany ceded the Shortlands, Choiseul, Ontong Java and Santa Isabel to Britain. The new territory was named the British Solomon Islands Protectorate, or BSIP.

Britain's main objectives in the Solomons were to keep order, stop head-hunting and cannibalism, and ensure that the islanders and their lands were not exploited. In 1896, Charles Morris Woodford was appointed the first resident commissioner.

Born in England in 1853, Woodford was the son of a London publican. He made for the South Seas at an early age.

Woodford had to control close to 100,000 Solomon Islanders, many of them head-hunters, with only a few Europeans and a small force of local police. His biggest problem was the people of New Georgia's Roviana Lagoon, who were intent on dominating all the western Solomons and were universally feared.

Woodford never carried a gun. His policy was to convince islanders of the futility of head-hunting and tribal warfare. He retired in 1915, having laid the foundations for organised government in the Solomons.

Education and health were left to the missions, as money was scarce and the Solomons had to be self-supporting. Although economical, this system produced new and deep divisions among villagers, as each missionary claimed his version of Christianity was right and the rest were wrong.

Island traditions were gradually eroded as missionaries declared many customs and ceremonies to be evil. Although sorcery and head-hunting rapidly diminished, population figures also declined drastically following regular epidemics of diseases introduced by Europeans.

Further alienation was caused by the islanders being subject to foreign ways. The Kwaio Rebellion on Malaita in 1927 was a clear rejection of European values. All but one of a government tax-gathering team were killed by highlanders who objected to paying for a foreign government they did not want. (See the History section of the Malaita chapter for more on this.)

Punitive measures afterwards cowed further resistance but left an enduring legacy of mistrust of Europeans in the area. In 1928 several Kwaio rebels were hanged in the then capital, Tulagi. One of these was Basiana, the rebel leader. Shortly before his death he defiantly prophesied 'Tulagi will be torn apart, and scattered to the winds'. Fourteen years later his prediction would come true in an unexpected fashion.

WWII

The 1930s was generally a period of calm in the Solomons, but peace was completely shattered in 1942. In early April, the Japanese seized the Shortland Islands. Three weeks later Tulagi was taken.

In the very early stages a few local people supported the Japanese, but the behaviour of the invaders soon alienated and disgusted the islanders. The Japanese defiled and robbed churches, demanded food at gunpoint, forced all healthy adult males to work for them without wages, and stole clothes and property. Worse, they looted villagers' gardens, destroying a year's hard work by seizing the crops, pigs and chickens needed to feed a family for the next 12 months.

In early June, Korean labourers were seen building an airfield (later known as Henderson Field) on Guadalcanal. If completed, the way would be open for further advances by the Japanese against Allied territory in Vanuatu, New Caledonia, Fiji – even Australia and New Zealand. It had to be retaken, whatever the cost.

Large-scale US landings in Guadalcanal occurred in August 1942. In the very early hours of 9 August, while the landings were still in progress, a Japanese naval force slipped out of Rabaul in Papua New Guinea. Its plan was to attack and destroy the US transports at Red Beach before they unloaded their supplies. Although seen three times – by a US Flying Fortress bomber, a US submarine, and an Australian Hudson pilot – no warnings got through.

The Japanese task force took an Allied naval squadron completely by surprise. Four heavy cruisers were sunk: three US ships, each with 12 huge 203-mm (eight-inch) guns, and one Australian, HMAS *Canberra*, with eight 203-mm guns. Another US heavy cruiser, USS *Chicago*, had its bow blown off by a torpedo.

This action – now called the Battle of Savo – was one of the heaviest defeats in US naval history. To make it worse, the survivors had to cope with frenzied shark attacks as well as their wounds. In all, 1270 Allied sailors were lost. Fortunately for the Allies, the Japanese failed to press home their advantage against the troop transports and instead retired, satisfied with the damage they had done.

The USA was soon able to establish daytime air supremacy around Guadalcanal. Japanese destroyer transports had to run close inshore under cover of darkness to deliver their cargoes of men and supplies. This occurred with such regularity they were called the Tokyo Express.

Once their loads were delivered, the Japanese warships would shell US positions on their way back to base. Routine nightly nuisance raids by two Japanese seaplanes, nicknamed Louie the Louse and Washing Machine Charlie, kept the marines awake.

The US forces gradually gained the upper hand, but at tremendous cost to life and limb on both sides. After six months of relentless bloodletting, the Japanese secretly withdrew to New Georgia. The fighting had cost them dearly in men and equipment, and had damaged their earlier aura of invincibility.

During the Guadalcanal campaign, six naval battles were fought and 67 warships and transports sunk on both sides. Although US casualties were heavy, with over 7,000 Americans killed, Japan's casualties were crippling. Of more than 24,000 soldiers lost, over a third died from disease, starvation or war wounds. Another 15,000 perished in sea actions. More than 800 Japanese aircraft were destroyed and over 2400 irreplaceable pilots and aircrew lost.

As 1943 progressed, more and more islands were recovered – though usually after fierce resistance. By the end of the year, only Choiseul and the Shortlands were still in Japanese hands. These were bypassed ignominiously; the Allies recovered them after the Japanese surrender in 1945.

The islanders' loyalty to the Allied cause was admirable. Although initially under British orders to fight an opponent they knew little about, Japanese misconduct in occupied areas quickly persuaded local people of the need for direct action. They conducted their own scouting and guerrilla operations against Japanese patrols in the north-western Solomons, and rescued Allied aircrew who had been shot down. They operated behind enemy lines as 'coastwatchers', led by government officials, soldiers, traders, planters and priests who had stayed behind when the Japanese invaded. A number of islanders were decorated for their bravery.

Several thousand other islanders, mainly Malaitans, went to Guadalcanal once it was secured. They served as labourers and orderlies at the huge US supply base at Honiara. The Americans treated them as equals, shared food with them and gave them presents – something their colonial masters had never done. Not surprisingly, islanders noticed the difference. Malaitans were particularly determined that their status should permanently improve.

Postwar Recovery
Recovery was slow after 1945. As Tulagi was gutted, the Quonset-hut township of Honiara replaced it as the capital. The economy was in ruins, with many private planters not bothering to return. A huge amount of abandoned war material littered the country, with some still here even now.

A nationalist movement sprang up in Malaita. Called Marching Rule, it was a self-reliant movement opposed to any cooperation with the restored British authorities – government or church. Its members were regimented into strictly ruled coastal villages dependent on community-based agriculture.

A cargo-cultist feature of the movement was the hope that huge quantities of US goods would be delivered to islanders by those US forces remaining behind in the Solomons after WWII. They also hoped the wealthy and generous USA would replace Britain as the country's ruler.

Though sympathetic, the USA could not accept this request. Mass arrests by the British authorities in 1947 and 1948 caused the movement to wane. It died out soon

after the last of the US forces withdrew from the country in 1950. But the movement did help Britain to see the need for a system of local government, and fledgling regional assemblies were introduced and refined in the ensuing years.

The early 1960s were years of political awakening in the Solomons, leading to the creation of an elected governing council in 1970. The British Solomon Islands Protectorate was renamed the Solomon Islands five years later and independence granted on 7 July 1978.

Independence
The post-independence era has not seen any major upheavals. Some older islanders look back to the British era with nostalgia, believing that the country's institutions were run more efficiently then.

In the countryside 'subsistence affluence' prevails, despite population increases and pressure for land, particularly in Honiara and Malaita. But as long as each family has sufficient garden plots, fruit trees, pigs and chickens, the pleasant life of independent means will continue.

Bougainville's attempts to secede from Papua New Guinea (PNG) has strained relations between the Solomons and its larger neighbour. The Bougainville Revolutionary Army (BRA) became active in 1988, and the PNG defence force responded by blockading the province in 1990. Shortland Islanders, who have close ties with Bougainvillians, have sometimes broken the blockade to help the rebels. At other times, BRA rebels have entered the Shortlands to steal supplies.

Occasional international incidents have occurred, with PNG forces pursuing BRA rebels into Solomons territory. Lives have been lost. Bougainvillian refugees regularly come to the Solomons seeking support and medical help, putting pressure on the nation's fragile finances. With the crisis seemingly escalating in 1997, as many as 10,000 refugees are expected to flee to the Solomons.

GEOGRAPHY

The Solomons is a scattered double chain of islands which extends 1667 km in a southeasterly direction from Bougainville Island in Papua New Guinea. Some of the islands are rugged, heavily wooded and mountainous; others are tiny, low-lying coral atolls.

The third-largest archipelago in the South Pacific, the Solomons covers over 1.35 million sq km of sea. The total land area is 27,556 sq km. Counting all the tiny atolls and cays the total number of islands is 992, of which 347 are populated. Its six largest islands are Guadalcanal, Malaita, New Georgia, Santa Isabel, Makira and Choiseul, which are between 92 to 181 km long and 24 to 56 km wide.

The country's highest peak, Mt Makarakombu (2447m) on Guadalcanal, is typical of most of the group's mountains – rugged igneous formations cleft by narrow valleys.

Much of the Solomons is covered with dense rainforest, with mangrove swamps occurring along parts of the coast. Most islands are girdled by coral reefs and lagoons. Many have formed around an initial volcanic cone which has since been overlaid with colourful, level-topped terraces of coral rock.

Other islands are former reefs lifted high out of the water by volcanic activity. In Rennell's case, this has happened five times, creating the most striking example of an uplifted coral atoll in the Pacific.

Coral Reefs

There are 600 species of coral in the Pacific. Coral is formed by a marine polyp, which looks and behaves like a plant but is actually a minuscule, primitive carnivorous animal. When a polyp dies, its hard white skeleton remains and is built upon by succeeding generations of polyps. In this way a coral reef grows by about 15 mm per year. It is the living polyps which give coral its colour, so not only is it environmental vandalism to pluck vivid coral from the ocean, but it's futile because it loses its colour when dead.

Coral reefs come in three varieties. A fringing reef lies close to land. A barrier reef is further out to sea, separated from the mainland by a channel of water. An atoll is a ring of, or horseshoe-shaped, coral-formed land, which encircles a shallow lagoon. An atoll, according to Charles Darwin's widely accepted theory, is the remains of a sunken volcanic island. The fringing reef of the original island continues to build up while the island itself subsides over the course of many millennia. The reef becomes a barrier reef in the process, until it is all that is left above the waves. ■

GEOLOGY
Volcanoes & Earthquakes

The Solomons is part of the Pacific Ring of Fire. This highly volcanic area is at the intersection of the huge Oceanic and Indo-Australasian tectonic plates. Pressing vigorously together, they cause constant seismic activity, including earthquakes and volcanoes – though less frequently here than in nearby Papua New Guinea and Vanuatu.

The Solomons has experienced up to 1900 earthquakes in some years, often with more than 40 measuring five or more on the Richter scale. The strongest one was in 1977, measuring 7.2 and causing landslides and damage to villages in Guadalcanal. Most seismic activity occurs in Temotu Province, Choiseul Island and the Shortland Islands, though earthquake damage and tidal waves are rare.

There are three land volcanoes and at least two submarine volcanoes in the Solomon Islands. The most active volcano in the last 40 years has been Tinakula, 42 km north of Santa Cruz Island. Its last violent eruption, in 1971, forced all the island's small population to evacuate. Savo Island, north-west of Guadalcanal, has a number of bubbling and boiling springs. Its crater has not blown its top since 1840; nonetheless, seismologists constantly watch it for warning signs.

In the New Georgia Islands, Simbo Island's Ove Crater emits sulphurous fumes but has not erupted within oral or recorded history. Further north there's a large area of hot springs and seething mud in north-eastern Vella Lavella.

The two main submarine volcanoes are both in Western Province. Cook is south-west of Vonavona Island, and Kavachi, the more active of the two, is south-west of Nggatokae. From time to time, the seas above them boil in brief but feverish activity. As the eruptions are in different spots each time, sometimes several km apart, each volcano may be made up of several cones lying close together on the ocean bed.

CLIMATE

The Solomon Islands' tropical climate is tempered by the surrounding sea. From late May to early December, during the country's dry season, the south-easterly trade winds produce pleasantly mild weather. Rainfall is usually light and several days apart.

During the summer months, from mid-December to mid-May, monsoonal winds come mostly from the west or north-west. This is the country's wet season and a time of higher temperatures, humidity and rainfall, particularly from January onwards. Short, sharp, torrential cloudbursts deluge the countryside and are followed by bright sunshine.

There's an average of seven hours sunshine per day. Sunrise/sunset is usually around 6.30 am/6.45 pm, and dusk lasts only 10 minutes.

Temperature & Humidity

Daytime coastal temperatures vary through the year between 21°C and 32°C, with an occasional maximum of 33°C. At night the temperature sometimes falls to 19°C as the air is cooled by land breezes off nearby mountains and hills. Inland temperatures at sea level can be rather higher, sometimes reaching 35°C, yet mountain air remains pleasantly cooler, averaging closer to 22°C.

Humidity is highest in the morning, regularly reaching 90%, but it falls off in the afternoon. Kirakira is the country's muggiest place, with 95% humidity in February! Humidity falls to a pleasant 69% in Honiara in August.

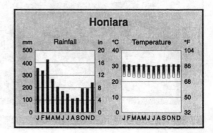

Even in the summer's hottest months, cool sea breezes along the shore keep the climate fresh. But once you go more than a few hundred metres inland, you really feel the heat.

Rainfall

There's an average 3500 mm of rain a year, with significant regional variations. Gizo, though rather humid, averages only 2900 mm a year, while Lata in Temotu Province occasionally gets twice that. Most rain falls from December to April, but this pattern is reversed in Choiseul.

Honiara and Henderson airport are in a rain shadow and have a lower than average annual rainfall. However, on Guadalcanal's southern coast over 12,500 mm has been known to fall in a year – a colossal 12.5m of rain. Falls of 8000 mm annually are quite common there. The south-eastern coast of Makira is almost as wet.

The windward side of an island always gets the most rain, as do the higher parts, with some mountains almost permanently shrouded in cloud. Steep water courses in highland catchment areas cause many rivers to flash flood after storms.

These high rainfall levels, together with the tall, rugged terrain, usually produce good-quality water. It's clean and unpolluted except where villages have grown up alongside riverbanks. In contrast, on the tiny outer islands and atolls there is often no surface water at all, and rainwater catchment tanks have to meet human needs.

Cyclones

Although winter is the Solomons' calmest season, strong winds can occasionally blow up to 50 km an hour or force four. Such storms can last 10 days at a time, bringing heavy rain – particularly in July along Guadalcanal's and Makira's southern, or 'weather', coasts. Once over, a storm is usually followed by days of fresh, light breezes and balmy weather.

On average there's at least one cyclone a year in the Solomons. Called hurricanes in the Caribbean and typhoons in the South China Sea, cyclones are destructive tropical storms which rotate around a central low-pressure zone. They usually occur between January and April but can arrive as early as November and as late as May – like Cyclone Namu in 1986, which took the lives of 140 villagers.

Most cyclones build up over the Coral Sea or the Solomon Sea, and tend to move south-west towards Vanuatu or Australia, gathering speed and strength as they go. When they strike the Solomons, they cause considerable damage to leaf-house villages, crops, water supplies and rainforests.

ECOLOGY & ENVIRONMENT

Tropical rainforest in the Solomons covers 79% of the country – but it used to be nearly 90%. Since 1984 the government has collected a 7.5% reforestation levy on timber harvests (the country's biggest export earner), but little of the revenue has actually been spent for this purpose. Fortunately, some local landowners are beginning to recognise that the short-term profits from wholesale logging does not compensate for the resultant environmental damage. Tourism development is seen by some as a more sustainable alternative.

The Solomons is not a mass-tourist destination, and efforts have been made to ensure that tourism develops on a low-impact, eco-tourism basis. The blueprint for eco-tourism resorts are those in the Marovo Lagoon which have been sponsored by the World Wide Fund for Nature and the World Heritage organisation (ie UNESCO). They attempt to conserve both the natural environment and traditional lifestyles. Organisations like Solomons Village Stay (see Accommodation in the Facts for the Visitor chapter) promote tourism that does not overwhelm the local communities.

Global warming is also an important issue for the Solomons. With the majority of people living by the sea, the predicted rise in sea levels could have a huge impact. Warmer seas cause coral bleaching, and many low-lying atolls could disappear under the waves.

⊳⊲⊳ ⊳⊲⊳ ⊳⊲⊳ ⊳⊲⊳ ⊳⊲⊳ ⊳⊲⊳ ⊳⊲⊳ ⊳⊲⊳ ⊳⊲⊳ ⊳⊲⊳ ⊳⊲⊳ ⊳⊲⊳ ⊳⊲⊳ ⊳⊲⊳ ⊳⊲⊳ ⊳⊲⊳ ⊳⊲⊳ ⊳⊲⊳ ⊳⊲⊳

The Value of Trees
Timber is an extremely important industry, in both economic and environmental terms. The rainforest shelters a rich diversity of flora and fauna which will be threatened by excessive logging. Deforestation would also threaten the traditional lifestyle of villagers as well as tourism. Other possible negative effects include erosion, climate changes, loss of water resources, and disruption to coral reefs.

Sustainable timber harvests in the Solomons are calculated to be 325,000 cubic metres per year but since the 1990s logging has exceeded these levels. Current estimates vary, but it's generally accepted that logging is around *three times* the sustainable limit. At these levels, the World Bank has estimated that accessible forests in the Solomons will be fully depleted within eight years.

The environmental cost, together with external pressures (notably aid inducements from Australia to promote sustainable logging) prompted Prime Minister Hilly to announce a 1994 moratorium on new logging licenses, with a ban on timber exports to commence in 1997. Solomon Mamaloni, upon being re-elected prime minister in November 1994, pushed the commencement of the ban back to 1999 and is perceived to be in the pocket of the logging industry, a view borne out by his government's attitude towards logging on Pavuvu Island in the Russell Islands.

Local Pavuvu landowners mostly favoured an ecological approach to forestry, but the Malaysian loggers were allowed to move in during Mamaloni's tenure, and a resettlement plan was announced for residents. Local reports of systematic abuses, confirmed by Greenpeace, include illegal logging on customary land, and logging of undersize and protected nut trees. But the government did nothing, and disenchanted locals protested by burning three of the loggers' bulldozers on 3 July 1995. On 30 October 1995 Martin Apa, an anti-logging leader, was murdered, apparently in retaliation. The government dragged its feet in commencing an investigation, and sought to repress media reporting of the incident.

The pressure to increase logging is understandable. Timber exports are worth millions of dollars, and in 1993 and 1994 contributed *over half* of total export earnings. Most of the logging is carried out by Malaysian companies, which moved into the Solomons when forestry protection measures were introduced in their own country. Around 50% of government revenue comes from log export levies but half as much again is lost through smuggling, under-reporting of timber harvests, and transfer pricing by foreign companies. And this after Mamaloni has already granted the logging companies increased exemptions and remissions, annually worth S$34 million in 1995 (up from S$5 million in 1994). Local communities are also susceptible to the immediate rewards logging can bring. The loggers offer to build schools and other facilities but sometimes renege on such agreements. Ultimately only 5% of logging profits stay within the local community.

In order to increase the pressure for more responsible logging, in December 1995 Australia withdrew a A$2.2 million allocation of annual forestry aid. The way forward seems to be to create community-based logging concerns, which will log at a sustainable level and process the logs locally. The move to this sort of logging is slowly gaining momentum, but the struggle between environmentalists and loggers will continue for years to come. ■

⊳⊲⊳ ⊳⊲⊳ ⊳⊲⊳ ⊳⊲⊳ ⊳⊲⊳ ⊳⊲⊳ ⊳⊲⊳ ⊳⊲⊳ ⊳⊲⊳ ⊳⊲⊳ ⊳⊲⊳ ⊳⊲⊳ ⊳⊲⊳ ⊳⊲⊳ ⊳⊲⊳ ⊳⊲⊳ ⊳⊲⊳ ⊳⊲⊳ ⊳⊲⊳

FLORA & FAUNA

The country is largely covered by tropical rainforest. Most of the bigger islands have a thick layer of tall trees, while the smaller ones are usually carpeted inland by a mass of scrub that is surrounded by a thin coastal belt of coconut trees and mangroves.

The Solomons' indigenous land mammals are few and mainly nocturnal, including bats, rats, possums and bush mice. Wild pigs living deep in the forests can be ferocious and have gored people. Insect life flourishes and small numbers of leeches live in the rainforest and freshwater creeks.

Reptile life is plentiful, with several species of lizard, snake and turtle, and two types of crocodile. The seas teem with fish, including sharks, and dugong and whales are occasionally seen.

Flora

The Solomons has over 4500 plant species, including 230 varieties of orchid. Many plants and trees are valued by islanders as sources of traditional building materials, food, medicine or clothing; tapa, for example, comes from the paper mulberry tree.

A common evergreen is the *sumai* tree, which blossoms at night. Its flowers fade and die as the daylight falls on them. Sumais usually grow close to the shore and are recognisable by the large number of dark-green, box-shaped fallen unopened fruit littering the adjacent ground.

The American vine was introduced from the southern states of the USA for use as a fast-growing natural camouflage around the WWII US installations east of Honiara. Since then, it has spread unrestrainedly in north-eastern Guadalcanal, choking indigenous vegetation.

The hibiscus is the flower of the Pacific. Honiara is a good place to see its many single or double varieties, including whites, yellows, oranges, pinks and reds. You'll also find white and pink-flowered frangipanis, red ginger plants, colourful bougainvilleas and many other varieties around the country.

Coconut Trees Bearing fruit for about 70 of its 75 years of life, the coconut tree provides leaves for roofing and weaving, sennit for rope, fibre for making fire, shells for containers, and trunks for house, bridge and canoe building. The plant tolerates sandy soils and is the only large tree which grows on atolls and sandbars without needing human help.

Hazardous Plants The large, purple-veined *nalato* leaf causes an unpleasant nettle-like rash. Your skin goes red at the site of the contact, and can itch for a week.

Islanders use the sap from the plant's roots or from beneath the bark as an antidote.

Another toxic plant is the *hailasi*. Its bark and sap can produce large blisters or swellings in some people, but not everybody. Some are affected just by coming close to it.

The *loya*, or lawyer, cane has hooks on the end of its leaves, and some of its five varieties also have barbs on their stems. Take care what you grab hold of when going up or down a hill.

Birds

The Solomons is home to 173 species of bird (over 300 including subspecies). Within this rich diversity are nine kinds of hawk and eagle, 20 species of pigeon, 11 species of parrot, eight kinds of kingfisher and seven types of starling. Some have distinctive names, such as the dollar bird, the marbled frogmouth, the buff-headed coucal, the midget flowerpecker and the spangled drongo!

Around 40 species are unique to the Solomons, including the cardinal lory – a familiar sight around Honiara and elsewhere. Some species live only on one island, such as the Rennell fantail and the slaty flycatcher of Vanikoro.

Nearly every major island group in the Solomons has its own quota of subspecies. These have evolved after birds became separated and then remained isolated by the country's wide seas. This helps explain why there are 10 types of white-collared kingfisher.

Frigate birds – blackish males, white-breasted females – are the principal birds of island folklore. Their large size, deeply forked tail, long canted wings, aerial skills and habit of forcing other birds to disgorge their food have made them a favourite motif in Melanesian art. They can't dive or swim because their wings aren't waterproof. But they are often seen along the shore, either hunting for skipjack or circling in their hundreds over their shoreside nests just before dark, gradually descending as the daylight disappears.

Male frigate bird in courtship display

The other two birds that appear in traditional tales are the megapode, or incubator, bird and the completely brown-plumaged Sanford's eagle. Local people often call Sanford's eagle the Malaita eagle, after the island where it is most plentiful.

Megapode birds can best be seen on Savo and Simbo, where they lay their eggs in the thermally warmed ground. They are found along sandy seashores or occasionally living inland, but seldom beyond 200m above sea level. Megapode hatcheries are specially prepared and farmed by islanders. See the Megapode Birds aside in the Central Province chapter.

Insects & Arachnids

Most of the huge variety of insects in the Solomons live in the upper reaches of the rainforest. Among those found lower down are butterflies, moths, wasps, beetles, mosquitoes, centipedes, scorpions and caterpillars – some with stinging hairs.

Butterflies Of the more than 130 butterfly species found locally, 35 are endemic. The two largest forms, the Queen Victoria birdwing and the blue mountain birdwing, have spans of over 250 mm. These large butterflies are present in small numbers all around the country, though they are seldom seen in towns (unlike the large, nocturnal moths).

Wasps The 12-mm-long Solomons fruit wasp is very common in Bellona, less so in Rennell and some other islands. It's not nearly as ill-tempered as the European wasp, but can give a mild sting if disturbed. It often lives in the wooden framework of leaf houses and usually feeds on pawpaws.

Centipedes & Scorpions Small centipedes may live in the roofs of leaf houses or be carried into a house in firewood. The large, dark-green centipede causes excruciating pain for about a day if it stings you. Use a mosquito net in the bush and in leaf houses to stop centipedes falling on you in the night. There are also scorpions, particularly in drier woodland areas, though it's unlikely you'll be stung by either creature.

Mammals

There are four types of rat larger than domestic cats! The largest one nests underground, mainly in Choiseul and Guadalcanal, eating nuts, fruit and insects. The others live in trees and inhabit Guadalcanal and Santa Isabel. There's also the Polynesian rat and the common brown rat;

the latter has become a pest, especially around coastal settlements.

The cuscus, or marsupial phalanger, is found on the larger islands, except those in Temotu Province. Ranging in colour from pure white through fawn and grey to nearly black, it's considered a delicacy. Its teeth are sometimes used as traditional currency.

The flying fox, or fruit bat, makes a popular village meal, while its teeth are collected for bride price on some islands. In the daytime, when they aren't fighting or barking at each other, fruit bats sleep in huge colonies at the top of tall trees.

Reptiles & Amphibians

Snakes There are eight species of sea snake in Solomons waters, mostly 60 cm to one metre long, with rudder-like tails. Although venomous, they are generally non-aggressive. One of these, the black-banded sea krait (also called the coral snake), is common along most island shores. It even inhabits fresh water, including Lake Te'Nggano on Rennell. The same lake is the sole home of the freshwater snake, the tugihono. It's extremely poisonous, but similarly placid.

There are also seven land species, three nonvenomous. The *typhlina* is a brownish-red nocturnal burrowing snake occurring in several subspecies and varying in length from 12 to 35 cm. The tree boa is limited to Temotu Province but is plentiful there, especially in the Reef Islands. It's two metres long and silvery coloured, with dark patches along its back. The ground boa is a similar length and greyish-brown, with a continuous serrated black line down its back. It usually hides under leaves waiting for its dinner (rodents) to come by. Both boas are called sleeping snakes, as they lie absolutely still as if asleep when disturbed by large creatures such as humans. They can bite repeatedly if annoyed.

Guppy's snake is the most aggressive of the four venomous land snakes, though even this seldom bites. It's a short snake, with a distinctive head and thin reddish-brown back, often with transverse bands.

Living in forests and near creeks, it's active during the day. The brown tree snake has occasionally bitten sleeping human babies. It has rear-facing fangs and noticeably big eyes. Its narrow body is two metres long, light-brown to khaki in colour and crossed with darker wavy lines. It lives in trees or empty houses in bush villages and is mainly active at night. The Solomons banded snake has striking yellow and black bands on its body and a whitish head. It grows to a metre long, is very docile and lives under rotting debris on the forest floor. The small Woodford's snake, also venomous but docile, is just 30 cm long. It has a dark-brown back and is only occasionally seen, usually living under rotting fallen timber and leaves.

Lizards The 1.5m monitor lizard (sometimes called a goanna) is plentiful around Lake Te'Nggano on Rennell and in the Three Sisters Islands off Makira, but uncommon elsewhere. The giant prehensile-tailed skink is about 75 cm long; the tail is as long as its body and it lives mainly in trees. Nocturnal, normally docile and slow moving, the skink can scratch and bite if severely provoked. Both these large lizards are eaten by villagers and taste like chicken.

Crocodiles The short-mouthed crocodile is the dangerous, human-eating saltwater variety which is wide-bodied and often four or more metres long. The long-mouthed crocodile is a slim, freshwater variant which is usually between one and two metres long. Although it eats mainly fish, at this size it is strong enough to take dogs, pigs or small children.

Freshwater crocodiles mostly favour clear or reedy, fresh, sparkling rivers like north Malaita's waterways and the Ulo River area of eastern Vella Lavella, but be on the lookout elsewhere too. Small numbers of saltwater crocodiles live in many of the country's mangrove swamps and tidal estuaries, though they're capable of travelling far inland up muddy, low-lying rivers.

The saltwater crocodile lives almost entirely in the ocean and can swim many km out to sea. They only swim upriver where there is salt water.

Saltwater crocs are reasonably plentiful in the Three Sisters Islands and southern and eastern Guadalcanal – particularly in the Lauvi Lagoon – while some have been found close to Honiara, near the Betikama Seventh Day Adventist (SDA) mission. Other habitats are the marshy and mangrove-ridden parts of the Nggelas, New Georgia, Vangunu, Nggatokae, Tetepare, Choiseul, San Jorge, Vanikoro, Makira, southern Santa Cruz, western Vella Lavella, eastern Kolombangara, southern Malaita and north-western Maramasike.

A few villagers are taken by crocs every year. If you are bushwalking and plan to cross muddy coastal rivers, marshes, estuaries or tidal flats, or to go near mangrove swamps, always ask if there are crocodiles about and whether they are long or short-mouthed ones. If there's any chance at all of crocs, don't go there. Children are always at risk.

Frogs & Toads The Solomons has several species of frog and toad, including a number of tree varieties, one horned frog and a giant edible form which grows to 45 cm long and carries its young on its back. Accidentally introduced in WWII and now a pest, the cane toad has poison glands on its back which can squirt venom one metre. Any animal eating a cane toad can expect to die from toxic poisoning within an hour.

Marine Creatures

Whales were plentiful until worldwide depredation by whaling fleets made them uncommon visitors to the Solomons. But dolphins and porpoises frequently play around inter-island boats. People in Malaita and Makira/Ulawa sometimes organise hunting parties to drive them into confined waters. Their flesh is eaten and their teeth are used for bride price.

Occasionally dugongs can be seen in the shallows eating seaweed, the female suckling her one pup on the surface.

On most voyages through the Solomons you will see flying fish skimming above the sea, their tiny, wing-like fins beating so hard that they look like fast-revolving wheels.

Two of the four turtle species frequenting the Solomons are quite common. The green and hawksbill turtles nest on most islands from November to February. The female digs her nest at night on a sandy shore, laying a clutch of about 100 eggs nightly at the same spot over several weeks. The baby turtles hatch at night after two to 2½ months.

Sharks Shark attacks are rare, but not unknown. It's always wise to seek the advice of local people before taking to the water. Islanders usually consider themselves adequately protected from sharks when they are inside a reef or swimming from a white-sand, or coral-debris, beach. Black sand, however, is usually volcanic in origin, and has no protective coral reef to form a barrier. Worldwide, most shark strikes occur either at beaches in only one metre of water or in tidal river mouths and estuaries.

If you're approached by a shark, stay as calm as possible and swim steadily away. See Health in the Facts for the Visitor chapter for how to treat victims of shark attack.

Dangerous Reef Dwellers The extremely poisonous stonefish is well named, its stone-like appearance making it very hard to see. Avoid touching any rocks that are small and odd-shaped, and always wear reef shoes when walking through coral shallows. Scorpion fish, in contrast, are easy to spot, with their attractive pink colours and silvery, but highly venomous, spines.

Not every type of cone shell is venomous, but several are, so don't touch any unless you have an islander along who's sure which ones are safe. Some cone-shaped shellfish have an extremely venomous proboscis, which extend rapidly, functioning as a dart-like stinging device. This can reach any part of the shell's outer surface, poisoning you as you handle the creature. Cone-shell venom can be fatal.

Clams and moray eels have something in common – they're nonvenomous but when they bite they don't let go! Leave clams alone, even though their jaws generally close too slowly to trap a human. Don't poke around small coral holes, where morays live. Finally, don't swim with anything shiny on or a barracuda may take a bite out of it – and you too!

Nature Reserves
East Rennell Island and New Georgia's Marovo Lagoon have been proposed for World Heritage listing, and both areas have introduced nature-conservation measures.

Oema Atoll and Oema Island are treated as bird sanctuaries by Shortlands people, and Tetepare has been proposed as a nature reserve. However, nothing official has been decided on these yet.

GOVERNMENT & POLITICS
The Solomon Islands became an independent country on 7 July 1978. It's a parliamentary democracy with a single legislative assembly. The British Crown, as leader of the Commonwealth, is head of state, with the governor general, chosen by Parliament, acting as the monarch's representative. Moses Pitakaka was appointed governor general for a five-year term in July 1994.

The judicial system is based on British law, with a high court, a court of appeal and magistrates' court. Local courts are conducted by village elders and there's a customary land appeal court that hears appeals over land-ownership matters – a major aspect of court business. An ombudsman investigates public complaints against national and provincial government bodies.

The Solomons has generally taken a quiet position in international affairs. The country is a member of the United Nations and most of its special intergovernmental agencies, the World Bank, two of the European Union (EU) subgroups, the Commonwealth, the South Pacific Forum, the South Pacific Commission, and the South Pacific Nuclear Free Zone.

National Government
The 47-seat parliament is in Honiara. The main party is the National Unity Reconciliation Progressive Party, which won power in the November 1994 election. The prime minister, Solomon Mamaloni, is in his second term. His previous tenure was ended in June 1993 by the government headed by Francis Hilly. Hilly was prime minister for only 17 months and was brought down largely by the powerful logging lobby.

The other main parties are the National Party, the National Action Party, the Labour Party and the People's Alliance Party. The parties are not strongly differentiated – members regularly cross the floor to attach themselves to emerging personalities. Elections are held within every four-year period. All citizens over 18 may vote.

Politics in the Solomons since Independence has mainly been about devolution.

There has been secessionist talk in Western and Temotu provinces, partly because they fear domination by the more heavily populated provinces.

Regional Assemblies

Each province is administered by its own provincial government which sits for a four-year term and is headed by an elected premier. Honiara is politically independent of Guadalcanal Province as it has its own municipal authority. The provincial assemblies have a reasonable degree of autonomy, though they are largely dependent upon the national government for financing.

In 1996 the national government introduced legislation to replace the old provincial assemblies. Each province would have a provincial council comprising the head of each of its newly formed area assemblies. The post of premier would disappear. Area assemblies would be composed of elected and nominated members, including chiefs and landowners. The plan was greeted with strong opposition from the existing provincial assemblies, and some (such as Western Province) won the right to defer introduction until 1999.

The new system will mean more people involved in local government but fewer powers for the provincial administration. It will also be a more expensive system, and it's questionable whether it can be afforded.

ECONOMY

The country's main natural resources are its trees (yielding fruit and logs) and its fisheries. The Solomons has allowed these prime assets to be mostly exploited by foreign companies who pay the government low taxes and take all the profit abroad.

In recent years, there has been considerable diversification from the copra-based, one-product rural economy of the colonial era. New interests include beef cattle, oil palms, cocoa and spices. There are mineral deposits of bauxite, phosphates, gold, silver, copper, manganese and nickel.

Employed people earn an average of S$4168 annually, yet the country's income

National Symbols
The national flag was first flown on Independence Day and is blue and green, divided diagonally by a thin yellow stripe. This stands for the narrow strand of sand separating the surrounding blue seas from the country's green forests. There are five white stars clustered at the top left corner, representing the Solomons' five main groups of islands.

The national anthem is *God Save Our Solomon Islands*. The coat of arms includes a shark, a crocodile, an eagle, two turtles and frigate birds, spears and a shield. The country's motto is 'To Lead is to Serve'. ∎

per capita is only S$134 per year. This is because the Solomon Islands is primarily a rural and subsistence economy, with approximately 75% of the population enjoying self-sufficiency from the assets of the land and the sea.

In 1995 only 34,200 people were formally employed in full or part-time work,

5% fewer than the previous year. Traditionally a village-based country, the Solomons is experiencing urban drift (Honiara is growing by 7% per annum), mostly through young men leaving their families and seeking their fortune in the city. When they can't find jobs, they find it hard to survive in a monied environment, especially as they're used to subsistence living and the support of their village *wantoks* (relatives or close friends).

Government finances are in a mess. The 1996 budget allowed for a deficit of S$100 million, and the Central Bank's annual report morosely commented 'how this will be financed is yet unclear'. Inflation is steady at around 10%. Commerce and industry are dominated by foreign interests, particularly Australian and Japanese.

Foreign Trade

In 1995 the Solomons achieved a small surplus on its current account, the first since 1984. This was mainly due to increased exports (value S$573 million, as against S$552 million in imports). Exports by percentage share were: timber 49%, fish 25%, palm oil 13%, copra 6% and cocoa 2%. At the same time a deficit in the capital account meant that the balance of payments showed its usual deficit, though the gap has narrowed since the early 1990s.

External reserves, falling since 1988, reached around S$55 million in 1995, enough to finance only five weeks' worth of imports. External debt was S$519 million, down from a peak of S$615 million in 1992. The Solomons' exports go to Japan (39%), UK (23%), Thailand (9%), Australia (5%) and the US (2%). Imports come from: Australia (34%), Japan (16%), Singapore (14%) and New Zealand (9%). The Solomons dollar experiences steady depreciation; in 1995 it depreciated 10% against the value of the currencies of its main trading partners.

Foreign investment was only worth S$6 million in 1995. Overseas aid mainly comes from Britain, Australia, Japan, New Zealand and Taiwan, albeit at a modest level.

Agriculture & Forestry

About 30% of land is cultivable in small parcels. The only large expanse of good agricultural soil is on the Guadalcanal Plains. Villagers in the Solomons are often described as living in a state of subsistence affluence. Gardens (providing fruit and root vegetables), fishing and livestock supply their basic needs, plus a modest cash income. Before WWII, plantations used to dominate the copra trade. Since then, villagers have become a significant economic force, owning 80% of the country's trees and producing 50% of its cocoa.

Palm-oil output, mainly from large projects in north-eastern Guadalcanal, continues to expand, though world prices have been very low for some years. New oil-palm plantations are still being established and are seen by environmentalists as simply a ruse for clearing the land by logging.

Natural forests cover 2.2 million hectares, or 79% of total land. Of this, 12% is considered viable for commercial logging. See the Value of Trees aside in the Ecology & Environment section of this chapter for information about how this valuable asset has been abused. The main forestry islands are Kolombangara, New Georgia, Shortland, Santa Isabel, Makira, Choiseul, Malaita, Guadalcanal and Santa Cruz. Most of the logs go to Malaysia, Japan, South Korea and Taiwan. Some timber is sawn locally at the country's small mills and now has an export value of S$10 million, exporting mainly to Australia, New Zealand and Korea.

Land Use & Ownership

Around 88% of land in the Solomons is owned under customary tenure. Neither the government nor expatriates may own it. The other 12% is known as registered land; the government owns over half, the rest belongs to custom owners. Foreigners may hold leases on this land for a maximum of 75 years, the average life of a coconut tree.

Traditionally, land belongs to people, not institutions. An individual's right to use land comes from their membership of a

Melanesian clan or Polynesian family claiming descent from the first people to settle there. Other people may only use this land with the consent of those who have inherited rights to it.

Land transfers beyond members of the same family require payment of compensation. In some areas this involves the exchange of shell money and a feast to signify publicly that this transaction has occurred.

Legal wrangles over land, particularly that desired by mining and timber interests, are common. This can make investment unpredictable, even unrewarding. Litigation between individual islanders is also frequent, usually between the current occupant and the descendants of a family that may have last used it some two or more generations ago.

Mining

Although there's a great diversity of minerals nationally, few exist in sufficient quantities and purity to justify development. Problems over compensation and customary land ownership, in addition to islanders' understandable concerns over inevitable destruction of their gardens and traditional ways of life, have often proved insurmountable. So far, mining for bauxite on Wagina, Santa Cruz and Rennell, and phosphate on Bellona, is on indefinite hold for these reasons.

Gold prospects in the Shortland Islands and the islands of Santa Isabel, Choiseul, Vella Lavella, Mbava and Marovo (beside Vangunu) remain unexploited, usually because of customary land access and ownership difficulties. However, commercial mining has recently started at Gold Ridge in Guadalcanal. Nickel laterite in Santa Isabel and San Jorge is likely to be the next in line for large-scale mining. Offshore oil exploration is also likely to begin in the next few years.

Fishing

The Solomons is an extremely rich fishing ground for tuna. Fish – mostly skipjack, yellowfin tuna and albacore – are usually caught by the pole-and-line method, and the bulk of the catch is frozen and exported to other markets.

Commercial fishing is the Solomons' second-biggest earner. In 1995, 35,000 tonnes of fish were caught by Solomon Taiyo Ltd. Its cannery at Noro is operating at full capacity (producing one million cases a year), yet strangely this part-Japanese-run company usually reports annual losses and therefore pays negligible taxes. National Fisheries Developments Ltd, Canadian owned, is the next largest concern, catching 21,000 tonnes. The government recently gave a licence to Ting Hong, a Taiwanese company, to catch and process fish, believing it would build a factory and employ islanders. The company did neither, instead shipping in its own floating factory and its own workers. Public outcry prompted the government to suspend the licence, which was still under review in late 1996.

The Solomons has proclaimed a 200-nautical-mile (376-km) exclusive fishing zone, but this is difficult to police and foreign boats have been caught fishing inside it (including a US boat, causing an incident which led to an expensive embargo on Solomons tuna by the USA). The sustainable level of fish caught annually is claimed by the government to be 120,000 tonnes, yet village fisherfolk have seen their subsistence catch diminishing in size and quantity in places. This is partly due to large-scale netting of baitfish in shallow waters.

Manufacturing

The Solomons' manufacturing sector is still very small, though boat building is a major activity in Tulagi. Most other industries are in Honiara and the Guadalcanal Plains.

Palm-oil milling and timber and fish processing are new activities, as is the making of paint, furniture, fibreglass canoes, water tanks, shell costume jewellery, buttons, biscuits, soft drinks, beer, clothing, soap, nails and coarse tobacco, and the baking of bread.

Tourism

Tourism is only a minor part of the economy. In 1994 the country received 11,919 visitors by air, of whom only 4,049 were tourists. There were also 3,742 people visiting on cruise ships. Tourism revenues were $53.3 million, though Solomon Islanders travelling abroad spent nearly as much.

Over 36% of visitors were from Australia, 12% were from New Zealand and 8% from Papua New Guinea. The average length of stay was 12 days. Tourism levels have dipped since the mid-1980s. Visits were about 10% higher in 1995 than in 1994, yet the government's target for 56,800 tourist visits annually by 2000 remains absurdly optimistic.

POPULATION & PEOPLE

The nation's population was estimated to be about 400,000 in 1996. The vast majority of Solomon Islanders – 95%, or 380,000 – are Melanesian. Polynesians number about 15,000, or 3.75%. There are also about 4500 Micronesian settlers from Kiribati – often called Gilbertese – and a smattering of expatriate residents and Asians.

The term Melanesia comes from the Greek words *melas* and *nesos*, meaning 'black' and 'island' respectively. Therefore, Melanesians are the black island people (of western Oceania). Polynesians are the people of the *polys* (many) islands in the eastern Pacific, while Micronesians come from the *mikros* (tiny) islands to the north. Of the indigenous population, the Melanesians tend to prefer the group's larger, mountainous islands, while the Polynesians live mainly on the isolated outer reefs and atolls.

The Solomons' population density of 14.5 people per sq km is one of the lowest in the Pacific. The nation's population has increased annually by about 3.5% since the early 1970s, due to a combination of high fertility levels and improved medical facilities. Figures released in 1996 indicated the annual rise had recently eased back to 2.4%. Death rates and infant-mortality rates are

Legendary People

Whether Kakamoras have ever lived, or still do, can only be guessed at. Similar doubt surrounds the existence of various other legendary races talked of by islanders. Little is known of the fierce Mumutambu from the Nggelas, the Sinipi of Choiseul, or the Mongoes of Santa Isabel.

People from Rennell and Bellona islands talk about the Hiti as if they really existed, and archaeological evidence supports this claim, even if it cannot confirm or contradict their belief that they were short and hairy. Archaeological evidence also suggests that the Afukere of Anuta might once have existed.

Kakamoras are the most widely reported of such legendary people. Islanders tell of a pygmy race of aboriginal pre-Melanesian people, who still hide in mountain caves on Makira, Santa Isabel, Choiseul, Guadalcanal, Vanikoro and Santa Cruz.

Kakamoras are said to be like humans, but are only about one to 1.5 metres tall and chatter in an unintelligible language. Allegedly, they are caught on rare occasions. Some say a male Kakamora was found on Guadalcanal in 1969 but got away. Others tell of seeing naked 'wild people' with very long, straight hair hanging to below their waists, short, sturdy legs and very strong, short, pointy teeth.

According to legend, Kakamoras are able to run very fast through the bush and to hop speedily across rocks and boulders. Despite their small size, an individual Kakamora is believed to be as strong as three men. While Kakamoras seldom attack people and are usually harmless and shy, stories abound of local females being carried off by them. ■

steadily falling, and life expectancy has shot up to over 70 years (from only 54 in the late 1980s).

A feature of the Solomons group is the large number of small villages, where nearly 75% of the population live. Excluding provincial capitals, there are 4180 settlements in the country, with an average of 71 people in each and six people per household. There is a problem with urban drift to Honiara, which is currently growing by about 7% per year.

Melanesians

Although Melanesians are all of the same race, their physical appearance and customs vary considerably. The people with the darkest skins live in the western areas and Choiseul, and are ethnically related to Bougainville Islanders in Papua New Guinea. People in the rest of the country are lighter.

Melanesian life is more democratic than the aristocratic and oligarchic system prevailing in Polynesian islands. Although there's plenty of intermarriage between the two races (particularly in the Reef Islands), there are occasional tensions too.

Polynesians

Some Polynesians, particularly those from Sikaiana, have slim, Asiatic features, due to a Micronesian mixing in the 19th century.

Gilbertese

Between 1955 and 1971, Micronesian settlers came from the Gilbert Islands (now Kiribati) under a British government resettlement scheme. Their own seriously overcrowded islands had been exhausted by a long period of drought. New land was offered on Ghizo, Shortland and Wagina.

Some have moved to White River Village in Honiara, or to Red Beach, just east of Henderson airport. Their dance, the *batere*, is a regular part of the capital's tourist scene. Yandina and Tulagi also have sizeable Micronesian communities now.

Asians

The small Chinese community lives mainly in Honiara's Chinatown. There are a few Chinese stores elsewhere in the country – at Gizo, Auki and Kirakira – though Tulagi's large prewar Chinatown has now gone.

The Japanese, and a few Koreans with them, work for the Noro-based Solomon Taiyo fishing fleet. Many veterans come to see the battlefields or to find the remains of war-dead compatriots still needing cremation according to traditional Shinto rites.

Expatriate Residents

Expatriate residents, known as expats, still hold many specialist and technical government posts, most of which are based in the capital. In contrast, most overseas volunteers work outside Honiara. The majority of expats are Britons, Australians, New Zealanders, Americans and Canadians, who generally hold jobs in medicine, teaching, technical trades or water supply. In the past, most expats were missionaries, doctors or government staff (or, occasionally, planters or traders). Consequently, local people sometimes have an overly idealised opinion of whites.

Islanders always assume all foreigners who speak English are wantoks. This can cause problems, as US Peace Corps staff report. Occasionally a foreign traveller ends up at some isolated spot bumming off villagers who are too embarrassed to confront the person. So they ask the local volunteer teachers either to persuade the visitor to leave or to start looking after the freeloader themselves.

Albinos

Albinos have white skin and pinkish eyes, resulting from a congenital melanin deficiency. Albinism is quite common in the Reef Islands, the Duff Islands and Santa Cruz.

Albinos have great difficulty with the strong light and heat of the tropics, and are often heavily clothed to protect against sunburn. Though sympathetically treated by their companions, they are considered to be

SIMON FOALE

SIMON FOALE

SIMON FOALE

SIMON FOALE

HOLGER LEUE

SIMON FOALE

SIMON FOALE

SIMON FOALE

A	B	C
	D	
E	F	
G	H	

A: Crab spider, Guadalcanal
B: Leaf-cricket, Sandfly Island
C: Dragonfly, Sandfly Island
D: Gecko, Malaita Island

E: Orchid, New Georgia Island
F: Cormorant, Rennell Island
G: Parrot, Malaita Island
H: Common rainforest flower, Sandfly Island

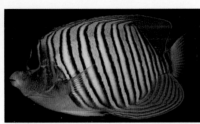
Regal angel fish
(*Pygoplites diacanthus*)

Male red-fin anthias
(*Pseudanthias dispar*)

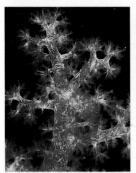
Soft coral at night

Golden damsel
(*Amblyglyphidodon aureus*)

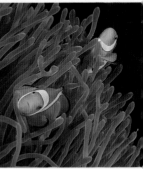
Anemonefishes
(*Amphiprion percula*)

Blenny
(*Ecsenius* sp.)

Cleaner shrimp
(*Periclimenes holthuisi*)

Giant clam
(*Tridacna maxima*)

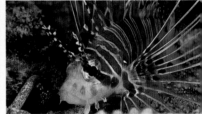
Nudibranch
(*Chromodoris coi*)

Ragged-finned firefish
(*Pterois antennata*)

All photographs taken by Simon Foale

clumsy. Their life expectancy is short, especially for females, and they seldom marry because of the likelihood that any children would inherit the gene leading to albinism.

EDUCATION

Education in the Solomons is neither compulsory nor free. The country has one of the lowest literacy rates in the Pacific; a 1991 government survey claimed 62% literacy but the true figure is probably much lower than this.

About 500 preprimary and primary schools teach children aged five to nine. About 10% of children up to age 14 receive secondary education in 21 schools; four national secondary schools and 17 provincial ones. The national secondary schools are more academic and have sixth forms in preparation for tertiary studies. Over 300 students a year undertake courses abroad, mainly in Fiji and Papua New Guinea. Others attend the Solomon Islands College of Higher Education (SICHE) in Kukum to study technical subjects.

There are two six-week school holidays annually: in December and January, and in June and July. The majority of primary school children are girls. However, less than half the secondary-school pupils, and only one in seven of the students attending tertiary studies overseas, are female.

The wage economy in the Solomons is very small, so finding paid employment presents a major problem for educated school-leavers.

Expatriate Schooling

There are five private primary schools in Honiara, of which the Woodford International School (☎ 30186) is the one most favoured by expat families. There are also three small private kindergartens for children under five years. Most foreign children return to their home country for secondary schooling at 10 or 11 years of age.

ARTS

In the past, many of the Solomons' artefacts were made out of materials which rapidly decomposed in the hot, humid climate. Others used for ceremonial purposes were destroyed with the onset of Christianity.

Certain crafts lost their market with the arrival of modern trade goods. Pottery, formerly made in the Shortlands, and possibly also in Simbo, Wagina and Kolombangara, is now only produced in north-western Choiseul.

Tapa clothing, decorated or otherwise, is more characteristic of the south-east Pacific, though elderly men sometimes wear it in the Polynesian outliers. It's also made on Simbo and Santa Isabel.

Before colonisation carving and weaving were skills basic to everyday living. Because of endemic warfare, every family had to fashion its own weapons. Weaving was required for domestic items such as bags, baskets and mats.

Carving

Carvings incorporated human, bird, fish and animal motifs, often in combination; they frequently represented deities and spirits. Frigate birds and sharks were particularly popular, and together with the human form, could appear on as diverse objects as stone mortars, canoe ornaments, house posts, fishing floats, shields and ritual staffs.

Carving represented a form of worship. Only the best reproductions of a god's image could ensure success in war, fishing, gardening and healing. Carvings were often inlaid with small pieces of chambered nautilus shell, chosen because it had a smooth, shiny surface and was a convenient material to work in.

Traditional and nontraditional motifs are used to decorate a wide range of goods, including coins and postage stamps. Carvings of *nguzunguzus* (canoe figureheads, also carved in miniature) and various animals are skilfully fashioned by Western Province craftspeople in modern flowing designs, using mainly light-brown kerosene wood.

Santa Catalina in Makira/Ulawa Province produces small, ornately decorated ritual bowls. Well away from the tourist mainstream, its products have a much more

Nguzunguzus

The most distinctive carved artifacts are *nguzunguzus* (pronounced 'noozoonoo-zoos'). These figureheads used to adorn the prows of war canoes, particularly on inter-island raids. Positioned on the craft's prow at the water line, a nguzunguzu's job was to ward off any water spirits which tried to upset the canoe, guide the craft past jagged reefs, protect the warriors aboard and guarantee success in combat.

Depending on the canoe's mission, the figurehead rests its chin on two clenched fists (war), a human head (head-hunting) or a dove (peace). Nowadays, nguzunguzus are usually carved in the head-hunting mode because that's what the tourists seem to like. The best of these figureheads are made of ebony; cheaper ones are carved from brown-streaked kerosene wood, and blackened with furniture polish. After carving, pieces of pearly nautilus shell are inlaid, making an extremely striking contrast against the smooth, highly polished, jet-black background. ∎

traditional look and are much sought after by collectors. Makira/Ulawa also has a tradition of large housepost carvings, often of naked human figures.

Miniature canoes are made as tourist souvenirs in Western Province, Malaita, Ulawa, Santa Ana and Nggela islands. Polynesians make small replica outriggers from hibiscus wood in Tikopia and Bellona, while model sailing canoes are occasionally crafted in the Reef and Duff islands. Shark-hooks are made from branches and roots, though bone and shell are used for miniature versions. Floats and handmade fish-hooks are used both for fishing and as tourist souvenirs.

Although nontraditional in design, masks are carved from kerosene wood in Western Province, and on the Rennell and Bellona islands. Their designs, complete with sombre, stylised faces and lengthened ears, have been adapted from Africa and Papua New Guinea.

Some lime boxes, used by betel-nut chewers throughout the Solomons, are made from gourds or coconuts. The best ones are from Guadalcanal.

Weaving

Most weaving is done without looms, using split bamboo, vines, cane and dried coconut and pandanus leaves. *Bukaware* baskets, trays, table mats and coasters are made in several parts of the Solomons, especially Guadalcanal. They're time-consuming to make as the very tough *asa* vine is used. Bukaware gets its name from the similar products created on Buka Island in south-eastern Papua New Guinea.

Mats are made throughout the archipelago. Gilbertese people make sturdy, brown sleeping mats out of pandanus leaf. Finely woven shoulder bags are produced on Rennell and Bellona from vine, while those made in the Reef Islands are decorated with tufts and tassels.

Music & Musical Instruments

Bamboo pipes are common on most of the larger islands – in particular Malaita and

Guadalcanal – and are made in sets, or singly like flutes. A typical bamboo band has three to eight performers.

When the music first developed in the 1920s, the ends of the larger bamboo tubes were struck with coconut husks to make a tune. Rubber sandals are usually used nowadays. The shorter bamboo tubes twang like a ukulele, the longer ones boom like a double bass.

Stamping drums are made from bamboo tubes in Ontong Java and Malaita and from hollow wood in Vanikoro. They're about one to 1.2m long and 15 cm in diameter. Dance sticks are made in Malaita and Santa Ana.

Traditional Dance

Dancing outside Honiara is mainly traditional, though you can also see this in the capital. There are regular performances each week at hotels, and around town at other times, particularly on Independence Day.

Villagers may invite you to custom dances. They will expect you to watch and not to participate unless specifically invited to do so. Be sure to obey their rules and do nothing *tabu*.

Grass skirts are rarely seen nowadays except at traditional dances and ceremonies. Rather than grass, they are actually made from betel leaf or hibiscus bark soaked in salt water for a week. Rennellese men often dance in tapa, dyed yellow with turmeric, at festivals.

Literature

The Solomon Islands has a tradition of telling custom stories, some of which are now published and available in Honiara's bookshops and souvenir shops. In the 1980s the University of the South Pacific (USP) encouraged writers from all over the Pacific to build up a body of written material about their countries.

Ples Blong Iumi: The Solomon Islands, the Past Four Thousand Years (USP & the Solomon Islands College of Higher Education, Suva & Honiara, 1989) by Sam Alasia and others, and edited by Hugh Laracy, con-

tains contributions by 14 Solomon Islanders about differing aspects of their country. These include culture, social change and the past. *Hostage* (USP, Honiara, 1988) by Sam Alasia is a book of personal poems.

Several works have been written by former parliamentarians and government officials. *Zoleveke: A Man from Choiseul* (USP, Suva, 1980) by Gideon Zoleveke recounts the story of a Choiseul man who became a Cabinet minister. *From Pig-Theft to Parliament: My Life Between Two Worlds* (USP & the Solomon Islands College of Higher Education, Honiara, 1989) by Jonathan Fifi'i, translated and edited by Roger Keesing, tells of the author's childhood in eastern Malaita, the Marching Rule Movement, and life as a parliamentarian. *Kanaka Boy* (USP, Suva & Honiara, 1985) by Sir Frederick Osifelo is the autobiography of the first Solomon Islander to be knighted.

SOCIETY & CONDUCT

The immense variety of the Solomons' culture and customs reflects the existence of about 100 indigenous languages and dialects among a population of 400,000. Dances, ceremonies, funerals, weddings, initiations, and systems of status and authority often differ from island to island, and sometimes from one district to another on the larger islands. Yet there are common themes, particularly the acceptance of the obligation to offer something in return for all services rendered. This is the same throughout the country.

Kastom

You will hear the word '*kastom*' (custom) used constantly when villagers refer to traditional beliefs and land ownership. If something is done in a certain way because of custom, this means it has always been done this way, and people consider it right to continue doing it this way. Breaches of custom are always deplored.

Dances, songs and stories depicting the past are still common. These usually celebrate war, hunting, the natural world or the harvesting of crops. Cultural displays are usually colourful and varied, with many islands having several dances unique to themselves.

Some islanders still believe in various forms of magic. In Malaita, in particular, some still believe the spirit of a dead person can live for a time in sharks, birds and reptiles. Where this is so, the creature is offered gifts and becomes tabu to eat. Ancestors, it seems, are particularly fond of returning as sharks.

Village Life

About 75% of Solomon Islanders live in villages. Most settlements are coastal and close to freshwater springs. Each family has a small coconut plantation for copra production and cash income, and a few scattered vegetable plots.

The nearby bush or rainforest provides traditional foods such as wild nuts, ferns and fruits, as well as material for leaf-house and canoe construction, rope and basket making, and firewood. Traditional crops such as taro are cultivated in village plots. There's always a church in the larger villages, often a primary school and a store, and sometimes a medical clinic and/or police post.

The Chief or Bigman

Inheritance is a major factor in determining who holds power in Polynesian society, but Melanesians adhere instead to the bigman cult. The bigman, or chief, is the most influential villager, either as a result of his wealth or his success at settling disputes.

Anyone may ask the chief for assistance. However, in return, his (or, in Vella Lavella, possibly her) word must be obeyed while there. The chief may consult other influential villagers before making a decision, for instance to determine whether a foreigner or group of foreigners can stay overnight in the village.

The Role of Women

Although these are the days of equal opportunity, a woman's main role in the Solomons is still to be a good wife and mother. Agriculture and domestic duties are treated as women's work, though heavier tasks are done by men. Girls have to learn adult ways earlier than boys, but they are expected to treat their brothers with respect – even the younger ones.

In the past, political power and control over customary land descended through females in certain parts of the country. As clan heads, women did and do exercise considerable power in Guadalcanal, Savo and Vella Lavella.

Women usually marry at 19, whereas men do so on average at 25. As a woman is traditionally paid for in marriage with some form of bride price, children belong to the husband's clan, not the wife's.

Despite legislation providing for equal employment and political participation, women still occupy mainly junior positions in the country. The proportion of female employees is gradually rising, but it's still only about 20%. About 50% of working women are nurses, teachers, government officials or clerical staff. The Solomons previously had a few female members of parliament, though there's none currently.

Wantoks

You will hear the expression 'wantok' repeatedly. In its simplest sense a wantok is someone who speaks the same dialect, and therefore has the same 'one-talk', or language. This is why many islanders tend to assume all English-speaking Europeans of the same religion are wantoks.

In Melanesian terms, all people from the same settlement are wantoks because of the communal nature of village land ownership and the ethic of sharing goods and property between relations. However, true wantoks are only those of an extended family, close friends and their immediate family.

Custom requires you always help your wantoks. This includes helping them build their house and providing them with shelter and food. To refuse help, however justifiably, is to bring shame on yourself, your family and your clan.

This is fine when you are surrounded by well-stocked gardens in island villages, but it breaks down in an urban, money-based environment. An islander who manages to find a good job and home in Honiara may soon be faced with wantoks, who have neither money nor jobs, arriving and expecting shelter and food.

Many shops are owned by Chinese who are not bound by the obligations of wantok relationships. If an islander opens a trade store, there's a risk relatives will come by and demand free food.

Dos & Don'ts

Solomon Islanders are usually very tolerant of outsiders' unintentional errors, but they do expect their rules to be observed. If you accidentally breach some minor rule, courtesy and friendly apologies are usually sufficient. However, private property is just that, so make sure you stick to the road when passing through a village. If you leave the highway to walk on a bush path, always ask the first person you meet for permission to use it. Either approval will be given straight away or you will be introduced to the chief for his ruling.

Land ownership and food growing are extremely delicate matters, so don't pick fruit and flowers growing by the wayside. They may look untended, but they still belong to someone, as do reefs.

Food-sharing is important in Melanesian society, even in dealings with foreigners. Generosity in this regard is considered a great virtue. Islanders will often offer food, usually a coconut or banana, on your arrival and won't expect more than thanks in return if you're only with them a short time. But if you stay longer, they will expect you to pay them back. When you eat with local people, don't tuck into your food straight away, but wait to see if grace will be said out loud.

In some remote traditional areas people – particularly young children – may wear few or no clothes. Middle-aged men and elderly women may be bare-chested, and young women may be naked or only wearing a grass skirt or a small T-piece. In all such regions, visitors should always be fully dressed.

Foreigners dressed in scant swimwear can cause a very negative reaction in a town. In some rural areas, this applies even on the beach. Indeed, many islanders often swim fully dressed as the display of thighs – especially by women – is considered tabu. Consequently, nude bathing and skimpy swimwear are always to be avoided, for either sex.

Some islanders, especially Gilbertese, might say 'yes' by simply raising their eyebrows and smiling. This can be unnerving until you get used to it, because it seems like a gesture of enquiry, as if they haven't heard your question.

In rural areas, get into the habit of saying 'hello' to people you pass on the path – it will be warmly returned. In the evening, passers-by commonly wish each other 'good night', even though they haven't previously met.

Shaking hands is a Western custom which even today some islanders find unnatural. Looking people directly in the eye is another habit islanders are only gradually getting used to. Traditionally, people would stand and look askance as a sign of respect; northern Malaitans took this to the extreme, requiring courting couples to stand back to back!

You'll see men holding hands with their male friends, and female friends doing likewise. But local men will not touch women in public. It's OK for Western couples to do this, but exercise restraint. It's disrespectful to step over somebody's outstretched legs, especially those of older people.

It is most unwise to collect geological specimens or pan for gold without the village chief's permission. If you do, you will be considered to be stealing from the landowners – both those of this generation and those as yet unborn.

Tabus

You'll frequently hear the word 'tabu' (pronounced 'tambu'), from which comes the English word 'taboo'. (On Polynesian islands, it may instead be pronounced 'tapu'.) In Pacific Island terms, this expression means 'sacred' or 'holy' as well as 'forbidden'. In its simplest form, it can even mean 'no entry' when written across a doorway or gate.

Tabu places can only be visited with permission from the owners. Visiting without it will cause much local ill feeling and you may be required to pay compensation.

Village and island life is beset with tabus, although rules can vary from place to place. Rural women's lives are particularly fraught with them. They may not stand higher than a male, nor can they step over a fire, as its smoke may rise higher than a man.

At the same time, men may not deliberately place themselves below women. So, walking under a woman's clothesline or swimming under her canoe is forbidden. If a male visitor does this in some areas, everything involved will have to be destroyed and he'll have to pay compensation.

Menstruation and birth are surrounded by all sorts of tabus. In more traditional areas – especially in certain parts of Malaita – each village has an area set aside for childbirth and menstruating women. The area is strictly tabu for men. Women have to remain secluded in the menstrual huts until their period is finished, though they can usually be visited by a young girl with food and firewood if need be. Menstruation and pregnancy tabus do not apply to women travellers in towns but may apply in villages and remote regions. Check with local women.

It would be a serious breach of custom if a woman refused to go into confinement while pregnant, and continued to go to her garden, fish, or cook publicly. She would have to pay compensation to the chief or leave the village, and in the past it would have meant death. Women are also barred from going near men's tabu places, such as skull shrines. Boys may visit these once they're initiated.

Islanders say foreigners who breach certain tabus or go to a tabu place can get sick. Apparently several expats who have done so have been suddenly struck down by strange illnesses. After falling sick one foreign woman lost her straight blonde hair; it eventually grew back black and curly! So, always ask an adult islander whether it's all right to go to a particular place or not.

Each sex has its own area for ablutions. If you're staying in a village, check which is your section as soon as possible after arrival.

Bad manners are exceptionally rare in Melanesia, and thoughtlessness and impatience are usually the preserve of foreigners rather than islanders. Most local people will act as if nothing has happened if you offend them, silently forgiving you for not knowing that you have broken a local rule. Malaitans and Shortland Islanders may be quite direct with you if you breach one of their tabus or act inconsiderately.

Custom Fees

Local villagers charge a landing, or custom, fee for some sites. This may be to see a collection of ancestral skulls, a cavern or a thermal area, or to visit a war site, reef, beach or tourist-oriented island village where ancient dances or ceremonies are regularly performed.

Unfortunately, prices as high as S$50 are occasionally asked, although figures between S$5 and S$10 are more common. If the price is too high, you could try suggesting what you're prepared to pay, but some villagers seem to be totally indifferent as to whether you see the place or not. Commissioning a local guide may shield you for the more extortionate demands, or you could try offering goods instead.

Recently, non-landowners have been making bogus claims for custom fees, but fortunately this practice hasn't yet spread beyond Malaita (see Charges & Custom Fees in the Malaita chapter).

Tattoos

Tattooing is common among both Melanesians and Polynesians. Many patterns have a traditional significance depending

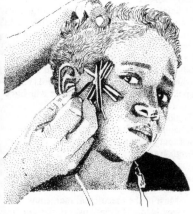

Facial engraving is a traditional practice

on the age and social position of the wearer. Some Polynesians from Ontong Java and Anuta are still heavily into tattoos.

Facial engraving is practised on Malaita. A grooved, unpigmented design is made using a bone to scrape the skin's surface. On some other islands, pigment is then applied, leaving a permanent design, usually in blue and black.

In northern Malaita, men are tattooed below the eye, while women decorate their breasts. Ontong Java's people prefer their tattoos on their foreheads, while the back of a woman's thigh is the usual spot in the Reef Islands. The chest can be tattooed in Tikopia, as it used to be in pre-Christian Rennell and Bellona.

Ornaments

Shell-money necklaces are used as personal decoration in both Malaita and Western Province, while oyster-shell pendants can be seen in Choiseul, Malaita and Guadalcanal. Forehead discs, made from turtle shell and clam shell, are called *kapkaps* and come from Nggela, Malaita and the New Georgia group. On several islands, necklaces and forehead decorations are made

from the teeth of porpoises, dogs, possums and flying foxes.

In Malaita, belts of red, black and white shell money are worn as armbands, and some people wear ear ornaments complete with beads and porpoises' teeth. Earrings of brown shell are preferred in Santa Cruz. In other places small, white cowrie shells are used as forehead or leg decorations. Combs are commonly worn as hair ornaments and on Malaita may have coloured fibres.

Currency

Several forms of *kastom mani* have evolved for paying bride price and for other specialised transactions, which are beyond the scope of normal traveller activity. Kastom mani is still in use in Malaita, where shell money costs up to S$400 for each 10-strand length, and in Temotu Province, where red-feather coils are occasionally used. Although previously used, large clam-shell rings in the New Georgia Islands, thin clamshell cylinders in Choiseul, and forehead apparel made from porpoises' and dogs' teeth in Malaita and parts of Makira/Ulawa are no longer traditional currency.

RELIGION

About 96% of the population are Christians. Some 35% of these are members of the Anglican-affiliated Church of Melanesia (COM) and about 20% are Roman Catholics. Both have resident archbishops, while the COM has assistant bishops in Isabel, Temotu and Makira/Ulawa provinces.

A further 18% of islanders belong to the South Seas Evangelical Church (SSEC), 11% belong to the Uniting Church, and 10% are Seventh Day Adventist (SDA).

Christian sects include the Bahais, Jehovah's Witnesses, or members of the Christian Fellowship Church, an indigenous breakaway movement from the Methodists which is active mainly in northern New Georgia and Vonavona. The remainder of the population are followers of pre-Christian religions, found in only a very few remote areas – mainly the mountains of eastern Malaita.

Warning

If you stay in remote villages or islands, you are sure to be asked what church, or 'mission', you belong to. It's not wise to be dismissive of religion, particularly Christianity, if you are a nonbeliever. Islanders are likely to dislike you strongly if you are hostile to Christianity. The message will get around very quickly and the nonviolent disdain shown towards you may be quite obvious. ∎

Most islanders are extremely devout and practically every village has a church. Many country people attend an early morning service daily. In some places aspects of traditional religion, such as the ancient ancestor cults of inland Malaita, are followed alongside Christianity.

During the early years of the Protectorate, health and education were in the hands of the churches. When the financial burden became too great for them after WWII, the government mostly took these over, though some hospitals and schools are still run by churches. Early 20th-century missionary-preachers often denounced followers of rival churches as unbelievers, and some were extremely strait-laced, banning traditional dances and art forms. Religious exclusiveness has since declined considerably.

All the main denominations are represented in Honiara, with worship often in Pijin. Some services are accompanied by lots of inspired singing. For information about service times call one of the following numbers:

Church of Melanesia	☎ 21892
Roman Catholics	☎ 21943/22795
South Seas	
Evangelical Church	☎ 22388
Uniting Church	☎ 61125/25041
Seventh Day Adventist	☎ 21191
Assembly of God	☎ 22847
Bahais	☎ 22475
Jehovah's Witnesses	☎ 22241

LANGUAGE

Officially, there are 67 listed indigenous languages and about 30 dialects. It's quite common for people from villages only a few km apart to speak mutually incomprehensible languages. For that reason people who aren't wantoks communicate in Pijin, which contains many English words and is spoken by most islanders. People who have received some education generally speak English – it's the language taught in many schools – so you can get by in the Solomons without learning any Pijin. However, English is perceived to be a 'serious' language. If you're able to converse in Pijin, people lose their shyness and really open up to you.

Most of the precolonial indigenous languages belong to the Austronesian, or the Malayo-Polynesian, language group. Another 15 are Papuan languages and dialects, that are thought to be considerably older than their Austronesian counterparts; they're spread at random through the archipelago (eg parts of Rendova, the Russell Islands, Savo and Vella Lavella, and Temotu). About 10 languages have under 200 speakers each and a few dialects are gradually becoming extinct. However, no effort is being made by the government to preserve them.

If you stay in one place a long time, try to pick up a few words of the local language – even being able to say 'hello' would please the locals.

Pronunciation

When speaking, many Solomon Islanders prenasalise, but this isn't uniform throughout the country. Consequently, problems with understanding names and words can easily occur, even when they're speaking Pijin or English.

You may hear the following pronunciation:

b	'mb' as in ramble
d	'nd' as in hundred
gn	'ny' as in onion and the Spanish 'ñ'

ng	as in singer
ngg	as in finger
nj	as in range
g	as in gate
kw	as in quickly
r	as in terrace
s	as in seal but sometimes pronounced as 'ch'
r	usually rolled

a	'ah'
e	'ay'
ee	'i'
o	'oh'
u	'ooh'
ae	'eye'
ao	'ow'
oe	'oy'

Pijin Blong Solomon

The national language of the Solomons is Solomon Islands Pijin, or Pijin for short. The name 'Pijin' could come from the Chinese for 'business', as the China coast was a frequent destination for early 19th-century sandalwood traders. Alternatively, it might have been derived from the word 'jargon', meaning 'broken' English, which was used for Pijin in the 1870s.

Early 19th-century sailors stimulated the evolution of Pijin. The recruitment of labour (including Solomon Islanders) from the 1860s to 1900s to work in Oceanic canefields and plantations and in mines spread the language all over the Pacific. By the 1930s, Pijin was being spoken by missionaries in many areas, helping to spread it further. Although English is now the official language of the administration, many government staff use Pijin in everyday conversation.

Solomon Islands Pijin – like similar languages in Papua New Guinea, Vanuatu, West Africa and along the old China coast – has been condemned by all and sundry, including the United Nations (UN). It's been called 'baby talk', a 'bastard language' and a 'mongrel lingo'. Pijin speakers use two versions. One is a simplified form used by

islanders to their English-speaking employers. The second is the true Pijin, which they use among their fellow countryfolk. Since the 1970s, linguists have been treating this version with respect.

Any time you spend learning this interesting language will be time well spent. You're sure to find plenty to say, once you get the hang of Pijin.

Grammar

Pijin is a blend of English words and Melanesian grammar. Many Pijin sentences express the performing of an action, and the subject comes before the verb, eg *nan i ranaot,* meaning 'the man ran out'.

Pijin has two grammatical features that English lacks. The first distinguishes between the first-person plural (we) when it includes the listeners *(iumi)* and when it excludes the listeners *(mifala)*. Secondly, Pijin distinguishes two and three from the general plural (see the following section on Pronouns).

There are a couple of other differences between the two languages. When two vowels are placed beside each other in Pijin, both vowels are always pronounced separately, unlike in English. An example is 'ia', meaning 'here'. Pijin also has no specific words for third-person pronouns (he, she, it), as does English. In Pijin the third person is hem, followed by 'i' and the word – eg hem i wanfala rabis man meaning 'he is a useless person'.

Useful Words

bathe/swim/shower
   waswas
be, stay, remain
   stap
do
   dum
have
   garem
want
   laekem
of
   blong

to, for, at, on, about, by
long
with
wetim

more
moa
better
moabetta
the best
nambawan

Pronouns

I
mi
you
iu
he/she/it
hem

we
the two of us including you
iumitufala
the three of us
iumitrifala
if more than three
iumi

you (plural)
the two of you
iutufala
the three of you
iutrifala
if more than three
iufala

they/all
olketa

Basics

Yes.
Ya.
No.
No/Nating.
Please.
Plis.
Thank you (very much).
tanggio (tu mus).
You're welcome.
No waris/No seksek/Hem oraet.

Hello.
Halo.
Good morning.
Gud moning.
Good afternoon.
Gud aftanun.
Good night.
Gud naet.
See you later.
Okei/Lukim iu.
How are you?
Hao iu stap?
I'm fine, thank you very much.
Mi orait, tanggio tumas.

I (don't) understand.
Me (no) savi.
Do you speak our language?
Iufala save toktok languis blong Solomon?

What's your name?
Watkaen nem blong iufala nao?
How old are you?
Haomas yia blong iu?
Who is he/she?
Hu nao hem?
What do you want?
Warem nao?
This is yours.
Desfala blong iufala.

white man/European
araikwao/waetimani tie vaka (in western areas)
white woman
misis/waetman mere
Gilbertese
sagabo
chief
sif/bigman
child
pikinini
woman
mere/woman
the interior, bush
bus

Around Town
Where is the ...?
Hem i wea ...?
airfield
eapot
clinic
klinik
post office
pos ofis
aircraft
plen
ship
sip
canoe
kanu
road
rod
car
ka
baggage
basket

How far is it?
Haomas longwe nao?
far
longwe
nearby
kolsap
this side
saedkam
that side
saedgo

Please may I use this telephone?
Plis kan mifala iusim telefon ia?
Please may I use this radio?
Plis kan mifala iusim redio ia?

shop
stoa
I would like to buy...
Mifala laek fo peim...
food
kaikai
traditional clothes
kastom kaliko

Accommodation
Where is the rest house?
Haos blong res hem I wea?

How much does it cost?
Haomas nao?
When can I eat here?
Wataem nao baebae mifala kaikaim ia?

bedroom
rum blong bed
bathroom
rum blong waswas
toilet
smol haos

Time & Dates
What is the time?
Waswe taem nao?
What day of the week is it?
Watkaen dei blong wik hem i nao tude?
It's one o'clock.
Taem hem save wan klok.
now
destaem noa
earlier
bifoa

Health & Emergencies
Come at once!
Kam fastaem!
Where is the police station?
Stesin blong pulis hem i wea?
Where is the hospital?
Hospitol hem i wea?
How strong is this cyclone?
Haomas strong disfela big win nao?
Go away!
Go-go baek!
diarrhoea
beleran

Numbers

1	*wan/wanfala*
2	*tu/tufala*
3	*tri/trifala*
4	*foa/fofala*
5	*faev/faefala*
6	*siks/sikfala*
7	*seven/sevenfala*
8	*eit/eitfala*
9	*naen/naenfala*
10	*ten/tenfala*
11	*eleven/elevenfala*

12	*tuel/tuelfala*
13	*totin*
14	*fotin*
15	*fiftin*
16	*sikstin*
17	*seventin*
18	*eitin*
19	*naentin*
20	*tuenti*
21	*tuentiwan*
30	*toti*
40	*foti*
50	*fifti*
60	*siksti*
70	*seventi*
80	*eiti*

90	*naenti*
100	*handred*
1000	*taosin*

Further Reading

Pijin Blong Yumi (A Guide to Solomon Islands Pijin) (Solomon Islands Christian Association, Honiara, 1978) by Linda Simons & Hugh Young is the best general guide to the language, though at present it only seems to be available in Honiara library's Pacific section. A handy booklet is *Wei fo Raetem Olketa Wod Long Pijin* (S$3, SICA Pijin Project, Honiara, 1995). It's described as a spelling guide but is more like a Pijin-English dictionary.

Facts for the Visitor

PLANNING
When to Go
The coolest months are from June to September. Humidity levels, perhaps a more important consideration, are usually lowest from October to December, though December can be hot, especially in Honiara. Cyclones sometimes occur towards the end of the year, but are more frequent from January to April. Outside the cyclone season, seas are calmer which is better for boat rides and for underwater visibility if you're scuba diving and snorkelling.

June to August is a time of public holidays and festivities. Seven of the country's nine provinces have their annual holiday at this time, and the Queen's Birthday and Independence Day – the best times to see traditional dancing displays – are in June and July respectively.

Maps
Ordnance survey maps are available at Ministry of Lands & Housing offices in each provincial centre. Stocks at some may be low, though the Honiara branch (☎ 21511) between Mendana and Hibiscus Aves has a full supply of large provincial and town maps, most dating from the British era. They cost from S$16 to S$30 each. Hema, an Australian cartographer, produces the only fold-up map (scale 1:1.2 million) of the Solomons, available in Honiara.

What to Bring
People wear light, cotton summer clothes all year round. The style is always casual. Most men wear short-sleeved, open-necked shirts and shorts to work, with a singlet (ie vest) underneath to absorb perspiration. Ties and jackets are seldom seen. Women's attire is similarly casual. For the less affluent male islanders, T-shirts, shorts and rubber thong-type sandals are standard gear (though many go barefoot, especially outside the capital). It's sometimes worth packing something dressy but cool for the odd special occasion.

For rain showers, bring a small collapsible umbrella or a lightweight poncho. Villagers use disposable banana leaves or old copra sacks instead. Bring a light pullover as sea travel can be quite cool, especially after scuba diving at night.

If you go reef walking you will need to wear special shoes. Razor-sharp coral tears through sneakers in a few weeks. Diving boots give the best protection but are rather expensive. Plastic sandals are ideal for canoe travel, but closed shoes should be worn around muddy villages because of possible hookworm infestation.

Sleeping bags or sleeping sheets are useful if you plan to camp or stay in simple village leaf houses. You'll also need strong, but light, footwear – canvas baseball boots are the best – if you plan to climb volcanoes or make your way through the undergrowth of a tropical rainforest. When walking through scrub, jeans or long trousers are always necessary to protect you against scratches, the stinging *nalato* plant and the blister-raising *hailasi* tree.

A small pack of fishing tackle allows you to catch your own food on board ship (hooks and lines are sold in many stores in the Solomons). Plastic bags are useful for wrapping your clothes and camera gear when travelling by motor canoe. Soft bags (travel packs, sports/sausage bags – preferably water resistant) are much better for canoe travel (as they fit easily aboard such craft) than backpacks and suitcases, which tend to be bulky and cumbersome.

Other useful items include candles, matches, a flashlight (torch), a water bottle, a corkscrew and a can-opener. If you're going camping or taking extended sea trips you'll need some cutlery and crockery – a light, plastic picnic set is ideal. A reader recommended taking a bag of balloons – they make excellent gifts for kids.

Tampons, sanitary towels and condoms can be bought in Honiara and other main towns, though your favourite brand may not be available and you may have to ask for these items by a brand name rather than by the generic name to be understood. Take sufficient supplies before venturing into rural areas.

HIGHLIGHTS

As a list of highlights precedes each regional chapter, this section merely gives a general overview.

In the Solomons you can have beautiful beaches all to yourself and meet friendly islanders who live a lifestyle virtually unchanged by time. Most people love to be photographed, so you can get some great photos here. Scuba diving and snorkelling are one of the country's biggest draws – the combination of coral and wreck dives is hard to beat.

The Western Province has some of the best attractions – be sure to view its breathtaking lagoons from the air. It's also worth experiencing rural life by staying in the ecotourist village in Marovo Lagoon, which is a proposed World Heritage Site. Lake Te'Nggano in East Rennell is another, and is a haven for birdlife. (Ornithologists have plenty to enjoy in the Solomons.)

In Guadalcanal there are a range of facilities in Honiara, WWII battlefields and some relaxing island resorts. Malaita has artificial islands, and villagers clinging to age-old traditions. Temotu gives a rare opportunity to visit extremely isolated communities, including some populated by Polynesians. If you can take a boat tour of this province, you're bound to be the centre of attention everywhere you stop.

TOURIST OFFICES
Local Tourist Offices

The Solomon Islands Tourist Authority (SITA) was renamed the Visitors' Bureau in 1997. There's only one office in Honiara. Limited information for tourists is also provided in Gizo and Auki – see the Western Province and Malaita chapters.

Tourist Offices Abroad

The Solomon Islands is part of the Tourism Council of the South Pacific (TCSP) which has its head office (☎ (679) 304 177, fax 301 995, PO Box 13119) in Suva, Fiji. It has branches in the USA (☎ (916) 5830 152, fax 5830 154) at Lake Blvd 475, PO Box 7440, Tahoe City, CA 96145; the UK (☎ (0181) 392 1838), 375 Upper Richmond Rd, London SW14 7NX; as well as in Belgium (Brussels), France (Grenoble) and Germany (Berlin). In Australia and New Zealand, plenty of Pacific-orientated travel agents will give you useful information.

VISAS & DOCUMENTS

Every tourist has to have a valid passport, onward tickets and adequate funds. The officials will usually ask to see your tickets but are unlikely to want to check your money. Sailors travelling on duty may use a sailor's book instead of a passport.

Visas

In theory, entry visas are not required for any tourist, as a visitor's permit for a stay of up to three months is granted on arrival. However, the guidelines are ambiguous for nationals from former or continuing communist countries, the Indian subcontinent, Nauru and Kiribati. Airlines may therefore refuse to allow people from these nations to board Solomons-bound aircraft if they don't have a visa, which can only be issued from Honiara. These nationals should ask for advice from the nearest Solomons embassy or consulate well before travelling; staff will probably contact Honiara to get a written assurance that a visitor's permit will be granted.

Visitor's permits can be extended for a further three months at the Immigration Office (☎ 22585) in Honiara, but after that you will have to leave the country for one year before you can enter again. The extension costs S$30 for each month.

Work & Residence Permits

If you want to stay longer than six months, you'll be expected to apply for a temporary resident's permit. There are quite high fees attached and the labour department will check you're not secretly working. There are immigration offices at Honiara, Henderson airport, Gizo, Munda and Korovou.

Anyone who is not a Solomons national must have both work and residence permits before working. Each lasts two years and covers both voluntary and unpaid workers. Work permits are issued by the Labour Division, Ministry of Commerce, Industries & Employment (☎ 21849, fax 25804), PO Box G26, Honiara.

The rules say your prospective employer can only apply for you while you're outside the Solomons unless you're waiting to extend an already existing permit. However, some applicants prefer to wait in Honiara, occasionally visiting the Labour Division, hoping to speed things up.

You would need specialist, useful skills to get a work permit; it's quite easy to get permission to work as long as the job you've been offered specifically involves training a local person to take over from you in due course, and the officials have received your new employer's letter or statement about you. The target waiting period for approval is one month, though it can sometimes drag on indefinitely without explanation.

The only exceptions to these rules relate to wives and children of expats who already have work permits, and a few special categories, such as pilots, aircraft engineers and scuba instructors. Self-employment is possible, but again you have to wait for your clearance. At any one time there are plenty of volunteer workers in the country, particularly Peace Corps from the USA and Voluntary Service Overseas from the UK; enquire of volunteer organisations in your home country.

Any visitors who are not authorised to work but do so, or who overstay their visitor's permits, are likely to be deported. They may have to face unexpected tax liabilities, and have their future applications to visit the Solomons refused. These restrictions also apply to researchers and prospectors.

Student Cards
Students should take their international identity card (ISIC card) – it's good for reductions with Solomon Airlines and *Ocean Express* trips.

Vaccination Certificates
Vaccination certificates against yellow fever are required of anyone arriving by air within six days of leaving or transiting an infected area (eg central Africa and northern South America).

EMBASSIES
Solomon Islands Embassies Abroad
Diplomatic representation abroad includes:

Australia
    High Commission of Solomon Islands: PO Box 256, 1st floor, JAA Building, Unit 4/19, Napier Close, Deakin, ACT 2600 (☎ (02) 6282 7030, fax 6282 7040)
    Consul General: GPO Box 850 Brisbane 4001 (☎ (07) 3221 7899)
    Solomon Islands Consulate: Level 5, 376 Victoria St, Darlinghurst, NSW 2010 (☎ (02) 9361 5866, fax 9361 5066)
    Honorary Consul: Level 5, 376 Victoria St, Darlinghurst, NSW 2010 (☎ (02) 9361 2033)
European Union
    Embassy of Solomon Islands Ave de L'yser 13, Bte 3, 1040 Brussels, Belgium (☎ (02) 732 7085, fax 732 6885)
Japan
    Honorary Consulate of Solomon Islands Kitano Arms, 16-15 Hirakawa-cho, Z-Chome, Shiyoda-ku, Tokyo (☎ (03) 5275 0515, fax 222 5959 5960)
New Zealand
    Honorary Consulate of Solomon Islands PO Box 21360, 3rd floor, Kean's Building, 35 High St, Auckland (☎ (09) 373 4676)
Papua New Guinea
    Honorary Consulate of Solomon Islands PO Box 419, Kund WY No 3, P/L Port Moresby (☎ & fax 213051)
United Kingdom
    Honorary Consulate of Solomon Islands 19 Springfield Rd, London SW19 7AL, England (☎ (0181) 296 0232, fax 946 1744)
USA & Canada
    Mission of Solomon Islands to the UN Suite 800, 820 2nd Ave, New York, USA (☎ (212) 599 6193, fax 661 8925)

Foreign Embassies in the Solomons

All foreign embassies are in Honiara. The British High Commission (☎ 21705) is adjacent to the Telekom office. Nearby in Mud Alley St is the Australian High Commission (☎ 21561). The Papua New Guinea High Commission (☎ 20561) is in the Anthony Saru Building, the New Zealand High Commission (☎ 21502) is in the Y Sato Building, and the Japanese Embassy (☎ 22953) is in the NPF Building. Only the Taiwanese Embassy (☎ 22187) is outside the capital's downtown area, two km away at Lenggakiki. No other nations are represented in the Solomons.

Applications for US visas can be routed through Keithie Saunders (☎ 22393) of BJS Agencies, Mendana Ave.

CUSTOMS

Customs officials meet every international flight at Henderson airport. There's also a customs branch at Honiara for all shipping using the capital's main wharf. Customs staff based at Munda also serve Noro, and there are officials at Gizo, Lata, Tulagi, Yandina, Viru Harbour and Ringgi to deal with any international shipping calling there.

As long as you're over 18, you may bring into the Solomons the usual 200 cigarettes, 250g of tobacco or 50 cigars, or a combination of these. Also, you can have two litres of spirits or the equivalent, and other goods up to S$600 (S$300 for children) in value.

All fruit and vegetables brought into the country need an import permit issued from the quarantine section (☎ 36014) in the Ministry of Agriculture & Fisheries in Honiara. Without it they'll be destroyed, even if they're in packets with unbroken seals. Also check there about the importation of cats and dogs.

Police permits are required for guns and ammunition and any other weapons. Pornographic books, pictures, movies and videos are all banned, as is the importation and use of drugs.

MONEY
Costs

It's possible to live cheaply in the Solomons. If you stay in budget accommodation you'll be able to self-cater. On this basis you can eat and sleep for S$50 a day if you avoid expensive tinned imports and dine mostly on local fruit, fish and vegetables. In villages accommodation might even be free if you are prepared to rough it in simple leaf houses, though you should always offer your hosts some cash, food or goods anyway.

Of course, you can spend much more if you want. Staying in higher-priced accommodation in Honiara, Gizo and Munda will mean you won't have access to a kitchen; so on top of more expensive room prices you would have to pay about S$60 to S$100 a day for prepared meals. Scuba diving, organised tours and car hire will also push costs up considerably.

Currency

The local currency is the Solomon Islands dollar (S$). Banks still call it 'SBD' – a relic from the days before Independence, when it was the British Solomons dollar. There are S$2, S$5, S$10, S$20 and S$50 notes, S$1 coins and 1, 2, 5, 10 and 20c coins.

Up to S$250 may be taken out of the country in local currency. However, there are no restrictions on bank transfers abroad of Solomons-derived earnings by expatriates.

Currency Exchange

Australia	A$1	=	S$2.78
Canada	C$1	=	S$2.61
United States	US$1	=	S$3.52
United Kingdom	UK£1	=	S$5.90
New Zealand	NZ$1	=	S$2.49
Germany	DM1	=	S$2.33
Japan	¥100	=	S$3.08
Papua New Guinea	K1	=	S$2.65
Fiji	F$1	=	S$2.52
Vanuatu	100VT	=	S$3.15

Changing Money

Three commercial banks are represented in the country. These are the National Bank of the Solomon Islands (NBSI), the Australia & New Zealand Bank (ANZ) and the Westpac Banking Corporation. Banks should have no difficulty with travellers' cheques in most major international currencies. Stick with the best known brands of travellers' cheque – Visa, Thomas Cook and American Express.

Banks all offer similar rates of exchange; the rate for cheques is slightly better than that for cash. Either way, no commission is charged, although Westpac charges S$20 to cash cheques. If you run out of money, the Honiara banks will accept telegraphic transfers and charge only a modest commission. Both the ANZ and Westpac banks in the capital acknowledge their own credit cards for cash advances. ATM machines have not hit town yet. Major hotels will change money, but at a less favourable rate.

Honiara has branches of all three banks. In the provinces, there are one or more banks only in Gizo, Auki, Munda, Kirakira, Lata and Tulagi, so you'll have to carry enough currency to get you between these centres. If you plan to spend a long time in more remote places, it might be worth opening a savings account with the NBSI to use at their 50-odd local agencies (mainly in post offices and stores) that are located throughout the country.

You may notice a few branches of the Development Bank of the Solomon Islands (DBSI) in the provinces. Their business is solely to offer small loans to Solomon Islanders (especially in rural areas) to finance local business schemes.

Credit cards are accepted by some businesses in Honiara, Gizo and Munda, including hotels, car-rental agencies, airlines, and tour and dive operators. Elsewhere, plastic money is very seldom used. Even places that accept Visa and MasterCard often won't accept American Express or Diner's Club, and any payment by credit card generally incurs a 5% surcharge.

Tipping & Bargaining

Neither tipping nor begging is acceptable in the Solomons, and visitors are asked to respect this. Melanesians consider that tipping or giving money to beggars creates an obligation which the receiver has to return. Naturally, a person can't return the favour if you are travelling through, so a friendly smile and 'thank you' are sufficient.

Bargaining is not really part of the nation's traditions. Shops and market traders, for example, have set prices. But it's becoming more common nowadays to ask for a 'second price' for things like handicrafts. When buying direct from craftspeople, you might gently suggest what you're prepared to pay, but don't get into long haggling matches. In souvenir shops you might also be able to get discounts, especially if you're buying several items.

Occasionally people in isolated areas will quote you grossly inflated prices for handicrafts, canoe rides, custom fees or accommodation, mainly because they have no idea what the current price would be elsewhere. A possible way round this is to offer food or goods instead of cash.

Taxes

There's a 10% government tax on hotel and restaurant prices. Some of the more basic places don't bother to charge it, and new businesses can often get a tax 'holiday'. Always enquire whether quoted prices include this tax. All prices given in this book are *inclusive* of tax.

POST & COMMUNICATIONS
Post

The only postal delivery is to a post office box or to poste restante. These are available at all post offices and at many of the 98 postal agencies. The international postal rate is only 50c for postcards (unfortunately, the postcards themselves are pricey) and S$1.10 for letters; domestic letters go for 30c. Air mail takes slightly less than a week to Australia and New Zealand, though surface deliveries take two months. Double these times for Europe and North America. For posting larger items, ask for the airlift/surface rate as a reasonable compromise between speed and cost.

Internal postal deliveries are frequent to the main islands. However, outlying areas are serviced solely by ships and may receive their mail only once every four to eight weeks. Mail generally takes longer to get to the provinces than it does to get from them.

Telephone & Radio

The telephone network is improving and expanding all the time. There are 12 automatic telephone exchanges serving the country's 6000 telephone subscribers, and a teleradio (ie radio telephone) network connecting isolated communities. Telephone boxes are becoming common in towns. It costs 60c minimum in a coin phone, yet only 16c in a card phone. The phone cards (S$10, S$20 or S$50) are collectable and widely available. Enquire at Telekom offices about making teleradio calls: for three-minutes it's S$3.70 for a station call (ie the message will be relayed later) or S$5.90 for person to person.

Service Messages If you want to send a message to a village or island where there is no telephone or teleradio yet, you can do it via a service message: villagers regularly listen in to daily broadcasts by the Solomon Islands Broadcasting Corporation (SIBC) between 6 and 8 pm in case there are any contacts of this type. To send a service message, go to SIBC in Honiara, Gizo or Lata; the minimum cost is S$18 for 20 words.

If possible, making contact by radio is preferable as the villagers won't have to pay money to respond. Honiara's Visitors' Bureau has a radio. If you're in an isolated part of the country and want to send a radio message, try the local clinic; you may be charged S$5 to S$10.

International Calls The new Domsat (ie domestic satellite) system allows international calls to be made from all parts of the country. You can dial ☎ 102 to make one, but it's cheaper to dial direct using a card phone. The cheap rate (6 pm to 8 am, and at weekends) is S$4.47 per minute to Australia and S$7.01 to most of the rest of the world. To call the Solomons the international dialling code is tel 677; there are no regional codes.

Fax, Telex & Email

Sending faxes via Telekom offices is expensive: per page (minimum two pages) it's S$6.25 nationally and S$18.75 internationally. Your hotel might do it cheaper. Faxes can also be received by Telekom (S$3.15 per page) where they are collected by the customer. Some branches (not Honiara) can deliver these to an addressee in the same town for S$6.25. Sending a telex through Telekom costs S$6.25 per page nationally and S$37.50 internationally.

Only a few businesses have email as yet, and there's no public facility.

BOOKS

Some of the books here are now out of print, but you may be able to obtain a copy through your library. The Pacific section of the National Library in Honiara should have them, and others, but you will have to read them there.

Guidebooks & Travel

The annual *Solomon Islands Trade Directory* is full of useful practical information. It's published by BJS Agencies (☎ 22393, fax 21017), PO Box 439, Honiara. Alan Lucas' *Cruising the Solomons* is a useful guide for those travelling by yacht.

An entertaining travelogue which ends up in the Solomons is Justin Wintle's *Heart Treatment: The Oriental Travels of an Amorous Hypochondriac*. He finds Melanesia to be just as intriguing as Asia, where his journey began. Paul Theroux wrote *The Happy Isles of Oceania* – his meanderings by plane and kayak took him to the Solomons.

History & Politics

The Search for the Islands of Solomon, 1567-1838 by Colin Jack-Hinton records the history of the exploration of the Solomons. Judith Bennett's *Wealth of the Solomons* is the third in the masterly Pacific Islands Monograph Series, and is a very informative history of the archipelago from 1800 to 1978. *Independence, Dependence & Interdependence: The First 10 Years of Solomon Islands Independence* is a series of essays by local leaders (SICHE & USP, Honiara, 1992).

Passage, Port and Plantation by Peter Corris is an illuminating history of the labour recruitment of Solomon Islanders for work on Queensland and Fijian plantations between 1870 and 1914. *Peter Dillon of Vanikolo* by JW Davidson, and edited by UHK Spate, deals with the Irish trader-explorer's discovery in 1826 of the remains of the lost French La Pérouse expedition. Hector Hothouse's *White Headhunter: The Extraordinary True Story of a White Man's Life among Headhunters of the Solomon Islands* is a reconstruction of the life and times of the esteemed Scotsman John Renton, who lived from 1868 to 1875 at Sulufou, Malaita.

Lightning Meets the West Wind: The Malaita Massacre by Roger Keesing & Peter Corris is the story of William Bell, the district officer killed by Kwaio tribesmen in 1927. It reveals the tensions created by colonialism and its effect on the people involved, particularly Bell himself and Basiana, the Malaitan tribal leader. *The Maasina Rule Movement* edited by Hugh Laracy (USP, Suva, 1983) is about noncooperation on the return of colonial authority after Malaita's comparative freedom during WWII.

WWII Wartime literature relates mainly to the Guadalcanal Campaign and coastwatch activities. Eric Felot's *The Coast Watchers* tells of their lonely and dangerous vigil far behind Japanese lines. H Macquarie's book *Vouza and the Solomon Islands*, celebrates the country's national hero Jacob Vouza, his daring wartime exploits and those of other similarly courageous islanders.

Savo by Richard F Newcomb tells the story behind the costly errors which caused one of the US Navy's worst defeats. *Guadalcanal Diary* by war correspondent Richard Tregaskis is an interesting eyewitness account of the fighting on Guadalcanal in August 1942.

The Big Death: Solomon Islanders Remember WWII (joint publication by the Institute of Pacific Studies, Suva, Fiji, and SICHE & USP, Honiara, 1988) by Geoffrey M White and others is a fascinating collection of stories told by various islanders who took part in WWII. Written from their viewpoint it dispels quite a few British-inspired myths about the war.

The US Navy, Marines and Army all published accounts of their part in the Solomons campaign.

Anthropology

Raymond Firth set the tone with his remarkable *We, the Tikopia* about his studies there in 1928 and 1929. Firth wrote several other books, including *History and Traditions of Tikopia*, in which he recorded the island's history.

Dr DE Yen & Janet Gordon's *Anuta: A Polynesian Outlier in the Solomon Islands* was based on their field trip made to Anuta in 1973. Richard Feinberg, who was on the same expedition, wrote several books based on material he collected at the time, including *Anuta: Social Structure of a Polynesian Outlier* (Institute of Polynesian Studies, Honolulu, 1981).

An American, Samuel Elbert, and two Danes, Torben Monberg and Rolf Kuschel, wrote extensively about Rennell and Bellona between 1965 and 1981. Elbert & Monberg's *From the Two Canoes* (Danish National Museum, Copenhagen, and the University of Hawaii Press, Honolulu, 1965) gives a vivid account of the history of the two islands and the dramatic desertion of their old ways in 1938.

The Voyaging Stars: Secrets of the Pacific Island Navigators by David Lewis uses islanders accounts to explain how immense trans-Pacific journeys were made by Micronesian and Polynesian canoeists, including Solomon Islanders, right up to the 1950s.

WG Iven's *Island Builders of the South Pacific* (Seeley Services, London, 1930) details the everyday life of the Lau people, builders of the artificial islands of north-eastern Malaita. *'Elota's Story: The Life and Times of a Solomon Islands Big Man* (Queensland University Press, Brisbane, 1978) edited by Roger M Keesing is the fascinating life story of one of Malaita's last warrior-chiefs, also a very capable peace-maker.

General

The most distinguished author to write about the Solomons is James Michener. His *Tales of the South Pacific* (Macmillan, New York, 1947) and *Rascals in Paradise* (Secker & Warburg, London, 1957) have plenty of racy tales in them.

Bring Another Glass (Angus & Robertson, Sydney, 1944) by Georgina Seton is a period thriller set on a mythical island with a strong resemblance to the Solomons. Ann M Kengalu's *Murder on the Mataniko Bridge* is fiction, but contains several informative asides which reveal how local people view both expats and certain other islanders. *Naismith's Dominion* by Peter Corris is an entertaining story set in a fictional British protectorate and has close parallels to the events of 1927 in Malaita.

Grass Roots Art of the Solomons – Images and Islands edited by John & Sue Chick has a wealth of detail about every kind of pictorial and sculptural art form found in the Solomons, including information on where these are still made.

Reflections on Melanesia by Michael McCoy is packed with beautiful pictures, above and below water, of both the Solomons and Papua New Guinea. For archaeologists, *Solomon Islands National Sites Survey* by D Miller lists a number of ancient sites around the country, especially in Simbo.

Pacific Women: Roles and Status of Women in Pacific Societies (USP, Suva, 1988), edited by Taiamoni Tongamoa, assesses the changing situation of Solomons women in one of its six chapters. Indu Baburam's *Island Cook Book* contains a range of mouthwatering local recipes, some of which have previously only been recorded orally.

A charming tale of the prewar colonial era is Gwen Cross' autobiography *Aloha Solomons* (USP, Suva, 1978). *Yours in His Service* (USP, Honiara, 1990) by George G Carter is the biography of Belshazzar Gina of New Georgia, who was ordained a Methodist priest in the late 1930s.

A good general book is Charles E Fox's *The Story of the Solomons*. Fox, a New Zealand missionary, spent the majority of his working life in the Solomons and writes as if he were himself a Solomon Islander. Janet Kent's *The Solomon Islands*, covers the same subject.

Bookshops & Libraries

Except for a couple of church bookshops, it's almost impossible to buy books outside the Honiara area. But at least there are libraries in the provincial centres Gizo, Tulagi, Auki, Lata, Kirakira, Buala, and Falamai on Mono Island. Their selections are limited and donations of quality books are always gratefully received. A few rest houses have small book collections. See the Honiara section for information on its bookshops, libraries and reading rooms.

ONLINE SERVICES

Simply get your Internet web browser to search for 'Solomon Islands' and you'll uncover loads of information, including web sites devoted to scuba diving and discussions of forestry issues. The TCSP (see Tourist Offices Abroad) site at http://www.infocentre.com./spt/ is a guide to the South Pacific.

NEWSPAPERS & MAGAZINES

The mostly widely read paper is the *Solomons Star*. It's an unusual newspaper, even down to its quirky grammar. There are lots of local features and interesting 'letters to the editor'. It costs S$1.60 and comes out on Wednesday and Friday. The *Solomons Voice* (S$1.70), every Friday, devotes more space to world news and is harder to find outside Honiara. Neither paper is afraid to be critical of the government.

Other newspapers are published infrequently, including the *Solomon Citizen* (S$1) and *The Solomon Times* (S$1.40). The government publishes *Solomon Nius* monthly and distributes it free of charge. In English, despite the Pijin name, it's partly official gazette, partly news tabloid. A 50c bimonthly publication called *Link* has a strong educational bias and an astute eye for issues. *Grasrut* (S$1.50) is a Pijin newspaper.

Stores in the provinces sell newspapers and stationery, though international publications are only sold in Honiara.

RADIO & TV

There are SIBC radio stations in Honiara, Gizo and Lata and long-term plans for two more at Auki and Kirakira. Programmes are in both English and Pijin, with local and overseas features, including news broadcasts from Britain and Australia. Programmes are broadcast on MW (1035 kHz) and SW (5020 kHz). Island Radio (101 MHz FM) is a new 24-hour Honiara station serving up pop classics. If you have a short-wave radio, you can easily find international broadcasts from Australia, New Zealand and further afield. The Australian Broadcasting Corporation (ABC) can be found at 630 kHz MW.

In 1997 domestic TV started up for the first time in Honiara, provided by an Australian company. Hotels with satellite TV can only pick up a few channels, mainly from Australia. Video is also available in Honiara's top hotels.

PHOTOGRAPHY

Avoid taking pictures in the midday sun. The best times for photography are before 9.30 am and after 4 pm. Otherwise, you may have to underexpose your shots slightly to avoid glare. If your camera is automatic, it may overcompensate for the Solomons strong light, causing dark-skinned faces and rainforest views to come out shadowy. Professional photographers recommend manual settings for such pictures.

Use a flash to take photos at evening cultural dances, for house interiors, or close-ups in the jungle dimness. A tele-photo lens is invaluable when something interesting is going on, but you'd prefer to remain unobtrusive.

Always ask before taking a photo of someone. Most people are very happy to be photgraphed, and don't expect money in return. Be sure, however, to get permission from the custom owner and pay any necessary fees before photographing custom sites. Children especially enjoy being photographed. The mere sight of a camera is often enough to make them leap for joy. In rural areas, young women are sometimes too shy to be photographed; older women may be a little embarrassed or amused but generally give their consent.

Film & Equipment

Bring enough film for your entire trip. The islands and people are very photogenic so you'll probably need twice as much as you expect. Film prices are high locally, and only 100 ASA print film is available in a few towns outside Honiara. In Honiara, 36-exposure 100 ASA film is about S$29 and 24-exposure 400 ASA film is S$27. Slide film is hard to find and will cost at least S$60 for 36 exposures (excluding developing). Likewise, bring your own camera, as there are only a few compact 35-mm ones for sale in Honiara. If you're transiting through Fiji, pick up cheap film duty-free in Nadi airport. Print film can be developed quickly in Honiara, though slides usually have to be sent overseas.

Film needs to be protected from heat and humidity in the Pacific. Sachets of silica crystals will protect your equipment from moisture but more important is to keep your camera and film in a cool place.

TIME

Clocks are set to UTC/GMT plus 11 hours, ie one hour ahead of Australia's Eastern Standard Time. Local time is the same as in Vanuatu, but one hour behind Fiji and New Zealand. When its noon in Honiara it's 1 am in London, 7 pm in New York and Toronto, 5 pm in San Francisco, and 11 am in Sydney and Port Moresby.

Time is fluid in the tropics. Things often happen a bit later than planned – people just shrug and explain things runs according to 'Solomons time'. However, businesses, airlines and tourist activities generally operate as scheduled.

ELECTRICITY & GAS

Power and lighting are provided only in urban centres such as Honiara, Gizo, Auki, Tulagi, Kirakira, Buala, Lata, Munda, Noro and Yandina. The current is 230/240 V, 50 cycles AC, and flat three-pin plugs and bayonet sockets of the Australian type are used.

In rural areas people have to rely on kerosene-fuelled hurricane lamps, though medical clinics, businesses and the more expensive rest houses often have electricity provided by a private generator.

There's no piped gas supply, but bottled gas is available in most large stores.

WATER SUPPLY

Towns have piped water supply, but not always of a drinkable quality – drinking water is often supplied via catchment tanks (see Health for information on water quality and treatment, and Drinks, both sections later in this chapter). Villages either have a communal tank with water supplied at particular times during the day, or a natural water pipe.

WEIGHTS & MEASURES

The old imperial system of miles, yards, feet, inches, pounds and ounces dies hard in the islands. Although the metric system has taken over in Honiara's shops and garages, market people still talk in terms of pounds, even when their scales are denominated in kg. Many people outside the capital continue to talk of miles (both statute and nautical), while fuel for motor canoes might still be measured in gallons locally. There's a metric/imperial conversion table at the back of this book.

LAUNDRY

Honiara's top hotels have a pricey 24-hour laundry service six days a week through the local laundry, Solclean (☎ 22055), in White River Village. Similar services are available elsewhere around the country at plusher lodgings. In more modest urban accommodation, staff might wash your things in their washing machine for a small charge. In a village, you could pay someone to do it by hand if you're unwilling to do it yourself.

TOILETS

Individual bowl toilets are found in towns and resorts, but they're a rarity elsewhere. Many villagers have to use the reef or the bush and have separate ablutions areas for women and men. There are public toilets at Point Cruz in Honiara.

HEALTH

The visitor to the Solomons can expect reasonably healthy conditions in the country's urban centres. Despite this, particular care has to be taken against malaria everywhere, including Honiara. According to World Health Organisation (WHO) figures, the Solomons had 460 malaria cases per 1000 people in 1992, making it one of the highest risk areas in the world, with Guadalcanal the most infected island. Happily, the national situation has improved since then, and a programme of spraying was effective in Honiara. In late 1996 Guadalcanal was down to below 20 new cases (per 1000 people) per month.

Other common illnesses in the Solomons are tuberculosis, gastric troubles and childhood respiratory infections. Water purity cannot always be relied on, and hookworm is endemic in the countryside and along beaches.

Health-Care Facilities

Basic medical services are free at hospitals and medical clinics, regardless of whether they are owned by the government or the church. The central referral hospital is in Honiara. There's also a hospital in each of the main towns, plus 130-odd medical clinics and aid posts spread throughout the country. See Medical Services in the regional chapters for more details. All hospitals should be able to sell you a mosquito net for only S$3 to S$5.

The facilities at clinics vary considerably. Some are large and have eight or more beds in them. Others have only one bed with no bedding, and only one old chair for the nurse and patients to share. Stocks of medicine can be equally variable.

The majority of doctors are based in hospitals, while a few others are spread around the capital. Dental care is available at Honiara, Kiluufi (Auki) and Gizo hospitals. The only two chemists are in Honiara, where malaria tablets are available without prescription. The country's only optician is also in the capital, so bring a spare pair of glasses.

Although the list of potential dangers can seem quite frightening, with a little luck, some basic precautions and adequate information few travellers experience more than an upset stomach.

Travel Health Guides

Staying Healthy in Asia, Africa & Latin America, Dirk Schroeder (Moon Publications, 1994) is probably the best all-round guide to carry, as it's compact but very detailed and well organised. *Travel with Children* by Maureen Wheeler (Lonely Planet Publications, 1995) includes basic advice on travel health for younger children.

There are also a number of excellent travel-health sites on the Web. There are links from the Lonely Planet home page (http://www.lonelyplanet.com) to WHO, Centers for Diseases Control & Prevention and Stanford University Travel Medicine Service.

Predeparture Planning

Health Insurance There is a wide variety of policies available with your travel insurance, so allow time to research the market. You may need (or prefer) to be treated as a private patient in the Solomons, in which case fees will be charged but you probably won't need a policy with higher medical-expense options.

Some policies specifically exclude 'dangerous activities' including scuba diving, motorcycling, and bushwalking.

You may prefer a policy which pays doctors or hospitals direct rather than you having to pay on the spot and claim later. If you have to claim later make sure you keep all documentation. Some policies ask you to call back (reverse charges) to a centre in your home country where an immediate assessment of your problem is made.

Check that the policy covers ambulances or an emergency flight home.

Medical Kit It's wise to carry one; it should include:

- Paracetamol (acetaminophen in the US) – for pain or fever.
- Antihistamine (such as Benadryl) – useful as a decongestant for colds and allergies, to ease the itch from insect bites or stings, and to help prevent motion sickness. There are several antihistamines so seek informed advice (some may cause sedation and interact with alcohol).
- Antibiotics – useful if you're travelling off the beaten track, but they must be prescribed and you should carry the prescription with you.
- Loperamide (eg Imodium) or Lomotil for diarrhoea.
- Rehydration mixture for more serious diarrhoea.
- Prochlorperazine (eg Stemetil) or metaclopramide (eg Maxalon) for nausea and vomiting.
- Antiseptic such as povidone-iodine (eg Betadine) for cuts and grazes (especially useful for slow-to-heal coral cuts).
- Calamine lotion or Stingose spray – for bites or stings.
- Bandages and Band-aids – for minor injuries.
- Scissors, tweezers and a thermometer (note that mercury thermometers are prohibited by airlines).

• Insect repellent, sunscreen, chap stick and water purification tablets or iodine. Consider taking multi-vitamins, too.

Health Preparations Make sure you're healthy before you start travelling. If you require a particular medication take an adequate supply. Also take the prescription, preferably showing the generic rather than the brand name (which may not be locally available).

Immunisations Officially no vaccination certificates are required for visiting the archipelago, apart from the usual requirements if you've come from an infected area. But some protection is recommended and anti-malarial tablets are essential. Plan ahead for getting your vaccinations: some require an initial shot followed by a booster, and some vaccinations should not be given together. Seek medical advice at least six weeks prior to travel. Ensure you're covered for typhoid (injection or oral capsules) and polio. Tetanus and diphtheria boosters are necessary every 10 years and protection is highly recommended.

Protection from hepatitis A can be provided in two ways. The antibody gamma globulin should be given as close as possible to departure because it is at its most effective in the first few weeks with the effectiveness tapering off gradually between the third and sixth month. Alternatively, the vaccine Havrix 1440 provides long-term immunity (possibly more than 10 years) after an initial injection and a booster at six to 12 months.

Protection against hepatitis B is advised for some travellers (see the Infectious Diseases section), especially if they are children or will have close contact with children. The vaccination course is ideally given over a six-month period, but this can be reduced to 21 days.

Basic Rules
Care in what you eat and drink is the most important health rule, but don't become paranoid – trying the local food is part of the experience of travel. Always wash your hands before eating.

Water Don't drink the water (including ice) unless you're certain it's safe. Don't even clean your teeth with suspect water. Islanders may say their water is OK because it comes from a rainwater catchment tank. But if the roof or guttering is dirty, so will be the water, and algae may be growing in the tank. Also, locals may consider the water clean because they've built up an immunity to whatever impurities may be in it. Take care with fruit juice, particularly if water may have been added. Young coconut milk is a pleasant and safe alternative to water.

Water Purification The simplest way of purifying water is to boil it thoroughly for five minutes. Otherwise, it should be treated chemically. Chlorine tablets (Puritabs, Steritabs or other brand names) will kill many pathogens, but not some parasites like giardia and amoebic cysts. Iodine is very effective in purifying water and is available in tablet form (such as Potable Aqua), but follow the directions carefully as too much iodine can be harmful. If you can't find tablets, tincture of iodine (2%) or iodine crystals can be used.

Food Salads and fruit should be washed with purified water or peeled where possible. Thoroughly cooked food is safest but not if it has been left to cool or has been reheated. Shellfish such as mussels, oysters and clams should be avoided as well as undercooked meat, particularly in the form of mince. Steaming does not make shellfish safe for eating. Busy, clean-looking restaurants where the food has not been left standing around are generally safest.

Nutrition Make sure your diet is well balanced. Eggs, beans and nuts are all safe ways to get protein. Peelable fruit and coconuts are safe and a good source of vitamins. Try to eat plenty of grains (including rice) and bread.

Make sure you drink enough during the Solomons' hotter seasons – don't rely on feeling thirsty to indicate when you should drink. Not needing to urinate or very dark yellow urine is a danger sign. Always carry a water bottle with you on long trips. Excessive sweating can lead to loss of salt and therefore muscle cramping. Salt tablets are not a good idea – instead, add salt to food.

Everyday Health Normal body temperature is 37°C or 98.6°F; more than 2°C (4°F) higher indicates a high fever. The normal adult pulse rate is 60 to 100 per minute (children 80 to 100, babies 100 to 140). You should know how to take a temperature and a pulse rate. As a general rule the pulse increases about 20 beats per minute for each °C (2°F) rise in fever.

Respiration (breathing) rate is also an indicator of illness. Count the number of breaths per minute: between 12 and 20 is normal for adults and older children (up to 30 for younger children, 40 for babies). People with a high fever or serious respiratory illness breathe more quickly than normal.

Medical Problems & Treatment

Self-diagnosis and treatment can be risky, so only do this in an emergency. Wherever possible seek qualified help.

If you're in an isolated area and you start feeling really sick, your best plan is to get aboard a plane and fly straight to the capital (your medical insurance should cover this).

Environmental Hazards

Sunburn In the tropics you can get sunburnt surprisingly quickly, even through cloud. Use a sunscreen and take extra care to cover areas of your body which don't normally see sun, including your feet. A hat provides added protection, and you should also use zinc cream or some other barrier cream for your nose and lips. Calamine lotion is soothing for mild sunburn. Protect your eyes with good quality sunglasses.

Prickly Heat Prickly heat is an itchy rash caused by excessive perspiration trapped under the skin. It usually strikes people who have just arrived in a hot climate and whose pores have not yet opened sufficiently. Keep cool by bathing often, use a mild talcum powder or resort to air-conditioning until you acclimatise.

Heat Exhaustion Dehydration or salt deficiency can cause heat exhaustion. Take time to acclimatise to high temperatures and make sure you drink sufficient liquids. Wear loose clothing and a broad-brimmed hat. Do not do anything too physically demanding.

Salt deficiency is characterised by fatigue, lethargy, headaches, giddiness and muscle cramps and in this case salt tablets may help. Vomiting or diarrhoea can deplete your liquid and salt levels.

Heat Stroke This serious, and sometimes fatal, condition can occur if the body's heat-regulating mechanism breaks down and the body temperature rises to dangerous levels. Long, continuous periods of exposure to high temperatures can leave you vulnerable to heat stroke. You should avoid excessive alcohol and strenuous activity when you first arrive in a hot climate.

The symptoms are feeling unwell, not sweating very much or at all and a high body temperature – 39°C (102°F) or more. Where sweating has ceased, the skin becomes flushed and red. Severe, throbbing headaches and lack of coordination will also occur, and the sufferer may be confused or aggressive. Eventually the victim will become delirious or convulse. Hospitalisation is essential, but in the interim get the victim out of the sun, remove their clothing, cover them with a wet sheet or towel and then fan continually.

Fungal Infections Fungal infections, which occur with greater frequency in hot weather, are most likely to occur on the scalp, between the toes or fingers, in the groin and on the body (ringworm). You get ringworm from infected animals or by walking on damp areas, like shower floors. To prevent these fungal infections wear loose, comfortable clothes, avoid artificial fibres, wash frequently and dry carefully. If you do get infected, wash the infected area daily with a disinfectant or medicated soap and water, and rinse and dry well. Apply an antifungal cream or powder like Tinaderm. Try to expose the infected area to air or sunlight as much as possible. Wash all towels and underwear in hot water and change them often.

Motion Sickness Eating lightly before and during a trip will reduce the chances of motion sickness. It can help to find a place that minimises disturbance – near the wing on aircraft, close to midships on boats, near the centre on buses. Fresh air also helps; reading and cigarette smoke don't. Commercial motion-sickness preparations, which can cause drowsiness, have to be taken *before* you feel sick. Ginger (available in capsule form) and peppermint (including mint-flavoured sweets) are natural preventatives.

Infectious Diseases
Gastric upsets are commonplace, but the chances of getting a hygiene-related illness, other than simple diarrhoea, are pretty negligible unless you go exploring in some very remote places. Seek immediate medical attention if you have any blood or mucous in your stools or fever, which may be indicative of serious illness.

Diarrhoea A change of water, food or climate can all cause the runs; diarrhoea caused by contaminated food or water is more serious. Moderate diarrhoea is a nuisance but probably not indicative of a serious problem.

Dehydration is the main danger with any diarrhoea, particularly for children who can dehydrate quickly. Fluid replacement is the primary remedy. Weak black tea with a little sugar; soda water; or soft drinks allowed to go flat and diluted 50% with water are all good. With severe diarrhoea a rehydrating solution is necessary to replace minerals and salts. Stick to a bland diet as you recover.

Lomotil or Imodium can be used to bring relief from the symptoms, although they do not actually cure the problem. Only use these drugs if absolutely necessary, eg if you *must* travel. For children under 12 years Lomotil and Imodium are not recommended.

Do not use these drugs if the person has a high fever or is severely dehydrated. An appropriate antibiotic would be required instead. This would also be the case for watery diarrhoea with blood and mucous, and persistent diarrhoea that has not improved after 48 hours.

Giardiasis The parasite causing this intestinal disorder is present in contaminated water. The symptoms are stomach cramps, nausea, a bloated stomach, watery, foul-smelling diarrhoea and frequent gas. Giardiasis can appear several weeks after you have been exposed to the parasite. The symptoms may disappear for a few days and then return; this can go on for several weeks. Tinidazole, known as Fasigyn, or metronidazole (Flagyl) are the recommended drugs for treatment. Antibiotics are of no use.

Dysentery This serious illness is caused by contaminated food or water and is characterised by severe diarrhoea, often with blood or mucous in the stool. There are two kinds of dysentery. Bacillary dysentery is characterised by a high fever and rapid onset; headache, vomiting and stomach pains are also symptoms. It generally does not last longer than a week, but it is highly contagious.

Amoebic dysentery is often more gradual in the onset of symptoms, with cramping abdominal pain and vomiting less likely; fever may not be present. It is not a self-limiting disease: it will persist until treated and can recur and cause long-term health problems.

A stool test is necessary to diagnose

which kind of dysentery you have, so you should seek medical help urgently.

Cholera Cholera vaccination is not very effective. The bacteria responsible for this disease are waterborne, so attention to the rules of eating and drinking should protect the traveller. Outbreaks of cholera are generally widely reported, so you can avoid such problem areas. Cholera is rare in the Solomons.

Hepatitis Hepatitis is a general term for inflammation of the liver. It is a common disease worldwide. The symptoms are fever, chills, headache, fatigue, feelings of weakness and aches and pains, followed by loss of appetite, nausea, vomiting, abdominal pain, dark urine, light-coloured faeces, jaundiced (yellow) skin and the whites of the eyes may turn yellow. **Hepatitis A** is transmitted by contaminated food and drinking water. The disease poses a real threat to the western traveller. You should seek medical advice, but there is not much you can do apart from resting, drinking lots of fluids, eating lightly and avoiding fatty foods. People who have had hepatitis should avoid alcohol for some time after the illness, as the liver needs time to recover.

Hepatitis E is transmitted in the same way; it can be very serious in pregnant women.

There are almost 300 million chronic carriers of **Hepatitis B** in the world. It is spread through contact with infected blood, blood products or body fluids, for example through sexual contact, unsterilised needles and blood transfusions, or contact with blood via small breaks in the skin. Other risk situations include having a shave, tattoo, or having your body pierced with contaminated equipment. The symptoms of type B may be more severe and may lead to long term problems. **Hepatitis D** is spread in the same way, but the risk is mainly in shared needles.

Hepatitis C can lead to chronic liver disease. The virus is spread by contact with blood usually via contaminated transfusions or shared needles. Avoiding these is the only means of prevention.

Typhoid Typhoid fever is a dangerous gut infection caused by contaminated water and food. Medical help must be sought.

In its early stages sufferers may feel they have a bad cold or flu on the way, as early symptoms are a headache, body aches and a fever which rises a little each day until it is around 40°C (104°F)or more. The victim's pulse is often slow relative to the degree of fever present – unlike a normal fever where the pulse increases. There may also be vomiting, abdominal pain, diarrhoea or constipation.

In the second week the high fever and slow pulse continue and a few pink spots may appear on the body; trembling, delirium, weakness, weight loss and dehydration may occur. Complications such as pneumonia, perforated bowel or meningitis may occur.

The fever should be treated by keeping the victim cool and giving them fluids as dehydration should also be watched for.

Intestinal Worms These parasites are most common in rural, tropical areas. A stool test when you return home is not a bad idea. They can be present on unwashed vegetables or in undercooked meat and you can pick them up through your skin by walking in bare feet. Always wear shoes when visiting villages or gardens. Hookworms are even found on 'toilet' beaches. Infestations may not show up for some time and, although they are generally not serious, they can cause severe health problems if left untreated. Consider having a stool test when you get home to check for worms.

Tetanus This potentially fatal disease, present worldwide occurs more commonly in undeveloped tropical areas. It is difficult to treat but is preventable with immunisation. Tetanus occurs when a wound becomes infected by a germ which lives in soil and in the faeces of horses and other animals, so clean all cuts, punctures or animal bites. Tetanus is also known as lockjaw, and the first symptom may be discomfort in swallowing, or stiffening of the jaw and neck; this is followed by painful convulsions of the jaw and whole body.

Rabies Rabies is a fatal viral infection found in many countries and is caused by a bite or scratch by an infected animal. Dogs, monkeys and cats are noted carriers. Any bite, scratch or even lick from a mammal should be cleaned immediately and thoroughly. Scrub with soap and running water, and then clean with an alcohol or iodine solution. A rabies vaccination is now available and should be considered if you are in a high-risk category – eg if you intend to explore caves (bat bites can be dangerous), work with animals, or travel so far off the beaten track that medical help is more than two days away.

Sexually Transmitted Diseases
Gonorrhoea, herpes and syphilis are among these diseases; sores, blisters or rashes around the genitals, discharges or pain when urinating are common symptoms. In some STDs, such as wart virus or chlamydia, symptoms may be less marked or not observed at all especially in women. Syphilis symptoms eventually disappear completely but the disease continues and can cause severe problems in later years. While abstinence from sexual contact is the only 100% effective prevention, using condoms is also effective. The treatment of gonorrhoea and syphilis is with antibiotics. The different sexually transmitted diseases each require specific antibiotics. There is no cure for herpes or AIDS.

HIV & AIDS HIV, the Human Immunodeficiency Virus, develops into AIDS, Acquired Immune Deficiency Syndrome, which is a fatal disease. HIV is a major problem in many countries, although the figures are low in the Solomons. Any exposure to blood, blood products or body fluids may put the individual at risk. The disease is often transmitted through sexual contact or dirty needles – vaccinations, acupuncture, tattooing and body piercing can be potentially as dangerous as intravenous drug use. HIV/AIDS can also be spread through infected blood transfusions; some developing countries cannot afford to screen blood used for transfusions.

If you do need an injection, ask to see the syringe unwrapped in front of you, or take a needle and syringe pack with you.

Fear of HIV infection should never preclude treatment for serious medical conditions.

Insect-Borne Diseases
Malaria This serious disease is spread by mosquito bites. It is a major problem in the Solomons, and the risk is higher in country areas and during the hot monsoonal summer. Off-shore islands bathed in fresh sea breezes are less risky.

Malarial symptoms range from headaches, fever, chills, sweating and abdominal pains to a vague feeling of ill-health. These may subside and recur. Without treatment malaria can develop more serious, potentially fatal effects. It can be diagnosed by a simple blood test. Antimalarial drugs do not prevent you from being infected but kill the parasites during a stage in their development.

There are a number of different types of malaria. The one of most concern is falciparum malaria, responsible for the very serious cerebral malaria. Falciparum is the predominant form in many malaria-prone areas of the world, including Africa, South-East Asia and Papua New Guinea. In the Solomons, about two-thirds of all cases are of this type. Contrary to popular belief, cerebral malaria is not a new strain.

The problem in recent years has been the emergence of increasing resistance to commonly used antimalarials like chloroquine, maloprim and proguanil. Newer drugs such as mefloquine (Lariam) and doxycycline (Vibramycin, Doryx) are often recommended for chloroquine and multidrug-resistant areas. Expert, up-to-date advice should be sought, as there are many factors to consider when deciding on the type of antimalarial medication, including the area to be visited, your medical history, and your age and pregnancy status. It is also important to discuss the side-effect profile of the medication, so you can work out some level of risk versus benefit ratio. If you intend to go diving it is worth mentioning this to your doctor as this may be relevant in deciding the drug to prescribe. Ask about dosages required for treatment, too.

Primary prevention must always be in the form of mosquito-avoidance measures, as no antimalarial is 100% effective. Travellers are advised to prevent mosquito bites at all times. The main messages are:

- wear light-coloured clothing
- wear long pants, socks (most bites are on the ankles) and long-sleeved shirts
- use mosquito repellents containing the compound DEET on exposed areas
- avoid highly scented perfumes or after-shave
- sleep under a mosquito net
- favour rooms with window screens and a fan, and burn mosquito coils

Seek examination immediately if there is any suggestion of malaria, even if symptoms occur several months after leaving an infected area.

Dengue Fever There is no preventative medicine available for this mosquito-spread disease; the message again is to avoid mosquito bites. A sudden onset of fever, headaches and severe joint and muscle pains are the first signs before a rash starts on the trunk of the body and spreads to the limbs and face. Full recovery can take up to a month or more.

Filariasis, a mosquito-transmitted parasitic infection, is not a problem in the Solomons.

Typhus Typhus is spread by ticks, mites or lice. It begins with fever, chills, headache and muscle pains followed a few days later by a body rash. There is often a large painful sore at the site of the bite and nearby lymph nodes are swollen and painful. Typhus can be treated under medical supervision.

There are usually ticks wherever cattle have been living. In the Solomons, this mainly means northern Guadalcanal, Kolombangara, the Russell Islands, around the Auki area of Malaita, south-eastern Vella Lavella and the southern part of the Three Sisters Islands. Seek local advice on areas where ticks pose a danger and always check your skin carefully for ticks after walking in a forest or long grass. A strong insect repellent can help, and serious walkers in tick areas should consider having their boots and trousers impregnated with benzyl benzoate and dibutylphthalate.

Santa Cruz Fever This is a scrub typhus carried by mites that feed on infected rodents, and mainly afflicts Temotu Province. Its fever is similar to malaria's but its effects are milder and are not usually considered to be life-threatening.

Cuts, Bites & Stings
Cuts & Scratches Skin punctures can easily become infected in hot climates and may be difficult to heal. Treat any cut with an antiseptic such as povidone-iodine. Where possible avoid bandages and Band-aids, which can keep wounds wet. Coral cuts are notoriously slow to heal and if they are not adequately cleaned small pieces of coral can become embedded in the wound. Avoid coral cuts by wearing shoes when walking on reefs, and clean any cut thoroughly.

Bedbugs & Lice Bedbugs live in various places, but particularly in dirty mattresses and bedding – spots of blood are a warning sign. Hotels in the Solomons, including most of the cheaper ones, maintain a high standard of cleanliness. You'll be most vulnerable in village leaf houses, which may have a worn old mattress or, more likely, merely a few old woven pandanus mats on the floor. Bedbugs leave itchy bites in neat rows. Calamine lotion or Stingose spray may help.

All lice cause itching and discomfort. They make themselves at home in your hair (head lice), your clothing (body lice) or in your pubic hair (crabs). You catch lice through direct contact with infected people or by sharing combs, clothing and the like. Powder or shampoo treatment will kill the lice and infected clothing should then be washed in very hot water.

Marine Dangers
Ciguatera This is an often-serious illness which occurs when a certain toxic organism in plankton is eaten by reef fish, which are themselves consumed by large flesh-eating species such as rock cod, trevally, sea perch, moray eel and barracuda. Only the oldest, and usually largest, are likely to contain sufficient toxin to be fatal to humans, but there are no outward signs that a particular fish is actually infected.

Ciguatera's symptoms include vomiting, diarrhoea and cramps, alternating fevers and chills, and tingling in the skin and mouth. Outbreaks of the disease seem to coincide with major traumas to reefs, such as cyclones, heavy rainfalls, earthquakes and major building or demolition works.

Some reef species, such as puffer fish, box fish and the prickly, ball-shaped porcupine fish, are toxic at all times. Eating them leads to muscular paralysis and respiratory failure. Seek medical attention if you think you may have fish poisoning.

Ciguatera is more of a problem elsewhere in the Pacific than in the Solomons, but ask local people for advice if you catch any fish close offshore. Open ocean and deep-water species are usually considered safe to eat in all seasons.

Sharks Victims of shark attack must be moved from the water as fast as possible to allow the application of pressure to any wounds and reduce blood loss. You may also need to treat the victim for shock, lie them down, cover with a towel or blanket and try to keep them calm.

Stonefish & Cone Shells Poisonous stonefish are rare but extremely painful for those unfortunate enough to step on one These ugly and well-disguised creatures lurk on the sea floor and stepping on one forces poison up spines in the dorsal fin and into the victim's foot. Heeding local advice about areas which may harbour stonefish and wearing shoes or thongs when walking in the lagoon is the best protection. If you do step on a stonefish, relieve the pain by immersing the foot or toe in very hot water and seek medical attention. You'll sometimes encounter stinging coral and the best solution is to avoid touching it. If you are stung treat it like a jellyfish sting; douse with vinegar and apply some calamine lotion to relieve the reaction and pain. Some cone shells can fire a dangerous, potentially fatal, dart if picked up. Treat any cone shell with caution, it you do get stung though, wash the area with antiseptic wash, or alcohol, and seek medical attention.

Women's Health
Gynaecological Problems Poor diet, lowered resistance due to the use of antibiotics and contraceptive pills can lead to vaginal infections when travelling in hot climates. Maintaining good personal hygiene, and wearing skirts or loose-fitting trousers and cotton underwear will help prevent infection.

Yeast infections, characterised by a rash, itch and discharge, can be treated with a vinegar or lemon-juice douche, or with yoghurt, or suppositories can be prescribed. Symptoms of serious infection are a smelly discharge and sometimes a burning sensation when urinating. Male sexual partners must also be treated.

Pregnancy Most miscarriages, which can occasionally lead to severe bleeding, occur during the first three months of pregnancy, so this can be a risky time to travel. The last three months should also be spent within reasonable distance of good medical care. Pregnant women should avoid all unnecessary medication, but vaccinations and malarial prophylactics should still be taken where possible. Additional care should be taken to prevent illness and particular attention should be paid to diet and nutrition. Alcohol and nicotine should be avoided.

WOMEN TRAVELLERS
Attitudes to Women
The Solomons is very tolerant of the many puzzling ways of the modern world, yet islanders are sometimes more accepting of the behaviour of foreign males than that of foreign females.

It's against custom for a young woman to be out at night by herself. Exercise normal caution in Honiara – after dark take a taxi and stay in busy areas. Female tourists swimming or sunbathing alone at isolated beaches might attract unwanted attention.

Foreign women travelling solo around remote villages are rare at present. Like men, you should see the chief on arrival at a village, preferably offering a gift. If you're allowed to stay, the chief will probably appoint a young local woman to look after while you're there.

Rape and sexual assault are rare, though solo expat women may experience a phenomenon called 'creeping', where a local man will stand outside her window and knock or hiss (hissing is a common way to attract attention in the Solomons). This means he wants to be invited in for sex; if she tells him sharply to go away, he will. It's unnerving rather than threatening.

What to Wear
As recently as the mid-1980s, local women wearing jeans, slacks or longish shorts were rare in the capital, let alone the rest of the Solomons. However, these are now acceptable in Honiara, and increasingly around the country, especially in Polynesian areas and the more cosmopolitan parts of Western Province, such as Gizo, Munda and the expat-managed plantations.

Local fashions inevitably change at differing paces, so ask first and take careful note of what others are wearing. Females showing their thighs in public is still tabu, so shorts should be knee-length. Shorts are even recommended for swimming, except in the self-contained resorts where Western standards apply.

GAY & LESBIAN TRAVELLERS
Homosexuality is illegal and subject to 14 years imprisonment, so discretion is called for. Prosecutions aren't common but are not unknown. Lesbians are not subject to any statutes.

DISABLED TRAVELLERS
There are no special facilities for the disabled. Getting around will be a real problem for wheelchair users – small domestic aeroplanes have narrow doors and shipping services don't have ramp access.

SENIOR TRAVELLERS
Check with relevant organisations before you leave home for advice and discounted travel packages. Once in the Solomons, you won't be eligible for any special deals.

TRAVEL WITH CHILDREN
See Lonely Planet's *Travel with Children* by Maureen Wheeler for useful advice. You can buy disposable nappies, infant formula etc in Honiara, but don't leave the capital without buying everything you need.

DANGERS & ANNOYANCES
Safety
Although people on some islands made a sport out of pig and taro theft in the past, there are other islands where stealing from neighbours was unheard of before white people arrived. However, criminal activity has recently increased in Honiara, where it is usually associated with alcohol abuse and youth unemployment. Some unemployed regularly do the rounds of shops, claiming falsely to represent certain local charities and asking for donations from both shopkeepers and customers.

Thieves occasionally steal money from cars parked in isolated spots or break into houses looking for alcohol or electrical equipment such as stereo systems and VCRs. There have been reports of hotel rooms being robbed, and bags have sometimes been snatched. An unusual crimewave hit in 1985 and 1986: prisoners in Honiara's jail were able to let themselves out at night, commit crimes, and return before sunrise to give themselves an alibi! (Prison security has since tightened.)

Violence towards expats or visitors is uncommon. In fact, it's usually quite safe for foreign males to walk around at night anywhere in the country. Female tourists should refer to the Women Travellers section earlier. Drunks may need to be avoided, as is the case anywhere. Islanders in Honiara walk close to the road at night to be in the light, because even now there's the danger of inter-island feuding.

Valuables are usually safe in your hotel room, but don't leave wallets or handbags visible in parked cars or lying around anywhere. It's just a matter of taking the same precautions as you would back home.

A very sensible extra precaution is to photocopy all your travel documents, including passports, travellers' cheques and airline tickets, keeping the copies with you but separate from the originals. Replacements are much easier to get if you have these duplicates.

Unexploded Munitions

Although WWII finished over 50 years ago, unexploded shells and grenades, mortar bombs and bullets are still being found, particularly around Honiara. Children sometimes unearth small arms ammunition and offer to sell it to you. Don't buy anything – warn them of the risks they run handling such volatile material and advise them to hand in their trophies to the authorities at once!

Flora & Fauna

There are a number of plants and animals to be wary of in the Solomons, though the likelihood of experiencing problems with them is small. See the Flora & Fauna section in the Facts about the Country chapter and the information about shell collecting in the Activities section of this chapter for more details. Don't sit under coconut trees, or shelter under them during a storm – falling coconuts can kill.

LEGAL MATTERS

You're not supposed to drink alcohol on the street in towns. Dope is illegal, and smoking it is not part of the local culture.

BUSINESS HOURS

Banking hours in Honiara are from 8.30 am to 3 pm, Monday to Friday; some branches outside the capital close for lunch between noon and 1 pm. Government offices are open Monday to Friday from 8 am to noon and 1 to 4 pm. Private businesses close half an hour later, and also operate on Saturday mornings till noon.

Shops in town are generally open Monday to Friday from 8.30 am to 5 pm and on Saturday till noon, though some open longer hours, including on Sunday. There are even a few basic provisions stores open daily 24 hours.

Village trade stores open whenever there are customers willing to buy. This includes Sundays if the shopkeeper's around rather than at church. However, it's very hard to persuade SDA members to open their stores on Saturday, their day of worship.

PUBLIC HOLIDAYS & SPECIAL EVENTS
National Holidays

Annual holidays in the Solomons are:

1 January
  New Year's Day
March/April
  Easter – Good Friday, Holy Saturday and Easter Monday
May
  Whit Monday – eighth Monday after Easter
June
  Queen's Birthday – usually second Friday
7 July
  Independence Day
25 December
  Christmas Day
26 December
  National Thanksgiving Day

SIMON FOALE

MARK HONAN

SIMON FOALE

MARK HONAN

SIMON FOALE

Top Left: Semegi Station on Sandfy Island, Nggela Islands, Central Province
Top Right: Lilisiana village, Malaita Island, Malaita Province
Middle: Olevuga village, Sandfly Island, Nggela Islands, Central Province
Bottom Left: Michi village, Vangunu Island, Marovo Lagoon, Western Province
Bottom Right: Tahanuku village, Rennell Island, Rennell & Bellona Province

HOLGER LEUE

SIMON FOALE

HOLGER LEUE

HOLGER LEUE

SIMON FOALE

Top Left: Children in Honiara, Guadalcanal Island
Top Right: Market in Honiara, Guadalcanal Island
Middle Left: Japanese war memorial, Mt Austen, Guadalcanal Island
Middle Right: US F4F Wildcat wreck, Vilu War Museum, Vilu, Guadalcanal Island
Botttom: Mamara Estate near Bonegi Creek, Guadalcanal Island

When a national holiday falls on a weekend, the accompanying public holiday is usually taken on the preceding Friday or following Monday, except for Holy Saturday. Expect aeroplanes and ships from Honiara to be full around Christmas time, as people return to the islands to be with their families.

Independence Day celebrations in early July are the Solomons' most important annual festival. Although there are festivities in every provincial centre, the largest are in Honiara. These include sporting events, a military parade and custom dances by performers from different islands.

There are also parades in Honiara on Whit Monday, when war veterans march to the war memorial opposite the central bank, and on the Queen's Birthday, when police march through the capital. This is followed by sporting events and custom dancing.

Keep an ear out for custom festivals and ceremonies performed at village level. You'd be lucky to happen on something, but it would be well worth witnessing.

Provincial Holidays

Each province has its own holiday:

Central	29 June
Choiseul	25 February
Guadalcanal	1 August
Isabel	8 July
Makira/Ulawa	3 August
Malaita	15 August
Rennell, Bellona	20 July
Temotu	8 June
Western	7 December

Provincial holidays, like national ones, are transferred to a weekday when they fall on a weekend. Isabel's holiday on the day following Independence Day is sometimes merged with the national holiday.

Other regional events include the annual yam-increase ceremonies in Santa Catalina in March, and Wogasia, the week-long marriage ceremonies and mock clan wars held in Santa Catalina around the end of May. Western Province used to have its annual

Festival of the Sea in December, though the 1996 event was postponed till May 1997 to coincide with the new (perhaps annual) Brisbane-Gizo yacht race.

ACTIVITIES

The outdoor life could keep you occupied for months – there's bushwalking, canoeing, mountain and volcano climbing, scuba diving, snorkelling, swimming, surfing, fishing, shell collecting, bird-watching, and caving on offer. Or if you'd prefer something less active you can laze on beaches, examine archaeological sites, observe ancient custom, search for war wrecks or take scenic drives near the capital.

The Solomons has great potential (as yet, largely unexploited) for ocean kayaking. You'd need to bring your own gear. Mountain biking is also possible along tracks too rough for vehicles. A dismantled bike can be taken as luggage on the small domestic aeroplanes.

Structured participation sports aren't very much in evidence, though golf, squash and tennis are available in Honiara. Every village of any size has a football (soccer) field – the kids would be thrilled (though perhaps shy at first) if you joined in their informal kick-abouts.

Bushwalking

The Solomons is often too hot and humid for bushwalks. But in the cooler months of the midyear, an island walking tour can provide a genuine insight into Melanesian village life. The Honiara area is usually dry then, though it's when Guadalcanal's southern coast has its heaviest rainfalls.

Islands like Nggela, Kolombangara, Nggatokae, Rennell, Santa Cruz, Vella Lavell-a and Savo suit a brief trip on foot, as long as you are well prepared and carry a reasonable stock of food, money and items to use as gifts.

In addition to village life, there are beaches, mountains, craters, waterfalls, hot springs, caves and lakes to see – depending which island you choose. Some, like Choiseul, have tracks from one side to the other or, like Malaita, Santa Isabel and Makira, along part of the coast.

When bushwalking, always watch the weather, as heavy rain in the hills can cause sudden and dangerous flash floods downstream. Take plenty of insect repellent.

Volcano & Mountain Climbing

Tinakula may be too sheer to climb, but there are other volcanic peaks on Simbo, Savo and Vella Lavella. Climbing either Rendova's or Kolombangara's peaks would require a strenuous but rewarding two-day hike, with magnificent views over Western Province from their summits. Guadalcanal has the nation's two highest peaks, but you would need to be very well prepared to consider climbing these.

Bird-Watching

There are 173 bird species for ornithologists to enjoy. The Honiara area is as good a place as anywhere in the Solomons to see most of the country's tropical birds, including the unfortunately named spangled drongo. If you want to see some very rare species, you must go to Temotu Province, Lake Te'Nggano on Rennell, or the highlands of Makira and Guadalcanal. If instead you prefer sea birds, you'll find plenty of these in Ontong Java, on the smaller offshore islands in the Shortlands group, and in the coastal parts of Makira/Ulawa Province. Try to see megapode birds at their hatcheries if you can. Savo and Simbo are the best places for these, though they are also present on several other islands.

Check Flora & Fauna in the Facts about the Country chapter for other creatures to keep an eye out for.

Viewing War Relics

Without doubt, scuba divers get the most thrilling view of the country's many wrecks. Even so, there are plenty more relics ashore in Guadalcanal, Central and Western provinces to satisfy any war buffs who aren't licensed scuba divers.

Hundreds of US and Japanese citizens come annually to see the battlefields. They find more than enough remains, including old planes, guns and vehicles, to evoke poignant memories of the events of 55 years ago.

Visiting Ancient Sites & Caves

There are ancient remains all over the country, with accessible sites in Malaita, Simbo, Bellona, Santa Cruz, New Georgia and Santa Ana. Some ancient sites may still be in daily use, especially the artificial islands in Malaita.

It's forbidden to remove (or even touch) anything from such places, especially personal objects such as skulls, without the traditional owner's agreement. It's also illegal to export custom objects. A difficulty may arise when locals disagree on what you may or may not do. In such a case, try to establish who is the true custom owner, and follow their wishes. As long as you're tactful and polite, you should be able to see most skull and traditional-money collections. A custom fee is often charged to visit ancient and tabu sites; likewise for certain natural wonders like caves, hot springs and waterfalls.

Rockshelters and caves are widely spread around the country. The largest concentration is in Nggela, though Bellona has several too. Other places with two or more rockshelters and caves are Santa Ana, Makira, Guadalcanal, Choiseul, Malaita, New Georgia, Kolombangara and the Reef Islands. If you want to see all Nggela's caverns, come prepared to camp, unless you're on a yacht.

Petroglyphs are much scarcer. There's a site close to Honiara, and another on Guadalcanal's southern coast. The remainder are in Simbo, Vella Lavella and Maramasike.

Shell Collecting

Anyone going beachcombing on the outer islands will find a huge range of beautiful shells; but beware of poisonous cone shells and stonefish. Go with an islander until you know what to avoid, and wear reef shoes.

You should ask permission before shell

ollecting. Each section of coral that can be reached on foot or by a skin diver (ie an islander diving without scuba tanks) has its own custom owner. Taking small shells will seldom be a problem, but large or distinctive shells may have a commercial value if sold at the local market, and a live one may represent food for the owner's family.

Fishing

There are some superlative fishing sites. Although most tropical marine life is colourful, it's usually small. If you're after larger fish, you'll find them mainly at the reef's outer edge.

You can try your hand at game fishing, particularly off the southern New Georgia Islands. Sailfish, marlin, shark, tuna, barracuda and wahoo are regularly caught. Game fishing is only permitted in deep waters, as coastal landowners ban it in shallow areas for fear of depleting traditional fishing grounds.

Trolling is the best way to catch large fish if you're in a moving boat. Just hang a baited line over the side whenever you take a ship or canoe ride, and pull fish in as soon as you feel them bite.

River fishing is also worthwhile, particularly for freshwater crayfish and prawns. Most of the larger islands have fast-flowing creeks where you can land some good-sized catches. But avoid any muddy coastal rivers which empty into shoreside swamps, as these are more likely to conceal human-eating estuarine crocodiles than fish!

As always in Melanesia, check whether the reef or river belongs to anyone before casting your line. To preserve fish stocks, spearfishing is often prohibited.

Swimming

There's a multitude of beaches around the country. Many are white or gold; in geologically young areas they're more likely to be blackish or grey. See Flora & Fauna in Facts about the Country for information about dangers from sharks.

Swimmers should strictly avoid crossing any offshore reefs. Beyond the reef are strong ocean currents which can quickly sweep you out to sea, so stay within a reef's calm, protected waters, close to land.

Surfing

Surfers have found some good waves at Pailongge on Ghizo, Poro on Santa Isabel and Tawarogha on Makira. Surf has also been reported at Beaufort Bay in southern Guadalcanal; Malu'u, Manu and Fakanakafo Bay in northern Malaita; Nemba, Byron and Kala bays on Santa Cruz; and between Nifiloli and Fenualoa islands in the Reefs group. However, some of these sports may be across coral rock rather than sand, and therefore could be dangerous.

Islanders have accommodated surfers quite readily in the past, but they expect you to respect their customs and rules. That means asking a village's permission before you surf, bathe, use their washing facilities, or stay there.

Diving

This is one of the main attractions in the Solomons. The extensive coral and fish life alone would merit a visit, but there are also hundreds of interesting WWII wrecks to explore. It's easy to combine both types of dive on the same day. Numerous wrecks are within reach of sports divers, including many in good condition and with interesting artefacts in-situ. The situation is perhaps even better for advanced and technical divers – the Solomons is rated one of the three best sites in the world. Many wrecks have been undisturbed for 55 years, and are overflowing with portable items and personal effects.

There are good dive sites off northern and south-eastern Guadalcanal, in Marovo and Vonavona lagoons and north-western parts of Roviana Lagoon, and off Ghizo Island, the Shortland Islands, north-eastern Vella Lavella, western Choiseul, north-western Santa Isabel, north-eastern Malaita, Sikaiana, Ontong Java and the Roncador Reef, the Russells, the Nggelas, south-eastern Makira, the Reef Islands, Utupua,

Vanikoro, and the Indispensable Reefs to the south of Rennell.

There are registered scuba operators in Honiara, Tambea, Gizo, Uepi and Munda. They all insist on seeing your certification before letting you dive. Contact details and prices are quoted in the relevant regional chapters, as are descriptions of the main dive sites they visit. Pigeon Island Resort in the Reefs also arranges scuba diving. Touring yachts with their own compressors find more out of the way diving places.

Scuba divers score over snorkellers and shell collectors as far as customary law is concerned. As traditional ownership of reefs is limited to as deep as an islander can free-dive, there's no need to worry about possible breaches of customary law as long as you're more than 10m down. But taking souvenirs from wrecks is looting, so don't be tempted.

Water temperatures in the Solomons are among the warmest in the world, though night diving can be rather chilly in the archipelago's cooler months. Wear something (at least a T-shirt) to limit the chance of getting grazes from coral or wrecks, and to protect you skin from abrasive BCDs. Lycra suits are usually warm enough even at night, yet most operators have standard-type wet suits for hire also. Many divers bring their own gear, but all Solomons dive shops rent full equipment, as do the live-aboard dive boats.

Underwater visibility is usually good to around 30m, unless you're diving in a busy harbour or inside the hold of a wrecked ship.

Learning to Dive If you're over 15 and healthy, you can learn to dive. Instructors train novice divers up to full scuba certification over an intensive period of five to seven days (costing from A$350), or provide one-day 'resort courses' (from A$85) for those who wish to have the thrill of diving without full training. Prices vary between the operators, so compare rates. If you intend learning to dive, check in advance whether you need a medical certificate. Honiara clinics can provide a scuba check-up for about S$55.

Decompression Facilities There's no decompression chamber in the Solomons despite the large number of scuba-diving tourists visiting the country. The nearest is at Townsville on Australia's northern coast.

Live-Aboard Dive Craft Bilikiki Cruises (☎ 20412, fax 23897, PO Box 414, Mendana Ave, Honiara, has two well equipped vessels which regularly take divers on luxury scuba trips (usually seven to 10 days' duration) around the country, particularly through the clear, blue water of the Russell Islands. The charge per person is US$445/296 a day for single/twin occupancy on the MV *Bilikiki*, and from US$296/215 on the MV *Spirit of Solomons*. The company also has a US office (☎ (800) 663 5363) and an Internet site (http:// www.3routes.com/scuba/sp/sol/).

Blue Lagoon Cruises (☎ & fax 25300, PO Box 1022), Honiara, charges from US$285 per day for similar trips on the MV *Solomon Sea*.

Dive Holidays To track down specialist companies organising package dive tours to the Solomons, ask your travel agent or read the scuba diving magazines. Australian based companies include Dive Travel Australia (☎ (02) 9970 6311), and Dive Adventures (☎ (02) 9299 4633 or (008) 22 2234. Dive Adventures, also with an office in Melbourne, does a complete package from Sydney to Uepi Resort for A$2300 including eight dives.

Snorkelling
Snorkellers can usually join scuba trips for between S$30 and S$60 a time. Otherwise there's a mass of coral around the country to view for free.

When snorkelling in the tropics, you'll find it's comparatively easy to enter the water off a coral ledge, but often fearfully hard to get back onto dry land again, especially if the sea is at all rough. Islanders always plan their exit point before they enter the water.

Avid snorkel fans won't need to be reminded to bring their own double-sealed mask, snorkel tube, diving boots and fins. There's often great coral where there's no rental gear available, and in any case, renting can be pricey.

WORK
Both voluntary and paid workers require permits to work in the Solomons. For more information see Visas & Documents earlier in this chapter.

Expatriate & Local Incomes
The minimum wage in the Solomons is around S$1.50 per hour, though expatriates would probably require a shade more than that. Average monthly income for locals is S$203 for sales workers, S$304 for service people, S$306 for clerical and related staff, and S$384 for professionals and technicians.

A single expatriate's annual expenditure if running a car, paying a reasonable rent, shopping freely, and enjoying a modest level of entertainment would be around S$25,000. A family with two children would probably spend above S$35,000 a year. Residence involves a tax liability for any income derived in or from the Solomons, and a stay of six months is sufficient to qualify. Tax levels range from 11% for annual earnings of S$5,100 to S$15,000, up to 47% for earnings above S$60,000.

Registering a Business
Getting a small business registered should not be too difficult as long as you have adequate funds, but really large capital investments can take up to four years to be approved or rejected. Registration is with the Foreign Investment Division (☎ 21928) in the Ministry of Commerce, Industries & Employment.

Tax is only liable for income which accrues in, is derived from, or is received in the Solomons, though double-taxation relief is available on overseas earnings. The tax rate for Solomons-incorporated companies is 35%.

ACCOMMODATION
The Solomons is not exactly overflowing with places to stay, though Honiara and Gizo provide a decent range of options. Only towns, resorts and a handful of villages have any sort of accommodation that caters for tourists. However, the few visitors who venture to villages off the beaten track should have no problem finding basic short-term shelter in a leaf hut. If you intend this, it's always worth first asking around in the provincial capital about village visitors' houses, local tabus and transport options.

Try to book accommodation ahead. Not only will you be sure of securing a bed, it will also enable your host to meet you at the airfield or port – useful in places where there is no public transport.

Camping
Camping is rare in populated areas but quite acceptable in the bush. The landowner's permission has to be obtained first; ask what wood you can use if you want to light a fire.

Staying Overnight in a Village
Most villages of any size in the Solomons have a basic leaf house which is available for visitors. These are mostly intended for wantoks and other islanders, though foreigners can use them. You could probably stay a night or two on such a basis. The charge will be nominal, or it may even be free. Even if there isn't a leaf house, it's likely something could be arranged to get a roof over your head – perhaps spending the night in the local school.

Villages rarely have electricity; lighting will be by hurricane lamp. The water supply will be from a stream or a communal tap. Washing will be outside, perhaps behind a partition. The toilet will be a hole in the ground, or a reserved place in the bush or on the reef. You would have to rely on other villagers for cooking facilities, so bring enough food to share around. Tinned meat or tuna, tea, coffee, sugar and fresh bread are all useful items to bring. Rats are the curse of village life, so hang your food up overnight.

Upon arrival at a village, see the chief and ask permission to stay. This may be refused, so don't arrive somewhere too late to move on the same day. It's always a good idea to have a gift or two to offer. Tobacco sticks, betel nuts, betel leaves and lime are often recommended as gifts for villagers. However, you may not want to encourage these unhealthy habits, and in any case, no SDA and few SSEC members touch them.

Other easily portable gifts include *lava lavas* (sarongs), T-shirts, fishing gear, knives, lighters and candles.

For isolated villages it's advisable to send a service or radio message well in advance to request permission to stay. This is particularly necessary if you want to stay more than a couple of nights.

Organised Village Stays Recently it has become possible to experience village life without relying on the kindness of villagers and becoming a burden to them. Visits can be pre-arranged, and you stay with locals who have an idea of what tourists want and expect. It is an authentic taste of traditional

Leaf houses are raised on stilts to allow for tidal flows

rural life. Visiting on this basis is highly recommended and helps pump money into the local communities. It also takes some of the uncertainty out of getting there, getting fed, and finding acceptable accommodation.

The World Heritage organisation and World Wildlife Fund have been active around the Marovo Lagoon, helping to set up eco-tourist lodges in villages in this beautiful area. Lodge owners well understand local environmental issues and are keen to demonstrate traditional lifestyles and activities. See the Marovo Lagoon section in the Western Province chapter for details.

A similar experience is provided by Solomons Village Stay, except you will be staying with ordinary villagers, rather than with lodge owners. Your host will act as your guide during your stay, and you must book in advance. Stays are for a minimum two nights, and there are participating villages in north and south-east Guadalcanal, West Honiara, west and north Malaita, Ghizo Island, Kolombangara and Vella Lavella. From 1998 it will also be possible to stay in east and south Malaita and the Nggelas. The A$40 daily charge (A$20 for children) includes accommodation, meals, and village-based activities. The main booking agent is Adventure Sports & Travel, 119 Logan Rd, Woolloongabba, Qld 4102, Australia. The booking fee is A$40; it's only S$20 if you wait till you get to Honiara and book through the local agent, SolTravel (see the Honiara section).

Rest Houses & Hostels
These comprise church hostels, provincial government rest houses and private rest houses. Most have room fans, shared washing facilities and a communal kitchen. They generally charge around S$35 per person per night. Most of your fellow guests will be islanders.

Rooms might have anything from two to five beds. Solo travellers can save money by sticking to places where the room is priced per bed rather than per room. In such cases they'll be expected to share on a dor-

mitory basis if the place gets full. They could opt instead to pay for the whole room, which is usually double the per bed rate, but enforced sharing doesn't happen too often, as proprietors will always allocate empty rooms first.

Drinking and (sometimes) smoking are often forbidden in budget places, particularly provincial government and church rest houses. Provincial government rest houses are primarily designed for visiting government staff; there's a possibility you may have to evacuate if an official wants a bed.

Hotels & Resorts
Comfortable, tourist-class hotels only exist in Honiara, Gizo, Munda and Auki. They generally have rooms with or without private shower and air-conditioning, depending on how much you're prepared to pay. A telephone, TV and tea/coffee-making facilities may be provided, but you're rarely able to self-cater. Some have restaurants and bars. Boat trips, scuba facilities and regular performances by island dancers may be on offer.

Self-contained resorts are found away from the towns, usually in idyllic island locations. They range from cheap and fairly basic places like Luelta Resort in Lata, up to elegant and expensive places like Tavanipupu Resort in Tavanipupu Island.

FOOD
Unless you can afford to dine in expensive hotel restaurants and resorts, food is not likely to be the high point of your visit to the Solomons. Only a few towns have any restaurants at all – most of the time you'll be self-catering.

Staple Foods
Vegetables you'll come across frequently are cassava, kumara (sweet potato), taro and yams. These and other foods are described in the glossary at the back of this book. Rice is another staple. Although fresh fish is usually readily available, most local town dwellers seem to prefer to eat tinned tuna! Tinned meats like corned beef and luncheon

meat are also popular, as are packet instant noodles. An enjoyable and cheap lunch (S$3 to S$4) is a portion of fish and chips, usually comprising tuna or reef fish in batter and kumara chips. Cassava starch can be processed into tapioca, which is used in puddings.

Coconuts The primary food of the Pacific is the coconut. In addition to being part of the staple diet, it has other valuable uses.

The coconut fruit provides food or drink through all stages of its development. When young, it yields refreshing coconut water. As it matures, white flesh forms round the hollow interior. Initially this is soft and jelly-like, and easily scooped out with a spoon. It gradually thickens and firms, yet remains tasty. The older, harder flesh is normally dried into copra. At its last stage the nut begins to shoot and the milk inside goes crispy, making what is known throughout the Pacific as coconut ice cream.

Vegetarians
Except for SDA members who avoid pork and shellfish, most islanders are not familiar with the practice of vegetarianism. As it is considered rude to decline food that has been offered to you, it requires both creativity and cultural sensitivity to maintain a vegetarian diet. In Honiara, vegetarian foodstuffs and restaurant meals are available, but elsewhere they'll be harder to find.

Markets & Trade Stores
There's no bargaining at markets, as prices are fair and cheap. Coconuts, bananas, pawpaws, betel nuts and kumara are always on sale, and taro, yams, *pana* and manioc are usually available also. In some parts of the country you'll find breadfruit, slippery cabbage, edible ferns, *mangou* and *ngali* nuts, as well as bush limes, oranges, starfruit, pineapples, mangoes and sugar cane.

Town stores stock a reasonable variety of goods, but don't expect too much of village trade stores. They mainly sell tinned meat and tuna, rice, noodles, soap, dry biscuits, tea and sugar. In larger places the selection

---

Betel Nut
Bia blong Solomon (Solomons' beer) is what islanders light-heartedly call the nut of the areca palm. The meat of the betel nut is chewed in a betel-pepper leaf with lime. It has a mildly intoxicating and tonic effect caused by the catalytic effect of nut, leaf and lime. Betel-nut chewers usually carry a lime box and leaves with them.

The nut is best chewed when the fruit is green and soft and juicy in the husk. First bite off the top of the nut, then hold it sideways between your teeth and bite it open. After this, roll up the leaf and chew it. Finally, use a spatula or finger to put the lime into your mouth.

Although some members of the Provincial Assembly chew betel nut during debates, very few expats have taken to it, despite its effects. Its acidity is a major drawback, and after prolonged use the juice stains the mouth crimson and makes teeth go black. The unpalatable mess of juice and chewed nut is spat out, which explains the red splotches frequently seen on the ground.

The lime eventually eats away the chewer's gums and can cause serious mouth ulcers, especially among people who chew 10 or more betel nuts a day. Nearly 20% of all local cancer cases – about 30 people per year – are associated with chewing betel nut. ■

---

may extend to cigarettes, cotton cloth, beer and soft drinks.

DRINKS
Nonalcoholic Drinks
Fresh water is usually abundant throughout the main islands but can be scarce on the smaller coral atolls, where local populations often depend on water catchment for their survival. There is also piped water at Munda, Malu'u and Noro and all provincial capitals except Tinggoa Bay. Although only a third of the rural population presently has drinkable water, the proportion increases yearly.

Town water is filtered and usually chlorinated. Even so, it's not always safe to drink. Only Buala's is clean and plentiful, while Auki has supply problems. Honiara's water is plentiful but variable in quality and so should be boiled or treated. Most hotels will provide boiled water on request.

The Solomons Brewery produces an excellent range of bottled soft drinks (S$2.50). In restaurants you can often get a refreshing glass of bush lime and water from only S$1.

Alcoholic Drinks

The Solomons recently started producing its own beer – an excellent German-style lager, Solbrew. It and the slightly stronger SB cost around S$4 a bottle, but the price rises the further you get from Honiara. These Solomon Brewery products have largely superseded Australian beers, though cans of Victoria Bitter (VB) are still available.

The only bars in the Solomons are those attached to private clubs or the more expensive hotels. Solbrew generally costs around S$5 to S$7 in such places. Hotels sell alcohol from 10 am to 10.30 pm. On Sundays, bars open from noon to 10 pm; only hotel residents may buy liquor between 2 and 7 pm. Many of Honiara's restaurants are licensed to sell alcohol.

Islanders make their own alcoholic beverage in Ontong Java and Sikaiana – a fermented coconut juice or palm toddy, sometimes called white beer. There is also a popular, but illegal, drink known as 'home brew'. The most common form, widely drunk on Bellona, is a coconut toddy fermented with yeast and sugar.

ENTERTAINMENT

Except for Honiara, which has discos and casinos, there's little nightlife. Elsewhere, islanders tend to spend the evening quietly with their family.

The only regular film screenings are in Honiara, Auki, Munda and Gizo. They show films on video, usually fast-paced thrillers, projected onto a screen or a large TV, depending on the size of the place. Elsewhere there'll be video shows in a school or public hall whenever a plane or a ship brings a film. Ask around locally and keep an eye out for posters advertising shows.

Outside the capital, modern dances can be hard to find. If you're looking for one, check out any public notice boards and ask around for *sisi*, the Pijin word for parties or dances.

SPECTATOR SPORT

Although every provincial capital is also the local sports centre, the best place to watch is in Honiara. It has the national sports stadium, the Lawson Tama, and other venues. Football (soccer) is the national sport, and the season takes up most of the year. Boxing, rugby, athletics, basketball, netball and volleyball are also popular.

THINGS TO BUY

The only specialised handicraft shops are in Honiara, though a few hotels and resorts elsewhere sell local crafts. Purchasing is often by direct contact with villagers themselves, particularly in the New Georgia Islands and Makira/Ulawa Province.

The Solomons' most distinctive products are *nguzunguzus* from Western Province, usually inlaid with pearl shell. They make great souvenirs. Another item unique to the country is shell money, which is made into headbands, armbands, belts and necklaces. Other things to look out for include woven mats and baskets, carved dolphins and bowls, model outriggers, and replica weapons. See Arts in the Facts about the Country for much more on local products – most would make fine souvenirs.

A lava lava is useful for both men and women as cool casual wear and to cover up when away from the beach. A tape of local panpipe music would make a good memento. Alexander McDonald (☎ 20396), Room 28, NPF Plaza, Honiara sells the cheapest tapes in town (S$30).

Restrictions on Artefact Exports

Many countries, including the USA, Australia and New Zealand, restrict the importation of the bodily parts of sea and land animals. Before buying some of the beautiful and rare shells for sale in the Solomons, make sure your country will allow you to bring them back home.

Turtle shell, though available in the Solomons, is severely embargoed overseas. Traditional currencies and ornaments incorporating the teeth of porpoises, bats and dogs are frequently subject to foreign customs controls. Red-feather money from Temotu Province is similarly regulated.

The Solomons government prohibits the export of original artefacts. A great deal of early material was destroyed in the early days of Christianity in the Solomons, or was eagerly scooped up by foreigners and museums at paltry prices. Consequently, there isn't much left. While there's no problem with replicas or modern carvings, restrictions apply to all original carvings as well as to most clam-shell money and products, as these haven't been made for many years now. Skulls from head-hunting collections are similarly embargoed.

Wrecks on a reef are treated as the property of the local custom owners, and those in the depths are national treasure. Looting results in heavy penalties, confiscation of what's been recovered and deportation. ∎

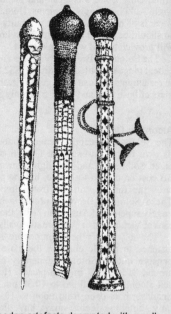

Wooden artefacts decorated with small pieces of shell

Getting There & Away

AIR

Airports & Airlines

The Solomons' only international airport is Henderson airport (air code HIR), 11 km east of Honiara. The current terminal building is very small. The departure lounge has a tiny duty-free/handicraft shop (with a poor selection) and a bar. In the general lobby there's a food and drinks shop, car rental desks and an NBSI foreign-exchange counter. The latter two are open for international flights only.

In late 1996 a S$60 million upgrade of airport facilities commenced, financed by the Japanese government. A new terminal building and other facilities will be built. Airport capacity will be quadrupled.

The Solomons is serviced internationally by Solomon Airlines, Air Pacific, Air Nauru and Air Niugini. Often these flights are on a code-sharing basis. This means two airlines sell tickets for the same flight, which will have a different flight number, depending on which airline you've bought the ticket from. Solomon Airlines flights are prefixed 'IE'.

The paucity of direct flights to the Solomons is one factor holding back tourism. Its only international services are to Eastern Australia and a few South Pacific neighbours, and flights from there are expensive, unless the trip can be completed using an add-on regional pass.

Buying Tickets

Always be clear about what restrictions and cancellation penalties apply before buying a ticket, and don't pay if you're only waitlisted for a seat. Budget tickets have the most restrictions, and may have inconvenient transit stops. The cheaper 'excursion fares' quoted below generally have a 30-day maximum stay, and may also have a minimum stay requirement.

Ask if airport taxes are included in the price, and deal with travel agents who are bonded in the event of bankruptcy (eg ABTA in the UK, ASTA in the USA). Low season fares are cheaper, though when low season falls varies between airlines – if your travel dates are flexible, you could make significant savings.

If you have special needs (eg vegetarian meals, wheelchair assistance, attending to or carrying a baby etc) let the airline know your requirements when booking and again on confirmation.

Regional Passes A variety of Pacific air passes are available, but the only one that currently reaches the Solomons is the Visit South Pacific Pass, valid for several regional airlines, including Solomon Airlines. Two to eight flights can be purchased and it's valid for six months. Fares per flight cost US$160 in group A (eg Honiara to Nauru), US$215 in group B (eg Honiara to Brisbane, Nadi, Port Vila or Port Moresby) and US$320 in group C (eg Honiara to Auckland). This is only available if added on to Round the World (RTW) or return tickets purchased in Europe, North America or Asia. Subject to government approval, Air Nauru will have a Visit the Pacific Pass that links Honiara to destinations in Micronesia, the Philippines, Nauru, Kiribati, Fiji and Australia's east coast. It will cost US$400 for three flights, and up to five extra flights can be added for US$75 each. It will be valid for 90 days. Air Nauru used to have extensive, cheap flights though the Pacific, but its services have contracted. Until the pass is introduced, there are no direct flights between Honiara and Nauru.

Australia

Solomon Airlines flies direct from Brisbane to Honiara every Monday, Thursday and Saturday, with the return flight leaving the following day. This is the only direct service to the Solomons from Australia. The fare is A$670 one way, or A$839 as an excursion return. The Solomon Airlines office is in Brisbane (☎ 3229 0000, fax 3229 1399); tickets are also sold in Brisbane, Melbourne, Sydney, Canberra and Adelaide by World Aviation Systems.

If you're in Australia en route from North America, Asia or Europe, it's much cheaper to get to Honiara using one of the regional passes above, rather than paying the scheduled fare.

New Zealand

On Tuesday morning Solomon Airlines flies from Honiara to Auckland, including a

---

Air Travel Glossary

Apex Apex, or 'advance purchase excursion' is a discounted ticket which must be paid for in advance. There are penalties if you wish to change it.

Baggage Allowance This will be written on your ticket: usually one 20-kg item to go in the hold, plus one item of hand luggage.

Bucket Shop An unbonded travel agency specialising in discounted airline tickets.

Bumped Just because you have a confirmed seat doesn't mean you're going to get on the plane – see Overbooking.

Cancellation Penalties If you have to cancel or change an Apex ticket there are often heavy penalties involved; insurance can sometimes be taken out against these penalties. Some airlines impose penalties on regular tickets as well, particularly against 'no show' passengers.

Check-In Airlines ask you to check in a certain time ahead of the flight departure (usually 1½ hours on international flights). If you fail to check in on time and the flight is overbooked the airline can cancel your booking and give your seat to somebody else.

Confirmation Having a ticket written out with the flight and date you want doesn't mean you have a seat until the agent has checked with the airline that your status is 'OK' or confirmed. Meanwhile you could just be 'on request'.

Discounted Tickets There are two types of discounted fares – officially discounted (see Promotional Fares) and unofficially discounted. The lowest prices often impose drawbacks like flying with unpopular airlines, inconvenient schedules, or unpleasant routes and connections. A discounted ticket can save you other things than money – you may be able to pay Apex prices without the associated Apex advance booking and other requirements. Discounted tickets only exist where there is fierce competition.

Full Fares Airlines traditionally offer first class (coded F), business class (coded J) and economy class (coded Y) tickets. These days there are so many promotional and discounted fares available from the regular economy class that few passengers pay full economy fare.

Lost Tickets If you lose your airline ticket an airline will usually treat it like a travellers' cheque and, after enquiries, issue you with another one. Legally, however, an airline is entitled to treat it like cash and if you lose it then it's gone forever.

No-Shows No-shows are passengers who fail to show up for their flight, sometimes because of unexpected delays or disasters, sometimes because they simply forget, sometimes because they made more than one booking and didn't bother to cancel the one they didn't want. Full-fare passengers who fail to turn up are sometimes entitled to travel on a later flight. The rest of us are penalised (see Cancellation Penalties).

On Request An unconfirmed booking for a flight, see Confirmation.

Open Jaws A return ticket where you fly out to one place but return from another. If available this can save you backtracking to your arrival point.

50-minute transit stop in Port Vila. The flight returns on the same route in the afternoon. The return fare is NZ$1972, or NZ$1376 as an excursion return (minimum/maximum six/60 days). World Aviation Systems (☎ (09) 308 9098) in Auckland represents Solomon Airlines. If coming from the South Island it might be cheaper getting a flight via Brisbane.

The Pacific

Solomon Airlines has offices in Nadi (☎ 722 831) in Fiji and Port Moresby (☎ 325 5724) in Papua New Guinea. It also

---

Overbooking Airlines hate to fly empty seats and since every flight has some passengers who fail to show up (see No-Shows) airlines often book more passengers than they have seats. Usually the excess passengers balance those who fail to show up but occasionally somebody gets bumped. If this happens guess who it is most likely to be? The passengers who check in late.

Promotional Fares Officially discounted fares like Apex fares which are available from travel agents or direct from the airline.

Reconfirmation At least 72 hours prior to departure time of an onward or return flight you must contact the airline and 'reconfirm' that you intend to be on the flight. If you don't do this the airline can delete your name from the passenger list and you could lose your seat. You don't have to reconfirm the first flight on your itinerary or if your stopover is less than 72 hours. It doesn't hurt to reconfirm more than once.

Restrictions Discounted tickets often have various restrictions on them – advance purchase is the most usual one (see Apex). Others are restrictions on the minimum and maximum period you must be away, such as a minimum of 14 days or a maximum of one year. See Cancellation Penalties.

Stand-By A discounted ticket where you only fly if there is a seat free at the last moment. Stand-by fares are usually only available on domestic routes.

Tickets Out An entry requirement for many countries is that you have an onward or return ticket, in other words, a ticket out of the country. If you're not sure what you intend to do next, the easiest solution is to buy the cheapest onward ticket to a neighbouring country or a ticket from a reliable airline which can later be refunded if you do not use it.

Transferred Tickets Airline tickets cannot be transferred from one person to another. Travellers sometimes try to sell the return half of their ticket, but officials can ask you to prove that you are the person named on the ticket. This is unlikely to happen on domestic flights, but on an international flight tickets may be compared with passports.

Travel Agencies Travel agencies vary widely and you should ensure you use one that suits your needs. Some simply handle tours while full-service agencies handle everything from tours and tickets to car rental and hotel bookings. A good one will do all these things and can save you a lot of money, but if all you want is a ticket at the lowest possible price, then you really need an agency specialising in discounted tickets. A discounted ticket agency, however, may not be useful for other things, like hotel bookings.

Travel Periods Some officially discounted fares, Apex fares in particular, vary with the time of year. There is often a low (off-peak) season and a high (peak) season. Sometimes there's an intermediate or shoulder season as well. At peak times, when everyone wants to fly, not only will the officially discounted fares be higher but so will unofficially discounted fares, or there may simply be no discounted tickets available. Usually the fare depends on your outward flight – if you depart in the high season and return in the low season, you pay the high-season fare. ■

has sales agents in Suva (☎ 315 755) in Fiji, Noumea (☎ 286 677) in New Caledonia and Port Vila (☎ 23878) in Vanuatu.

Fiji Air Pacific and Solomon Airlines share a weekly schedule between Honiara and Nadi (pronounced 'nandi') in western Fiji, routed via Port Vila. It leaves Honiara on Saturday afternoon and returns on Sunday morning. The one-way fare is F$813.

If travelling via Fiji from the USA, it's much cheaper to use the South Pacific Pass to continue to Honiara.

Papua New Guinea Solomon Airlines and Air Niugini code-share on the service from Port Moresby to Honiara on Wednesday and Sunday mornings. The flight between Port Moresby and Honiara takes two hours and twenty minutes. Excursion fares (minimum 10 days, maximum 30 days) cost S$1160 one way and S$1501 return. The normal return fare is S$2310.

Vanuatu Services to Honiara from New Zealand and Fiji are routed through Vanuatu's capital, Port Vila. From there to Honiara costs S$1096/34,800VT.

Asia

The most direct route to/from Asia is via Port Moresby in Papua New Guinea, though depending on your starting point, connections may be more frequent and cheaper going via Brisbane. Garuda connects Indonesia to Australia's east coast (Brisbane, Sydney or Melbourne). The low-season, one-way fare to Sydney is A$765 from Jakarta and A$646 from Denpasar, with a free stopover allowed.

Qantas can get you from eastern Australia to Singapore during low season for A$839 one way or A$1129 return; it sometimes has cheaper one-off deals.

For tickets purchased in Honiara, Solomon Airlines charges S$3367 to Manila, S$4469 to Hong Kong, S$4075 to Singapore and S$3828 to Seoul and four Japanese airports, including Tokyo. These destinations involve connecting flights with

other airlines and all flights are routed via Brisbane.

Europe

London is the best place in Europe to find cheap fares, though Amsterdam and Athens are also good. STA Travel (☎ (0171) 361 6262), 86 Old Brompton Rd, London SW7, has branches worldwide. It also has many affiliated agents, including NBBS Reizen (☎ (020) 624 0989), Rokin 38, Amsterdam, and ISYTS (☎ (01) 322 1267), 2nd floor, 11 Nikis St, Athens. Another budget operator knowledgeable about South Pacific routes is Trailfinders (☎ (0171) 938 3939) at 194 Kensington High St, London W8.

There are no direct flights to Honiara – the cheapest returns are via Australia. A charter flight from London to Melbourne, Sydney or Brisbane could cost as little as UK£500 return, but there may be lots of restrictions, such as a maximum six weeks' stay. Scheduled flights start at around £600 in low season.

Travelling west via the USA and Fiji is also a possibility. London-Los Angeles is about £300 return, then you can pick up Air Pacific's flight to Nadi (£470 return).

A RTW airline ticket may work out cheaper than a return ticket. A low season RTW including Brisbane could cost under £700, onto which you could add Honiara as a side trip.

Solomon Airlines' office (☎ (01959) 540737) in Kent, England, sells Air Pacific tickets.

North America

Air Promotions Inc (☎ (800) 677 4277 or (310) 670 7302, fax (310) 338 0708) is the general sales agent in North America for Pacific-based airlines, including Solomon Airlines. It has offices in Los Angeles, New York and San Francisco, and an Internet site at http://www.pacificislands.com.

The best route between the USA and the Solomons is via Fiji. Air Pacific (☎ (800) 227 4446) flies from Los Angeles to Nadi for US$798/949 one way/return in July, US$1107/1144 in December. It departs LA on Tuesday, Thursday and Saturday, and returns from Nadi on Tuesday, Friday and Saturday. If you don't want to stay over-night in Nadi en route to Honiara, you'll have to use a different carrier and may end up paying more.

Council Travel, the budget/student chain, has a student fare from San Francisco to Honiara for $1112 in June and $1258 in December. Return fares from Los Angeles to Nadi/Brisbane are about US$890/ 1325 in December and US$1600/ 1100 in June. From Canada, it would also be easiest to go via Fiji or Australia. Return fares in December are about C$1600 Vancouver-Nadi and C$1800 Vancouver-Brisbane.

SEA
Cruise Ship
Cruise ships occasionally visit Honiara – check with your travel agent for details. It would be a more expensive option than flying, although food, accommodation and entertainment would be included in the cruise price.

Freighter Travel
Gone are the days when tramp steamers plied the world's oceans, picking up stray travellers with little or no fuss. Yet it's still possible to book a passage on a freighter with the help of an experienced travel agent in a major port. Few cargo lines take pas-sengers, but you could ask the captain. The usual answer is that there's only accommo-dation for the crew.

The largest travel agency in the USA for freighter travel is Freighter World Cruises (☎ (818) 4493106, fax 449 9573), Suite 335, 180 South Lake Ave, Pasadena, CA 91101.

Yacht
It is much easier to get to the Solomons by yacht than by cargo boat. The best way if you don't have your own boat is to hang around yachting marinas. There are plenty of good places on the US west coast and along Australia's north-eastern seaboard. Auckland, Tahiti, Noumea and Vila all have

sizeable yachting communities where you might find a boat.

Conversely, if you're in Honiara and want a ride onwards, try the Point Cruz Yacht Club, where yacht owners sometimes leave notices up saying 'crew wanted'. Yacht skippers may charge around US$15 to US$25 a day. They will drop you off before leaving the Solomons, unless you to have an onward or return air ticket from their destination country.

Before going on a long trip, spend a few days sailing on the yacht to get your sea legs. That way you'll also be able to see how prone you are to seasickness – espe-cially if you've been put to work in the galley. If you're sensitive to seasickness, every moment will be torture and you will only be a burden to your skipper.

Customs & Immigration Yachts should clear customs and immigration at the first opportunity. This can be done at Honiara, Gizo, Munda, Lata and Korovou. The offi-cials will want to know your planned port of departure.

Canoe
There is a very rarely used route between Ontong Java in Malaita Province and Nuku-manu in Papua New Guinea. Both destina-tions are well off the beaten track – see the Ontong Java section in the Malaita Province chapter.

ENTRY & DEPARTURE TAXES
The S$40 airport tax is charged on interna-tional flights only. The only exemptions are transit passengers who don't leave the customs and immigration area at the airport, and children under two years old.

There's a rather discouraging light fee for yachts sailing in Solomons waters. This is for the use of lighthouses and buoys, and is collected at customs offices. The cost is a flat S$100 fee plus 10c a tonne.

ORGANISED TOURS
Package tours are ideal for those with limited time to spare and little inclination to

experience the challenges (and rewards) of independent travel. A well-selected package holiday can actually turn out cheaper than a budget trip, and will have high-class facilities thrown in. Package tours also include free car hire, subsidised hotel prices, voucher for dining out around the capital, and free sporting activities, including some on or under the water.

Several travel agents in Australia and New Zealand specialise in the South Pacific. The Pacific Island Travel Centre in Sydney (☎ (02) 9262 6555, fax 9262 6318) and elsewhere is one place to try. The further from the Solomons you start, the fewer the package options that will be available. In Europe the only package deals you're likely to find will be through a travel agent specialising in scuba-diving tours.

An all-in deal might be the best way to explore a specific interest. Scobie's Walkabout Tours (☎ & fax (049) 570458, email p.scobie@hunterlink.net.au), PO Box 43, Newcastle 2300, Australia, takes groups on culture and nature trips to the two proposed World Heritage sites – Marovo Lagoon in July and East Rennell Island in January. Both trips last 11 days and cost A$1650

Honiara to Honiara (international transfers not included).

See Diving in the Facts for the Visitor chapter for companies specialising in dive trips.

WARNING

This chapter is particularly vulnerable to change: prices for international travel are volatile, routes are introduced and cancelled, schedules change, special deals come and go, and rules and visa requirements are amended. Airlines and governments seem to take a perverse pleasure in making price structures and regulations as complicated as possible. You should check directly with the airline or with travel agent to make sure you understand how a fare (and ticket you may buy) works. In addition, the travel industry is highly competitive and there are many lurks and perks. The upshot of this is that you should get opinions, quotes and advice from as many airlines and travel agents as possible before you part with your hard-earned cash. The details given in this chapter should be regarded as pointers and are not a substitute for your own careful, up-to-date research.

Getting Around

Getting around in the Solomons can be both a challenge and a pleasure. Air services usually stick to their scheduled timetable, but with other forms of transport the stretchable nature of 'Solomons time' becomes apparent. Always allow plenty of leeway for unexpected delays in getting back if you venture far off the beaten track. Around Christmas much of the country is on the move, so reserve seats well in advance.

AIR
Domestic Air Services
Flying is a great way to get around. The Solomons' lagoons and islands look fantastic from the air, and in these small planes you're always by a window. As they cruise at only around 2000m you see plenty of detail on the ground.

The most extensive domestic routes are flown by Solomon Airlines. It provides regular services to over 20 airfields around the country. Nearly all flights originate in

Honiara, but several airports may be visited (especially on Western Province routes) before the return leg to the capital. The dates of booked flights can be changed without penalty. Reservations can be made without paying up front, but make sure you know when payment is due – if you don't pay by then the booking will be cancelled.

Solomon Airlines' competitor is Western Pacific Airline (☎ 36533, fax 36476), PO Box 411. This is an SDA airline – you don't know whether to be comforted or alarmed when the pilot leads passengers in a pre-flight prayer! More importantly, it means there are no flights on Saturday. Some of its services overlap with those of Solomon Airlines, but there are a few small airfields it visits exclusively.

A few Solomon Airlines fares are slightly higher than the equivalent trip with Western Pacific. However, the latter has no discounts or passes. If you have an international ticket with Solomon Airlines, you

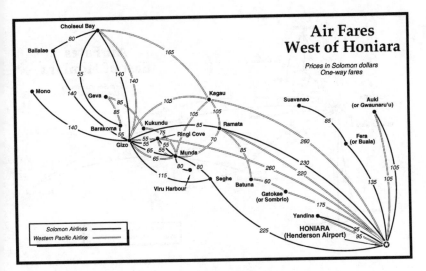

Air Fares West of Honiara

Prices in Solomon dollars
One-way fares

will get 10% off all its domestic flights, making it the cheaper choice. Even if you don't hold such a ticket, you'll probably get the discount if you prove you're a foreign visitor. Students get a 25% discount: this is only supposed to apply to trips to/from college, but rural agents may give it anyway if you flash an ISIC card.

Domestic flights do fill up, especially around Christmas, so make reservations well in advance. If a particular flight is already full, you can be put on the waiting list. Both airlines operate charter services if required, and both restrict the free baggage allowance to 16 kg per person. You are more likely to be charged excess baggage at Henderson airport than elsewhere if you're slightly over the limit.

Air Passes

Solomon Airlines has a domestic air pass, the Discover Solomons Pass, which needs to be purchased before arrival and in conjunction with an international ticket. It's valid for 30 days and gives four flights for US$250 (UK£159). It's well worth getting if you're going to further-flung destinations

such as Choiseul Bay, Santa Cruz and Gizo, but for other trips you might not make any savings on the standard fare. However, connecting flights on the same day count as one flight only, so you may be able to construct itineraries that make it worthwhile adding extra flights (four maximum) to the pass at US$50 (UK£32) each. The pass is not available in Australasia.

SEA

Boats are a fun way to get around and a good place to mix with islanders, but they are slow and prone to delays. The country's division into numerous islands, with many small settlements and a low population density, has made inter-island shipping the country's main means of transport. Air transport carries 50,000 internal passengers a year, yet ships move this number every seven weeks. Despite this, shipping services to remote areas are irregular, even more so since the government-owned Marine Division was privatised and became National Shipping. Services to Temotu and Rennell and Bellona have been particularly affected by this. Wharves are infrequent, so vessels

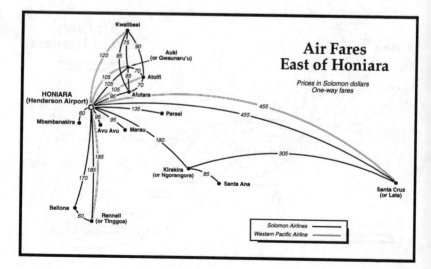

visiting the outer islands often have to use canoes and their dinghy to ferry people to and from the shore.

Ships occasionally sail several days earlier or later than scheduled. Details of shipping movements are posted up in company offices at main ports, or announced over the radio in the service-message segment, but the captain's decision to leave is final – so keep your eye on the vessel. Once the cargo is loaded, the skipper may not wait. Boats that primarily provide a passenger service, such as the *Ocean Express*, tend to stick to their timetable. Copra and cargo boats nearly always have room for some passengers.

When your ship is travelling from island to island, there's usually ample time to go ashore at each stop. The captain can tell you when the boat will be leaving each anchorage. He'll stick to his word.

Larger vessels usually offer three choices: deck/economy, 1st class, or cabin. Prices are very reasonable: for Honiara-Gizo, Malaita Shipping charges S$74 in economy, S$100 in 1st class and S$132 for a cabin. This compares to S$280 by air, though for some other trips flying isn't that much more expensive than taking a cabin. Shipping fares do vary between companies, so shop around.

Inter-Island Shipping Services

Most shipping organisations have an office near the main wharf in Honiara. The largest is National Shipping (☎ 24935, fax 26039, PO Box 1766), with eight ships (though they're rarely all in service): *Baruku, Belama, Betua, Bulumako, Butai, Leili, Marona* and *Vele*. It tries to keep to fortnightly services to Lata/Reef Islands, Makira, Malaita and Choiseul, and monthly services to Temotu, Rennell and Bellona and Malaita's atolls. In practice, services are less frequent, especially those in the monthly category. Schedules are advertised on SIBC radio, not in the newspapers.

Across the street is Malaita Shipping (☎ 23501, fax 23503, PO Box 584). It has two ships, *Ramos I* and *Ramos II*, and keeps

a reliable timetable to Malaita and Western Province. Its monthly schedules are advertised in the *Solomon Star*. Fares in economy, 1st class and cabins are offered.

Down the road is the Commodities Export Marketing Authority (CEMA tel 22528, fax 21262), which also advertises. Its ships primarily transport cargo, particularly copra, and go to all provinces. Passengers are taken, but the CEMA vessels are not the most comfortable to ride on.

Opposite (and close to National Shipping), is Florida Shipping (☎ 20210), which goes frequently to the Nggela Islands, including Tulagi. Its 15m-vessel *Florida II* has one cabin (S$10 extra per bed). In an adjoining office is Sasape (☎ 32193), which also runs to Tulagi. Facing the wharf is Tavuilo Shipping (☎ 21445). Its MV *Faalia* plies regularly between Honiara and Auki.

Just east of National Shipping is the Isabel Development Company (☎ 22122, fax 22009), which sends two ships to its namesake province: *Ligomo V* has no cabins, but *Ligomo IV* has four, with a surcharge of S$50 for each bed.

Next door is Olifasia (cargo only) and Universal Shipping (☎ 25119, fax 24868). The latter's vessel *Bulawa* goes to Temotu, Rennell and Bellona, and Ontong Java, but to no set schedule. It has three cabins and room for 120 deck passengers.

Wings Shipping Ltd (☎ 22811, PO Box 9), at the eastern end of Hibiscus Ave, has the *Iuminao* and the *Compass Rose II*. *Iuminao* is the larger vessel and concentrates on Western Province It's pretty stable in rough seas, but economy, 1st-class (with seats) and cabin rates are a little higher than those charged by Malaita Shipping for the same trip. *Compass Rose II* only has economy and 1st-class fares (S$14 surcharge) and alternates between Malaita, Makira and Isabel. Another ship, the *King Solomon*, will probably service Choiseul when it comes back from repair.

Around the corner is the Church of Melanesia's warehouse (☎ 21892, fax 21098). It has three mission boats, *Southern*

Cross, Charles Fox and *Koporia* – which might go anywhere depending on the demands of the diocese. Passengers can be taken – the *Koporia* has four cabins.

The Guadalcanal provincial government (☎ 20041) owns vessels which regularly circle the country's main island. Its offices are east of the main wharf in Honiara's Mendana Ave. Opposite is Ocean Navigation (☎ 24281, fax 24280, PO Box 966), which operates the *Ocean Express*. This keeps to a regular schedule, visiting Auki, Buala and Kirakira on a weekly basis. It's fast, but rolls in rough seas. In fact, it was really designed as a river boat, and it won't be many years before the salty sea water erodes its thin hull.

KHY (☎ 30134), with offices in Ranadi (Honiara's factory area) and also facilities at Gizo, has a small vessel, the MV *Hiliboe*, which goes to Western Province and sometimes Choiseul and Malaita.

More information on shipping can be found in the regional chapters.

Life Aboard Ship Deck travel is all right for a short journey. For longer trips, 1st class is often OK, but hire a cabin if you can afford it. In addition to having somewhere to spread your baggage, your cabin is a place to go when the sea gets rough. While everyone else is seasick, you can be happily sleeping on your bunk until the weather improves. The below-deck cabins get pretty hot and stuffy, but the cabins on the upper deck are usually kept cool by sea breezes on otherwise steaming hot nights.

No-one will go into your cabin unless you invite them to, but an open door at night on board ship means it's all right for deck passengers to sleep there too. So shut your door, or else the next morning you might find a number of sleeping bodies curled up on your floor!

There's a good chance you'll be the only foreigner aboard. Many of the other passengers will tell you about their home islands, and show you around them when the ship gets there.

Travel to Traditional Areas

You should think carefully before visiting the more remote and traditional areas of the country where there's an ambivalent attitude to tourism and tourists. The Moro area of south-eastern Guadalcanal has strict rules for both its members and visitors, while the Kwaio people of east-central Malaita don't appreciate fellow islanders, let alone outsiders.

Many outlying areas are very isolated, and are visited by only one vessel every four to six weeks – less frequently if the seas are rough. Exploring the smaller islands for a few hours while your ship is anchored offshore is never a problem, but staying any length of time may well be. You should give the chief ample warning by radio if you want to stay – and be prepared to accept no as an answer. ∎

What to Take Mattresses are provided in the cabins, but you'll need a sleeping sheet or bag, and a sleeping mat if you prefer to go deck class. The cabin life jacket makes a serviceable pillow – it will feel less hard if you put it under the mattress.

There's usually plenty of drinking water aboard, and hot water almost constantly on the boil in the kitchen. But no utensils are provided, so you'll need cutlery, a plastic cup and high-rimmed plate, and a small cooking pot. You can get by without the latter if you can live off two-minute noodles which will soften enough to eat when you pour boiling water over them in your plate.

Bring enough food for the entire trip. If you end up with too much, give some away. Your new friends are sure to repay your generosity with unexpected kindnesses throughout the trip.

Crew members will often trail a line from the stern. When a large fish is caught, everyone gets a helping. If you want to do some fishing of your own, colourful squid lures are particularly good for catching kingfish and tuna. Although you might expect villagers to sell you bananas, coconuts and pawpaws at every stop, surprisingly they seldom do, except on the Honiara-Western Province run.

Canoe

Fibreglass-hulled outboard-motor boats, commonly known as motor canoes, or just simply canoes, are found everywhere. They sometimes cover considerable distances – up to 80 km each way in often choppy seas – but are much better suited to protected lagoons, such as those around New Georgia and northern Malaita.

Always dress for wet weather when you take a motor-canoe ride. Although there's usually an enclosed area in the bow where your baggage should remain dry, everywhere else aboard gets wet! The driest part of the boat is near the front, but the front end bounces up and down uncomfortably.

If you look around a motor canoe for safety equipment, you won't find much, except perhaps spare fuel, paddles and a bailer. Flares, life jackets and fire extinguishers will be conspicuous by their absence. Yet safety is an important consideration – every year some canoes are lost at sea. Don't take a canoe across open seas in rough weather. In any weather, think twice about getting into a canoe without alternative means of propulsion (eg a paddle). Make sure the driver has enough fuel to cover the whole trip.

Motor-canoe prices can be alarmingly high because a new fibreglass boat, plus a 25 to 30-horsepower engine, costs S$9000 or more. Fuel in some parts of the country costs up to S$3.30 a litre, despite being S$1.85 a litre in Honiara. Fuel consumption can be anything from seven km per litre (heavy load, big engine) up to 15 km per litre (light load, slow 15-horsepower engine).

Canoe charters can cost anything from S$50 per day up to S$150 or more (eg in Malaita). This should include the canoe, driver and engine hire, but probably won't include fuel. When fixing a price, always be clear which of these four elements is and isn't included. Charter rates for specific trips can be arranged, but the driver will have to allow for the return trip, even if you're only going one way. The provincial fisheries department of the local government usually has canoes available for hire, and at lower rates than asked by private owners.

At these prices, it's obviously better if you can split the cost between several people. Even the smaller canoes can safely take four or five passengers, plus the driver. You'll probably have to organise the group yourself, as unfortunately canoes tend not to operate on a fare-paying, set-route basis like buses. If you *can* find this sort of shared motor-canoe ride, fares are reasonable (around one-sixth of the charter rate). You'll have your best chance of getting such a ride to and from markets. Otherwise, hooking into a shared canoe ride is a very hit-and-miss affair. Start asking around as soon as possible, and be prepared to wait – perhaps for a day or more.

Paddle canoes are still commonly used in sheltered waters, especially by children. In fact, wooden dugouts or outriggers are preferred to motor canoes on remote islands where fuel supplies are uncertain. You may see some using a palm leaf for a sail, but sail-driven craft no longer venture far offshore for fishing and trading as they did in past.

CAR & MOTORCYCLE

There are 1300 km of motorable roads in the Solomons, mainly in Guadalcanal, Malaita and Western Province. Only about 85 km of these are bitumen sealed – mostly in and around Honiara. The remainder are coral or gravel surfaced. There are also about 1500 km of secondary plantation and forestry roads varying from all-weather quality to tracks suitable only for tractors and trailers.

International driving permits are accepted, as are most current national driving licences. People drive on the left-hand side.

Rental

Hire cars and 4WD vehicles are only available in Honiara – see that section for rates (which are rather high).

HITCHING

Hitching is never entirely safe in any country, and we don't recommend it. Travellers who decide to hich should understand that they are taking a small but potentially serious risk.

If you want a ride through the countryside, flag down a passing vehicle and ask the driver the cost of a lift. Many will give you a free ride, but others will charge between 10c and 20c a km. However, if you charter someone, or get them to go far out of their way, you will have to pay more – maybe 50c a km.

WALKING

Footpaths vary from clearly defined trails over a metre wide to indistinct tracks less than the width of an adult. Some islanders, particularly in Santa Isabel and Choiseul, talk lightly of roads through the bush, when they really mean footpaths. Always ask how wide the road is if you suspect your informant is talking about a path.

If you need directions in the vicinity of a village, young children will often be asked to show you the way. There are sometimes dozens of paths – all unsignposted – leading in many different directions.

If you need to use isolated footpaths in the bush or over mountains, you should hire an adult guide. Fees for their services vary from island to island, but they are usually around S$12 to S$20 a day, or slightly higher if the guide also acts as your bearer. In addition, you should pay for any nights your guide is away from home, and for whatever meals and accommodation they need during the journey.

If you're going through really dense undergrowth or over rugged mountains, it's wise to have a companion as well as a guide. If one of you is seriously hurt, the guide will know where to find help, leaving the companion to comfort the injured person.

Avoid leaving the path in a rainforest, as it's quite possible to get completely lost within 30m of your route. Crossing fast-flowing rivers can also be very hazardous.

LOCAL TRANSPORT
The Airport

It's rarely a problem getting to/from airports, even the small ones located on uninhabited islands. Often you can get a ride with the Solomon Airlines agent.

Minibus & Truck

Public minibuses are only found in and around Honiara. Try to tender the correct fare. Smoking is banned on most buses. In Malaita and parts of Guadalcanal, people pile into open-backed trucks to get around. Elsewhere, the lack of roads means there's not much scope for public transport.

Taxi

Taxis are only plentiful in Honiara, but you sometimes see them in other large towns (eg Auki). They do not have meters, so agree beforehand on the price. This may be slightly higher at night. Most drivers have some small change, though few will have anything bigger than a S$10 note. Taxi drivers don't expect a tip. Hiring a taxi by the day is a good alternative to hiring a car – it costs about the same and you don't have the hassle of driving.

ORGANISED TOURS

Tour operators are based in Honiara and Auki. See the Guadalcanal and Western Province chapters for details. They usually have a set programme of excursions, but given the small scale of most operations, it's often possible to arrange a tailor-made tour based on your own special interests. From Honiara, tours of WWII battlefields are popular. In Gizo, dive operators sometimes combine scuba diving with local land-based attractions.

Guadalcanal Province

Guadalcanal is the largest island in the Solomons group and a province in its own right. It is known in Pijin as Galekana, or just simply as Solomon.

Guadalcanal's northern coast is the hub of the nation. Government, commerce and tourism are all centred in the capital, Honiara, and access is relatively easy to anywhere along its adjacent coast. Development in this part of the island has proceeded apace.

In contrast, the southern coast is much less accessible. Here life moves slowly, always dependent on the weather and giving rise to its name, the Weather Coast. While transport around the north is normally on four wheels, any visit to the southern coast is likely to involve travel by foot or boat.

HISTORY

A cave on the Poha River, north of Honiara, is believed to have first been occupied about 6000 years ago, and then again around 1000 BC. European discovery was not until 9 April 1568, when the crew of the 30-tonne Spanish skiff *Santiago* first sighted Guadalcanal.

Gallego, the vessel's commander and one of the leaders of the Mendaña expedition, named the island after his home village of Wadi-al-Canar in southern Spain. A month later, Mendaña himself formally claimed it for the Spanish king. The island's name was later anglicised to Guadalcanar, becoming Guadalcanal in the 19th century.

The Spaniards are believed to have searched for gold in rivers along the island's northern coast. Despite legends to the contrary, they probably failed to find any. They sailed away two months after arrival.

No other Europeans visited Guadalcanal for over 200 years. Then two Britons, Shortland in 1788 and Captain Alexander Ball in 1790, sailed by. They were followed three years later by the French admiral Bruni d'Entrecasteaux.

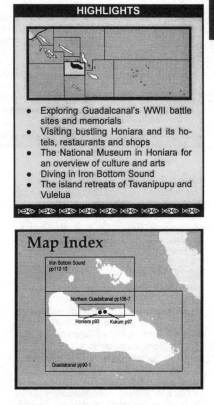

HIGHLIGHTS

- Exploring Guadalcanal's WWII battle sites and memorials
- Visiting bustling Honiara and its hotels, restaurants and shops
- The National Museum in Honiara for an overview of culture and arts
- Diving in Iron Bottom Sound
- The island retreats of Tavanipupu and Vulelua

Map Index

Iron Bottom Sound pp112-13

Northern Guadalcanal pp106-7

Honiara p93   Kukum p97

Guadalcanal pp90-1

By the 1890s, a few traders and missionaries were living on Guadalcanal Island. On 6 October 1893, the British government proclaimed a protectorate over most of what is now the Solomon Islands, including Guadalcanal.

In the following years the islanders' lives remained basically unchanged, although fighting and killing diminished as the influence of missionaries and the Protectorate government spread throughout the island.

GUADALCANAL

Local Hero
Prior to the US arrival in 1942, the sole Allied force on the island consisted of 12 islander volunteers and one Australian-born officer. One of the 12 was Sergeant-Major Jacob Vouza. When found carrying a US flag by the Japanese, he was tortured in the hope that he would reveal the US marines' position. He was tied to a tree and bayoneted through the chest, neck and both cheeks. Left for dead, Vouza managed to free himself, swim a creek with his hands still bound, and crawl three km back to the US lines. Although exhausted, he refused medical treatment until he had revealed the enemy position.

While recovering, Vouza told his incredulous admirers, 'When I was a police-boy before the war, I often was naughty and caused plenty trouble for the government. So I told myself to do something good for King George to pay him back for all that trouble I gave'. Vouza was later knighted for his efforts and there's a memorial to him outside the police headquarters in Honiara. ■

WWII & After

The events of 1942 changed all that. First there was the panic-stricken departure of colonial Europeans, followed by the arrival of Japanese forces on 8 June. Then an immense US fleet appeared, followed by the landing of US marines at Red Beach on 7 and 8 August. Six months of desperate fighting followed until the Japanese secretly withdrew from Cape Esp,rance in early February 1943.

The Guadalcanal campaign was pivotal to the course of the war in the South Pacific. Admiral Tanaka, one of Japan's most successful fleet commanders, said of his country's defeat, 'On that insignificant shore, inhabited only by islanders, Japan's doom was sealed'.

Once WWII was over, Honiara replaced Tulagi as the national capital, and Guadalcanal became readily accepted as the most important island in the group. Large agricultural projects were begun in 1976 along the northern coastal plains. Following Independence, government, commerce, transport and tourist services were concentrated in the Honiara area – a process begun in the closing days of British colonial rule.

GEOGRAPHY

Guadalcanal is 160 km long by 48 km wide and has an area of 5336 sq km. The island has a mountainous spine lying close to its southern coast, making the interior a forbidding landscape of sheer and ragged peaks. It includes Mt Makarakomburu (2447m) and Mt Popomanaseu (2330m), the nation's tallest peaks.

Guadalcanal's north-western corner is composed of quiescent volcanic cones rising to 700m. On the north-eastern coast these mountains descend into wide alluvial plains thickly planted with coconut palms, cacao trees and oil palms.

Guadalcanal's rivers are short and prone to flash floods. Similarly, treacherous currents, fierce seas and strong undertows, especially along the southern coast, make the island's anchorages hazardous for small craft, even in moderate conditions.

CLIMATE

Guadalcanal has two main weather zones. The southern coast is exposed to the south-easterly trade winds, which blow straight across it, releasing very heavy rainfall. In contrast, the northern coast is in a rain shadow, sheltered by the island's central mountain chain. As a result, Honiara usually enjoys calm and pleasant weather.

Honiara

The average annual rainfall in the capital is 2154 mm, raining on average 196 days a year, mostly from December to April. Honiara's morning humidity reaches 89% in March, but averages 85% through the year. Afternoons are always much less humid, with the reading falling to 69% in August. Annual maximum and minimum temperatures are 31°C and 21°C respectively. Guadalcanal's weather diversity is such that Henderson airport, only 11 km east of Honiara, is 10% drier than the capital.

The Weather Coast

Although Guadalcanal's southern coast is commonly called the Weather Coast, a better name would be the Bad-Weather Coast or the Wild-Weather Coast. Heavy rain frequently causes floods, with vegetable gardens and even houses occasionally washed away. Heavy seas often prevent ships anchoring.

The Weather Coast averages 5000 mm of rain a year, with its heaviest falls from July to September. Choghiri, halfway along this coast, holds the province record for the heaviest annual rainfall. In 1972 an astonishing 13,452 mm fell there. Similarly, over a 13-day period in July 1965, Avu Avu, 23 km further to the east, received 3125 mm of rain.

FAUNA
Birds

Bird-watchers need only go up to the ridges just behind Honiara to see a huge range of birds. However, to see species endemic to Guadalcanal you must search highland areas. A Guadalcanal subspecies of the thicket warbler only lives above 500m, while the Guadalcanal mountain owl has only been seen around the island's tallest peaks.

Crocodiles

Most large estuarine rivers and coastal swamps in Guadalcanal have resident saltwater crocodiles. There's a particularly large concentration in the Lauvi Lagoon.

The closest crocs to Honiara are those in the Lungga River and its connecting creeks. Small numbers are likely to be in every sizeable northern coastal river or estuary (even in quite small creeks) east as far as Marau Sound.

The same applies along the southern coast. Villagers warn of crocodiles in the Hoilava River and most other large or muddy waterways east of it.

ECONOMY

Honiara is the nation's business centre. The plains are the only large flat and fertile expanse of land in the country, and since 1976 successful large-scale copra, palm-oil and cattle-raising projects have been located there. There is a clam farm at Aruligo, and commercial piggeries and poultry farms have been set up elsewhere along the northern coast.

Many creeks in the island's central mountains have grey shale beds – some are gold-bearing. Several of the wide alluvial rivers along the northern coast have similar features.

A few villagers in the highlands of central Guadalcanal regularly pan for gold, especially along the Matepono River. In 1996, Ross Mining of Australia reached an agreement with local landowners to start mining at Gold Ridge; it expects to extract 2,835 kg of gold per year.

POPULATION & PEOPLE

Honiara is the Solomons' melting pot. People from all over the country come here for work, for holidays, or just to shop. Its population has grown from 2600 in 1959 to something in excess of 40,000. Of the remaining 60,600 people in Guadalcanal, most are coastal dwellers, with about 7500 living in small, isolated hamlets in the highland interior. Although there is a continuous line of settlements along the southern coast, only about 14,000 people live there at present.

Many people from the Marau Sound area are descended from Malaitan settlers who migrated there between the 17th and late 19th century. Some still follow old Malaitan customs such as using shell money to pay bride price. This tradition has now spread to other parts of the southern coast and into the isolated highlands.

GUADALCANAL

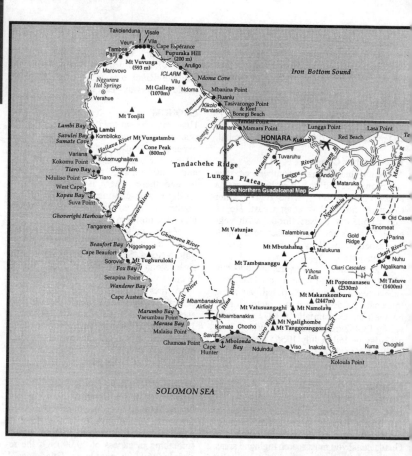

ARTS

The main artistic products created in Guadalcanal are *bukaware* baskets, trays, coasters and table mats. Bamboo panpipes are also produced, as are decorated lime containers for use by the omnipresent betel-nut chewers.

Turtle-shell pendants, incorporating a frigate-bird design fixed to a crescent-shaped piece of gold-lipped oyster shell, are made on the southern coast. Pendants, earrings and bracelets are made in Marau Sound.

ACCOMMODATION & FOOD

If you plan to travel around the southern part of the island, call into the subprovincial headquarters and the Guadalcanal provincial government offices in Honiara's town centre. Staff members should know where you can camp, or which villages have an empty hut for visitors to use and who you should see once you're there.

Honiara has a range of food stores, some open 24 hours. Elsewhere, only larger villages will have a basic shop. These only serve limited foodstuffs, and sometimes run

Guadalcanal

short, so take a few supplies with you when you leave the capital. Fresh fruit is only available in season and can be hard to find, especially in isolated mountain villages.

Honiara

The word Honiara is derived from the islander name Nahoniara ('facing the northeast winds') used for a piece of land 400m to the west of Point Cruz. The capital is ad-

ministered separately to Guadalcanal Province by the Honiara municipal authority.

The national museum is here and excursions can be made to WWII relics and other sights. Several companies operate regional sightseeing tours and there's one scuba-diving company. Restaurants, cafes, bars and handicraft shops will help you fill the rest of your time.

Not all reminders of the wartime Guadalcanal campaign have been removed. When a major building project is underway, human bones or unexploded munitions are often found – as was the case in 1996 during work on the new terminal at Henderson airport. If you hear a series of short, sharp booms, you can be sure old shells are being detonated at the bomb-disposal centre beside Alligator Creek, north of the airport.

History

Honiara owes its life to the huge military-supply depot the USA built between Kukum and Point Cruz in 1943. To support its war effort in the north-western Solomons, the USA constructed wharves, roads and storage sheds and completed the airfield at Henderson. With the US army's departure at the end of WWII, the British moved their capital from the devastated Tulagi to Honiara to make use of these brand-new facilities.

Originally built along a narrow coastal strip, the capital has spread inland onto several nearby ridges, many of which were battlefields in WWII.

Orientation

Although there's a constant stream of minibuses, the best way to see Honiara is on foot. The central area from the Solomon Kitano Mendana Hotel (locally known as the Mendana Hotel) to Chinatown can be covered in a 20-minute stroll along Mendana Ave, the town's main thoroughfare.

In this compact sector are national and provincial government offices, the nation's largest port complex, shops, embassies, banks, hotels, restaurants and churches.

The capital's 12-km-long urban sprawl has within it several separate communities. To the west are the settlements of Rove and White River Village, while immediately to the east of the Mataniko River (pronounced 'muh-tanny-koh') are Mataniko Village, populated by settlers from Ontong Java, and Chinatown. Beyond them are Kukum and the industrial area of Ranadi.

Behind the main town and larger suburbs are many recently built housing areas, some of which started life as squatters' camps. New settlements on the ridge overlooking Honiara and Iron Bottom Sound

The Capital in Perspective

At first impression Honiara is a dusty, uneventful small town, with only a meagre selection of restaurants and some undistinguished shops. A couple of weeks in the provinces changes all that. After village life with no cars, no electricity, nowhere to eat out and (if you're lucky) a one-shelf store, the capital undergoes a magical transformation. It takes on the guise of a bustling and cosmopolitan metropolis, replete with culinary choices, shops heaving with consumer goods, and all the trappings of modern life, including traffic jams. ■

offer breathtaking views. Among these are Lenggakiki, Vavaea and Mbokonavera west of the Mataniko River, and Kola'a Ridge, Vura, Naha and Panatina to its east.

Maps The souvenir shop in the Mendana Hotel sells Hema maps of the Solomons for S$19, and cheap postcards.

Information

Tourist Office The old Solomon Islands Tourist Authority was reborn in 1997 as the Visitors' Bureau (☎ 22442, fax 23986, PO Box 321). It's been of limited help in the past, but a newly installed radio should make it possible for staff to pre-book accommodation in isolated locations. The office is beside the Mendana Hotel in Honiara's town centre, and is open Monday to Friday from 8 am to 4.30 pm and Saturday from 9 am to noon.

Money Foreign exchange is handled by all three banks. The National Bank of the Solomon Islands (NBSI), the Australia & New Zealand Banking Group Ltd (ANZ) and Westpac Banking Corporation all have branches in Mendana Ave. The NBSI and Westpac also have Chinatown branches, and NBSI has one in Ranadi too.

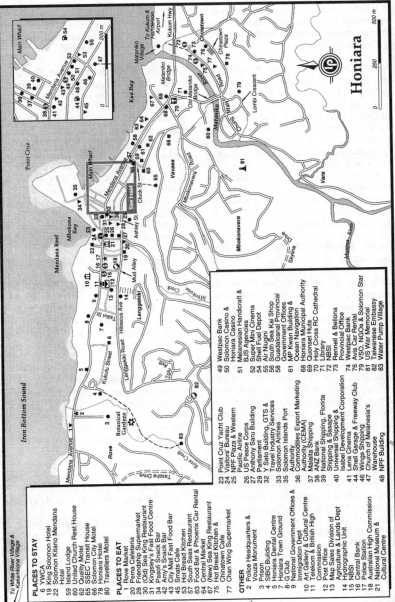

To White River Village &
Kakambona Village

PLACES TO STAY
6   YWCA
19 King Solomon Hotel
22 Solomon Kitano Mendana
    Hotel
59 Island Lodge
60 United Church Rest House
62 Quality Motel
65 SSEC Transit House
66 Solomon City Motel
76 Honiara Hotel
80 Travellers Motel

PLACES TO EAT
1   Rove Market
20 Pema Cafeteria
28 Friendship Supermarket
30 (Old) Sea King Restaurant
31 Kingsley's Fast Food Centre
34 Pasoti Snack Bar
42 Amy's Snack Bar
43 City Mall Fast Food Bar
45 Smata Cafe
55 Hot Bread Kitchen
57 South Seas Restaurant
63 Food Bar & Phoenix Car Rental
64 Central Market
67 (New) Sea King Restaurant
75 Hot Bread Kitchen &
    Chinatown Cafe
77 Chan Wing Supermarket

OTHER
2   Police Headquarters &
    Vouza Monument
3   Prison
4   SIBC Building
5   Honiara Dental Centre
7   Honiara Town Ground
9   G Club
8   National Government Offices &
    Immigration Dept
10 Art Gallery & Cultural Centre
11 Telekom & British High
    Commission
12 Post Office
13 Map Sales Division of
    Agriculture & Lands Dept
    Hydrographic Unit
14 NBSI
15 NBSI
16 Central Bank
17 Police Station
18 Australian High Commission
21 National Museum &
    Cultural Centre

23 Point Cruz Yacht Club
24 Visitors Bureau (SIVB)
25 NPF Plaza & Western
    Pacific Airline
26 US Peace Corps
27 Anthony Saru Building
29 Parliament
32 Y Sato Building, GTS &
    Travel Industry Services
33 Solomon Airlines
35 Solomon Islands Port
    Authority
36 Commodities Export Marketing
    Authority (CEMA)
37 Malaita Shipping
38 ANZ Bank
39 National Shipping, Florida
    Shipping & Sasape
40 Universal Shipping &
    Isabel Development Corporation
41 Lena Cinema
44 Shell Garage & Freeway Club
46 Wings Shipping
47 Church of Melanesia's
    Warehouse
48 NPF Building

49 Westpac Bank
50 Solomon Casino &
    Honiara Casino
51 Melanesian Handicraft &
    BJS Agencies
52 Super Mini Cinema
54 Shell Fuel Depot
56 South Sea Kai Shop
58 Guadalcanal Provincial
    Government Offices
61 Air Niugini
    NPF Kwan Building &
    Ocean Navigation
68 Honiara Municipal Authority
69 Quonset Huts
70 Holy Cross RC Cathedral
71 Library
72 NBSI
73 Rennell & Bellona
    Provincial Office
74 Westpac Bank
76 Avis Car Rental
79 VSO, NGOs & Solomon Star
81 US War Memorial
82 Taiwanese Embassy
83 Water Pump Village

The Mendana and King Solomon hotels will change foreign currency and travellers' cheques outside normal banking hours, but at a reduced exchange rate.

Post & Communications The main post office, just off Mendana Ave, is open Monday to Friday from 8 am to noon and 1 to 4.30 pm and Saturday mornings. Its postage, parcel and poste restante services are all reliable. The cheap stationery shop on site sells first-day covers, as does the Philatelic Bureau round the corner. There is a new post office in Ranadi.

Solomon Telekom, on Mendana Ave, has a very expensive fax and telex service, as well as card and coin telephones. It's open weekdays from 8 am to 4.30 pm and Saturday from 8 am to noon.

Travel Agencies & Tour Operators Guadalcanal Travel Services (☎ 22587, fax 26184, PO Box 114), commonly called GTS, is in the Y Sato Building. It is the only international travel agency in the Solomons, offering hotel and flight bookings, plus tours and itineraries.

Tour Solomons (☎ 21205 ext 188, fax 20022) is based in the King Solomon Hotel and has a few full and half-day tours from Honiara. Tour Solomons was in financial difficulty in late 1996 and wasn't offering all its advertised tours, so enquire on arrival. SolTravel (☎ 22476, fax 24065, PO Box 597) books for Solomons Village Stay and does tours.

Bookshops & Stationers Acor Stationer by Solomon Airlines on Mendana Ave sells newspapers, including the British *Weekly Telegraph*. Newspower (☎ 22069) in the Anthony Saru Building is generally more expensive but has Australian newspapers, paperbacks, and is the only place in the Solomons that stocks Lonely Planet books. National Stationery Supplies, round the back, is the same company. Between the two entrances is a place that does photocopies for only 30c a copy.

The University of the South Pacific (USP) in Kukum has a bookshop with texts on the Solomons and the Pacific. The souvenir shop in the Honiara Hotel sells some interesting locally published books.

Libraries & Reading Rooms The town's public library is near the Mataniko Bridge and is open Monday to Friday from 10 am to 5.30 pm, Saturday from 9 am to noon and Sunday from 2 to 5 pm; it's closed Wednesday and holidays. Behind it is the National Library, open weekdays from 10 am to noon and 1 to 4.30 pm. It has a large Pacific reference section, including many out-of-print titles on the Solomons. USP's library has material from all over Oceania.

The embassies and high commissions in Honiara (see the Facts for the Visitor chapter) have reference materials on the Solomons, as well as newspapers from back home to read.

Organisations such as the Peace Corps and Voluntary Service Overseas (VSO) have extensive literature on the Solomons. The Peace Corps (☎ 21612) is on Mud Alley, but is expected to move soon to Kukum. The VSO (☎ 21168), along with other non-governmental organisations (NGOs), is by the Solomon Star newspaper in New Chinatown.

Film & Photography Several places stock and process photographic film but prices are high. Slide film is hard to get in the Solomons. The Agfa Photo Lab, also called Honiara Photographic Supplies, in the NPF Plaza offers a choice of film speeds and usually has slides too, and a few compact 35-mm cameras. It also has a one-hour service for processing prints but the service at the Technique Radios Centre in the MP Kwan Building works out slightly cheaper.

Water & Electricity Supply The quality of Honiara's piped water is varied, and it's not advisable to drink it without first boiling or treating it. Many rest houses have a tank to catch rainwater for drinking. Honiara has electricity, but there are daily short power cuts.

Medical Services The Central Hospital (☎ 23600) in Kukum, known colloquially as Nambanaen, provides free medical attention. You may be able to avoid queues by making an appointment. There are also various public and private clinics in the Honiara area; you'll have to pay in the latter but you'll get quicker service. Typical charges are S$30 for a consultation, S$5 for a prescription and S$80 for a medical. Ask your hotel or embassy for a recommendation. The Honiara Dental Centre (☎ 22029) is on Mendana Ave and the Bartimaeus Vision Care Centre (☎ 24040) is on China-own Ave.

There are two chemists. The Pharmacy (☎ 22911) is in Ashley St, and the Honiara Dispensary (☎ 23587 or ☎ 23595 after hours) is in the NPF Plaza and generally has lower prices.

Emergency For urgent service you can call the following:

Ambulance	☎ 25566
Police	☎ 22266
Fire	☎ 20235
Marine rescue	☎ 21611

In a life-threatening emergency call ☎ 999.

Dangers & Annoyances Honiara is the place you're most likely to encounter crime in the Solomons. By international standards it's pretty small-scale stuff (the theft of 10 basketballs from a school made the front page in late 1996!) but there are signs it's getting worse.

Lock your room where possible. It's still safe to walk around after dark, though some people recommend not walking in the Mataniko Bridge area at night – take a taxi instead.

Point Cruz
On 12 May 1568, Mendaña and his men erected a cross at a spot traditionally called Kua by islanders, renaming it Point Cruz. They then said their prayers and claimed for Spain their discoveries in the Solomons.

Island legends maintain the site of this historic event is where a medium-sized tree now stands, beside Point Cruz's public toilets.

Since the 1950s, this generally low-lying spur of land has been greatly extended with wharves and copra sheds. Boat services reach out from Point Cruz to the remotest destinations in the island group. There's always a busy scene here as copra boats and inter-island passenger vessels load and unload.

Parliament
This distinctive conical building on the hill above Ashley St opened in 1993. You can watch proceedings from the public gallery on weekdays from 11 am to noon and 2 to 3 pm. Ask at the desk and the sergeant at arms will probably give you a tour. The building cost US$5 million and was funded by the USA, but there's no money forthcoming for the ambitious next phase which includes members' offices, tennis courts and a swimming pool (see the model in the lobby).

National Museum & Cultural Centre
The National Museum (☎ 22309) is opposite the Mendana Hotel and is open Monday to Friday from 9 am to 4.30 pm and Saturday from 9 am to 1 pm. Entry is free, though donations are welcome. There is only one room, but it includes displays on dance, body ornamentation, currency, weaponry and archaeology. Behind it is the open-air Cultural Centre with eight traditionally constructed houses, each from a different province. The Makiran building is particularly striking, with boldly carved black statuettes adorning its front. There's a canoe inside the tall structure from Marovo.

To the west of the museum is a green Japanese howitzer, believed to be one of the guns which were collectively known as Pistol Pete. Pistol Pete destroyed many parked US aircraft and huge stocks of fuel at Henderson airfield in late 1942.

Central Bank

This large, modern building beside the police station contains some interesting displays, including very fine woodcarvings from Rennell and Makira. Exhibits of traditional local currencies include Santa Cruz red-feather money, Malaitan dolphin-teeth and shell money, *mbaravas* from New Georgia, and clam-shell currency from Choiseul.

Opposite the Central Bank is the **Art Gallery & Cultural Centre**, which should open up in 1997.

Botanical Gardens

Beside the SIBC Building is a track leading past the prison to the botanical gardens. They have a herbarium, an orchid garden, a cascading creek, and a selection of bush plants and trees, most of them typical of any rainforest area in the country. The gardens are always open, but the herbarium and orchid greenhouse only open during office hours.

A path crosses Rove Creek and leads to **Water Pump Village**, next to a pump house which feeds water up to Lenggakiki, a housing area behind Honiara. Water Pump Village is similar to many others in the Solomons and gives a good idea of rural life if your only stop is the capital.

White River Village

This friendly Gilbertese settlement about four km west of the centre is where the Sendai Trail started. The Japanese Sendai Force cut this track in October 1942 to outflank the US position at Bloody Ridge. After dragging several heavy guns along the trail, they were repulsed by the Americans once they finally emerged. Villagers will point out where the route starts.

A wartime jeep track called Tasahe Drive follows several nearby ridges from Rove and is a back route to White River Village.

Kakambona

This village has a 1.5-km grey-sand beach: ask before you swim here as some local people may regard it as village property. There's a Sunday market which stretches for about one km along the south side of the road; prices can be slightly higher than in Honiara's Central Market. Kakambona is the final stop for 'White River' minibuses.

Skyline Drive

You can still follow this wartime jeep track for the five km between Honiara and Valeatu. As it leaves Honiara, Skyline Drive overlooks the Mataniko River, providing a magnificent view of village life below it in Vara. Enjoy it from the **US War Memorial**, a compound of marble slabs bearing detailed descriptions of battles fought during the Guadalcanal campaign. It was unveiled on 7 August 1992, the 50th anniversary of the US beach landings. It's a hot 20-minute walk up from Mendana Ave – consider going about 5 pm when it's cooler, and staying for the sunset (it's supposed to close at 4 pm, but they don't seem to lock the gates).

A little further on the track reaches a ridge above the Musona River and its several small cascades. It then continues on to Valeatu, passing one km to the north of Galloping Horse Ridge – a WWII Japanese strong point – as it approaches the village.

This whole area is good bird-watching country. Cardinal lories, pigeons, parrots, dollar birds, Sanford's eagles, and the brown and white-plumaged Brahminy kites can often be seen.

Once you've reached Valeatu, ask local people to show you the footpaths from there back to Tasahe Drive or Honiara.

Mataniko River

Either side of the mouth of the river are shanty towns of flimsy dwellings. The area looks seedy but the people are friendly, and the kids are eager to be photographed. In the shallows off the east bank are the remains of a Japanese tank.

A short distance west of the Mataniko River are six US-built WWII **Quonset huts**, now used by the provincial government. On the hill opposite is the Roman Catholic **Holy Cross Cathedral**.

Chinatown

This is immediately east of the Mataniko River. Chinatown's main street, **Chung Wah Rd**, is 400m of colourful stores. Most have high porches and all bear Oriental names. To the west of Chung Wah Rd is a recently built area called New Chinatown. Close by is the tiny, rather run-down **Independence Park**. Its arch was presented to the town of Honiara in 1978 by the town's Chinese community to celebrate Independence.

Kukum

The district to the east of the Mataniko River is known as Kukum. This whole area lines the southern side of the Kukum Hwy, with several roads leading off to the hillside housing estates of Koloale and Kola'a Ridge.

Honiara's Central Hospital is known colloquially as Nambanaen. Built in Kukum by the US army, it was given the wartime name of 9th Station, thus its Pijin name. Opposite the hospital is the large, open-sided Church of Melanesia Cathedral of St Barnabas, where there's a small memorial to Bishop Patterson, killed at Nukapu in the Reef Islands in 1871.

Despite the large number of people living in Kukum, it has only a very small centre. You'll find what little there is beside the Kukum Market.

Ranadi

To the east of Kukum is the Ranadi (pronounced 'ranandi') trading estate, named after the Marine Division's old training ship which was formerly moored here. Ranadi is the country's principal light-industrial zone.

The Honiara Golf Course is next to the remains of Fighter Two, a US wartime airstrip. Modern buildings now cover the WWII tarmac. Beyond the golf course is Ranadi Beach. The black-sand shore

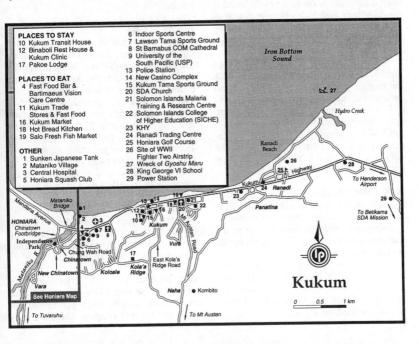

PLACES TO STAY
10 Kukum Transit House
12 Binaboli Rest House & Kukum Clinic
17 Pakoe Lodge

PLACES TO EAT
4 Fast Food Bar & Bartimaeus Vision Care Centre
11 Kukum Trade Stores & Fast Food
16 Kukum Market
18 Hot Bread Kitchen
19 Salo Fresh Fish Market

OTHER
1 Sunken Japanese Tank
2 Mataniko Village
3 Central Hospital
5 Honiara Squash Club
6 Indoor Sports Centre
7 Lawson Tama Sports Ground
8 St Barnabus COM Cathedral
9 University of the South Pacific (USP)
13 Police Station
14 New Casino Complex
15 Kukum Tama Sports Ground
20 SDA Church
21 Solomon Islands Malaria Training & Research Centre
22 Solomon Islands College of Higher Education (SICHE)
23 KHY
24 Ranadi Trading Centre
25 Honiara Golf Course
26 Site of WWII Fighter Two Airstrip
27 Wreck of *Gyoshu Maru*
28 King George VI School
29 Power Station

Iron Bottom Sound

Hydro Creek

Ranadi Beach

Highway

Kukum

Ranadi

To Henderson Airport

To Betikama SDA Mission

Panatina

Mendana Avenue

Mataniko Bridge

HONIARA
Chinatown
Footbridge

Independence Park

Chung Wah Road

Chinatown

New Chinatown

Vara

Koloale

Mt Austen Road

Vura

East Kola'a Ridge Road

Kola'a Ridge

Naha ● Kombito

See Honiara Map

To Tuvaruhu

To Mt Austen

Kukum

0   0.5   1 km

extends all the way from here to Poposa, near the eastern tip of Guadalcanal.

Sporting Centres & Clubs

Kukum has an Indoor Sports Centre. Outside are tennis courts; contact the Honiara municipal authority (☎ 21133) if you want to use them. The Honiara Golf Club (☎ 30181) at Ranadi has the only golf course in the Solomons. Green fees are S$50, caddy fees are S$6/12 for nine/18 holes. Its bar is open to visitors from 10 am to 6 pm. The Honiara Squash Club welcomes visitors to its courts on Chinatown Ave, Kukum. The charge is S$10 each per hour.

Diving & Snorkelling

The temperature of the water at Honiara's dive sites is between 27°C and 28°C, and visibility is usually good to 30m. Most of the sites are within easy reach of the capital. Island Dive Services (☎ 22103, fax 21493), open daily from 8 am to 5 pm, is based in the Mendana Hotel. It offers comprehensive scuba trips, including dives among brightly coloured tropical fish and through sunken WWII wrecks.

The basic cost per dive is S$115; S$185 includes full equipment rental, after which the day's second dive costs S$115. Snorkellers can accompany divers for S$42 (S$75 including equipment). A resort course can be done for S$260. The price of full PADI certification is at least S$750, depending on the number of people taking the course. Island Dive Services also arranges excursions on live-aboard dive boats.

Dive Sites Mendana Reef is only 250m from the Mendana Hotel and is a good place to learn scuba diving. There's an American fighter plane offshore: one wing is in the shallows near the hotel, the other is by the cockpit 10m down.

The *Gyoshu Maru* is a Japanese tuna boat 21m down off Ranadi Beach. There are other, more distant sites, including the popular Bonegi wrecks (see the Around Guadalcanal Island section).

Swimming

Honiara's sea swimming is rather a disappointment. There's a small stretch of sand in front of the Mendana Hotel and Point Cruz Yacht Club, but the water's murky and islanders don't swim there. The nearest beaches (dark sand) are at Ranadi and Kakambona, four and 6.5 km away respectively.

Organised Tours

GTS run tours of the Eastern Battlefields (S$80), Western Battlefields and Tambea Resort (S$150), Western Sights (S$100), and Vulelua Island (S$180). Tour Solomons basically covers the same ground, and also has bushwalking to Tenaru (S$95) and Mataniko Falls (S$60), and a Savo Island tour (S$400). All prices are per adult; children go half-price.

Heli Solomons (☎ 30033, fax 30713) can arrange excursions by helicopter: a 20-minute battlefield tour costs S$270 per person.

Places to Stay

Honiara has plenty of places to stay, catering for all budgets. The options below don't exhaust the possibilities. Most places are conveniently close to the centre; even those a little out of the way in Kukum are reasonably close to a minibus route. All bottom-end places have shared shower/toilet, and a communal kitchen – essential if you want to save money on evening dining. These places also generally have rooms with anything from two to five beds, which may be priced per bed or per room. If the former, solo travellers may have to share if the place gets full.

All of the rooms in the middle and top categories (except Honiara Hotel's budget rooms) have private shower or bath and toilet, and tea/coffee-making facilities. There are no communal kitchens.

Bottom End The *SSEC Transit House* (☎ 22800, PO Box 16) in Vavaea has five rooms and charges S$25 per person, or S$40 for married couples. There's a cosy kitchen and lounge area; smoking and drinking are strictly forbidden. It's only a five-minute walk downhill to the centre once you've discovered the pathway. The closer, larger *United Church Rest House* (☎ 20028, PO Box 18), just up the hillside at the southern end of Cluck St, is also good. You'll meet lots of interesting islanders here, and there's a good view from the terrace. This clean place has 10 rooms and charges S$33 per bed.

Island Lodge (☎ 23139, PO Box 737), near Cluck Street, has simple singles/doubles for S$66/88. The view is completely masked by the building in front, which was built later. Along the road to the east is the *Solomon City Motel*, with multi-bed dorms for S$35 per person and family rooms for S$80. A canteen is planned, and they show free videos at 7 pm nightly.

The *YWCA* (☎ 22661, PO Box 494) in Kukutu St has two rooms available for female travellers, and charges S$40 (S$30 for members).

The *Travellers Motel* (☎ 25721, fax 25735, PO Box 56) is in what's known as the Fijian Quarter, a residential area near the old Mataniko Bridge. It is tidy and well run; no alcohol is allowed. The price per twin-bedded room is S$66, or from S$77 with private shower/WC.

Binaboli Rest House (☎ 25211, PO Box 63) is a friendly, pleasant place next to Kukum Clinic, with 11 twin rooms. The cost is S$33 per bed or S$55 per room. *Kukum Transit House* (☎ 24810, PO Box 878, is nearby. It has six rooms and costs S$33 per bed.

Pakoe Lodge (☎ 21336, PO Box 679) is on Kola'a Ridge, Kukum. It has lots of rooms and charges S$66 per bed, including three meals.

Middle The *Quality Motel* (☎ 25150, fax 25277, PO Box 521) is a new place overlooking the Central Market. There's a pleasant balcony, and meals are available. Twin rooms with two single beds cost S$132, or S$165 with air-con. Units with a double

bed, single bed, TV, kitchen and dining area are S$231, or S$275 with air-con.

The *Honiara Hotel* (☎ 21737, fax 23412, PO Box 4), just south of Chinatown, has 67 rooms at a range of prices. Small double rooms with shared facilities are S$94. Singles/doubles in the old wing (with private shower/WC) are S$176; those in the new wing cost from S$253 and have TV and air-con. The hotel has a swimming pool, restaurant, bar and other facilities, and also offers airport transfers for S$10 each way.

The *Airport Motel* (☎ 36446, fax 36411) is a 10-minute walk east of Henderson airport and has free airport transfers. Rooms with often noisy air-con start at S$115/145. There's a bar and restaurant. The owners plan to open a motel by the beach.

Top End All rooms in this category have air-con and telephone, and the hotels have ample parking facilities. The Mendana and King Solomon hotels have conference facilities.

The *Solomon Kitano Mendana Hotel* (☎ 20071, fax 23942, PO Box 384), Mendana Ave, has an excellent oceanside location with a swimming pool, restaurant and open bar area, but some of its rooms are beginning to look a little shabby for the price. Standard rooms cost S$187/209; those for S$240/260 and up have a TV. There's no lift.

The revamped *King Solomon Hotel* (☎ 21205, fax 21771, PO Box 268), Hibiscus Ave, offers the best central rooms, as well as a bar, restaurant, swimming pool and novelty funicular lift (though you still have to climb stairs to most rooms). Deluxe rooms with TV and air-con cost from S$23/75 for singles/doubles. The standard rooms on the ground floor (from S$154/198) are older and plainer, but still OK.

Lelei Resort (☎ 20720 or tel 22970, PO Box 235) is about three km west of Honiara, by the sea. The resort has only six rooms but they are new, stylish, and have all the facilities visitors could want, except for a

TV. Singles/doubles are S$275/319 and each room has two double beds.

Places to Eat

Eating places are cheap and plentiful in Honiara in the daytime. But the budget places mostly shut by 5 pm, leaving pricey hotel and Chinese restaurants the only alternative to self-catering. Don't take opening times too literally, as places may shut early if there are no customers.

Hotel Restaurants The best dining is in the top hotels mentioned under Places to Stay. One of the two restaurants in the *King Solomon Hotel* serves pizza – it's a bit pricey but makes a change. The best is *Tomoko Restaurant* in the Lelei Resort, named after the scale-model war canoe inside. Lunches cost around S$20 to S$40, and dinners anything from S$30 to S$65. There's a wide selection, including chilli crab and char grills.

The *Honiara Hotel Restaurant* is also very good nowadays and has similar prices. On Wednesday (Island Night) and Sunday (Roast Night) a two-course buffet is S$38.50.

Chinese Restaurants Eating in the mid-price category basically means eating Chinese food – there are six or so places to choose from. They're usually open daily, for lunch and dinner, but strangely there are none in Chinatown! They're all OK, if a little more expensive than you might expect. Look out for cheaper dim sum lunches at the weekend.

The *South Seas Restaurant* (☎ 22363), Cluck St, is pretty good and at the lower end of the price range. The noodle dishes from S$15.40 are the best cheap option. Main courses are S$25.30 or more, and a bowl of plain rice is S$1.10.

The old *Sea King Restaurant* (☎ 23621) in Ashley St has six 'fast lunches' for S$22, including vegetables and soup. Evening meals are S$20 to S$99, though it also has tasty hamburgers for S$9 (closed Sunday evening).

The other, newer *Sea King Restaurant* (☎ 23678) near Mataniko Bridge is large, quite plush and rather expensive (closed Sunday). It's popular with expats.

Snackbars & Cafes The NPF Plaza has a section at the front with small food stalls where you can pick up cheap meals, snacks, drinks and ice cream.

The *Pasofi Snack Bar*, opposite the Solomon Islands Ports Authority, is perhaps the best of the budget places. It has an excellent selection of dishes, both meat and vegetarian, mostly in an Oriental style. They all go for S$11, except for noodles with meat for S$6, and portions are sizeable. Eating is alfresco under leaf roofs, and there are drinking coconuts for S$1.50. Opening hours are weekdays from 7.30 am to 5 pm and Saturday from 8.30 am to 3 pm, but they may start evening hours soon.

Amy's Snack Bar serves up palatable rice/noodle meals for around S$10, plus fish and chips for S$3.80 and drinking coconuts for S$1.20. It closes daily at 6 pm (4.30 pm Sunday). The new *City Mall Fast Food Bar* on Mendana Ave is under the same ownership.

Pema Cafeteria, Hibiscus Ave, is the hut in front of the Girl Guides Association. It serves two dishes at lunch, each for S$10, and is open weekdays only. Drinking coconuts are S$1.20. Also on Hibiscus Ave is *Smats Cafe* with pleasant surroundings, table service and a choice of lunches for S$11. Smats shuts at 4 pm (12.30 pm on Saturday; closed Sunday), but eat around noon before the best dishes sell out. Bush lime costs S$1 a glass.

Kingsley's Fast Food Centre in Ashley St is open from 7.30 am to 7.30 pm on weekdays and 8 am to 5.30 pm on weekends. It serves simple fare such as noodles, rice, chicken and burgers. You can eat reasonably well for under $10.

Beside the South Seas Restaurant in Cluck St is the spartan but clean *South Sea Kai Shop*, serving snacks and noodle/rice dishes for under S$10. It closes at 6 pm and is open Monday to Saturday. Nearby, on a side road overlooking Central Market, is

Food Bar, open Monday to Saturday from 9 am to 4 pm. It has various rice/noodle dishes for S$9, and T-bone steak for S$12.

Lots of places serve fish and chips for around S$4. One of the best is a no-name snack bar next to Chinatown's NBSI, just off Kukum Hwy. It's busy at lunchtime.

On Chung Wah Rd is the *Chinatown Cafe*, with a tidy, fan-cooled dining area. It has the usual selection of snacks, noodles (from S$6) and rice dishes (S$11). It's closed on Sunday and from 5 pm on weekdays and 3 pm on Saturday. The *Fast Food Bar* by the optician at the eastern end of Chinatown Ave is similar; it closes at 7 pm and on Sunday.

Supermarkets & Stores The big supermarkets generally have lower prices, but there's surprisingly little price advantage compared to some of the smaller stores. Also, a particular store may be cheap for some items but expensive for others, so you can certainly save a few cents if you can be bothered to shop around.

The *Wings Supermarket*, at the back of the NPF Plaza, has a broad range of groceries, including fresh beef flown in from Australia. It is open to 6 pm on weekdays and to 1 pm on Saturday. The *Friendship Supermarket* on Ashley St has a good range and good prices, and keeps long hours. There are several stores open 24 hours daily, such as *ELO 24* on Cluck St.

The *Hot Bread Kitchen*, is open daily from 6 am to 8 pm. There are branches on Mendana Ave, Chung Wah Rd, and Kukum Hwy. Next to the Chinatown branch is an unnamed self-service shop with a good range of spices, cereals and dairy products. Across the road is Chinatown's largest store, *Chan Wing Supermarket*, which stocks European beers.

Markets Markets open Monday to Saturday, sometimes even on Sunday. Although small by Asian standards, the *Central Market* is the country's principal food market and worth visiting for the atmosphere alone. Produce comes from outlying villages along the northern coast and from Savo island. In addition to fruit, vegetables and fresh fish, Malaitan shell money and souvenir shells are sometimes on sale. Fish and chips and drinking coconuts will also be on offer. Business is brisk and some foodstuffs sell out by about 11 am. Shop around for the best price.

The other markets are all open air. The small *Rove Market* (pronounced 'rove-y') is opposite the prison. *Kukum Market* often has cheaper prices than the Central Market. There's also the *Salo Fresh Fish Market*, opposite Kukum's SDA church. Further east, there's a new market near the King George VI school.

Entertainment

Cinemas Honiara is well stocked with movie halls showing videos. Programme changes are frequent, with fast, action-packed movies the favourites.

You'll find the *Lena Cinema* in the town centre, opposite the ANZ Bank. It has screenings at 10 am, noon, 2 pm and 5 pm, and entry costs S$4. It's the largest cinema: films are projected onto a reasonably large screen and there are proper cinema seats.

There are also several *Super Mini cinemas*. The most central two are immediately west of the Hot Bread Kitchen and there's another on the western side of the Central Market.

Bars & Clubs The *Point Cruz Yacht Club* (☎ 22500) is the best place to meet expats, yachties, volunteers and divers. Solbrew beer is only $4.50, and lunches and dinners (around S$20) are available daily except Sunday. Would-be yacht crew members should check the noticeboard. Tourists can simply sign in for free admittance, though longer term visitors would need to become members. Special events are weekend discos, bingo on Tuesday and videos on Sunday; an admission fee may apply.

The *G Club* (☎ 20796) – the G is for Guadalcanal – is another private club and has a bar with a pool table, darts board and weekend discos. Outside are a swimming pool, tennis courts and a large Japanese WWII howitzer. However, the club is rather seedy and rundown nowadays. Reportedly, expats and tourists flashing money around will attract pickpockets and prostitutes.

The *Mendana Hotel* bar is a good place to meet other expats or visitors. The King Solomon Hotel has the *Pipeline* bar and disco, where Solbrew costs S$5.50. But the best place for dancing is the *Freeway Club*, known simply as Freeways. It's open from 9 pm to 2 am, Thursday to Saturday, and gets packed with both expats and islanders. There's an entry fee of S$20 and drinks are S$5. There's no sign outside: enter from behind the Shell garage on Hibiscus Ave.

Casinos Honiara has four casinos, including a new one on Kukum Hwy, though there is a public campaign to reduce this number. *Solomon Casino* and *Honiara Casino*, next to each other on Mendana Ave, are both open daily from around 11 am to 3 pm. There's no entry fee and minimum stakes are S$1 for roulette and S$5 for blackjack and baccarat. There are also plenty of video and poker machines. Each club has a VIP room.

Club 88, on Chinatown Ave, is open from 9 pm to 3 am, Wednesday to Saturday, and 6 pm to 3 pm on Sunday. It has an entry fee of S$10 and higher minimum limits.

Kastom Music & Dancing If you don't manage to see an authentic *kastom* festival during your travels, the evening shows put on at the top hotels are almost as good. You may have to pay a small entry charge for some of these. The *Mendana Hotel* has a cultural group on Saturday, Tamure dancers on Sunday, and Mao dancing and panpipes on Wednesday. The *Honiara Hotel* hosts 'Are'Are panpipers and Tamure dancers on Wednesday, and the *King Solomon Hotel* has panpipes on Sunday.

Amateur Dramatics The Honiara Hams are a group of friendly, mainly British expats who get together fortnightly to monthly beside the Honiara Squash Club

courts for evening plays, pantomimes, folk club meetings and films. Events are advertised around town. Entry fees are modest and there's a bar.

Spectator Sport
Football (soccer) is the most popular spectator sport in the Solomons. Try to see a game at Lawson Tama Sports Ground in Kukum – the crowd is almost invariably good-natured. Entry fees are only about S$2 and the season stretches from around March to December. The stadium also hosts rugby and athletics; volleyball and softball can be viewed at the Honiara Town Ground. Since the British left, interest in cricket has waned, though there are attempts to revive it. Boxing has an ardent year-round following at the Kukum Indoor Sports Centre.

Things to Buy
Handicrafts for sale include skilfully crafted wooden carvings from Western Province, traditional items from Makira/Ulawa, personal weaponry and masks from Rennell and Bellona, and basketware and lime containers from Guadalcanal.

There are souvenir shops on Mendana Ave and in the NPF Plaza. Islanders sell their wares on the pavement outside Mendana Hotel, plus the hotel has a carvers stall by the car park. Melanesian Handicraft is opposite the Shell fuel depot and has reasonable prices. It's part of BJS Agencies, packagers and removalists, who also sell an annual trade directory.

Also with good prices are the King Solomon Arts & Crafts Centre, near the Lena Cinema, and the shop in the National Museum. The Honiara Hotel also has a souvenir shop.

Getting There & Away
Air Henderson airport is the hub of domestic services – nearly all flights to the provinces originate in the capital. Less-visited destinations may only receive one flight a week, whereas places like Gizo get several flights a day. See the regional chapters for specific information. The Getting

There & Away chapter has details on international flights.

The airlines flying into or around the Solomons have offices in Mendana Ave. These are Air Niugini (☎ 22895); Solomon Airlines (☎ 20031); and Western Pacific Airline (☎ 36533), at No 26 in the NPF Plaza. Travel Industry Services (☎ 36533), next door to GTS, represents Air Pacific and Qantas.

Sea Cruising yachts usually arrive at Honiara's main wharf, where customs and immigration can be cleared. See the Getting There & Away chapter for details.

Most of the Solomons' shipping companies are based in Honiara, so services tend to start from the capital. Operators are listed in the Getting Around chapter; specific services are covered in more detail in the regional chapters.

Motor canoes travel around Guadalcanal and to neighbouring islands. The best places to find them are at the small beach beside the Point Cruz Yacht Club and at Central Market.

Getting Around
The Airport Taxis are always hanging around. The standard fare into town is S$30. When you first arrive and don't know your way around, it might be worth getting a taxi, especially if you can split the cost with other travellers. For subsequent trips, a minibus should be more than adequate unless you've got loads of luggage (a backpack is no problem). The fare is only S$2. Wait under the trees by the main road. All minibuses going west will take you into Honiara, a 15-minute journey. Going to the airport, take any minibus marked CDC 1, 2 or 3. They go past every 15 minutes or so, but may be hard to find before 6 am or after 6 pm.

Bounty Taxi (☎ 36444) is reliable for early-morning trips to the airport (book the day before).

Minibus The cheapest way around Honiara is by minibus. Just flag one down: it will almost always stop unless it is already full. A near continuous stream of minibuses travels between King George VI School (which may be written as KGVI or KG6 on their signs) and Rove during daylight hours. Many also turn inland at Kukum to Naha. Though minibuses are less frequent after dark, you can still catch them, particularly returning to the town centre, up to 9 or 10 pm. The flat-rate fare around town is S$1; fares are S$2 and up for destinations east of KG6.

Car You need to be quite pushy when driving in Honiara. You can wait for ages at an intersection before someone will let you into the traffic stream. The only solution is to push in. Many of the side roads round town are unsealed. Even on Mendana Ave vehicles have to dodge huge potholes.

Rental Unless you take a tour, car is the easiest way to visit the north coast and the battlefields, but rental prices are high. Phoenix (☎ 20444, fax 25357) overlooks the western side of the Central Market, and Budget (☎ 23205, fax 23593) is by the Visitors' Bureau. At either place the cheapest car costs about S$175 per day, including unlimited km. This includes the compulsory collision damage waiver (CDW) and tax. Avis (☎ 24180, fax 23489), on Chinatown Plaza and in the Mendana Hotel, works out more expensive.

Before renting, investigate the possibility of hiring a taxi for the day instead. The rate from 8 am to 4 pm should only be about S$200, and you won't have to pay petrol or have the hassle of driving. Petrol per litre in Honiara costs S$1.47 for super and S$1.44 for diesel.

Taxi There are no taxi stands in Honiara, just lots of taxis available for hire during daylight hours. There are fewer after dark, but you can still find them quite easily right up to midnight. The best place to hail a taxi is outside Solomon Airlines, in Ashley St, or outside the Mendana Hotel.

None have meters, so agree on a fare

before getting aboard. You should only pay around S$3 a km, which is also the minimum fare. Fares go up slightly after dark. Some drivers quote inflated prices; if the fare seems too high, decline it, as another cab will be along in a minute or two.

To book a taxi, telephone Bounty Taxi (☎ 36444), Sombagi (☎ 24333) or Vineyard Cabs (☎ 39333).

Walking Most places in Honiara's central area are under 10 minutes apart on foot. Pedestrians should take particular care crossing roads, especially in Ashley St and in Mendana Ave between the Y Sato Building and Solomon Airlines.

In Kukum, the worst place to try to cross the road is from the northern side of Kukum Hwy over to Chinatown. Few motorists will slow down for pedestrians crossing the road.

Around Guadalcanal Island

Many of the sights along the north coast are easily reached on day trips from Honiara.

Arts

Visitors to the south-coast villages and the central mountains can still find armbands and belts woven from red and yellow-dyed fibres.

Plain black wooden bowls, now made with metal tools instead of stone, are still in common use.

Medical Services

There are rural health centres at Visale, Mbinu, Ruavatu, Aola and Totongo on the northern coast, and Tangarere, Kuma, Avu Avu and Manikaraku on the south coast. Inland health centres are at Kolochulu, Turarana, Mbambanakira, and near Kolosulu. There are also some mission clinics, private clinics and aid posts.

Organised Tours

See Honiara for information on tour operators. Visits to the northern battlefields are the most popular tours. Compare itineraries – especially if there's something you're particularly interested in – as tour operators don't all visit the same sites.

Getting There & Away

The central point for arrivals and departures in Guadalcanal is Honiara; see its Getting There & Away section.

Getting Around

Air Guadalcanal has three airfields on the southern coast: Mbambanakira, Avu Avu and Marau. They are only served by Solomon Airlines and only receive return flights from Honiara. Each gets one on Saturday. On Monday, there are flights to Avu Avu (S$75) and Marau (S$95), on Wednesday to Avu Avu, on Thursday to Mbambanakira (S$60), and on Friday to Marau.

Sea The Guadalcanal Provincial Government (☎ 20041) has two ships, the *Kangava* and the *Wango*. They each go round the island on a weekly basis in opposite directions, usually loading on Monday and leaving on Tuesday. Enquire at the shipping division in the Honiara offices. Fares from Honiara are: Visale S$24, Tiaro and Brande S$31, Wanderer Bay and Aola S$37, Viso and Babasu S$43, Suhu and Kopiu S$48, and Makaruka S$49. The *Ocean Express* stops at Manikaraku (Marau Sound) on its run to Makira.

Guadalcanal's all-weather anchorages are at Rere Point and Makina on the northern coast, and Wanderer Bay, Ghoverighi Harbour, Kopau Harbour, Tiaro Bay and Lambi Bay in the south. Talise is used in calm weather. Ships also often call in at Inakona.

Kopiu Bay, Mbalo and Savuna are only suitable when north-westerly winds blow, from mid-November to mid-April, while Aola and Haimarao are only feasible from late April to early November, when it's the season for south-easterlies. Guadalcanal's ship anchorages may be suitable for yachts during calmer weather.

Mixed fuel for canoe journeys costs about S$1.80 per litre in Honiara.

Land The island has approximately 450 km of roads and tracks. There's a main trunk route from Lambi Bay in the north-western part of the island through Honiara eastwards to Aola. A number of feeder roads extend out from the northern highway, particularly across the Guadalcanal Plains and towards the central foothills. In the south there's a road from Kuma to Avu Avu, a rough track form there to Sukiki, then a tractor trail on to Manikaraku in the southeast. Footpaths join Lambi Bay with Kuma, while a combined footpath and canoe route links Makina with Aola, thereby completing the island circuit.

There are two or three ill-defined tracks across the mountains that some villagers know and use occasionally. However, they are exceedingly strenuous and difficult to follow, and not recommended.

See the Honiara Getting Around section for information about car rental. Petrol and puncture repair facilities are only readily available in Honiara, so fill your car up before you set out. Along the north coast, only the 70-km stretch of road from Ndoma to Mberande River is sealed, and you'll need a 4WD vehicle to get much beyond Tambea. Watch out for villagers and animals on these very quiet roads.

Public Transport Public-transport vehicles can be identified by their number plate: they have white lettering on a black background, as opposed to the normal black on white. There are regular minibus services between Kakambona and White River Village to the west of Honiara, and Henderson, CDC 1, 2 and 3 (Mbaravuli, Nini and Karoururu respectively) to the east. Although infrequent minibuses go as far west as Tambea (S$7), for longer-distance travel you need to rely on trucks, which generally don't run on Sunday. They go from Honiara's Central Market to Aola in the east

and to Lambi Bay in the west; fares are about S$1 per 10 km. The general pattern is for trucks to set out for the capital early in the morning and return from the market about mid-afternoon, though you can sometimes get trucks in either direction at other times of the day. Ask around locally.

Along the southern coast, the Guadalcanal provincial government runs tractors which sometimes take passengers. Fares are low, but depend on the local substation. You may be able to charter a tractor.

Private vehicles often stop if you flag them down. Payment is by agreement and usually around 10c to 20c a km.

Walking There's an excellent booklet by JLO Tedder and A Clayton called *Walks on Guadalcanal*. Although written some years ago, it'll help if you're contemplating doing some bushwalking. The National Library will have a copy.

EAST OF HONIARA

The Guadalcanal Plains extend from the Lungga River to Kaoka Bay. At the Matepono River, the plains widest point, they reach 12 km inland.

Most of the WWII battlefields are in the vicinity of Henderson airport. They are hallowed ground to US war veterans. Pilgrims also come from Japan, some searching for the bones of relatives to give them a proper cremation according to Shinto tradition.

Mataniko Falls

This spectacular double-sided waterfall thunders down a cliff into a cave full of stalagmites and swooping swallows and bats. During WWII this cavern and others nearby were hide-outs for Japanese soldiers trying to evade capture by the Americans.

It's a two-hour walk from Honiara, starting on the 2.5-km road from Chinatown to Tuvaruhu. At Tuvaruhu, cross the river and follow its course south, mostly walking along the top of the ridge. The trail is often steep. It's probably best to seek a guide after Tuvaruhu; they'll want about S$10 per person. The custom fee is also S$10.

Some people opt to swim a stretch of the river on the way back to Tuvaruhu, but watch out for storm clouds – flash floods do occur, and there have been fatalities. Tour Solomons does a five-hour trek to the Mataniko Falls for S$60 per adult.

Mt Austen Road

The road to Mt Austen begins in Kukum and passes through Vura before climbing up to the historical sites where Japanese troops doggedly resisted the US advance.

The **Solomons Peace Memorial Park**, about four km south of Kukum, has a large, white memorial. It was built by Japanese war veterans in 1981 to commemorate all who died in the WWII Guadalcanal campaign. There's a magnificent view over Honiara and towards Savo and the Nggelas.

Continuing south three km, the thick bush opens to reveal an elevated clearing about 200m west from the road. This is the site of the **Gifu**, named by its wartime Japanese defenders after a Japanese district. Very fiercely defended, it was the Japanese forward command post, important in their efforts to capture Henderson. It finally fell

to the USA in mid-January 1943 after its starving defenders were wiped out making a final banzai attack. To the north-west is **Sea Horse Ridge**, a Japanese strong point in 1942. It was given this name by US aviators because it looked like a sea horse from the air. Skirting the ridge is a scenic trail that leads to Tuvaruhu and Chinatown.

One km south of the Gifu is the summit of **Mt Austen** (410m), where a clearing by the roadside offers a marvellous view northeastwards over Henderson. Americans in WWII dubbed this spot Grassy Knoll. At the northern end of the hilltop are the remains of a small dugout, which acted as an observation post for the Japanese artillery bombarding Henderson. You may be able to stay in the SSEC hut up here, though it's mainly used for prayer. Ask locally about the viability of walking back via the Mataniko Falls.

Betikama

On the way to Henderson airport, and about 600m beyond the King George VI School, a charming sign spans the road with 'Welcome' and 'Farewell' in English and

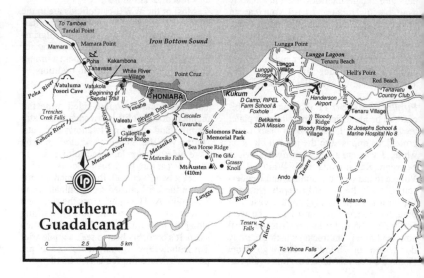

Pijin. (Half the welcome has fallen down, but happily, that's not symbolic.) Just beyond, about 6.5 km from Honiara, is the turn-off southwards. It's a 1.5-km walk along here to the Betikama SDA Mission.

Within the grounds is a large handicraft shop, Betikama Carvings, specialising in Western Province products and stylish modern copperware. Much of the carving is done by school children who've come to Betikama from SDA villages in the New Georgia Islands. The quality is good and the prices are reasonable; it's open daily, except Sunday, from 8 am to noon and 1 to 5 pm. A small donation is expected if you don't buy anything.

There's a small **WWII museum** with an outdoor collection of salvaged material (mostly US aircraft), two small Japanese antitank guns and a well-preserved British Bren gun carrier. Inside, at the rear of the handicraft shop, is a collection of WWII photographs and memorabilia. Just behind the nearby hedge is a sturdy-looking US military bulldozer.

Two saltwater crocodiles reside in the small pen between the museum and the

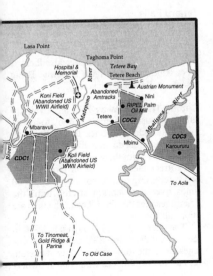

carvings shop. Both were taken from the nearby Lungga River.

If you ask them, the carvers will point out the *tita* tree that's growing nearby. The tree's nuts produce a resin which is used by canoe builders to render their craft waterproof.

Lungga Village

About 50m across Lungga Bridge, beside a tree on the eastern side of the main road, is the original foxhole. It was named after Colonel Fox, a US marine stationed here in 1942. This small, concrete-lined hole in a bank was the colonel's command bunker.

A track goes up a bank on the southern side of the road by the bridge. A small opening in the ground leads to the old US underground command post, known as D Camp, where radios, field telephone systems, maps and plotting rooms once were. Now it's empty except for a few bats. You'll need a torch to look around. About 30m up the track at the top of the same bank, and on the south-eastern side of an intersection, is a Japanese anti-aircraft gun, placed here as a trophy.

Just beyond Colonel Fox's command bunker is a track through the grounds of the Russell Islands Plantation Estates Ltd (RIPEL) Farm School. About 50m along on the southern side of the track is a very rusty and wrecked Quonset hut. This was General Vandergrift's first command post in the Guadalcanal campaign. The route then circles the 300m or so round to the Japanese gun above D Camp. If you meet any RIPEL staff, ask them to point out these sites, and get their permission to see them.

Lungga Lagoon

There's a four-km track from Lungga Village out to the lagoon. Turn north (left) after 2.6 km and continue 1.4 km to the end of the track. At the end of a long, sandy beach are the ocean-battered remains of a US Navy jetty. Fifty metres away is a small landing craft. Beached for repairs, it's now immobilised forever by a large tree which has grown up right through its centre.

About 50 to 200m offshore from Lungga Lagoon are six sunken US pontoons in about eight metres of water. They can easily be seen from the air.

Henderson Airport

A small memorial outside the airport entrance honours US forces and their Pacific Islander allies. In front is a Japanese anti-aircraft gun. Inside the airport terminal are plaques explaining how Henderson Field – as the Americans called it in WWII – was named after a US flier of the time. About 100m to the west of the buildings is the scaffold-style WWII control tower, disused since the early 1950s.

There's a very ambitious long-standing plan to create a Solomon Islands WWII museum at the airport, including restored WWII planes that will give joyrides. Don't hold your breath!

Bloody Ridge

A track running either side of the airport leads south to several small leaf-house settlements, including Bloody Ridge Village at the bottom of Bloody Ridge. This village has a small hut on top of a tall pole, reserved for young men and teenage boys.

Bloody Ridge is also called Edson's Ridge, after Edson's Raiders. Commanded by Colonel Merritt Edson, they defended the ridge against the Japanese in 1942 in their determined but unsuccessful attempts to seize the airfield. About one km beyond the village a Japanese war memorial honours the 2000 or more Japanese killed during these actions.

Hell's Point

There's a wooden monument surrounded by long grass at Hell's Point 50m back from Alligator Creek's exit to the sea. This is a poignant site for Japanese visitors. According to the inscription, the Japanese Colonel Kiyono Ichiki and his 800 men 'died honourably' there on 20 August 1942 after a banzai attack from the eastern side of the creek against US machine guns and artillery mounted on its western bank.

A sunken pontoon in 10m of water 30m from the shore at Hell's Point is clearly visible from the air. The large US troopship *John Penn* was bombed and sunk about four km offshore. It's complete with gun turrets and dense schools of open-ocean fish, but at 36m to 50m down it's on the deep side for scuba.

To get to Hell's Point, take the first track northwards after the bridge just east of Henderson airport. Once you reach the sea, walk 200m westwards until you reach the creek. The northward track takes you through the RIPEL cocoa plantation, with restricted access, so at the first opportunity ask permission to continue.

Tenaru Village

A road turns south from the main road and follows the west bank of the Tenaru River. After 1.5 km there's **Marine Hospital No 8**, the first wartime hospital in Guadalcanal. This operated until the Americans built Honiara's Central Hospital. It's in the grounds of St Joseph's School, Tenaru. Many of the old WWII buildings and the concrete base remain.

Tenaru Falls

This 63m waterfall tumbles on two sides into a deep swimming hole and the cascades beyond. Here, as at all mountain creeks, watch out for signs of rain because there is a constant danger of flash flooding. Bring insect repellent and sunscreen.

Getting There & Away Take the seven-km side road, past St Joseph's School, to its terminus at Ando. The track then follows an old logging route down to the Tenaru River. Beyond this point there are many footpaths. The correct one cuts across the river's many bends, crossing and recrossing it up to 20 times over a seven-km stretch until the Tenaru reaches the Chea River. The falls are 300m up the Chea.

Travellers have had to pay up to S$50 in fees to visit the falls – S$5 each to three villages along the route and two lots of custom fees to the two villages who contest ownership of the falls. Consider commissioning a guide at Ando (where you'll need to ask permission to proceed anyway) – you won't get lost and you may end up paying fewer fees. Tour Solomons' six-hour trek to the falls costs S$95 per adult.

Red Beach

On this long sandy beach a lonely, very rusted Japanese gun, placed here by US veterans, points forlornly out to sea. This is the only reminder of the US landings here in 1942.

The *Tenavatu Country Club* (☎ 31174), with tennis courts and a fully licensed bar, is open from 4 to 10.30 pm on weekdays and from noon to 10.30 pm on weekends. Nonmembers are welcome.

Koni Field

This abandoned US airfield can still be seen near the main road. A few km north by a side track is a Seebee memorial and a wartime hospital. Continue north one km to reach a radio bunker, then follow the track another three km as it veers south-west to find a communications bunker.

Gold Ridge

After alluvial gold was found here in 1931, on the western edge of Mt Tatuve, there was a brief gold rush. Local village names such as Tinomeat and Old Case are reminders of the time. The ridge is now being mined commercially, so enquire if visits are allowed before setting out. Gold Ridge is a four-km walk from the end of the side track.

South of Tinomeat, an 11-km hike leads to Ngalikama. At this village, pick up a guide and get permission to visit the **Chari Cascades**, a long line of attractive shallow cascades on the Chari River about one km from Ngalikama.

Tetere

On both sides of Tetere thick palm-oil plantations, popularly known as CDC1, 2 and 3, line the road. They were planted in 1976 by a British-owned company, and are now owned by RIPEL. The large **palm-oil mill**

halfway towards the beach is also owned by RIPEL – tours may be possible if you ask.

A few metres before reaching the shore of **Tetere Beach**, take the track westwards to reach 30 or more abandoned amtracks. Many of these rusty relics are shielded by prickly thorns, and the access route is overgrown. They're beside a small cemetery and opposite a group of three small shoreside leaf houses. If you go looking for the amtracks without paying the S$10 custom fee, you may be charged much more by the custom owners as an unofficial fine for trespassing.

Returning to the beach road, continue about 300m along the shore to the east. Standing about 50m in front of a white house is a cross commemorating four Austrian explorers from the *Albatross*. They were part of a 25-person party, under the leadership of geologist HR von Foullon Norbeeck, which attempted to climb Mt Tatuve (1400m) in 1896. Local people believed that if white people climbed this tabu mountain, all the villagers would die. When the party continued the ascent, the islanders attacked and the foursome were killed – and two of them eaten!

Mbinu

The road crosses the Mbalisuna River one km beyond Mbinu, a subprovincial headquarters, and passes through the large CDC3 palm-oil plantation at Karoururu.

A thick, green vine grows over the natural bush once you leave the plantations behind. Called American vine, it was introduced from the southern states of the USA as a fast-growing natural camouflage during WWII. Since then, it has spread unrestrainedly over indigenous vegetation along the road between Karoururu and the Mbokokimbo River.

Tiua

Most villages east of Tiua (pronounced 'djew-ah') have houses built on stilts, raised variously from a half to two metres above ground. The road finally reaches the sea at Ruavatu, seven km further on. A six-km walk west of here is **Taivu Point**, where a black-sand beach extends two km inland. Many of the riverbanks around here and at Tasimboko Bay have populations of megapode birds that hatch their eggs in the sandy alluvial soil. Take great care crossing rivers in this area, as there have been occasional shark and crocodile attacks.

By the Mbokokimbo River is Komuniboli. The *Komuniboli Training Centre* (☎ 23760, PO Box 556) teaches Pijin and aspects of traditional culture. It has cheap dorm beds for $15 a head, plus two twin rooms. Toilets are basic. Meals and guided rainforest walks are available.

Vulelua Island

This two-hectare, almost circular island is 68 km east of Honiara. It's surrounded by sand and only 250m in diameter. Also known as Neal Island, Vulelua has a tiny neighbour 400m to its north-west called Pikinini (ie baby) Island, which in fact is no more than a raised sandbar and reef.

The *Vulelua Island Resort* (☎ & fax 29684, PO Box 96) is the island's only development, and a relaxing retreat. Its six units with own shower/WC can accommodate a total of 24 people. Meals, based on island-type foods, are delicious, with succulent seafood lunches for S$38 a head. The all-inclusive rate is A$80 (about S$215) per day, but enquire about discounts for local bookings.

There's excellent snorkelling (decrepit equipment provided) almost all around the island, especially on its western and north-western sides. Guests can go on free fishing trips, with the catch subsequently served up at mealtimes. There's a bar, a small aviary and a volleyball court. Avoid weekends, when it's full with Honiara's expats. Yachts are welcome.

Getting There & Away The boat to Vulelua leaves from Komuninggita car park, eight km east of Ruavatu's school. It's about a 75-minute drive from Honiara (longer by truck). The three-km speedboat ride from there to/from Vulelua is free as long as you eat or stay at the resort. Phone ahead to arrange for their boat to meet you, and flash headlights or a mirror if it's not waiting when you arrive. The waves can be quite strong at Komuninggita, so be prepared to get wet when getting in and out of the boat.

Tour Solomons' day-tour to Vulelua costs S$120 and includes a diversion to see the Tetere Beach amtracks. The GTS tour costs S$180 but includes lunch at the resort.

Aola

The prewar capital of Guadalcanal, now a subprovincial headquarters, is 76 km east of Honiara. The road ends here and this is as far as trucks can travel. Only footpaths and a short stretch of logging track continue beyond.

There's an extensive coral reef on the northern side of **Rua Sura Island** and a narrow white-sand beach. A chartered motor-canoe ride for the 13 km from Aola takes an hour each way. To its east is tiny, sand-surrounded Surakiki Island.

Vatupochau Falls are in very dense bush three km due north of Mt Vatupochau, a 17-km hike from Aola. You'll need to hire a guide in Aola.

Rere Point

Rere Point and its sandy beach are connected to Aola by a clearly marked, 15-km shoreside footpath. There's a custom site near the village where skulls are stored – ask villagers to show you.

Ten km on is Simiu River, one of Guadalcanal's largest water courses. Care is needed in crossing it. There's another custom site 7.5 km inland along the river.

Mbo'o, seven km south, is at the mouth of two very deep waterways – the Mbo'o and Singgilia rivers. Ask the villagers to canoe you across. Similarly, you'll need a canoe to cross the Kaoka River to Papara.

Poposa

Opposite this village are three small, coconut-covered, sand-fringed islands: Pari, Komukomutou (or Symons) and

Arona. They form a line extending from two to four km offshore, and are all about 1.5 km apart. Less than five km inland from Poposa is another custom site.

You can get from Poposa to Manikaraku in Marau Sound on foot, but the path is alongside swamps for the next 11 km to Savekau. The next seven km are better, though there's more swamp at New Marere. The route finishes with a 2.5-km tractor trail between Makina and Manikaraku.

It's much easier to charter a motor canoe for the 20.5 km from Poposa to Manikaraku. However, canoes can be scarce in Poposa, and you may have to wait several hours. A charter will cost around S$70.

MARAU SOUND

This lagoon at the eastern tip of the island has Guadalcanal's largest expanse of fringing reef and its best sea fishing. It also has several clusters of islands, reefs, shoals and coral gardens.

Particularly dazzling are the Paipai and Aaritenamo reefs which enclose the tiny, sand-girthed Paipai, Kosa and Rauhi Islands. This whole area is a favourite of scuba divers, and looks fantastic from the air. Domestic air services use Marau airfield.

Manikaraku

This village is a subprovincial headquarters and has government offices, stores and a clinic. There's a *provincial government rest house*, but it hasn't been maintained and is barely operational. Much nicer is the *Gower Rest House* (☎ 29055) which runs two houses and charges S$50 per person. One house has electricity and is on the coast; the other house is nearer the village centre, with no electricity. Kitchen facilities are available, and the owners can arrange canoe pick-up from Marau airfield, a 15-minute walk away, near Komunimbaimbai village.

Tavanipupu Island

A 20-minute canoe ride through the lagoon from Marau airfield, this 16-hectare island lies only about 100m from its much larger neighbour, Marapa Island.

The island is owned by two expats, Keith Paske and Denis Bellotte. Over the past 12 years they have built up an idyllic retreat here, complete with many items of Pacific art and landscaped walkways and gardens. Accommodation is in six stylish, high-roofed *vales* with solar power, each sleeping up to four people. Excellent meals are included; dinner is usually preceded by a get-together in the bar. There's a hill providing a fine view, sandy beaches and mangroves. Snorkelling is excellent (gear provided) and there are several sand-fringed islands close by. Novels and board games are available. Yachties are welcome.

The *Tavanipupu Resort* (☎ & fax 29043, PO Box 236) costs A$220 (about S$590) per person per day inclusive, but enquire about special deals for local bookings. Canoe transfers to/from the Marau airfield are provided.

WEST OF HONIARA

The seas between Guadalcanal's north-western coast and Savo Island were the site of constant naval actions between August 1942 and February 1943. By the time the Japanese finally withdrew, so many ships had been sunk it became known as Iron Bottom Sound.

Some of the wartime wrecks have become encrusted with coral and are turning into reefs. Fish swim in and out of the holds and decks, while steel hulls have become carpeted with marine growth. A few of the wreck sites are accessible to snorkellers and many are well within sports-diving levels.

Trenches Creek Falls

These small falls tumble 40m into a narrow gorge. They are a five-km hike south of Vatukola, where you should ask permission to see them. Villagers will direct you up the Trenches Creek (or Kohove River, as it's also called). The creek splits about half a km south of the village, and you follow the eastern branch. Around 1.5 km further on it splits, and again you take the more easterly course. Half a km later you take the western

GUADALCANAL

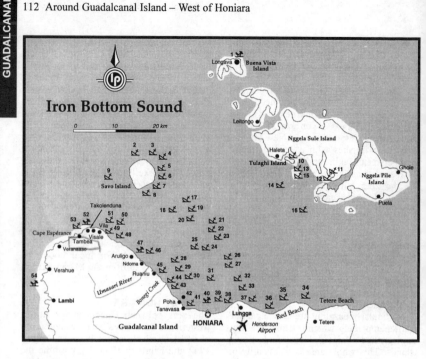

Iron Bottom Sound

stream, followed by an eastern stream a short while afterwards. Some of the route is along dry creek beds or requires scrambling over rocks, and there are several cool swimming pools along the way. Always watch out for storm clouds, as this creek is very prone to flash flooding through its narrow gorges.

Poha

There's a war memorial in this village. A Japanese floating crane, wrecked in 1957, lies partly submerged close to the shore – you can easily snorkel around it.

A trail alongside the Poha River follows the eastern bank for 1.5 km, until it reaches a steep cliff and cave shelter. This is the **Vatuluma Posori Cave**. Lapita-style petroglyphs on the cave walls were probably carved around 1000 BC, although some remains found on the floor go back 3000 years earlier. There are 26 wall carvings.

Some are hard to identify, others clearly show fish, snakes, a skull and a woman in childbirth. The cave is strictly protected by both the Poha villagers and the National Museum. Ask the museum's help if you want to see it, and be prepared to pay a custom fee to the landowners.

About 500m offshore from the mouth of the Poha River is the *Solsea*. This inter-island schooner, scuttled in 1980 and now sitting on a ledge 18m to 30m down, is an underwater photographer's delight. The wreck, covered in soft corals, is the home of many colourful fish.

Mamara Point, 1.5 km west, is a good scuba site with coral formations, as is Tandai Point, a further one km west. The latter also a good spot for night divers who want to see turtles sleeping.

From Mamara Point to Ndoma, 13 km to the north-west, many of the coconut trees are scarred with WWII bullet holes. Most of

UNITED STATES
1 B-24 Bomber
2 Heavy Cruiser Vincennes
5 Destroyer Duncan
7 Heavy Cruiser Astoria
8 Heavy Cruiser Quincy
12 Tank Landing Ship LST 325
13 Tanker Kanawa
14 Destroyer Barton
16 Transport George F Elliott
19 Destroyer Benham
20 Destroyer Walke
21 Destroyer Preston
22 Destroyer Laffey
23 Destroyer Cushing
24 Destroyer Blue
25 Light Cruiser Juneau
26 Transport Gregory
27 Transport Little
28 Destroyer Monssen
30 Heavy Cruiser Northampton
33 Transport Calhoun
34 Tug Seminole
36 Troopship John Penn
39 Cruiser Atlanta
40 Wildcat Fighter
47 B-17 Flying Fortress Bomber
48 PT Boat PT43
49 PT Boat PT112
50 PT Boat PT44
54 B-17 Flying Fortress Bomber

AUSTRALIA
4 Heavy Cruiser Canberra

NEW ZEALAND
10 Minesweeper Moa

JAPAN
3 Submarine I-3
6 Destroyer Fubiki
9 Heavy Cruiser Furutaka
11 Destroyer Kikutsuki
15 Destroyer Kikizuki
17 Destroyer Ayanami
18 Battleship Kirishima
29 Destroyer Takanani
31 Destroyer Yuduchi
32 Battleship Hiei
35 Heavy Cruiser Kinugosa
37 Destroyer Akatsuki
43 Transport Bonegi II
44 Transport Bonegi I
45 Transport Kyushu Maru
46 Transport
51 Destroyer Terutsuki
52 Wrecked Plane
53 Submarine I-23

MODERN VESSELS
38 Japanese Tuna Boat Gyoshu Maru
41 Inter-island Schooner Solsea
42 Japanese Floating Crane

their trunks have orangey moss, which, against a blue sky, makes for a striking photo.

Bonegi Creek & Beach

Two large Japanese freighters sank here, with appalling loss of life, on the night of 13 November 1942. Scuba divers call them simply *Bonegi I* and *Bonegi II*, as their true names were not known until recently. Growing on the wrecks are fan corals, sponges, coral polyps and gorgonia sea fans.

Bonegi I, a 6800-tonne transport, also known as the *Hirokawa Maru*, is in three metres of water descending to 55m. As this 172m ship is only 20m to 30m offshore, snorkellers can easily reach its bow. You can swim through its engine room and bridge amidst hundreds of colourful fish. There's a display of brass ammunition in open cases 12m down, and a 75-mm gun pointing to the sea bed at 35m.

As the upper works of *Bonegi II* break the surface, it can be snorkelled, though its stern reaches down to 24m. This ship was the 132m *Kinugawa Maru*. It's 300m north of the first wreck and has become a fascinating garden of coral and small fish.

To use Bonegi Beach there's a custom fee of S$5 per carload and S$20 per minibus. The fee is included if you go with a dive company.

Tasivarongo Point & Reef

Just past the Bonegi II site, and around 300m before you reach Tasivarongo Point, there's a bush track off to the south. It runs about a quarter of a km to a well-preserved US Sherman tank called *Jezebel* which was used for wartime target practice once the Guadalcanal campaign was over.

There are plentiful soft corals and colourful tropical fish at Tasivarongo Reef in depths of five to 35m. A site 400m beyond is very good for night scuba dives, with numerous small coral heads, drop offs and shells.

Ruaniu

Three km short of Ruaniu village is a 6500-tonne Japanese transport, believed to be the *Kyushu Maru*. This 140m vessel was lost on the same day as *Bonegi I* and *Bonegi II*. The vessel lies six to 45m down; its stern is fairly intact, though the bow is broken up. The colourful tropical fish here are very tame and enjoy being hand fed. Access to the wreck is through the Kikolo Plantation.

Ndoma

Ndoma is about 22 km from Honiara. There are plans to build a luxury resort here, overlooking the attractive 400m beach of dark-grey sand. Straight out from a creek and 100m from the shore is a US B-17 Flying Fortress bomber. Encrusted in soft corals, it's in 15m of water, with its engines and 0.5-calibre machine guns still intact.

Vilu

A turn to the south from the coastal road brings you within one km to the Vilu War Museum. There are US and Japanese memorials, four large Japanese field guns and the remains of several US aircraft, including a Wildcat fighter whose wings can still be folded as they were for naval carrier-borne operations. Entry costs S$10 and it's open daily.

The collection receives wildly mixed reviews from visitors – Tambea Resort divers often call in on the way back from Bonegi Beach.

Aruligo

If you continue one km west along the main road you'll come to the International Centre for Living Aquatic Resources Management (☎ 29255) or ICLARM. It protects and farms several marine species, particularly giant clams. These clams have been heavily overfished in the Solomons recently because of the high price the creature's adductor muscle fetches in the Chinese marketplace. The farm grows giant clams until they are large enough to be safe from predators when placed on a reef. Once in their natural habitat they reproduce and create small clam colonies of their own. ICLARM (open daily from 9 am to 4 pm) charges S$5 to show visitors round.

Cape Espérance

Named by D'Entrecasteaux in 1793 after the *Espérance*, it was from here that the Japanese successfully evacuated most of their 13,000 starving men at the end of the Guadalcanal campaign in January and February 1943. Many of them were also sick or wounded. They assembled on 200m Pupuraka Hill just behind the cape to wait for evacuation, and were then given one hour to board the waiting ships. Some fell to their deaths as they stumbled down the steep and slippery hillside in total darkness.

The narrow, sandy beach here continues for 2.5 km in each direction. Immediately to the west is **Vila**, which is a good place to find a shared canoe ride to Savo Island. Another one km west is **Visale**. The large Roman Catholic mission here has the interred remains of Bishop Epalle, who was murdered on Santa Isabel in 1845. Close by is **Takolenduna**, where a wrecked Japanese plane lies on the reef. Local villagers will know where it is.

Veuru

The Japanese I-class submarine *I-23* is 350m from the shore on a nearby reef. Local villagers here are custom owners of the site and will canoe you out to a point above the wreck. They charge both a waiting and a custom fee.

The submarine lies from three to 30m down, and parts can be snorkelled. It was blown open by salvagers, so you can dive through much of it, exiting close to the stern. To add to the fun there are said to be two live torpedoes still aboard!

Tambea

This is the location of the *Tambea Holiday Beach Resort* (☎ 23629, fax 20376, PO Box 4). This was the other main evacuation site for Japan's exhausted troops in early 1943. Next to the swimming pool is a small Japanese monument commemorating the

200 soldiers who died before evacuation; they were buried here.

The resort has 24 Melanesian-style bungalows with verandah, overhead fan, shower/WC and tea/coffee-making facilities. They're reasonably comfortable and are being upgraded. The price for a single/double/triple is S$176/231/269.

Meals in the restaurant are around S$20 for lunch and S$40 for dinner, but the food is disappointing. There's also a bar, swimming pool, volleyball court and barbecue area.

The resort welcomes day-trippers (and yachties) who can use the facilities free of charge, but they would be expected to buy drinks or a meal.

Activities The resort has its own dive shop. One/two dives cost S$90/145, or S$155/185 with full equipment rental. A resort course costs S$165 and full PADI certification is S$660.

All **scuba** sites between Bonegi Beach and Verahue (to the south) are regularly visited. This includes nearby Paru, where three km offshore two large coral heads (bombies) rise to three metres below the surface. Fish congregate around them in huge numbers, and underwater visibility is always good. Dreadnought Reef is close to the resort and features a two-metre-high dreadnought (ie battleship) anchor lying on a reef. Offshore caves provide an amazing labyrinth of coral caverns, most no deeper than 15m and some just two metres below the surface.

Snorkelling off the beach is not bad; equipment is free for guests and hired to day-trippers. Water-skiing, kayaking and windsurfing are all possible. **Horse-riding** and **fishing** trips are also offered, as well as tours to Savo (S$150), north-coast war sites (S$110) and local attractions (S$110).

Getting There & Away Tambea resort does transfers to/from Henderson airport for S$15 each way. Occasional minibuses make the 45-km trip to/from Honiara (S$7). They depart Tambea around 6 am and 2 pm, returning from Honiara at about 11 am and 4 pm. Trucks regularly do the same trip (except Sunday) for S$5. The Honiara Hotel (which is under the same ownership) offers transport to the resort, departing at 8 am and returning from Tambea about 5 pm. The return fare is S$20; book at the Honiara Hotel the day before. GTS and Tour Solomons both include Tambea on their itineraries.

Verahue

A US B-17 Flying Fortress bomber lies close to shore at a depth of 10m to 18m. Its 50-calibre guns are still intact and there's easy access to the cockpit. The Nggurara Hot Springs are five km inland. The track is hard to find, so you'll need a guide.

Nine km south is **Lambi Bay**, the end of the track and a subprovincial headquarters. The southern coastal route continues on as a footpath from here. The bay features two-metre surf.

THE WEATHER COAST

The southern shore's poor weather conditions have discouraged human settlement. Although there's a string of villages along the southern coast, most of these have only small populations.

There's a long strip of variously grey or black-sand beach eastwards from Viso, broken only by occasional wide alluvial rivers. Fast-flowing creeks tumble down the steep sides of tall, jagged mountains, some in a continuous chain of small cascades. Ridges covered in thick, green bush fall abruptly to the shore.

Making a journey on foot around the Weather Coast can be very hard indeed, often requiring a guide. Small creeks regularly swell to raging torrents in a few minutes, especially during the local wet season (July to September).

It's a four to six-day coastal trek from Lambi Bay to Kuma, with fine scenery all the way. Although there's a shoreside path most of the time, be prepared for quite a bit of rock-hopping by the water along some stretches of this route, as well as diversions over small hills and through bush to bypass the occasional rocky promontory.

GUADALCANAL

The three to four-day walk from Kuma to Marau Sound is along the most interesting part of the island's southern coast. Alternatively, you can catch the occasional vehicle along the road from Kuma to Avu Avu, or a tractor from Avu Avu to Marau Sound. Much of the route is beside long, narrow black-sand beaches.

Kokomughailava
The Hoilava River reaches the sea here. In its shallower parts are boulders decorated with carvings. The designs include a giant, canoes, the sun and a shield. There are also hungry crocodiles lurking near this river's crossing point and in many other squally creeks. Tiaro Bay to the south has some pleasant sandy beaches, particularly near West Cape.

Tangarere
Provincial government vessels stop at this subprovincial headquarters, which has a decaying *provincial government rest house*.

Ghove Falls is at the 200m mark to the south-east of 800m Cone Peak. The 12-km hike from Ghoverighi Harbour (where you should acquire a guide) is initially through lowland country along the banks of the Ghove River.

There's a good **surf beach** near the mission at the northern end of Beaufort Bay. The Ghausava River in the southern part of the inlet can be hard to cross when it's swollen after heavy rain. Beyond the river is **Sorovisi**, where there's a very attractive beach in a small cove. The route on to Fox Bay and Wanderer Bay requires some walking on shoreside rocks.

Wanderer Bay
Benjamin Boyd, an Australian sheep farmer, landed here in October 1851, planning to take control of Guadalcanal Island and import sheep on a large scale. He named the place Wanderer Bay after his ship the *Wanderer*, and went ashore alone to shoot game but was never seen again. Several British warships searched the area for him without success.

The route eastwards requires more boulder-hopping, both to Marumbo Bay and to Marasa Bay. After that, the path goes inland to **Mbambanakira**. This village, next to the wide Itina River and Mbambanakira airfield, is a subprovincial headquarters. There is only a simple *provincial government rest house*.

Komate
The path from Mbambanakira passes over a 100m hill before reaching the sea at Komate. It then follows the beach for about six km, rising again to around 100m before descending to the Noro River, crossing at the shore.

The next major crossing is the Koloula River, some 17 km east. July and September rains frequently make it an impassable floodwater channel up to 400m across.

Kuma
There are a number of custom sites very high up in the adjacent mountains between 1500m and 2000m above sea level, in areas of very heavy rainfall. You will need a local guide and adequate bush clothing and supplies. If the guide says the sites are tabu, you shouldn't dispute this.

Avu Avu
This is a subprovincial headquarters and has its own airfield. There's a small, unmaintained *provincial government rest house* with two rooms and shared facilities.

Just to the west is the Mbolavu River, which regularly floods to as much as 500m wide during the midyear wet season. However, it's often dry at other times of the year. None of the rivers east of Avu Avu present too much difficulty, except after especially heavy rain.

Lauvi Lagoon
The brackish waters of this four-sq-km lake are separated from the ocean by a narrow sand spit, though it overflows into the sea following heavy rain. As well as herons, cormorants, eels, river prawns and plentiful fish, there are some crocodiles living at the

lake's swampy edge, so don't swim in it. Mosquitoes also are a problem.

If you are looking for a guide to show you the best places to view the local wildlife, enquire at Bubuvua, the nearest sizeable village.

Korasahalu Island
Until very recently, this 70-hectare, quarter-moon-shaped island was just a reef. Submarine earth movements have raised it in the last 15 years so that it now stands a few metres above high tide level. It is covered in dark-green foliage.

Komuvaolu
Komuvaolu is the coastal Moro village where the Moro chief and the majority of influential Moro people live. Anyone wishing to visit Moro villages needs to get permission first from the chief, and may be required to wear skimpy traditional dress during their visit.

Talk to the Principal Administration Officer (☎ 20041) in the Guadalcanal provincial offices in Honiara in the first instance.

Many ancient manual arts are being preserved by the Moro people, including the making and wearing of tapa. Shell money, sacred stones and traditional tools such as stone axes and weapons are collected and stored in the custom houses in Komuvaolu. You can see inside the buildings if you ask first. Moro people formerly lived Marakura, a village to the west, but they were expelled in 1992. Most of them moved to Komuvaolu, though some dispersed to their native villages.

Valahima Falls
These falls are three km inland from Veramakuru. To get there, follow the river 1.5 km inland until it forks, then stay with the eastern channel for another 1.5 km as far as the waterfall.

The Moro Movement
This nationalist movement began quietly in 1953 but took off in 1957 when its leader, Moro, called on local people to return to their old customs. He claimed he dreamt about a spirit who told him to lead the Marau-language speakers of south-eastern Guadalcanal. A short jail sentence made him a hero.

In 1965, the movement's leaders offered the British Protectorate government the equivalent of A$4000 for the independence of Isatambu (their name for Guadalcanal) but were refused. Even today, the Moro Movement retains a significant following. ■

Central Province

Central Province is 1000 sq km and comprises the Melanesian islands of the Nggela (or Florida) group, Savo and the Russells.

Despite the presence of the large fishing base at the provincial capital of Tulagi, and the huge coconut plantations owned by RIPEL in the Russells, the province is one of the country's poorest, with most of its 18,500 people engaged in subsistence farming.

The Nggela Islands

Initially called Flora, and later the Florida Islands, by the Spanish in 1568, the Nggela group consists of four largish islands and about 50 others of various sizes. Lying between Guadalcanal and Malaita islands, the Nggela group is 57 km across and covers an area of 391 sq km. There is a rural population of about 8500, in addition to the 2000 inhabitants of Tulaghi – a small island half a km from the south of Nggela Sule Island.

The two main islands are divided by a long, sinuous channel called Mboli Passage. West of the passage is Nggela Sule, or Big Gela, while Nggela Pile, or Small Gela, is to the east. At the group's western extremities are the two other sizeable islands, Sandfly and Buena Vista.

These four larger islands have fairly rugged interiors and convoluted coastlines (they look great from the air on the Honiara-Auki flight). Long white-sand beaches flank the northern coasts of Nggela Sule and Nggela Pile and skirt the group's many small islets. There are also mangrove swamps, some with a resident crocodile population, though Tulaghi people insist their island is free of these cunning reptiles.

Locally, the entire group of islands is known simply as Nggela.

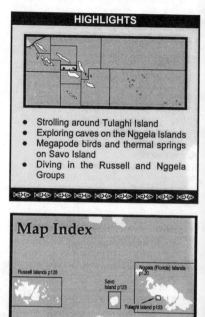

HIGHLIGHTS

- Strolling around Tulaghi Island
- Exploring caves on the Nggela Islands
- Megapode birds and thermal springs on Savo Island
- Diving in the Russell and Nggela Groups

Map Index

Russell Islands p128

Nggela (Florida) Islands p120

Savo Island p125

Tulaghi Island p123

History

The Nggelas suffered the same fate as many other Pacific islands during the early days of blackbirding in the late 1860s. In two months in 1867 over 100 men were forcibly carried off to Queensland to become virtual slaves, and another 18 were murdered. By the late 19th century, islanders were departing voluntarily to work overseas, but this, combined with intervillage warfare and the introduction of new diseases, contributed to a steep population decline.

In the 1930s, the secessionist Chair & Rule Movement from Santa Isabel became

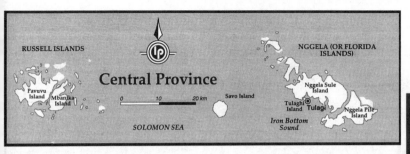

CENTRAL

popular in the Nggelas. When they experienced US wartime generosity, Nggela people, along with Malaitans, tried to buy US rule. Although the British authorities quickly insisted that any money paid to the USA should be returned to the islanders, some people believed they had bought a new government.

Arts
Forehead discs similar to *kapkaps* but called *biru* in the Nggelas are produced from clam and turtle shell and are worn on ceremonial occasions. Small model canoes and dog-teeth necklaces are also made.

Legendary People
The Nggela Islands' legends tell of an early race called the Mumutambu – a wild, hairy, cannibalistic race. Nothing is known of their demise.

Medical Services
Tulagi has a small hospital and the Church of Melanesia has a large clinic at Taroaniara. Other clinics include those at Salesape, Ndende, Siota, Mboromole and Leitongo.

Getting There & Away
Air There are no operational airfields in the Nggelas at present, though Anuha should reopen once the resort does. An airfield serving Tulagi has been proposed for Makambo Island, but it's only in the planning stage.

Sea Florida Shipping's *Florida II* spends each weekday running between Honiara and the Nggelas (S$20). Routes vary; sometimes it circles the islands, other times it goes through the Mboli Passage. It often (but not always) visits Tulagi and Taroaniara; it may overnight in the Nggelas though it usually returns to Honiara the same day. Sasape Shipping's *Thomas E*, a larger boat, regularly does similar trips. National Fisheries Developments Ltd goes frequently between Honiara and Tulagi, but its boats no longer take passengers.

There are sheltered bays and anchorages throughout the Nggelas. In addition to Tulagi Wharf and Sasape, Tulaghi Island has the Solomon Tulagi Base, though yachties may find this too busy for their liking due to trawler activity. There are other anchorages are at Leitongo, Taroaniara, Ghavutu Island, Siota, Tanatau Cove, Mbike Island and Hanesavo Harbour.

Getting Around
There's a track around Tulaghi, and a footpath along Nggela Sule's coast between Mboromole and Rara. There's another from Siota in Nggela Pile to Toa, though the going is difficult in places. Otherwise travel is by canoe, which you'll probably have to charter.

NGGELA SULE ISLAND
Most of thickly wooded Big Gela's inhabitants live along its northern coast from Rara to the Mboli Passage. There are also a few

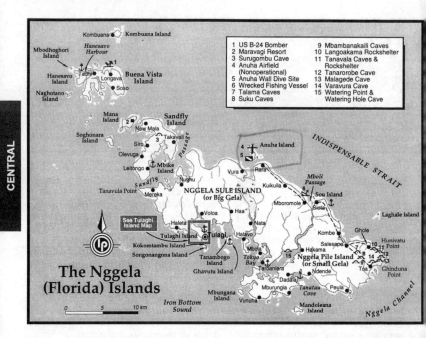

1 US B-24 Bomber
2 Maravagi Resort
3 Surugombu Cave
4 Anuha Airfield
   (Nonoperational)
5 Anuha Wall Dive Site
6 Wrecked Fishing Vessel
7 Talama Caves
8 Suku Caves
9 Mbambanakaili Caves
10 Langoakama Rockshelter
11 Tanavala Caves &
   Rockshelter
12 Tanarorobe Cave
13 Malagede Cave
14 Varavura Cave
15 Watering Point &
   Watering Hole Cave

The Nggela (Florida) Islands

villages on the southern coast, including Halavo, the island's subprovincial headquarters and former Australian WWII seaplane base.

The Japanese destroyer *Kikutsuki* lies half submerged in Tokyo Bay near Mbola. Sunk beside it is its tender. The beached bow section of the US tank-landing ship *LST 325* is about 1.5 km north-east of Taroaniara, its stern submerged. Taroaniara has white, sandy beaches on both its northern and southern sides.

Watering Hole Cave

Villagers can direct you to the water pipe running out from the shore at the bottom of Mboli Passage. Built by US forces in 1943 and used to supply their ships with drinking water, it runs 12 km from an underground stream high inland.

You can follow the pipe up the cliff face to a small cave called Watering Hole Cave.

You will need a powerful torch (flashlight). In a grotto inside are giant stalactites. Beyond a pool is another cave, followed by a larger cavern called the Cathedral, which is alive with bats. It has dripping stalactites and extends 500m to a natural sinkhole through which water cascades from above. In these caves is a rare spider-shaped scorpion whose sting has not yet been analysed, so beware.

Mboromole

About half a km offshore from Mboromole, on the island's east coast, is a very picturesque, small, sand-surrounded, coral-fringed island. Around 1.5 km further out to sea, beside tiny Sou Island, is a large coral bank with a small wrecked fishing vessel at its north-western tip. You can see the sunken vessel's skeleton very clearly from the air, with its bow protruding above the surface.

There's a path along a sandy shore from here to Rara, where canoes can take you to Anuha Island. This well-populated area is extensively planted with crops.

ANUHA ISLAND

Only two km offshore from Nggela Sule is Anuha, which means 'peace' or 'sanctuary' in the Nggela language. This lush 64-hectare island, with white-sand beaches in a deep-blue coral lagoon, was the site of the luxurious *Anuha Island Resort*. The resort was burned down in 1987, allegedly by villagers engaged in a land dispute. There are plans to rebuild it on stilts over the sea, with accommodation in air-conditioned thatched bungalows. Anuha's airfield will reopen once the resort does.

The island is renowned for its scuba sites. The best is Anuha Wall: beside this coral cliff face are huge gorgonia sea fans, sea whips, trumpet shells and black coral. Turtles and manta rays are occasionally seen.

From Anuha you can also make great dives among lobsters and large pelagic fish such as tuna, whaler shark and barracuda. Tanavula Point in Sandfly Passage offers a wall dive plus an unexpected submarine current.

MANA ISLAND

This small island has the recently opened *Maravagi Resort*. There are 12 beds, with more cabins planned. Rooms are leaf-style and have private shower/toilet; lighting is by hurricane lamp. Meals (tasty and substantial) are included in the daily charge of only S$126.50. The Vistors' Bureau should be able to make reservations by radio; otherwise write to Mathias Sake, PO Box 36, Tulagi. Canoe transfers per person are S$50 from Honiara or S$25 from Tulagi.

There's not a great deal to do on the island except relax, though there are snorkelling and scuba-diving spots nearby. A short canoe ride away on Sandfly Island is Olevuga, Mathias' home village. A twenty-minute walk from Olevuga is the **Surugombu Cave**, now occupied by nesting swiftlets, headhunted skulls and ancient hieroglyphics (S$10 custom fee).

BUENA VISTA ISLAND

This island was given its name by the Spanish explorer Gallego because it seemed so fertile. It's 18 km north-west of Nggela Sule and has a long, sandy beach on its southern shore. Extremely clear waters make it ideal for snorkelling and scuba diving, especially on the reef in Hanesavo Harbour.

About 1.5 km north of Longava is a sunken US B-24 bomber from WWII.

NGGELA PILE ISLAND

Also known as Small Gela, this island has a path from Siota to Toa which runs along golden-sand beaches much of the way. Some inland sections of the path are hard to follow, especially near Salesape, and you may need to walk along the beach instead. Three km north, offshore from Ghole, is the tiny, sand-surrounded Laghale Island.

Nggela Pile's Caves

The eastern tip of Small Gela is pockmarked with caves and rockshelters. If you want to see any of them, you'll need a guide and permission from the custom owners at Salesape and Ghole. Accept any restrictions; the owners will want to be sure you don't touch or disturb anything.

Salesape to Toa There's a six-km footpath inland over the hills to Toa, past three groups of caves. The Talama Caves are about two km along the path and 400m to the east of the path. The Suku Caves are one km further on, close to the footpath and on the same side. The Mbambanakaili Caves are one km beyond and about 800m to the west of the path. From there it's only two km to Toa and the sea.

You'll probably find it easier taking a motor canoe from Toa back to Tulagi, rather than pressing on along the often very indistinct paths around Nggela Pile's southeastern coast to Hakama, the island's subprovincial headquarters.

CENTRAL

Ghole to Ghinduna Point If instead you follow the shore between Ghole and Toa, you will find 13 more caverns – six rockshelters and seven caves. The majority of these sites are around one km inland, though five are close to the shore. The most interesting caves are called Varavura, Malagede and Tanarorobe. There is also a rockshelter at Langoakama, and two caves and a rockshelter at Tanavala.

Langoakama Rockshelter is 1.5 km along the shore from Ghole. The three Tanavala sites are at Hunivatu Point, while Tanarorobe Cave is about 1.25 km to its south. You'll find Malagede Cave by crossing a small creek about 150m south of Tanarorobe and then going inland for about 750m. Varavura Cave is inland and one km north-west of Ghinduna Point.

MANDOLEANA & MBUNGANA ISLANDS

Both of these small, attractive islands to the south of Nggela Pile are completely surrounded by sand. In 1880, several of the crew of HMS *Sandfly* were killed on Mandoleana. The US WWII transport *George F Elliott* lies in the depths about three km to the south of Mbungana.

TULAGHI ISLAND

Most of the south-eastern end of Tulaghi Island (pronounced 'too-lar-gie') is occupied by the town of Tulagi (same pronunciation, different spelling). Boat building and the administration of provincial government are its main activities.

The island's largest complex is the National Fisheries Development Tulagi Base. Formerly a fish cannery, it's now a fishing-boat maintenance centre. The Sasape Marine Base II slipway at Tulagi builds and repairs ships up to 300 tonnes, as does the smaller Sasape Marine Base I at Sasape.

History

Tulagi was established as the capital of the Solomons in 1897, four years after the Protectorate was proclaimed, because of its central position in the archipelago and its

deep-water anchorage. By 1910, Burns Philp, the large Pacific trading company, had opened a store, Chinese boat builders and carpenters were at work, and a government hospital was in operation on nearby Tanambogo.

By 1927, 30 of the country's 35 government officials lived at Tulagi, and the island's population numbered 1000. Most Europeans fled in panic and disarray the day before the Japanese invaded the island in May 1942.

Early on 7 August 1942, US forces landed at Blue Beach, recapturing Tulaghi the next day. However, the Japanese were dug in on the tiny nearby islands of Ghavutu and Tanambogo, inside deep, reinforced dugouts and caves. As in similar actions elsewhere, the Japanese refused to surrender, preferring to hide, fight and die in these deep caverns.

Once Tulaghi was secured, US forces operated a PT boat base from the wharf, and a seaplane base at Ghavutu. A number of buildings and relics remain from those times, including several rusty and ungainly pontoons rotting on the island's shore at Sasape and Blue Beach. After the war, Tulagi was too badly damaged to be reconstructed as the national capital, so the honour passed to Honiara.

Orientation

The Cutting, a north-south gash through bare rock, was dug by prewar jailbirds. It leads from Tulaghi Wharf to Bokolonga, the administrative centre, which has a number of Gilbertese settlers.

The town of Tulagi occupies the shoreside area from the main wharf to the east of the Cutting, and north to and including the National Fisheries Developments Tulagi Base. The latter is beside where Tulagi's Chinatown used to stand, though this has now completely disappeared.

Immediately to the west of the Tulaghi Wharf is the Sasape Marine Base II slipway. There's a wrecked trawler close to shore about 300m to the north. Beyond the National Fisheries Developments base are the remains of a WWII Nissen hut.

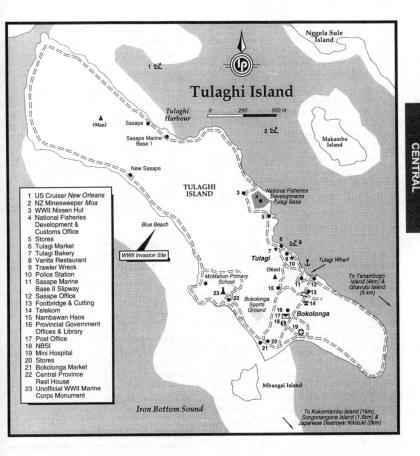

Tulaghi Island

Nggela Sule Island

Tulagi Harbour

0   250   500 m

(94m) Sasape

Makambo Island

Sasape Marine Base 1

New Sasape

TULAGHI ISLAND

National Fisheries Developments Tulagi Base

Blue Beach

WWII Invasion Site

Tulagi (56m)

Tulagi Wharf

To Tanambogo Island (4km) & Ghavutu Island (5 km)

McMahon Primary School

Bokolonga Sports Ground

Bokolonga

Iron Bottom Sound

Mbangai Island

To Kokomtambu Island (1km), Songonangone Island (1.5km) & Japanese Destroyer Kikizuki (2km)

1   US Cruiser *New Orleans*
2   NZ Minesweeper *Moa*
3   WWII Nissen Hut
4   National Fisheries Development & Customs Office
5   Stores
6   Tulagi Market
7   Tulagi Bakery
8   Vanita Restaurant
9   Trawler Wreck
10 Police Station
11 Sasape Marine Base II Slipway
12 Sasape Office
13 Footbridge & Cutting
14 Telekom
15 Nambawan Haos
16 Provincial Government Offices & Library
17 Post Office
18 NBSI
19 Mini Hospital
20 Stores
21 Bokolonga Market
22 Central Province Rest House
23 Unofficial WWII Marine Corps Monument

CENTRAL

Information

Bokolonga has provincial government offices, a post office, an NBSI branch, a library and a small hospital (☎ 32008). The Telekom office (☎ 32185, fax 32180) is south of the Cutting, though there are often problems with phone connections to/from Tulaghi.

Things to See & Do

Dominating the south is Nambawan Haos, where CM Woodford set himself up as first resident commissioner. It's currently in private use. A footbridge leads over the Cutting, and from the path that runs north-south in front of the house magnificent views can be seen.

Behind the Bokolonga sports ground is a very unofficial US marines' WWII memorial. It's the figure of a small, naked woman fashioned in concrete on a slab of natural rock and concealed among thick shrub. You will need local people's help to find it, as there's no obvious footpath to it.

The island lacks attractive beaches, but there's a short stretch of white sand in a small cove about 200m to the south of the large McMahon Primary School, itself about 1.5 km to the north-west of Bokolonga. The shore from there on to New Sasape was the site of the US landings at Blue Beach in August 1942. Now only litter-strewn sand remains. It is a leisurely two-hour walk following the nine-km gravel track around the island. At New Sasape, ask locals to point out the 18th-century gravestone by the path.

The sunken New Zealand minesweeper *Moa* lies 20m down on the sea bed between Sasape and Makambo Island. About 600m north-west is the wreck of *New Orleans*, a US cruiser.

Places to Stay & Eat

The six-room *Central Province Rest House* beside the Bokolonga sports ground has two beds per room and costs S$30 a head a night, including shared washing and kitchen facilities. Bookings are through the provincial government office (☎ 32100, ext 18). Phone in advance as it's often booked out. There are two stores and a market near the sports ground for basic provisions.

The *Vanita Restaurant* (☎ 22246, fax 32186) is in Tulagi and has eight twin-bed rooms at S$80 per room. There is a bar with a pool table and a garden/patio, but no kitchen. The restaurant serves lunch from about S$22 and good dinners for S$28 and up. If you reckon S$18 or more is too much to pay for breakfast, nip next door to the *Tulagi Bakery* (same ownership) for a couple of rolls and eat them in the restaurant with a cup of tea or coffee (S$1.80). There's a tiny market across the road, and several stores nearby for self-catering.

TULAGHI'S SMALL NEIGHBOURS
Makambo Island

In prewar days, Makambo was the British logging company Levers Brothers' national headquarters. It was the Solomons' commercial centre when Tulagi was the country's shipping and administrative base. There's a very rusted vessel beached near the island's south-western end.

Ghavutu Island

The Japanese made a last-ditch stand at Ghavutu and its tiny neighbour Tanambogo, to which it is joined by a narrow causeway. Once the USA began using Ghavutu as a seaplane base, the Japanese bombed it repeatedly. Old and rotting parts of wrecked US warplanes litter the wharf, including rusting Catalina aircraft engines which are now used as bollards. There's a sunken Catalina seaplane eight metres down close to the wharf. Snorkellers can also see the dim underwater shapes of two others in the same area.

The oysters growing on the jetty belong to local islanders. Don't take any without asking permission first.

Kokomtambu Island

This islet is often illuminated by fireflies at night. Close by in 25m of water is the 14,500-tonne armed tanker USS *Kanawa*. Sunk by Japanese bombs, and still leaking oil, its silent anti-aircraft guns point vainly to the surface.

Songonangona Island

Under one km south-east of Songonangona and 18m down is the sunken Japanese destroyer *Kikuzuki*. About 6.5 km to the south-west and in much deeper water is the US destroyer *Barton*.

Savo Island

Savo is a 31-sq-km island lying 14 km north of Guadalcanal. It is an active volcano with a pair of dormant but potentially dangerous craters, one enclosing the other. The island has a number of hot springs and thermal areas containing mud pools.

Savo's 2300 inhabitants speak a Papuan tongue called Savosavo. It's similar to that of the Russells and thought to be older than the languages of most neighbouring islands.

Much of the island is fringed by coconut groves. The continuous beach is mostly grey in colour, with golden sand along the southern side and a light-brown shore in the north-western corner. There's a resident population of megapode birds, and its waters teem with sharks, dolphins and flying fish.

History

Mendaña's expedition saw Savo erupting in April 1568 and called it Sesarga. In 1840 it erupted again, with considerable loss of life. Despite this, Savo was one of the first islands in the Solomons group to be visited by a European trader (1869). At the beginning of the 20th century, before several devastating epidemics seriously reduced numbers, Savo's population was about 4000.

Information

The main clinic is at Panueli and there is another at Kaonggele. The island's sub-provincial headquarters is in Mbonala.

Only some places have a piped water supply, but even in these places the water is often too sulphurous to drink. Wells are still used – their water is often quite warm. Always boil or treat any water before drinking it. There's no electricity.

Custom fees are payable to visit the megapode field and the hot springs; these may be up to S$25 for each site.

Hot Springs & Thermal Areas

Ground temperatures rise to nearly 85°C (185°F), and mud boils in several spots in Savo's centre. Thermal sites ring the main crater. The largest is Fisher Voghala, churning out hot, sulphurous water day and night. Nearby Mbiti Voghala is an area of boiling mud. Voghala has spectacular mud pools and geysers, and extends 600m southwards along the Poghorovuraghala River.

At Mbokiaka the Tanginakula River has several sectors which flow alternately warm and cool, making it a favourite haunt of freshwater prawns. Ask the villagers for permission before catching any. Two km from the large village of Kaonggele is Vutusuala. This large hot-spring site has boiling water and heated ground.

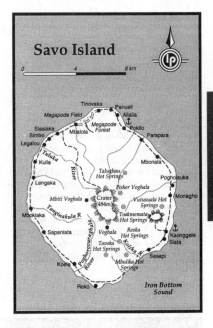

CENTRAL

The three hot springs near Sesepi, called Reoka, Mbulika and Tavoka, are all small sites, yet hot enough to make the nearby Kolika River run warm. The ground is hot underneath but only a limited amount of water boils up. The two other hot-spring sites, at Talughau and Toakomata, are hard to reach and concealed by thick bush.

Organised Tours

Tour Solomons of Honiara does a full-day trip for S$400 a head (children S$200). It includes lunch at Tambea Resort in west Guadalcanal; the hot springs and megapodes are visited in the morning. Tambea does its own Savo tour for S$150 per person, starting early and including breakfast at Legalou. You can also arrange trips to Savo through J&L Carriers & Escorted Tours (☎ 20626), Room 29 in Honiara's NPF Plaza.

CENTRAL

Places to Stay & Eat

The *Legalou Nature Site Village* is six km south-west of Mbalola. There are two rooms, both have four beds, and the price is S$30 per person. Meals are available. Villagers may be able to offer very informal accommodation elsewhere on the island.

Getting There & Away

Canoes are the only option. They travel regularly between Mbalola and Vila (north-western Guadalcanal). A shared ride is about S$15 and takes 45 to 60 minutes, depending on the weather. You should also be able to find a ride from Honiara: to Mbalola or Kaonggele is about S$25 and takes 1¼ hours or more. Enquire beside the Point Cruz Yacht Club or at the Central Market. If you can't hook into a shared ride, taking an organised tour may not work out much more expensive than chartering – it'll certainly be easier.

There are anchorages at Kaonggele and Alialia (both are exposed to easterly winds).

Getting Around

There's a 23-km route around the island. The northern half is reasonable and can be cycled; that would be hard going in the south, and impossible through the heavy undergrowth from Sesepi to Reko. You will need to walk along the beach from Sapaniata to Koela.

MBALOLA

The megapode field is about half a km north-east of Mbalola and extends for around 400m along the beach. Halfway between the megapode field and Mbalola is the megapode forest. During the day you can hear the birds calling and can sometimes see them perched high up in trees.

Nearby is **Tinovaka**. The USA had a gun base here in WWII to close off the northern approaches to Iron Bottom Sound. There are a few remains, including a complex of concrete pads and spars where the batteries once were.

Megapode Birds

Even by tropical standards, this chicken-sized bird, with a yellow beak and stocky, orange legs, is an oddity. Known in Pijin as *skrab dak* or *scrab faol*, they are usually dark-brown in colour.

Megapodes dig an unusually deep hole in the warm volcanic sand for their eggs. After a long incubation period of eight to nine weeks, the young hatches fully feathered and fully developed, possibly because of the very high proportion of yolk within the white or pinky-brown eggs. Once the chick has pecked its way out of its shell, it scratches its way upwards through the soft sand to the surface. The young bird can run immediately and fly shortly afterwards and doesn't need maternal care.

Megapodes have an attractive two-tone song which you can hear throughout the day around Mbalola. The megapode field is divided into small family plots, separated by fences, or lines, of young yellow hibiscus trees, on which the megapode birds roost prior to laying their eggs.

Villagers clear the warm, grey volcanic soil, leaving dozens of shallow depressions in each family plot. These are the mega-podes' hatcheries. From about 3 am nightly throughout the year, hundreds of female birds come to the megapode field. They dig down to about 90 cm, where the temperature (33°C) is ideal to incubate their eggs. This subterranean heat is generated by a nearby underwater volcanic fissure.

The megapodes are still running around at 9 am but fly off once the villagers come to harvest the eggs, which are eaten as custom food. Each sells for about S$1.40 on Savo and S$2 in Honiara. Unfortunately, megapode numbers are much lower than a few years back, so think twice before buying these eggs. ■

The megapode bird is a ground-dwelling bird that does not hatch its own egg.

KAONGGELE

The easiest access to the Vutusuala hot springs is from this village. You need to ask here for permission to go to the springs, and it is here that you should pay the custom fee and acquire a guide. A footpath from Kaonggele follows the course of a small, warm-water creek part of the way to Vutusuala, where boiling steam billows out of the ground. Villagers heat their food in holes in the adjacent earth, taking two to three hours to cook a full meal.

The Russell Islands

There are two main islands in the Russells group, Pavuvu and Mbanika, plus 70 smaller islets, mainly to their north and east. Occasionally also known simply as Cape Marsh, this group's pre-European name was Laube. It's 210 sq km in size, with about 5000 residents, a third of whom are Tikopians or Rennellese imported to work in the local plantations or to tend cattle. There's also a sizeable number of Malaitans and Gilbertese. Many children and young adults in the Russells have blonde or brown hair.

History

Captain Ball was the first European explorer to see these islands, sighting them in 1790. In the late 19th century, warriors from Savo and New Georgia's Roviana Lagoon made regular head-hunting forays to the Russells.

The Americans made unopposed landings on both Pavuvu and Mbanika in February 1943. Despite repeated air-raids, the US soon built two large airfields on Mbanika. Huge quantities of supplies were stockpiled, most of which were dumped in the sea at the end of the war.

This abandoned war material has become an underwater mecca for divers. In 1988 a stockpile of US mustard-gas shells was found locally. At first the US refused to acknowledge responsibility, but it finally disposed of them in early 1991.

Information

There are clinics at Yandina on Mbanika and at Pepesala on Pavuvu.

Much of the Russells is owned by Russell Islands Plantation Estates Ltd (RIPEL) and you are expected to have somewhere to stay before you arrive. This applies to Solomon Islanders as much as to foreigners. If you have a personal invitation, there's no problem. Otherwise, contact RIPEL first, via the Honiara office (☎ 22528, fax 23494), or the Yandina head office (☎ 29039, fax 21785), where the company rest house is located.

Dive Sites

Live-aboard dive boats such as the MV *Solomon Sea* and MV *Bilikiki* do regular trips around the Russells from Honiara.

The two inlets on either side of Lever Point, called Rokovan Bay and Meomavaua Bay respectively, are excellent dive sites. A vast quantity of war relics lie in only 24m of water. Much of it is now coral encrusted and the home of colourful fish.

Wernham Cove still has a number of PT-boat mooring points. Sponges and large sea fans have converted these into a submarine woodland. Neatly lined up nearby and 36m

CENTRAL

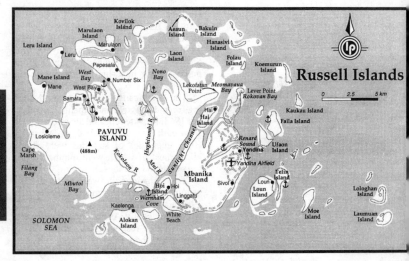

down are several abandoned wartime vehicles.

Two of the Russells' most exciting dives are through submarine caverns. People who've dived them say they are at their most impressive when illuminated by the noonday sun.

Reef growth is prolific, especially around Kovilok, Aeaun, Hanasivi, Folau and Koemurun islands to the north of the main islands. Several small islets are fringed with sand and have attractive coral gardens, especially Lologhan and Laumuan islands to the south-east of Mbanika.

Getting There & Away
Air Yandina is serviced from Honiara by Solomon Airlines on Wednesday and Saturday and by Western Pacific on Monday and Friday; both charge S$95. The Solomon Airlines agent (☎ 21779) in RIPEL's Yandina offices can arrange transport to/from the town.

Sea Yandina is the first stop out from Honiara for the Gizo-bound passenger boats; on either *Iuminao* or *Ramos I* the economy fare is S$36. Yandina-Gizo is slightly cheaper on *Ramos I* (S$66).

Yandina is one of the Solomons' main deep-water ports and has customs facilities but no immigration. Crews need prior permission before stopping at Yandina's wharf though it's usually granted quite readily for brief visits. There are wharves or jetties at Yandina, Nukufero and Telin Island, and other anchorages at Wernham Cove, Renard Sound, Nono Bay, West Bay, Samata and Faila Island.

Getting Around
There are 48 km of roads and tracks on Mbanika and Pavuvu. The longest stretch is between Lever Point and White Beach on Mbanika. Hitch a ride with any plantation vehicles going your way.

Visits to some of the two main islands' small, sandy island neighbours are restricted, so enquire before making plans to charter a canoe. Remember to arrange your trip back with the driver.

To some destinations you may be able to hitch a lift on one of RIPEL's canoes or barges.

HOLGER LEUE

SIMON FOALE

SIMON FOALE

Top: Islands in Blackett Strait, Western Province
Middle: Haroro village, Nughulau Island off Nggela Sule Island, Central Province
Bottom: Kangava Bay, Rennell Island, Rennell & Bellona Province

SIMON FOALE

SIMON FOALE

Top: Rugged southern coastline of Sandfly Island, Nggela Islands, Central Province
Bottom: Sunset at Sandfly Island, Nggela Islands, Central Province

PAVUVU ISLAND

The largest island of the Russells group, Pavuvu is almost 17 km across. It's thick with coconut palms, especially around West Bay and the Tikopian settlement of Nukufero. There are extensive reefs to the north and many small, sandy islands within them. Some have large coconut plantations, especially Marulaon Island. Pavuvu has been the site of wholesale logging by Maving Brothers, a Malaysian company, despite strong local opposition.

MBANIKA ISLAND

Separating Mbanika from Pavuvu are the deep waters of the Sunlight Channel. Mbanika is covered with coconut palms, as are its eastern neighbours, Loun, Ufaon, Faila and Telin islands. The coconut palms often grow right down to the water's edge.

Yandina

Yandina, on Mbanika Island's east coast, is the Russells' subprovincial headquarters and RIPEL's company town. Its wharf and Quonset huts (now used as copra sheds), and the group's large network of roads, were all built by the US army during WWII.

RIPEL's *guest house* is behind the company's offices, 500m from the wharf.

The nightly charge is S$35 per person, and there's a kitchen. Reservations should be made in advance. Guests can use the bar, library, tennis courts and swimming pool at the company's Mbanika Club.

There's good-quality fresh beef available for sale in Yandina, and a market selling fish, vegetables, fruit and other produce.

White Beach & Wernham Cove

White Beach is the best beach in the area and is also where villagers often barter shells to visitors. The nearby inlet of Wernham Cove was a small, temporary PT-boat base in 1943, and there are still some large wartime guns close by.

John F Kennedy served here before going on to Rendova, though the main patrol boat base in the Russells was on Hoi Island, immediately opposite.

BAKUIN ISLAND

Nicknamed Elephant Island, this island has a beach and a reef offers excellent fishing. It's a 20-minute canoe ride from Yandina. A resort is planned, but in the meantime the owner is happy for people to visit free of charge. Contact Alex Bartlett (☎ 22151) in Honiara.

CENTRAL

Western Province

The Western Province is an essential stop on any itinerary. Its combination of pristine lagoons, prime dive sites and lush forests have immense appeal to visitors. The many lagoons are a visual delight from the air. The combination of dark greens (tree-covered islands), white strips (sandbars and beaches), light blues (coral-bearing shallows) and dark blues (deeper seas) is breathtaking.

Formerly the largest administrative area in the Solomons, Western Province was reduced to 5279 sq km in size when Choiseul and Wagina departed to form a new province in late 1991. The region is often colloquially called the West, with its people describing themselves as westerners.

Western Province's speciality during the 19th century was head-hunting, so for self-protection most people lived on easily defended ridges. Evidence of abandoned inland settlements, such as standing stones, defensive walls and house foundations, can be found throughout the area. The interior has now reverted to thick forest, with most cultivation in shoreside villages cooled by fresh breezes.

In 1978, talk of a Western Solomons secession from the newly created Solomon Islands led to a local boycott of the country's Independence celebrations. Westerners have since been prominent in subsequent Solomons governments, believing their interests are now better protected by unity than division. However, in 1996 secessionist murmurings were given new impetus through dissatisfaction with the central government's legislation for regional Area Assemblies.

Western Province's economy relies on logging, plantations and fishing. The province is also the hub of tourism in the Solomons. Local landowners are currently faced with a choice between making a quick buck from wholesale, unsustainable logging

WESTERN

HIGHLIGHTS

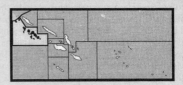

- Magnificent aerial views of verdant islands and azure lagoons
- Excellent diving and snorkelling at a variety of sites, including coral reefs and WWII wrecks
- Gizo, the provincial capital and a diving and excursions centre
- Kolombangara Island, an archetypal conical volcano with a crater rim 1770m high
- Megapode birds and skull shrines on Simbo, one of the first islands to welcome foreigners
- The pink and blue orchids at Munda and the crocodile farm at Roviana Lagoon
- Marovo Lagoon, a proposed world heritage site with eco-tourism villages and skilled wood-carvers
- Custom dances at Mbangopingo and bamboo panpipe bands

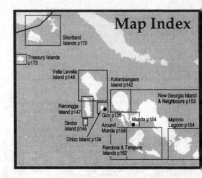

Map Index

Shortland Islands p170
Treasury Islands p173
Vella Lavella Island p149
Kolombangara Island p142
New Georgia Island & Neighbours p153
Ranongga Island p147
Gizo p136
Munda p164
Marovo Lagoon p164
Simbo Island p145
Around Munda p158
Ghizo Island p134
Rendova & Tetepare Islands p162

130

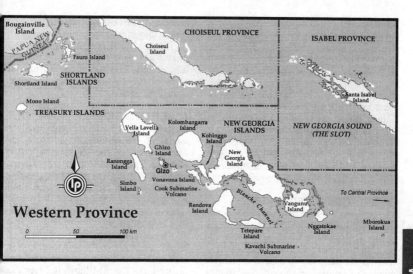

...r preserving the environment and making a sustainable return from eco-tourism. Happily, some have opted for the latter course, but logging concessions – many of which are yet to be taken up – have still been issued for vast tracts of forest.

The logging lobby remains extremely strong, and there will be many battles fought over this natural resource in the coming years.

POPULATION & PEOPLE

Western Province has 57,000 people. Most chiefs are male, but some are female, particularly in Vella Lavella.

Intermarriage with expatriate traders has been common, as there has been continuous European contact in this province longer than elsewhere in the country.

Gilbertese Resettlement

Over 2500 Micronesian people from what is now Kiribati – formerly the Gilbert Islands – were resettled in the Solomons between 1955 and 1964. Their home islands had become seriously overcrowded and were frequently devastated by drought. The main Gilbertese settlements in the province are in Ghizo and Shortland.

The larger Gilbertese villages have a *maneaba*, or village meeting house, where dances, marriages, feasts, communal sing-songs and village meetings are held.

ARTS

Bamboo panpipe bands are popular in the New Georgia and Shortland groups. Performances can be seen at festivals and at the Gizo Hotel.

Nguzunguzus were originally figureheads on war canoes and nowadays make distinctive souvenirs. They are made throughout the province.

SOCIETY & CONDUCT
Shell Money

Clam-shell money worn around the neck used to be a mark of status in the New Georgia group, but the custom is now rare. This traditional currency is made of pure-white clam-shell rings between 10 and 25 cm across. The smaller pieces have a higher value, while the most prized items bear traces of yellow.

Mbaravas

A *mbarava* was a Western Province symbol of chiefly authority, and held such mystique that no chief could claim authority without one. Mbaravas were white clam-shell carvings, either shaped like a lattice-work plaque and depicting human figures, or moulded into a hollow ring with a bird or human motif above. The carvings were made using stone drills and fibre saws.

Mbaravas were deliberately fractured at a chief's death to signify that his life was finished, and then placed by his graveside. Consequently, few have survived intact.

ORIENTATION & INFORMATION

The majority of Western Province's population and land area is in the New Georgia group. This consists of 12 large and well-populated islands – of which New Georgia itself is the largest – plus a considerable number of smaller neighbours. The islands extend diagonally from Vella Lavella and Simbo south-eastwards past Nggatokae and Tetepare to isolated Mborokua.

The region's three large lagoons are often said to be among the Pacific's most beautiful spots. The Roviana and Marovo lagoons hug New Georgia's coast, while Vonavona Lagoon separates Vonavona from neighbouring Kohinggo.

Submarine volcanoes in the region have occasionally erupted from the sea. Some have made regular appearances, others have rapidly sunk into permanent obscurity.

In 1942, the New Georgia Sound between the island group and Santa Isabel was a favourite corridor for the Japanese Navy. US forces called it the Slot and the nickname is commonly used today.

The influence of the church and missions in the province is clear from the biblical names of some of the New Georgia group's villages. Bethany, Jericho, Nazareth, Nineveh, Paradise and Sidon are just a few examples.

Custom land in the New Georgia Islands differs from place to place. Skulls and sacred objects are cited as evidence of continued occupation. Land disputes are fre-

quent and may be over parcels of empty ground unoccupied for over 60 years.

The rest of the province is made up of smaller islands in the Shortlands and Treasury groups. Located at the westernmost point of the Solomons, they are rarely visited by tourists.

ACCOMMODATION

Western Province offers a range of accommodation options markedly lacking anywhere else in the Solomons outside Honiara. These encompass international-quality hotels in Gizo and Munda, isolated island resorts in the lagoons, and simple leaf houses. Communication is generally good in the area, so making advance bookings is usually easy.

Staying at missions is a possibility in the remote areas, but you'll need to arrange this well in advance. Enquire at the church head quarters: the United Church in Munda and the Roman Catholic Church in Gizo. If they accept your request, they'll send all the necessary radio messages. Missions are often very welcoming, but contributions toward their expenses should always be made.

THINGS TO BUY

Western Province is home to the Solomons' most prolific woodworkers. Even though carvers now cater mainly to European taste, their carvings still show exceptional skill.

Nguzunguzus vary in size, price and quality. The smallest and simplest start at around S$35, while larger, more elaborate versions may be anything between S$200 and S$600. Carvings are sold at some hotels, or carvers may approach you in the street. If buying direct and the price seems too high, ask for a 'second price'.

Other carvings include masks, sharks, dolphins, turtles, canoes and paper knives made from kerosene wood or black ebony. They are often inlaid with pearly nautilus shell. Forehead discs called *kapkaps* are also produced. Thin carved strips of turtle carapace are placed over a circular piece of clam shell to produce a most distinctive facial ornament.

Domestic products such as pandanus sleeping mats are mainly made by Gilbertese women. These two-metre long brown mats are always sturdy and long lasting, yet only cost about S$20.

GETTING THERE & AWAY

Air

The major settlements are well serviced by aircraft. Gizo – the provincial capital – has several flights per day. There are three airfields on New Georgia Island, two on Kolombangara and Vella Lavella, and one each on Shortland, the Treasuries, Ramata, Vangunu and Nggatokae.

Sea

Wings Shipping's vessel the *Iuminao* makes a twice-weekly return journey through the New Georgia Islands to Gizo. It departs Honiara on Sunday at 10 am and Wednesday at 3 pm. Western ports visited en route are Mbili Passage near Nggatokae, Gasini, Chea and Patutiva in the Marovo Lagoon, Viru Harbour, Ughele on Rendova, Munda and Noro in New Georgia and Ringgi in Kolombangara. Plan to do at least part of your trip to/from the province by boat (certainly the Marovo Lagoon). It's a fantastic journey and takes 28 hours or more.

Malaita Shipping's *Ramos I* leaves Honiara for the Western ports at about 7 pm every second Saturday, visiting the same destinations. KHY's MV *Hiliboe* travels between Honiara and Gizo via New Georgia's Roviana Lagoon. The province owns the *Western Queen* which has lots of cabins and usually does the Honiara-Gizo trip, but it breaks down regularly, and is likely to be sold. National Shipping plans to start services to the Western Province in 1997. Local stores often act as booking agents for ships. If there's no agent, just pay on board.

GETTING AROUND

As elsewhere in the Solomons, to get outside the main shipping routes you have to rely on canoes, either charters or shared rides. Ask locals where canoes are berthed.

Ghizo Island

Once called Guizo and Injo, Ghizo is 11 km long and about five km wide. The total land area is 37 sq km, with Maringe Hill (180m) the highest point. Ghizo is often humid inland and in certain months it seems to rain every afternoon.

Ghizo's population is about 6000. Its main town, Gizo (same pronunciation, different spelling), is the second largest in the Solomons, with around 4500 people.

Diving and snorkelling fans are well served here. War wrecks and coral gardens provide some of the Solomons' best dive sites.

History

The first foreigners to see Ghizo were the Americans Read and Dale from their ship the *Alliance* in November 1787. In 1869 the first outsiders took up residence on Ghizo, finding this island much more peaceful than many of its neighbours. Trading contacts expanded, so in 1899 the government's second station in the Solomons opened at Gizo to administer the western half of the Protectorate.

Ghizo Island suffered badly during the 1930s Depression. There was a great deal of resentment among villagers over poor wages when copra prices declined to a quarter of their 1920s level. Then, in WWII, the Japanese used the town of Gizo as a barge-repair base. Although they withdrew before the town was liberated by US marines, it was severely damaged by wartime bombing.

Information

There's a large hospital (☎ 60224) at Gizo. Gizo has water-supply problems causing daily restrictions despite frequent deluges of tropical rain. Most accommodation places have their own water tanks to top up supplies; check this out before you book. A new plant should be providing drinkable water in Gizo from 1997.

WESTERN

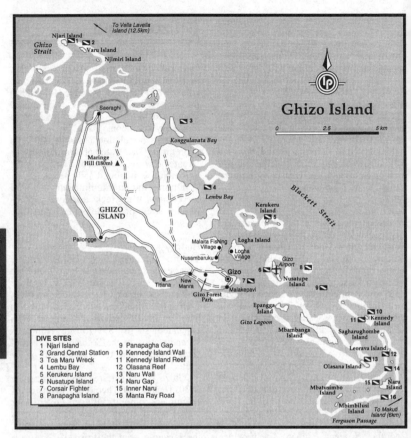

Ghizo Island

0   2.5   5 km

DIVE SITES
1 Njari Island	9 Panapagha Gap
2 Grand Central Station	10 Kennedy Island Wall
3 Toa Maru Wreck	11 Kennedy Island Reef
4 Lembu Bay	12 Olasana Reef
5 Kerukeru Island	13 Naru Wall
6 Nusatupe Island	14 Naru Gap
7 Corsair Fighter	15 Inner Naru
8 Panapagha Island	16 Manta Ray Road

WESTERN

Getting There & Away

Air Gizo's airfield is on Nusatupe Island and receives more flights than anywhere except Honiara. It has three Solomon Airlines flights a day to Honiara (S$280), which usually call at Munda (S$65) and sometimes Seghe (S$115). The flight from Gizo to Choiseul Bay (S$140) is daily except Tuesday. Flights from Gizo to Ballalae (S$140) depart on Wednesday and Thursday. Ramata (S$85) is visited on Monday and Thursday. Gizo also has Solomon Airlines connections to Ringi

Cove (S$55) and Barakoma (S$55) on Monday, Mono (S$140) and Viru Harbour (S$115) on Tuesday and Kagau (S$115) on Wednesday.

Western Pacific Airlines connects Gizo to Ramata (S$85) on Sunday, Kagau (S$110) on Monday and Friday, Munda (S$65) on Monday, Ringi Cove (S$55) and Geva (S$90) on Wednesday and Choiseul (S$140) on Friday.

Sea The *Iuminao* arrives from Honiara at 1.30 pm on Monday and 10 pm on Thursday. The return journey commences about an hour later. The Gizo Hotel is a ticket agent. The one-way fare costs S$79 in economy, or S$105 in 1st class and S$143 in a cabin. The fortnightly *Ramos I* arrives at about 10 pm on Sunday, departing for Honiara at 4 am on Monday. Gizo to Chea in the Marovo Lagoon costs S$47/75/109 on the *Iuminao*.

Smaller Gizo-based boats tour the region on cargo runs, but to no set schedule. *Matari* and *Wataro* sometimes go to Choiseul, and *Parama* goes to Shortlands. The *Ozama Twomey* visits Choiseul, Vella Lavella and Ranongga, and *Ferguson Express* goes to Kolombangara and Vella Lavella.

The shipping department (☎ 60250) in the provincial government offices may be able to tell you what's going where.

Gizo's daily market guarantees regular motor-canoe traffic between neighbouring islands – just ask around near the canoes. Friday is usually the best day for finding shared rides to other islands. The provincial fisheries (☎ 60107) sometimes has canoes available for charter: the daily rate is S$70 for the boat, driver and engine.

Getting Around

The Airport Motor canoes meet flights, charging S$10 each way between Nusatupe and Gizo.

Bus & Truck You can walk along the beach from Gizo to New Manra. Beyond there you'll need to use the road. The only way to Saeraghi at Ghizo's north-western tip is to take a tour bus, or hitch a ride from a passing truck. Passenger trucks go from Gizo market to Titiana, several times a day.

GIZO

You will see Gizo's best aspect on arrival by motor canoe from Nusatupe. Small copra boats line the wharf, with poincianas and coconut trees forming a backdrop. The town's waterfront covers a compact one km along Middenway Rd. This highway is named after the district officer for the western Solomons who was resident here

for part of the 1920s. Above and behind the harbour are residential areas, most of them with spectacular views.

Population & People

A large number of Gilbertese moved to Ghizo in the mid-1950s once their home islands in Kiribati became overcrowded. Many of these newly settled Micronesians, like the Chinese community, work in local shops and are active members of the town's business community.

Information

Tourist information is available from the Ministry of Culture & Tourism (☎ 60251, fax 60154, PO Box 36), Middenway Rd. It's hard work getting anything useful out of them, but this should improve as staff get more experienced. Opening hours are weekdays from 8 am to 4.30 pm, and sometimes also Saturday morning. The police station (☎ 60111) is opposite.

The Immigration Office (☎ 60214) is near the Catholic Church. Branches of the ANZ Bank and NBSI are on Middenway Rd, as is Telekom (☎ 60127, fax 60128). The small public library is across from the football field, and is open weekdays from 9 am to 1 pm and 2 to 4.30 pm. The post office is by the market.

Communications Service messages can be sent via SIBC's Radio Happy Lagoon (☎ 60160). The Roman Catholic Church maintains regular radio contact with several missions around the province. If you want to ask to stay at a mission, enquire at the priest's house near the church.

Lookouts

Near Paradise Lodge, breaks in the trees and tall grass allow views of Gizo Harbour and nearby Logha Island, with Kolombangara in the distance. Perhaps even better is the view of Nusatupe Island, with Kolombangara looming behind, seen from the bend in the turn off for Phoebe's Rest House. A similar perspective can be gained from further up Timpala Rd. Also on

WESTERN

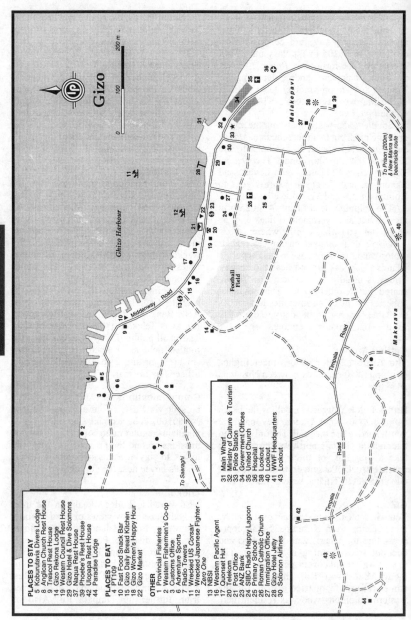

Gizo

PLACES TO STAY
5 Koburutavia Divers Lodge
8 Anglican Church Rest House
9 Trescol Rest House
14 Gizo Rekona Lodge
16 Western Council Rest House
29 Gizo Hotel & Dive Solomons
37 Naqua Rest House
39 Phoebe's Rest House
42 Ulopapa Rest House
44 Paradise Lodge

PLACES TO EAT
4 PT109
10 Fast Food Snack Bar
15 Gizo Daily Bread Kitchen
18 Gizo Women's Happy Hour
22 Gizo Market

OTHER
1 Provincial Fisheries
2 Western Fishermen's Co-op
3 Customs Office
6 Adventure Sports
7 Radio Towers
11 Wrecked US Corsair
12 Wrecked Japanese Fighter -
    Zero One
13 NBSI
16 Western Pacific Agent
17 Quonset Hut
20 Telekom
21 Post Office
23 ANZ Bank
24 SIBC Radio Happy Lagoon
25 Primary School
26 Roman Catholic Church
27 Immigration Office
28 Gizo Hotel Jetty
30 Solomon Airlines
31 Main Wharf
32 Ministry of Culture & Tourism
33 Police Station
34 Government Offices
35 United Church
36 Hospital
38 Lookout
40 Lookout
41 WWF Headquarters
43 Lookout

Timpala Rd, the south-eastern panorama from above the prison is excellent, encompassing tiny islets, surf breaking on the reefs of Gizo Lagoon, and Vonavona and Rendova beyond.

Monuments

There are two monuments in front of the police station. One monument is to Captain Ferguson of the *Ripple*, who used to trade between New Georgia and Shortland, but was killed in 1880 on Bougainville. Ferguson was such a popular figure that the Shortlands' Chief Gorai avenged him by burning the village where Ferguson was murdered. Another monument commemorates Captain Woodhouse, who traded in these waters between 1876 and 1892, dying in Gizo in 1906.

Malakepavi

This friendly suburb stretches from the hospital to the jail. At low tide you will see many of its residents combing the onshore reef for shellfish. **New Manra** is 2.5 km beyond, along the shoreside. This small fishing village was the first Gilbertese resettlement site in the Solomons. The beach route is much cooler than the walk along the inland road, although the latter does take you past the **Gizo Forest Park**, 1.5 km out of town.

This is a Forestry project to identify the best trees for future reforestation programmes. Paths are overgrown and you'll need the explanatory booklet from the tourist office to get much out of a visit.

Activities

Gizo has two outfits that organise diving trips and other excursions. **Diving** is the main activity, but both will be prepared to do almost anything if there's the demand, including combining dives with land-based sightseeing. On request, they'll even go as far afield as Choiseul or the Shortlands Islands. For diving, there's little to choose between them – both have enthusiastic and knowledgeable dive instructors. If you've pre-booked, make sure you're picked up by the correct company (there have been reports of customers being poached at the airport). Note that diving prices are in Australian dollars.

Adventure Sports (☎ 60253, fax 60297, PO Box 21), at the western end of Middenway Rd, is the longest established business; Dive Solomons (☎ 60199, fax 60137, PO Box 120) is conveniently located in the Gizo Hotel. Both charge A$45 for a one-tank dive and A$85 for an introductory resort course for novices. Dive Solomons has slightly lower prices for a two-dive trip including equipment (A$100), full open-water certification (A$350), and **snorkelling** trips (A$25/14 with/without equipment). For information on dive sites, see the Ghizo Island Dive Sites section.

Fishing trips can be arranged by both companies, and they can tell you about sailing boat charters. Dive Solomons has kayaks for hire. Dive Solomons' regular outings include visits to Ghizo Island's Saeraghi village (S$70 per person), Skull Island in the Vonavona Lagoon (S$200 per person), Kolombangara Island for the Ringi Cove waterfall tour (S$195 per person) and trips to Ranongga Island to see the stone carvers (S$250 per person).

Adventure Sports can undertake similar excursions; prices depend on the number of people going so you may be able to get a cheaper deal. A trip to Simbo Island, for example, could be as low as S$160 per person, plus custom fees. Wilson Hisu, a local character, takes people on **bush-walks** up Voruku Hill. This costs S$35 per person through Adventure Sports, including refreshments and transfers to/from Titiana.

Places to Stay

At the bottom end of the scale, avoid the *Western Council Rest House*, which charges S$3 for a bunk in a four-bed dorm. There's no bedding, mattresses, fans, water or locks, and the place is filthy.

The cheapest available accommodation is provided by *Anglican Church Rest House* (☎ 60159, PO Box 93). For S$25 you get a bed with a thin mattress in a simple one-to-

WESTERN

three bed room. There's a verandah and basic kitchen facilities.

One of the best budget deals is *Gizo Rekona Lodge* (☎ 60296, PO Box 91). Family-run and newly opened in October 1996, it's spick and span throughout. There's a kitchen and good views from the balcony. Four double rooms have good beds and a fan; price is S$35 per bed. It's conveniently central, accessible by footpath from the western side of the football pitch.

Almost as good but a little out of the way is *Ulopapa Rest House* (☎ 60289, PO Box 126), also known as Noah's after the owner. The charge is S$35 per bed in doubles or triples with fan, and there's a kitchen.

The convenient *Naqua Rest House* (☎ 60012, PO Box 127) charges the same as Ulopapa. Rooms have one to five beds with thin mattresses, and the walls are thin, but there's a nice kitchen and balcony (good view), and a tiny store.

Along the road *Phoebe's Rest House* (☎ 60336, PO Box 61) has four double rooms, again for S$35 per bed. There are cooking and laundry facilities, and good balcony views. It looks scruffy from the outside, but the owner is very friendly and the lounge has interesting knick-knacks.

Trescol Rest House (☎ 60090, PO Box 1), Middenway Rd, has a kitchen and beds for S$38.50, but the rooms aren't as good as in the places mentioned above. Nearby is *Koburutavia Divers Lodge* (☎ 60257, PO Box 50). It charges A$20 per bed (kitchen facilities available) but doesn't offer anything extra than the S$35 places, except a location by the water.

The friendly *Paradise Lodge* (☎ 60021, PO Box 60) has a fine ocean view. Downstairs are backpacker rooms with beds for S$38.50, and a kitchen. Rooms upstairs have private shower and toilet and smarter fittings, plus tea/coffee making facilities. The smaller rooms sleep two people and cost S$143, the larger ones sleep three or four and cost S$286. Meals are served. Staff normally drive people to/from town, otherwise it's a long walk.

The top choice is the *Gizo Hotel* (☎ 60199, fax 60137, PO Box 30), beside the harbour, which offers a range of rooms and prices, all with own shower/toilet, fan, telephone and tea/coffee-making facilities. Backpackers who dive with Dive Solomons can use dorm-style quad rooms for S$55 per bed. Standard singles/doubles are S$151/197 a night; air-con rooms start at S$260/320. The hotel has a restaurant, bar and other facilities on the premises.

Places to Eat

The *Gizo Market* operates beside the harbour daily except Sunday. There are always plenty of fish, fruit and vegetables for sale, or look out for tasty crepes for S$1 each. The *Western Fishermen's Co-op* sells fresh fish on weekdays and Saturday morning.

There's fresh bread daily at the *Gizo Daily Bread Kitchen*. The *Fast Food Snack Bar* does takeaway snacks only, and is open weekdays from 9 am to 5 pm.

The *Gizo Women's Happy Hour* is run by local women. It's the white hut by the market and is open for lunch weekdays, and some Saturdays. Two tasty choices are on offer for S$8 each.

Trescol Island Restaurant, part of the Trescol Rest House, recently underwent extensive renovations and serves local, Western and Chinese food for around S$6 to S$15.

The following three hotel restaurants serve good food to a similar standard and are all licensed for alcohol. *PT109*, part of the Koburutavia Divers Lodge, occupies a pleasant site by the water and is open for all three meals. Breakfast (from S$11) is good. There are usually two evening choices: for around S$33 you get three courses (tea or coffee is included if you ask for it). Take your shoes off by the door.

The *Paradise Lodge Restaurant* serves pre-ordered meals. Prices start at S$13.20 for breakfast, S$22 for lunch and S$35 for dinner. On Sunday night there's a buffet for S$44.

The *Gizo Hotel Restaurant* is open for

ll meals in a large leaf-style building. Breakfasts are variable, but there's a good choice of palatable evening dishes from about S$30. It puts on free shows for diners: Monday features Gizo singers/musicians, Wednesday it's a bamboo panpipe band, and Friday (which is also barbecue night for S$45) it's Gilbertese singers/dancers. You can watch the performances even if you're only having a drink.

Entertainment

The bar at the Gizo Hotel is popular with the town's expats, who congregate there from 4 pm. There's a disco every second weekend.

Video films are shown in the Quonset Hut which also houses a store. Screenings take place daily at noon and at 7 pm. Adults pay S$2, children S$1.50.

Things to Buy

Carvers often gather around hotels, especially the Gizo Hotel. Adventure Sports has carvings and souvenirs for sale. Plenty of shops stock film, but nobody sells slide film on a regular basis. Always check the expiry date.

AROUND GIZO

The main road out of Gizo skirts the shore to Saeraghi at the island's north-western end. The first stretch is through rainforest and can be very humid.

All distances are from Gizo's main wharf by road unless otherwise specified.

Nusambaruku

- 1 km by canoe

This village is clearly visible across the water from Gizo, and has several houses raised on stilts above the sea. About one km further on is the Malaita fishing village, populated by Malaitan settlers.

Although a long track connects Nusambaruku and the Malaita fishing village, it's much quicker to travel between the two by motor canoe. Once you get to either place you should ask the villagers' permission to land, and tell them what you're doing.

Titiana

- 4 km

Ghizo's main Gilbertese village is often pronounced 'sisiana'. In its centre is a large maneaba. About 500 Micronesians came to Titiana and New Manra between 1955 and 1962. They were from drought-stricken Manra Island in eastern Kiribati.

Pailongge

- 6 km

Pronounced 'pye-long-y', this neat, shore-side Melanesian village's two main features are friendliness and 2.5m surf. Surfers are welcome as long as they act respectfully. Unfortunately, in the past some people have not done so, causing embarrassment to villagers and making them wary of visitors.

Saeraghi

- 11 km

The road runs parallel to golden, sandy beaches, which are completely empty. Immediately across the water is Ranongga.

Saeraghi has a protecting reef with plenty of coral and small, colourful fish. The reef system spreads out to around three km from shore, and encloses several sand-surrounded islands. Saeraghi also has one of the Solomons' most beautiful beaches, about half a km before the village begins.

Saeraghi people are very friendly and will greet visitors with displays of seashells for sale. Some of these are excellent value, such as large cowries for S$1. (Although customs may not allow you to bring them home.) There's a small custom fee for visiting both the beach and the village.

Logha Island

There is a sandy beach on this green-canopied island's north-western side. The only settlement is Logha village, one km north of Gizo on the west coast.

Nusatupe Island

Narrow one-km-long Nusatupe is two km east of Gizo. It has an attractive coral garden on its western side and a sandy beach at its northern tip. In the south-east is the ICLARM clam farm (☎ 60022). For S$10, staff will show you round, explain what they do there, and let you snorkel over the giant clams in the ocean. Some clams are as big as an armchair, and have very colourful lips. The island is serviced by a motor canoe that meets flights (S$10 each way) – the trip is free for Gizo Hotel guests.

Kennedy Island
Seven km south-east of Gizo is Kennedy Island, also known as Plum Pudding or Kasolo. It is surrounded by sand and coral shoals. This is where John F Kennedy and his 10 shipmates swam ashore after their patrol boat *PT 109* was cut in half by the Japanese destroyer *Amagiri* in August 1943.

Mbambanga Island
Only four km south-east of Gizo and also called Long Island, Mbambanga is inhabited by Gilbertese settlers. It has a sandy beach at its north-western end, an offshore reef extending all the way to Olasana, and plenty of lobsters.

▧▧ ▧▧ ▧▧ ▧▧ ▧▧ ▧▧ ▧▧ ▧▧

The Sinking of *PT 109*
After their vessel *PT 109* had been sunk by the Japanese destroyer *Amagiri*, John F Kennedy and 10 fellow crew members clung to their boat's still-floating bow section all night, drifting with it to Sagharughombe Island. As there were no coconuts or water there, they moved over to Kennedy Island. Kennedy then swam via Olasana to Naru Island to salvage some supplies from a wrecked Japanese barge. Four days after their shipwreck, they were found by two islander scouts, who took them to Quomu Island, north of Vonavona, and later on to Patuparao, a nearby islet. Two days later they returned to the US base on Lumbaria Island next to Rendova Island. The whole ordeal lasted six days. The film *PT 109* was made of this memorable event in 1960. ■

▧▧ ▧▧ ▧▧ ▧▧ ▧▧ ▧▧ ▧▧ ▧▧

Olasana Island
This sand-surrounded island, 1.5 km south-east of Mbambanga, has marvellous coral, particularly at its north-western tip. Like Kerukeru Island, it's a favourite spot for Gizo picnickers. The Gizo dive companies arrange excursions here for around S$65 per person, including lunch.

Gizo Lagoon
This shallow coral formation encloses the islands from Epangga southwards to Mbambanga, with another stretch between Kennedy and Mbimbilusi. Clear, blue water with sand or coral bottoms is the norm for both areas.

Several of these islands have long sandy shores, including Leorava, Epangga, Mbatusimbo, Mbimbilusi and Naru.

DIVE SITES
The Ghizo area's dive choices include drop-offs, wrecks, walls, caves, drift dives, coral gardens, tropical fish, manta rays, eels, turtles, and pelagic fish such as groupers, barracudas and sharks. Top dive sites line Ghizo's eastern edge all the way from Njari to Naru Island.

The following locations nowhere near exhaust the possibilities. In the past, yachts have damaged coral by visiting sites independently; go with one of the dive companies – you'll probably get a better dive anyway.

Gizo Harbour Sometimes dived at the end of a dive trip, if you have enough air left in your tank. Because of constant port activity, poor visibility and local water pollution (which has caused some divers ear problems), great care should be taken when viewing these sites.

Zero One This wrecked Japanese fighter is only 10m beyond the market and in five metres of water. It was dumped here after WWII by salvagers. This is a busy spot for canoes and is therefore a hazardous dive. About 150m further offshore is a US Corsair fighter in 17m of water.

Njari Island Barracudas usually collect here and make good viewing.

WESTERN

Grand Central Station Excellent fish/coral dive off Varu Island. Named because of the huge variety of fish shoals swimming in constant procession. When the current is swift it's a good spot to see feeding sharks.

Toa Maru One of the best wreck dives around. This well-preserved 140m wrecked Japanese freighter lies off Kololuka Island. The *Toa Maru* sank after being torpedoed near her bow. There's still crockery, unopened saki bottles, a motorcycle and two small, two-person tanks aboard. Lying on her starboard side, the vessel is only 100m from shore and resting from about 18m down at her bow to around 37m at her stern.

Lembu Bay This inlet has very beautiful gardens of staghorn, plate and table corals.

Kerukeru Island Staghorn corals grow on the reef on the north-eastern side of the island.

Nusatupe Island There are gigantic clams, gorgonia sea fans and black coral nine metres down on the island's western side. This is a popular night-dive site.

Corsair Fighter Lying between Nusatupe and Gizo, this US WWII aircraft is on the sandy sea bed accompanied by clown fish and nudibranches.

Panapagha Island There's a beautiful coral garden to the south-east of the island.

Panapagha Gap This is a busy site for moving fish, and there are often sharks sleeping or resting on the sea bed 27m down.

Kennedy Island Wall This wall-dive site along the eastern side of the island offers 30m visibility and the chance of seeing large pelagic fish.

Kennedy Island Reef The southern side of the island is a shallow dive along a colourful reef and good for snorkellers, too. Both Kennedy Island sites are good night-dive spots.

Olasana Reef This shallow, sloping reef is also suitable for snorkelling. There's a range of corals, large sponges and eels as the reef shelves to a sandy sea bed. It's another favourite night-dive venue.

Naru Wall This one-km-long drop-off is to Naru's north and falls to a depth of 60m. It's covered with soft and plate corals.

Naru Gap Large pelagic fish, black corals and sea fans abound to the north-west of Naru Island.

Inner Naru This 18m dive is among very colourful fish and an immaculate coral garden.

Manta Ray Road The sea bed to the south-east of Naru Island is sandy 30m down. You're almost guaranteed to see manta rays here, sometimes as many as 15 at a time.

The following dive sites are further east but still easily visited from Gizo. See the Munda Vicinity map for locations.

Joe's Wall This spectacular wall dive has a 300m drop-off, and is to the north-east of Makuti Island. Attractive coral gardens are in the shallows nearby.

Grumman F6F Hellcat This US WWII naval fighter was ditched in October 1943 in a perfect water landing. It's still intact, complete with guns and ammunition. The plane is 11m down and 200m south-east of Quomu Island.

Shyoshu Maru No II This Japanese trawler lost the transducer from its hull when it clipped a reef. It slowly filled with water without the crew realising until too late. The vessel lies 35m down and about two km west of the north-west tip of Vonavona Island. It's hard to find because of poor underwater visibility.

Around Ghizo Island

All islands mentioned in this section can be visited on excursions with the Gizo-based dive companies. Although Gizo's Paradise Lodge doesn't (yet) arrange excursions, the owners can sometimes help with canoe transport. Together with Ghizo, the islands are sometimes (and confusingly) known as the Central Islands of Western Province.

KOLOMBANGARA ISLAND

Nduke, as many islanders call Kolombangara, is a classic, cone-shaped volcano. The island is 685 sq km in size and 30 km across. It rises from a one-km-wide coastal plain through flat-topped ridges and increasingly steep escarpments to the rugged crater rim of 1770m Mt Veve. Inside the crater, this four-km-wide extinct volcano falls abruptly to its deepest point 1000m below.

Most of Kolombangara's 4000 people live along its south-western shore, with no village further than 500m from the sea. Three-quarters of the island is uninhabited.

Logging has been a major activity for the past 80 years. As much of the original

WESTERN

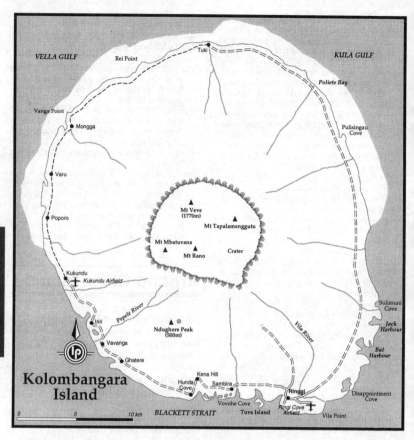

WESTERN

VELLA GULF

KULA GULF

Tuki

Rei Point

Poliete Bay

Vanga Point

Mongga

Pulisingau
Cove

Varu

Poporo

Mt Veve
(1770m)

Mt Tapalamenggutu

Mt Mbatuvana

Mt Rano

Crater

Kukundu
Kukundu Airfield

Sulimuri
Cove

Pepele River

Jack
Harbour

Iriri

Ndughore Peak
(500m)

Vila River

Bat
Harbour

Vavanga

Ghatere

Kena Hill

Hunda
Cove

Sambira

Ringgi

Disappointment
Cove

**Kolombangara
Island**

Vovohe Cove

Ringi Cove
Airfield

Vila Point

0   5   10 km

BLACKETT STRAIT

Tuva Island

rainforest has now gone, there are considerable efforts to replace it with timber plantations.

History

There are several 500m long stone platforms on Kolombangara's ridges. These were built for defence against 19th-century head-hunters. Despite such measures, the population had shrunk by the 1890s to a mere 150 people. The survivors congregated along the south-western coast, leaving the rest of the island deserted. Between

1905 and 1931, agreements were drawn up giving the British company Lever Brothers logging rights to two-thirds of Kolombangara.

The island was an important Japanese base in WWII, particularly around Ringgi and Vila Point, with about 4000 men garrisoned on it. When nearby Vella Lavella was liberated by the Allies in October 1943, they rapidly withdrew.

With the return of peace, logging resumed. By 1968, however, 90% of Levers' concession was logged out. Disputes with the custom owners of the remaining land led to the company's withdrawal in 1986. Since then, the Kolombangara Forestry Project Ltd (KFPL) was given a concession to grow commercially useful timber in plantations in the south, leaving rainforest to regrow on the rest of the island.

Information
Clinics are found at Ringgi, Poitete Bay, Ghatere and Kukundu. There are a few places to stay on the island – see the following sections.

Ringgi
This is the main base for KFPL's operations on Kolombangara. The very comfortable *KFPL Guest House* (☎ 60230) charges S$60/80 for singles/doubles; most rooms have private shower. There's a kitchen, though meals are also offered: breakfast and lunch are S$15 each, dinner is S$30. Guests have free use of KFPL's Nduke Club, a staff facility with a bar, tennis court, swimming pool and TV.

Vila Point & Around
Vila Point was the principal WWII Japanese base on Kolombangara Island. Some 150mm guns are still hidden in the bush, although their brass casings have been stripped. The guns were positioned by the Japanese to cover the eastern end of Blackett Strait between Kolombangara and Kohinggo islands. Saltwater crocodiles live in the Vila River area.

Nearby, at **Disappointment Cove**, several downed aircraft and abandoned guns from WWII can still be found in the undergrowth, while two Japanese freighters and a submarine lie offshore. They are shallow enough to be reached by divers.

Seven km north is **Sulimuni Cove**, also called Bennett Cove, where there's a sunken Japanese destroyer whose stern is partly exposed. You'll need a boat to get aboard it, even at low tide.

A further 20 km north is Poitete Bay, where it may be possible to stay in the old Forestry Department *rest house*.

Vanga Point
A cache of shell-money rings, now in the Honiara museum, was found here in the 1970s. It was hidden under some small cliffs inside the local mission's land. Custom valuables were often buried during periods of head-hunting raids, or when missionaries appeared and advocated the destruction of cult objects. There's a rural training centre here which might be able to provide food and lodging.

About three km inland from nearby Mongga there's an array of ancient stone walls extending over nearly 700m. Between two and three metres high, they were built as a defence against head-hunters.

Kukundu & Around
A narrow golden-sand beach extends for half a km on either side of this large SDA mission village. There's also a *rest house* here.

About a 40-minute walk south is **Iriri**, sometimes called Iririri. This friendly village gives a warm welcome to visitors, and has a leaf-style *rest house*. There's a cool swimming spot in the nearby Pepele River, and a large bat's cave to explore. Iriri also has a small lake.

Ghatere & Around
Six km inland on 500m Ndughore Peak is a small hot-spring site. Nearby are the remains of some abandoned 19th-century fortified villages. There is a leaf-style *rest house*.

Seven km round the coast is **Hunda Cove**. There are several archaeological sites nearby, including a number of ancient fortifications at Kena Hill.

Some 2.5 km from the hill is **Vovohe Cove**. The Japanese built several underground tunnels near this inlet in WWII which they used for ammunition storage. Ringgi is five km further on.

Climbing Mt Rano
Most walkers depart from one of five places on Kolombangara's western side. These are Ghatere, Vavanga, Iriri, Kukundu and

Vanga Point. All have guides available for hire, but several are SDA, so avoid Saturdays. If you want to visit the remains of abandoned fortified villages, go via Iriri, as several custom owners live there.

The Moss Forest is near the top of the mountain, or crater, as it is called locally. The mountain's upper reaches are thickly wooded, and rainfall is so heavy that the trees are covered in moss. Trees even coat the interior of the crater. Although the summit is often clear of clouds in the early morning, it's regularly covered in mist by noon.

It's about a 15-km climb, and this extremely strenuous trek takes seven or eight hours. To get the 'shrouded in mist' feeling, sleep overnight in the forest at what people call the *Professor's Camp*, over a five-hour walk up from Vavanga/Iriri. You'll have magnificent views from the top early in the morning before the cloud sets in.

Guides to the crater cost S$20 a day, and there's a S$50 custom fee (valid for up to six people). There are freshwater sources en route. Bring camping gear for your night out on the mountain.

Getting There & Away
Air Solomon Airlines flies Honiara-Munda-Ringi Cove-Gizo-Barakoma-Choiseul Bay on Monday mornings; the return leg misses out Munda. Western Pacific visits Kolombangara Island on Wednesday, on a flight that goes Honiara-Ringi Cove-Gizo-Geva-Choiseul Bay, before returning the same way.

It also has a flight on Friday, covering Honiara-Batuna-Ramata-Munda-Kukundu-Geva, which returns the same route. Honiara to Kukundu (sometimes spelled Kukudu) takes three hours and costs S$285.

Ringi Cove airfield is two km from Ringgi. Kukundu airfield is beside the SDA mission.

Sea The *Iuminao* calls in to Ringgi on its twice-weekly Honiara-Gizo run. The economy fare from Ringgi is S$75 to Honiara and S$23 to Gizo.

There are anchorages of varying qualities at Vanga Point, Ringgi, Vila Point, Jack Harbour, Sulimuni Cove, Pulisingau Cove, Tuki, Mongga, Kukundu, Ghatere, Hunda Cove and Sambira.

Kolombangara to Gizo is 35 minutes by motor canoe; expect to pay up to S$20 per person if you can find a shared ride at Gizo market. The cheapest ride will be with the Catholic Mission's boat that goes from Vanga Point to Gizo market on Monday, Wednesday and Friday mornings, returning the same afternoons. A charter from Gizo to Iriri would cost about S$50 each way.

Getting Around
A tractor trail extends 38 km around the island to Tuki in the north. This continues as a footpath to Kukundu, where it meets a track from Ringgi. A number of logging roads follow the inland ridges, with one from Ringgi penetrating eight km into the interior.

SIMBO ISLAND
Simbo is eight km south of Ranongga and 31.5 km south-west of Ghizo. This 7.5-km-long, 12-sq-km island is home to 1300 people. A fertile isthmus separates north and south.

Simbo is dominated by two young volcanic cones in the south, both over 300m high, giving rise to an active thermal area where megapode birds nest. A submarine volcano about five km south of Cape Satisfaction was active in 1964 but has been dormant since. Simbo's northern coastline has coral-sand bays.

History
In pre-European times, Simbo people traded with New Georgia exchanging megapode eggs and vegetables for turtle shell and handicrafts. Ancient pottery shards of unknown origin have been found on the island.

Simbo was one of the first Solomon islands to welcome foreigners, with European traders living there permanently from the 1840s. Known variously as Eddystone,

isn't a problem – you can either camp or lodge with a family (enquire in advance by service message). The owner of Gizo's Paradise Lodge is from Simbo and she may be able to arrange accommodation and transport.

The only medical clinic is at Lengana.

Narovo

Simbo's main village is connected by footpaths to Nusa Simbo, Righuru and Tapurai. There's a colourful reef to the north-west of Narovo, and a small island called Uelai with surrounding coral gardens at the harbour mouth.

Four km north is Tapurai, where there's a beach. A dead volcanic crater is on the nearby hillside, now occupied by Lake Pughele.

Archaeological Sites

These sites are sacred to Simbo people, even if they appear neglected. You must get permission, hire a guide and pay any custom fees required before you visit them. A clam-shell collection can be found at Mengge.

Skull Houses The most important skull site is Pa Na Ghundu, which has 12 coralstone reliquaries complete with skulls and clam-shell money. It's concealed by trees close to the western base of Mt Matindingi. Another one is Pa Na Ulu, which is on the small headland just to the north of Mt Patukio, while a third site is at Gurava, close to the abandoned settlement of Ove village. Some of these sites are centuries old and contain the skulls of highly regarded ancestors and head-hunting victims.

Petroglyphs There are two petroglyph sites at Righuru, and another just to the west of Nggagho. The most interesting one is at Vareviri Point, where rocks bear canoe and bird symbols.

Bonito-Increase Shrines Although these structures are small, bonito (ie tuna) worship was important in Simbo ritual and

Narovo, Simbo or Mandeghughusu Island, it had become a regular stopping place between eastern Australia and the Chinese coast by the 1860s. Yet Simbo, along with Ranongga, was a notorious head-hunting centre in the 19th century. Sorties against Choiseul and Santa Isabel were routine, with one raiding party coming back with 93 heads!

Arts

Blue-green tapa is made by washing it in the hot volcanic springs. Rare examples have been stained brown this way.

Information

Villagers charge a custom fee of S$20 to see each important custom site, and that includes the thermal area.

There's no organised accommodation on Simbo Island, so most people go only as day-trippers. Staying overnight probably was intended to guarantee large catches of the fish. There are two sites east of Nusa Simbo village and a sizeable one at Ove Lavata which is a line of large individual stone piles.

Abandoned Villages The coral-slab house bases on the western side of the path beside Lake Ove are all that remain of Ove village, abandoned since its inhabitants were driven out by volcanic activity earlier this century. You'll also see other isolated sites around the island, including some beside the harbour, just to the south-west of Narovo.

Thermal Area
Before visiting this part of the island, get permission from the land owners, who live in Narovo. They are trying to preserve megapode numbers, so access probably won't be allowed during August and September.

Lake Ove is deep green because sulphur drains into it from the nearby hillside. There's a hot spring at the lake's south-eastern end, making the waters nearby too hot for swimming. Villagers often cook fresh megapode eggs there in the naturally heated waters.

Ove Crater, on the western edge of the 335m Mt Matindingi, is yellow and sulphur-covered. There are fine views of Lake Ove and Simbo's western coast from its top. There's also a place about 200m south-east of the crater where the ground is so hot that food placed on it cooks in only a few minutes.

The mildly steaming crater has several outcrops of pure-yellow crystalline sulphur in it which is collected by islanders as a cure for skin infections. There's a fumarole at the shoreside immediately below the crater.

There are two **megapode hatcheries** on the mountainside, one above the lake and the other very close to the crater. There are also megapode holes at the bases of some nearby trees. The warm, soft ground around the hatcheries is cleared and raked by villagers, and small thatched roofs are

placed over it to entice the birds to use its shelter when laying. There's also a hatching area nearby, where eggs are left uncollected to prevent overfarming. A stick with fruit on it placed outside any one of the hatcheries means you are forbidden to enter.

Nusa Simbo Island
This two-km-long island is joined to its larger neighbour by a small bridge at the base of Mt Patukio. There's a hot spring 100m to the south of the bridge by the west coast. The water's always warm here.

You'll find more megapode hatcheries in Nusa Simbo village. Ask the custom owner of the site if you can see them. At Simbo Mbatuna are the remains of a coral-walled fortress and an accompanying dance circle.

Getting There & Away
As there's no regular scheduled shipping to Simbo Island, you'll probably have to get a canoe. The best hope for a shared ride is at Gizo Market on Monday and Friday afternoons; expect to pay about S$25 to S$30 each way.

Seas are very rough between Ranongga and Simbo, so wear wet-weather gear and don't risk the trip in blustery conditions. From Gizo, seas can also be quite choppy in the afternoon; mornings are calmer.

Narovo has the island's only wharf. On arrival, yacht crews should see the Simbo Area Assembly regarding staying, washing, drinking water, etc, and follow any instructions closely.

Getting Around
Movement is mostly on foot, though the thermal area is best reached by canoe. Moor at Ove Lavata beside a small coral garden and wade ashore across very slippery boulders. There's a footpath from there which goes beside Lake Ove and up to the Ove crater.

RANONGGA ISLAND
Ranongga is a 28-km-long, rugged, narrow island. Its high western coast falls abruptly

heated water and use it to cook their food. A custom fee is usually charged to see or use it.

History
Ranongga, also known as Rononga, Ghanongga and Vesu Ghoghoto, was first seen by foreigners when the Americans Read and Dale sailed through Western Province in November 1787. Like Simbo people, Ranonggans were keen head-hunters, particularly in the 19th century, and made routine raids on Choiseul and Santa Isabel. The island's last head-hunting party sallied forth in 1936.

Society & Conduct
Even now grandparents tell children stories based on memories of head-hunting raids. In the past no man was permitted to marry until he had been on one of these expeditions. Once he had done so, he was allowed to sleep with a woman captured from another tribe. The resulting offspring became full members of his clan, with rights to own land on the island.

Information
Clinics are at Koriovuku, Pienuna and Keara.

There are no rest houses on Ranongga, though larger villages, such as Koriovuku and Pienuna, may have an empty leaf house you could borrow. So send a service message to the chief, and come prepared to camp. Bring food to eat and exchange, as stores are few and far between.

Getting There & Away
There's no regular scheduled shipping services to Ranongga, though cargo boats sometimes make the trip from Gizo, or you might be able to find a shared canoe ride from there (about S$20 per person to Pienuna). Fuel sometimes runs short on Ranongga, which might delay your return to Gizo. Be wary of rough seas on the trip from Ranongga to Simbo.

The only anchorages are at Emu Harbour, Renjo and Keara. The eastern side

into deep water, while the eastern coast is much lower, with terraces and onshore reefs. Its tallest point is the 869m Mt Kela.

Ranongga has 3900 people in its 145 sq km. Most of these live along the sheltered eastern coast, especially in the south. The people of Ranongga and Simbo often treat each other as *wantoks*. Consequently, young Ranongga men are keen to find Simbo wives and bring them back to Ranongga to live. Unfortunately for them, Simbo women know that Ranongga's coastal villages have food gardens high up on the island's hillsides. The thought of clambering up to these gardens daily often crushes any romantic feelings Simbo girls have for their Ranonggan suitors.

The only dwellings on Ranongga are leaf houses. Cooking is often on wood fires, as gas and kerosene are still relatively uncommon. A hot-spring site lies 500m south of Mondo. Villagers bathe in the thermally is usually calm from October to May, while the western coast is rough (the reverse applies from 1 June to 30 September).

Getting Around

A footpath along the eastern coast from Emu Harbour leads down to Lale on the south-western tip of the island. However, these footpaths are sometimes only 30 cm wide and not very clear. You will need a guide, and should ask each village you come to for permission to pass through it. The same applies to the crossing over the island's 400m high central mountains between Pienuna and Mondo. It's a half-day hike each way. -The best way around Ranongga's western coast is by motor canoe.

VELLA LAVELLA ISLAND

Usually known simply as Vella, and formerly as Mbilua, the island is wooded and mountainous. Together with its small neighbour, Mbava, it's 670 sq km in size and has a population of 7500 people who speak a Papuan language and live mostly on its eastern shore.

Mt Tambisala in Vella's north-east is 790m high, yet its crater floor is close to sea level. Inside is a swampy flood plain and hot sulphur steam vents. Four km to the south-east, the Ulo River passes through an active thermal area.

Volcanoes in the island's north-west have produced a series of smaller cones, notably the Songga and Sukoe hills. In the south another quiescent volcano, the 520m Supato Peak, is bounded by coastal swamps.

History

Vella Lavella was first seen by foreigners in November 1787 when Read and Dale viewed it from their vessel the *Alliance*. More recently, the Japanese occupied the island in WWII, but lost several large warships trying to prevent the Americans wresting it back from them. When the US lost the light cruiser *Helena* off Vella, about 175 survivors swam ashore and were hidden by the islanders until rescued 10 days later by the Americans. The Japanese

WESTERN

Japanese Stragglers

When Japan withdrew from Vella Lavella Island, 300 troops were left behind. Many of them disappeared into the bush and hills to avoid capture by the Allies.

Since 1959, locals have reported seeing Japanese men hiding in Vella's rainforest. Similarly, elderly men with loin cloths and long beards have been seen stealing food from villagers' gardens. For a while Japanese veterans made frequent visits to Vella to find them.

In 1965, one Japanese straggler was located after first being seen by a woman in her garden. The Japanese ambassador flew over the area distributing leaflets saying 'The war is over!', so the man gave himself up, returning home to receive full national honours.

There have been further sightings since then, including one in 1989 near Vorambare Bay, close to where the Japanese made their last stand. Although it's about 55 years since the Japanese withdrew, some villagers think there may still be one or two stragglers left. Island cynics suggest instead the more recent 'sightings' may simply be a ruse to lure more Japanese visitors. ■

---

were finally driven out in October 1943 by a joint US and New Zealand force after more than a year's occupation.

Fauna

Vella has a wide range of wildlife in its rainforest, and marlin and sailfish can occasionally be seen breaking the surface in Vella Gulf. Bird and insect life is prolific, including megapode birds in the Ulo River area, and parrots and butterflies everywhere. Snakes are also plentiful, especially the small nonvenomous burrowing snake.

Crocodiles Villagers report seeing freshwater crocodiles in the sulphurous Ulo River (pronounced 'ooh-low') and its adjacent creeks, hiding by day and active at

night. Although they mainly eat fish, the larger ones are potentially dangerous to dogs and very small children. Apparently no human-eating saltwater crocodiles live in the Ulo River, but there are small numbers in the Oula River (pronounced 'oh-lah') and its tributaries on the island's swampy western side. Vella people call them alligators to distinguish them from the comparatively retiring freshwater species.

Information

There are clinics or nurse-aid posts at Vonunu, Kolokolo, Karaka, Iringgila, Maravari, Lambulambu, Paramata, Varese and Dovele.

Vella is not often visited by tourists, but ask around about accommodation possibilities. Reportedly there's a new resort near Lambulambu and plans for other rest houses. Bring food.

Liapari Island

This former plantation island now has a fish farm, and permission is required to go there. Liapari is protected by reefs which join it to its two small neighbours, Mbarambatu and Karokoni islands, at low tide. There are sandy beaches here. Good snorkelling sites are on the western sides of Karokoni and Mbarambatu islands, and near the wooden bridge between Liapari and Vella.

Vonunu & Around

The south's main village is connected by a 100m long sandbar to tiny Kalanga Island. Vonunu is close to Barakoma airfield and is a good place to look for shared canoe rides to Gizo (Monday to Friday).

Three km north, at Pusisama, a track leads to **Serulando Point** on the west coast. Petroglyphs depicting former chiefs adorn the top of the hill overlooking the point. There are more on the shore at Supato two km further on. Beyond at Oula is a long, sandy beach. About seven km north of Pusisama is **Maravari**, which has a simple leaf *rest house*.

Kolokolo

There are attractive coral gardens in the shallows at Kolokolo. At **Niarovai**, 2.5 km further north, a war memorial commemorates the New Zealand forces who landed here in September 1943 to reinforce the US marines already in action on Vella. **Orete Cove** is another six km north. There are several one-metre-high blow holes at Mbeiporo and Kundurumbangara points, either side of this attractive inlet.

Lambulambu

A Japanese freighter sank in the harbour here in WWII. It's 12m down but under-water visibility is poor. Nearby is an ancient stone tower. Villagers will show you the high walls constructed locally for defence in head-hunting days. Valapata, four km further on, has similar ruins.

The Matiuru family has reportedly opened the *Uriaupo Resort*, a 15-minute walk south of Lambulambu. They have radio contact and will take people on tours.

Simbilando

This large village is imposingly positioned on a hillside facing the sea. The reef 2.5 km away at the eastern tip of nearby Tambi-tambi Island is particularly colourful. There are more coral gardens 2.5 km due north at Paroana.

Ulo River Thermal Area

The first thing you'll notice at Paraso Bay is the brown volcanic sand heated by thermal activity. The footpath to the hot springs is about five km long and it takes one to 1½ hours to get there. You cross two small creeks immediately beyond the beach and then cross the Ulo River twice before reaching several large trees on its southern side. These have deep holes in their bases and are hatcheries where megapode birds lay their eggs in the thermally heated ground. A few people live in the area and harvest these eggs, but it's a small operation compared to those on Savo and Simbo.

Immediately beyond is a mud pool on the southern (left) side of the path. After this there are two km of hot springs known colloquially by islanders as the Volcano. It's very desolate compared to the thick bush along the Ulo River. The only plants growing in the thermal area are bracken and dozens of small pandanus trees.

You can go further and climb nearby Nonda Hill, Kumba Hill and Mt Tambisala, where there's more thermal activity, but you'll have to camp out if you do. Villagers will let you sleep in Simbilando, Paroana or Karaka if you're late back from the thermal area or rough seas delay your return.

The custom owners of the Ulo River thermal area live at Simbilando, so you'll need to call in there first. The custom fee is S$20 to see the whole two-km-long site, or S$2 just to view the first mud pool. They'll also provide one or two guides; pay them about S$5 each for half a day, though kids may do it for nothing.

Mbava Island

Known also as Baanga, Baga, Bagga or Bag Island, most of the coastal part of this 36-sq-km landform is low lying and marshy, except for the 230m quiescent volcanic peak on the island's eastern side. The only permanently occupied part of it is tiny Inia Island off Mbava's eastern coast. However, this may change, as Mbava is believed to be gold bearing. There are anchorages at both Somolo and Singgataravana harbours.

Getting There & Away

Air Vella Lavella Island has two airfields. On Monday Barakoma has connections to both Gizo (S$55) and Choiseul Bay (S$80) with Solomon Airlines. Western Pacific flies into Geva. It links this airport to Honiara, Batuna, Ramata, Munda and Kukundu on both Monday and Friday, and to Honiara, Ringi Cove, Gizo and Choiseul Bay on Wednesday.

Sea Vella doesn't receive regular shipping services, but Gizo-based boats like *Ozama Twomey* and *Ferguson Express* sometimes make the trip. There's also a passenger speedboat on Monday and Friday that starts at Mboro around 6.30 am, makes stops along the coast as far as Kolokolo, then starts the 90-minute trip to Gizo. It returns to Vella mid-afternoon from Gizo's main wharf. Fares from Gizo are S$25 to Lambulambu and S$30 to Mboro.

There are anchorages of varying quality at Liapari Island, Pusisama, Lambulambu, Kokolope Bay, Simbilando, Mboro, Liangai and Iringgila.

Getting Around

The WWII US-built road connects Liapari Island with Ruruvai, although many of its bridges have been washed away. A rather worn-out track continues on to Lambulambu, and there's also a track to Supato. Other places must be reached by canoe.

West New Georgia

This area includes the islands of Vonavona, Kohinggo, Rendova, Tetepare and New Georgia itself, together with many smaller neighbours. Munda, on New Georgia

Island, is the most developed area for tourism and makes a suitable base for exploring this part of the province.

NEW GEORGIA ISLAND

The largest island in the New Georgia group, New Georgia Island is nearly 85 km long, 41 km wide at its broadest point, and 2145 sq km in area.

The island, given its name by Shortland in 1788, is fringed by several lagoons and their many tiny, coconut-covered sand and coral islets. In contrast, New Georgia's coast is mainly swamp. Inland are several breached volcanoes (most notably Mt Mase and Mt Mahimba) whose craters radiate outwards in massive, narrow-crested ridges.

The eastern coast of New Georgia Island borders the magnificent Marovo Lagoon, which is dealt with later in a separate section.

History

Head-hunting was New Georgia's former claim to fame. The practice developed because people believed the skull contained the life-force of a person. The purpose of head-hunting raids was therefore to acquire the victim's personal power by capturing his skull. Oral traditions from the Roviana Lagoon tell of war canoes covering distances of over 250 km each way in raids on southern Guadalcanal, Santa Isabel and Choiseul.

Raiding parties usually returned with male heads and female captives. These warlike forays were particularly devastating to Santa Isabel, decimating the population along its southern shore.

On returning from a raid, some of the captives were killed and eaten while others were enslaved. Slave women's children however, were given full customary rights to tribal land.

Not surprisingly, these head-hunting expeditions were greatly feared. The less warlike among New Georgia's people settled inland on hilltops so they could see their enemies coming. Sentinels were posted day and night.

WESTERN

WESTERN

Traditional Land Ownership

In head-hunting days, there was always the danger that a man would be killed; although women could be enslaved, their lives were usually spared. For this reason, inheritance of land is matrilineal in New Georgia, with women being regarded as the land's custodians. The chief allocates tribal land to a woman's descendants subject to her death-bed wishes. Consequently, newborn girls are as welcome as boys. ■

By the late 19th century, all European axes and guns had made killing too easy and New Georgia's head-hunting and slave-raiding reached a peak. British trading interests in the area could not permit this lawlessness to continue so HMS *Royalist* was ordered to suppress it. Every village in the Roviana Lagoon was shelled or burnt, and the fortress at Nusa Roviana was destroyed in 1892.

In October of the following year the Protectorate was proclaimed over much of the Solomons, including New Georgia. One of its principal aims was to suppress head-hunting. It took many years, however, to bring lasting peace. The scourge of head-hunting was mainly laid to rest by WWI, though there were still isolated incidents up to the 1930s. British law, together with the influence of Methodist missionaries, gradually put an end to cannibalism, slavery and sorcery.

New Georgia was the scene of very fierce fighting in WWII. Coastwatcher Donald Kennedy's small group of islanders near Seghe made many daring guerrilla raids against the Japanese until they were relieved in June 1943 by US forces. During the following two months, there was violent combat, particularly around Munda and Mbaeroko Bay, until the island was finally cleared of Japanese occupation late that August.

Climate

New Georgia's annual rainfall is recorded at Munda and averages 3552 mm. It rains on about seven days in every 10, with morning humidity at 89% or more from January to September. The afternoons are much milder, with humidity usually around 76%. Temperatures vary between 22°C and 32°C.

Population & People

Most of the island's 19,000 people live along New Georgia's southern shores. There are four main languages spoken, of which Roviana (the old name for western New Georgia) and Marovo are the commonest.

Arts

The traditional war canoe, or *tomoko* (also *tomago*), is only made nowadays for ceremonial purposes. In the past, those produced in the Roviana area could carry 30 to 40 fully armed men on a head-hunting raid. Their sides were heavily decorated with shell inlay and carvings of insects and birds. At the stern was mounted a *kesoko* – a seated, bird-headed, spirit creature whose presence was believed to guarantee good fishing and a safe journey.

Information

In addition to the hospital at Munda, there are clinics at Noro, Viru Harbour, Seghe, Paradise, Biula, Olive and Arara, and on Vakambo and Keru islands.

Except for a leaf house in Paradise, accommodation is limited to Munda and nearby island resorts.

Things to Buy

Very highly polished carvings of nguzunguzus are made at Munda, Viru Harbour and in the Marovo Lagoon. Small, smoothly polished replicas of sharks and dolphins are also carved from kerosene wood. These are sometimes inlaid with pearly nautilus shell. Pendants, earrings, bracelets, hair ornaments, napkin rings, pandanus-leaf handbags and floor mats are also made and sold relatively cheaply.

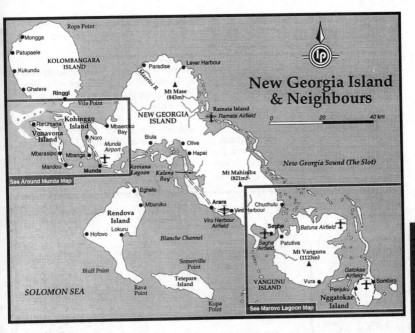

New Georgia Island & Neighbours

WESTERN

Getting There & Away

Air Munda airport has a tarmac runway. The terminal building has a customs and immigration office and a Solomon Airlines counter (☎ 61152). Other airfields are at Seghe (see the Marovo Lagoon section), Ramata Island, and Viru Harbour.

Solomon Airlines connects Munda with Honiara (S$245) and Gizo (S$65) several times a day. From Gizo, flights often continue to other destinations (eg Choiseul Bay). Munda is linked to Ramata (S$70) on Monday and Thursday, and to Viru Harbour (S$80) on Tuesday and Wednesday; most days there's a flight to Seghe (S$80).

Western Pacific has a direct Honiara-Munda flight on Thursday that takes 70 minutes each way (S$245). On Monday and Friday its flight to Munda is part of a Honiara-Geva routing that also includes Batuna, Ramata and Kukundu. An additional flight on Monday links Munda with Gizo, Honiara and Kagau (S$110). On Sunday Western Pacific flies between Ramata, Gizo (S$85) and Honiara ($230).

Sea The *Iuminao* and the *Ramos I* make stops along the south coast of New Georgia Island – see Getting There & Away at the start of this chapter. From Honiara, the Wings Shipping economy/1st class fare is S$63/93 to Viru Harbour, S$71/100 to Munda and S$72/102 to Noro. From Munda, it's S$37/64 to Viru, S$38/64 to the Marovo Lagoon stops and S$36/64 to Gizo.

Passenger ships stop about two km offshore from Munda, riding anchor between Munda Point and Hombuhombu Island. Hordes of motor canoes then come out to take people ashore; they charge S$10 per person. Most other vessels use the Munda Wharf at Lambete. At Noro you can disembark from the passenger ships directly at the wharf.

Anchorages around New Georgia are of varying holding and comfort. These are at Munda (ie Lambete and Kokenggolo), Canaan, Kalena Bay, Viru Harbour, Seghe, Lever Harbour, Paradise, Valuli Point, Rice Harbour, Mbaeroko Bay, Noro, and Mbuini Tusu, Vakambo and Keru islands.

Getting Around

The only roads in New Georgia are the US-built crushed-coral tracks around Munda, the new road from there to Noro, and the logging route from Viru Harbour to Kalena

Bay. Elsewhere transport is by motor canoe, small copra launches or on foot.

Munda

New Georgia Island's largest settlement is a collection of small villages stretching six km along the shore from Ilangana to Kindu. The whole area is called Munda.

Although all is peaceful now, the Munda area was the scene of frenetic WWII activity, as it was an important Japanese base of 4500 troops. Once it had been captured by the Americans, its size was greatly in-

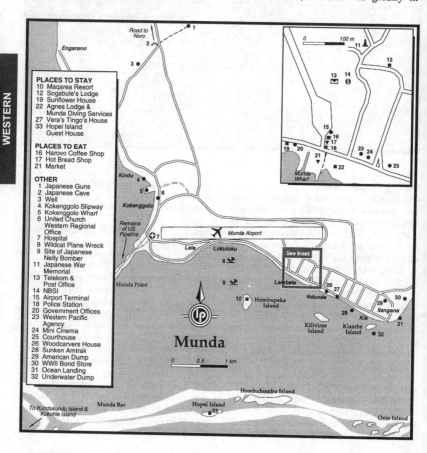

PLACES TO STAY
10 Maqarea Resort
12 Sogabule's Lodge
19 Sunflower House
22 Agnes Lodge &
    Munda Diving Services
27 Vera's Tingo's House
33 Hopei Island
    Guest House

PLACES TO EAT
16 Harovo Coffee Shop
17 Hot Bread Shop
21 Market

OTHER
1 Japanese Guns
2 Japanese Cave
3 Well
4 Kokenggolo Slipway
5 Kokenggolo Wharf
6 United Church
   Western Regional
   Office
7 Hospital
8 Wildcat Plane Wreck
9 Site of Japanese
   Nelly Bomber
11 Japanese War
    Memorial
13 Telekom &
    Post Office
14 NBSI
15 Airport Terminal
18 Police Station
20 Government Offices
23 Western Pacific
    Agency
24 Mini Cinema
25 Courthouse
26 Woodcarvers House
28 Sunken Amtrak
29 American Dump
30 WWII Bond Store
31 Ocean Landing
32 Underwater Dump

creased by lengthening the airfield, laying an extensive network of roads, and building many Quonset huts. Plenty of wartime structures remain.

Munda is also well known for its many pink and blue orchids and shoreside freshwater pools. Ask the owners' permission before you photograph their orchids or inspect the pools.

Information The most developed part of Munda is Lambete village, in the centre of the line of villages. Here you'll find the airport terminal, government offices, an NBSI branch, a Western Pacific agency, a police station (☎ 61135) and many stores. There's also a Telekom office (☎ 61149, fax 61150) next to a post office. Helena Goldie hospital (☎ 61121) is three km west, near Munda Point.

Dangers & Annoyances Women should take care at night; two sexual assaults were reported in Munda in December 1996.

East of Lambete There are two freshwater pools at **Ndunde** – both containing turtles and fish – and a small crocodile farm (S$3 entry). The owners will show you them on request.

Kiambe Island is only 100m from the shore near Kia. Behind it is a US dump: landing craft carrying jeeps were scuttled here in water between five and 10m deep. More accessible, behind **Kia**, is a huge pile of war material rotting in the bush. It's known locally as the American Dump; head inland a few steps beyond the eastern tip of Kiambe. Amid thick trees are rusting aircraft parts, tractor, truck and bulldozer chassis, two small Japanese guns and several broken-up US landing craft. There are also big spiders and plenty of mosquitoes. It's about a 20-minute walk from Agnes Lodge and worth the S$10 to S$20 custom fee you may have to pay.

There's a number of corrugated iron huts by the shoreside, each with a rusty open petrol drum protruding from it. These are copra dryers which islanders have made from the huge number of empty petrol drums left here after WWII. Just 20m out from the small coral jetty in front of the dump is what looks like a sunken US amtrack. It's in two metres of water.

Four large rusting pontoons lie half submerged in the shallows along Kia's waterfront, and many small, colourful fish have made their home inside the badly corroded frames.

About a five-minute walk further on is **Ilangana**. This village is immediately behind a huge concrete pad supported by old 44-gallon petrol drums, also filled with concrete. This pad once supported several Quonset huts used in wartime as store sheds, and were collectively known at the time as the Bond Store. To one side is a small, reinforced-concrete hut where the paymaster kept the soldiers' wages until pay day.

West of Lambete About a 10-minute walk brings you to **Lokuloku**, where two aircraft lie in shallow water; both can be seen by snorkellers. Furthest away, about 600m from shore and four metres down, is a Japanese Nelly bomber. Locals will canoe you to the spot. Closer in is a US Wildcat. It's only 200m out from a fish trap.

A long, rusting pipeline leads north from the shallows at **Munda Point** to Kokenggolo. World War II tankers used to unload here at the rate of 3000 tonnes of fuel per day.

Inland from the point is the start of the three-km **airport runway** begun by the Japanese. They needed a base to help them capture the US WWII airfield at Henderson on Guadalcanal. The Japanese tried to keep their plans secret, even going so far as connecting the tops of trees in Munda's coconut plantation. Their aim was to cut away most of the trunks, leaving only a few trees to act as supports for the remainder and their overhanging palms fronds. This was discovered within two weeks by islanders who immediately informed the Americans. The US reaction was to bomb the site regularly, effectively depriving the Japanese of the airfield's use. There's a simple **Japanese war memorial** at the eastern end of the runway.

Noro Road This road runs west along the north side of the runway. You may be able to hitch a ride on a Taiyo truck bound for Noro. About a 45-minute walk from Agnes Lodge is a rutted track to the right, at the junction with the road leading south to Kindu. Follow this track for about 500m through bush to a concrete pad where there are two **Japanese anti-aircraft guns**. There's a small memorial post between them.

On returning from the guns, turn northwards (right) up the Noro road. About halfway up on the left of the first hill, there's a small **cave** where several Japanese hid. The entrance was sealed up, leaving them entombed inside. There are several other caves by the airfield where Japanese hid; they are visible from the road.

Nearby Islands You can visit nearby islands from Munda by canoe. **Hombuhombu Island** is 2.5 km south of Munda. There's a sunken motorised pontoon in shallow water just beyond the island's small jetty. It's complete with driver's cab, now colourfully encrusted in coral. **Kundukundu Island** is about four km west. This sand-surrounded island has a long, white sandbar at its north-eastern end, and coral gardens only 100m from its eastern shore.

Close by is **Kokohle Island**, pronounced 'co-coh-high-ly'. This islet has a sand beach along half of its eastern side. Turtles come here to lay their eggs.

Diving & Snorkelling Solomon Sea Divers operates from Agnes Lodge and visits numerous wall, wreck and reef dive sites. It quotes in Australian dollars. The basic price is A$55/90 for one/two dives, though equipment hire could add A$36 per day. A snorkelling trip costs A$28.

One reason prices are higher than those charged in Gizo is that sites aren't so close to base, meaning transport costs are higher.

PADI open water certification costs A$425 and a resort course is A$90. Dive sites visited include:

SBD Douglas Dive Bomber This US plane lies 12m down in the Rendova Lagoon. The pilot survived the 1943 crash. You can sit in the cockpit just as the pilot did when he returned over 50 years later.

Casi Maru This small WWII Japanese freighter sank at her mooring, together with a barge and another boat which lie alongside 16m down.

Ndokendoke Island A freshwater pool in the centre of this volcanic island leads via caves and caverns to an 800m reef wall. There are lots of fish, sponges and soft corals.

Rainbow Passage Diverse corals and plenty of fish, including sharks and turtles.

Organised Tours Go West Tours is based in the Agnes Lodge. Prices depend on the number of people going – those quoted here are the *minimum* you'll pay. Tour destinations include Skull Island off Vonavona (S$40), and Roviana Island's Dog Stone together with Piraka Island's skull shrine (S$80). Activities range from a mountain hike to Bau (S$100) to a custom-cooking demonstration and tasting (S$40).

The Maqarea Resort organises snorkelling, windsurfing, fishing and lagoon trips. If you just want a paddle canoe to yourself, ask local villagers. They are likely to only charge you a couple of dollars whether you have the craft for a few minutes or all day.

Places to Stay – Munda Some villagers offer accommodation. *Vera Tingo* has a house in Ndunde with two rooms that can sleep up to five for S$20 per person. There's a kitchen and a verandah, but no electricity. It's a brown-wood house with a metal roof. If no-one's around, ask the neighbours or enquire at the Woodcarvers House, 150m west in Ndunde.

Sunflower House, by the government offices in Lambete, is a very attractive leaf house with two rooms sleeping up to seven people. Price is S$33 per bed and there's electricity, kitchen, garden, and paddle canoe (no charge). The owner, Merle Aqorau (☎ 60170, PO Box 150), lives across the road in the pale blue house.

Sogabule's Lodge in Lambete, also called Soba's Lodge, has three rooms and shared washing and cooking facilities for S$33 a night. It has fans and a small lounge.

Agnes Lodge (☎ 61133, fax 61230, PO Box 9), by Munda Wharf in Lambete, has a choice of rooms. Three-bed backpacker rooms with shared showers are S$33 per person. Smallish doubles with private shower/toilet are S$150, while large rooms and suites in a newer wing start at S$240 per person. Eight new self-contained cottages have been built that go for S$220. The lodge has a pleasant location by the sea; facilities include a bar and restaurant but no kitchen.

Places to Stay – Islands near Munda

The *Kundukundu Leaf House* on Kundukundu Island, is merely a roof over your head for S$6 a night. You need to build a fire to cook, and bring everything with you. There's no toilet or running water. Canoe transfers are S$10 each way. Enquire at the Woodcarvers' House, Ndunde.

Hopei Island has two self-contained cottages, and more are planned. Bring your own food. The cost is S$140 per night, which includes transfers. Agnes Lodge should be able to give more information, as the two were formerly under the same management.

The *Maqarea Resort* (☎ 61164, fax 61165, PO Box 66) (pronounced 'mangarea') is on Hombupeka Island and about 700m from Munda. There are four bungalows each with twin beds and bathroom but no kitchen, though there is a bar and restaurant. The single/double charge is S$94/150, including transfers.

Places to Eat

There's a very small fruit and vegetable market by Munda Wharf, but the market behind the hospital is cheaper.

By the airport terminal is *Harovo Coffee Shop* which has fish and chips and snacks

for about S$3. It's open weekdays from 7 am to 4 pm and Saturday from 7 am to noon. In the same block is a *Hot Bread Shop* (open similar hours, plus Sunday morning) and a 24-hour store.

The only place to eat evening meals is the *Agnes Lodge Restaurant*. Good fish dinners start at S$35 – some choices need to be pre-ordered by 6 pm. Lunch and dinner specials chalked on the board start at about S$20; breakfast is from S$6.

Entertainment

There's a mini cinema in Lambete. It shows films at noon and 8 pm, Monday to Saturday, and charges S$3. The bar in Agnes Lodge sometimes puts on custom dances.

Around Munda

The wartime road around Munda has been extended northwards to Noro. To the east, access by motor vehicle is now only as far as the Mbareke River, though walkers can continue as far as the Piraka River.

Nusa Roviana The notorious head-hunter Ingava ruled from this coral-walled fortress on Roviana Island until it was destroyed in 1892. His tribe had a wild dog as its totem and worshipped at a rock carved like a dog before going on head-hunting forays. The Dog Rock is still there, but it's now broken.

The fortified village was built of layers of coral, with the Dog Rock on top. The path to this stronghold was lined with shells to give warning of any intruder's approach.

The fortress was up to 30m wide in some places. Over 500m of coral wall still remain, though forest has now covered much of the area. There's also a giant's cave nearby. Expect custom fees to be charged at both sites. The island is a four-km canoe ride east of Munda.

Holupuru Falls This 10m waterfall is just north of the bridge over the Mburape River. Below the falls is a three-metre swimming hole (and a custom fee is payable). You'll need a guide to show you the falls and an interesting bats' cave nearby.

TOP 10 or lonely plants beach

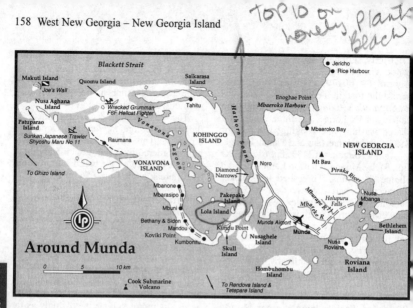

Blackett Strait

Makuti Island
Joe's Wall
Quomu Island
Saikarasa Island
Jericho
Rice Harbour
Nusa Aghana Island
Wrecked Grumman F6F Hellcat Fighter
Tahitu
Enoghae Point
Mbaeroko Harbour
Patuparao Island
Sunken Japanese Trawler Shyoshu Maru No 11
Raumana
Vonavona Lagoon
KOHINGGO ISLAND
Hathorn Sound
Mbaeroko Bay
NEW GEORGIA ISLAND
To Ghizo Island
VONAVONA ISLAND
Noro
Mt Bau
Piraka River
Diamond Narrows
Mbaerope R
Holupuru Falls
Nusa Mbanga
Mbanone
Mbarasipo
Pakepake Island
Mbaere R
Mbuni
Lola Island
Bethany & Sidon
Mandou
Kundu Point
Munda Airport
Munda
Nusa Roviana
Bethlehem Island
Koviki Point
Kumbonitu
Nusaghele Island
Nusa Roviana
Roviana Island
Around Munda
0   5   10 km
Skull Island
Cook Submarine Volcano
Hombuhombu Island
To Rendova Island & Tetepare Island

Mt Bau More than 10 stones and pillars stand on raised platforms deep in the bush atop Mt Bau, and represent ancestral spirits. Villagers treat these monuments very seriously and will refuse to take anyone who they suspect will act disrespectfully at the site. It is believed that anyone who doesn't act reverently will get a custom sickness.

Getting There & Away The site is about nine km inland from the coast at Ilangana on a very overgrown bush trail towards Enoghae Point. You will need a guide and should expect to pay a custom fee.

Noro Noro, 16 km to the north-west of Munda, is where the pole-and-line boats operating in Western Province are based. There's a large Solomon Taiyo cannery here, employing hundreds of people and processing thousands of tonnes of tuna. Noro is a major port and the fastest-growing town in the Solomons, with a population of 2700.

Noro's facilities already include an NBSI branch, a Westpac agency, a police station, a Hot Bread Kitchen, electricity and piped water. The 10-room *Noro Lodge* (☎ 61238) charges S$33 per person in six-bed shared rooms. Standard rooms are S$110 and studio rooms are S$165. It's a five-minute walk from the government wharf.

Getting There & Away Catch a ride with the Taiyo trucks that take Munda workers to the cannery early in the morning, and back again late in the afternoon.

New Georgia's South Coast
Roviana Lagoon The lagoon is protected by offshore islands 20 to 40m high and extends 52 km eastwards from Munda to Kalena Bay. Within it are many small islets formed from coral shoals. **Nusa Hope Island** has a crocodile farm (S$10 entry). There are also plenty of wild crocodiles in the waters nearby and in the lagoon's river mouths further east.

The crawl was swum here centuries before the rest of the world latched onto this efficient swimming stroke.

Directly below **Araroso Point**, at the eastern end of the lagoon, are three caves containing shell valuables and skulls.

Viru Harbour A further 30 km south-east, this was formerly an important WWII base for the Japanese. It's now a logging and saw-milling centre. Traditional carvings and fish-hooks are made at **Tombe**, the cliff-top village overlooking the eastern side of this inlet.

Ships approach Viru Harbour between tall coral cliffs while small canoes paddle across the one-km-wide port. Houses are right at the shore, many of them standing on stilts over the water. In the 19th century five coral-stone bastions protected the sea entrance from head-hunters. Three ancient fortresses are close to Tombe; another is near **Tetemara** on the harbour's western side. The oldest and most impressive one is inland. There are several stone monoliths or coral-rock platforms on nearby ridge tops, usually enclosed by rings of upright stones or coral walls. There are also some caves which were used in head-hunting days as burial places or hide-outs. Locals can show you these sites.

A more modern relic – a large Japanese gun from WWII – keeps a lonely vigil on the cliffs above Tetemara. Boats constantly cross the harbour between Tetemara and Tombe; it should be possible to pick up a free ride.

New Georgia's North Coast

There's a small custom fee to see attractive **Vakambo Island**, which has a village. It's a convenient access point for visits to the sand-fringed Tatama and Kotu Kuriana islands.

About 13 km north is **Mondomondo Island**. The small bay on the eastern side of this island is noted for its fishing. Yachts find trolling particularly successful. **Ramata Island** and airfield is 18 km northwest. It has sandy shores and a pleasing offshore islet, tiny Keru Island.

Ramata is just south of **Tokovai Lagoon**. This eight-km lagoon is the home of many wood carvers.

Paradise This large village welcomes outsiders. It's in an attractive position behind a string of reefs, on the southern bank of the Maerivi River. Two km upstream from the village are sparkling rapids.

Paradise is the centre of a religion known as Etoism. Its followers attend the Christian Fellowship Church (CFC). In 1959, followers of Silas Eto – later called the Holy Mama – broke away from the Methodist Church in New Georgia. The CFC is formed along kinship lines, and members' land belongs to the church so that communal progress can be achieved through village cooperation. The movement is strongest between Wilson and Rice harbours in north-eastern New Georgia.

There is a *village rest house* and the CFC can help to arrange accommodation in other nearby villages if necessary.

The villagers are the custom owners of many archaeological sites in the nearby mountains. They can guide you to these, including to Mt Mase's crater rim at 843m.

Mbaeroko Bay There was a very determined wartime Japanese garrison here. It held the besieging Us forces off for five weeks before finally being overwhelmed in August 1943.

A silent reminder of WWII is the **sunken Japanese freighter** near the shore. Its masts protrude above the water, with the upper works visible to snorkellers at low tide.

The freighter was bombed as its crane was loading cargo on to an adjacent barge. The derrick is still swung out with the rear axle of a truck hanging over its tender, which also sank. The ship is still leaking oil.

Crocodiles commute between Mbaeroko Bay and Hathorn Sound in New Georgia, and Vila River on Kolombangara. They can sometimes be seen on the surface, gliding across the two km stretch of open water before proceeding more furtively under New Georgia's mangrove shores.

Enoghae Point, at the jutting northern lip of the bay, has several large Japanese WWII anti-aircraft guns still hidden in the scrub, along with a pile of live ammunition.

VONAVONA ISLAND

To the north-west of New Georgia, and separated from neighbouring Kohinggo by the beautiful Vonavona Lagoon, Vonavona is a mainly flat 70-sq-km coral-limestone island. Alternatively called Wana Wana or Parara, Vonavona has about 3500 people. Rarumana and the area around Mbanone and Mandou are the island's two main centres of population.

Local fisherfolk make nets from vines collected from the bush. The nets are put to sea and dragged towards the shore, a juice in the vine stunning the fish, which are then easily caught.

Mandou is a CFC village, and outside each house is an *aroso*. This is a structure composed of two poles connected at the end by a bamboo rod. Below this rod, which is decorated with orchids and hibiscus flowers, are two shorter poles. The aroso is said to vibrate violently at various times throughout the day. These vibrations have religious significance to the CFC.

Bukaware baskets, trays and shields are made in **Mbuni**, while baskets and pandanus handbags are produced at **Mbarasipo**. They can be purchased direct from the weavers.

Getting There & Around

Vonavona can only easily be reached by canoe. There's a great deal of reef in the area and the only recognised anchorage in Vonavona is at Bethany. However, the lagoon's shallow, sheltered, often sandy-bottomed waters should offer plenty of comfortable moorings.

A three-km footpath runs along the coast at Rarumana in the north-west, and another 10-km stretch joins Mbanone to Kumbonitu in the island's south-east. Otherwise, transport is by canoe.

VONAVONA LAGOON

This lagoon extends for 28 km between the tiny islets of Blackett Strait and the long, sandy island of Nusaghele. Within this area are many islets, ringed by coral-encrusted shallows interspersed with deeper seas.

Most of the inner chain of islets along Blackett Strait are surrounded by white coral-debris beaches. You can walk between some of these at low tide, as there's often only a very narrow sandbar connecting them. The small islands in and around the western edge of the lagoon are surrounded by coral reefs. They're regularly visited by diving groups from Gizo – see the Dive Sites section under Ghizo Island earlier in this chapter for descriptions.

Skull Island

The tiny islet at the tip of Kundu Point (Vonavona) has a skull house, or reliquary containing the skulls of many chiefs. They date from the 1920s, right back to early head-hunting days of 300 years ago. The skull house is a small, triangular-shaped casket which also contains the chiefs' clamshell-ring valuables.

The custom owners live at Kumbonitu on Vonavona Island. They charge a custom fee of S$10 to see the skulls.

MARK HONAN

· SIMON FOALE

SIMON FOALE

Top: Reef off Sandfly Island, Nggela Islands, Central Province
Bottom: Baitfish on a reef off Sandfly Island, Nggela Islands, Central Province

SIMON FOALE

Diver at submerged reef, Sandfly Island, Nggela Islands, Central Province

Cook Submarine Volcano

This volcano, first reported by HMAS *Cook* about nine km south-west of Mandou (Vonavona Island), erupted in 1964 and 1983. Another eruption was reported in 1963 about 17 km west of Koviki Point.

Kohinggo Island

Also called Arundel, Kohinggo has about 850 people. It nestles between Vonavona and New Georgia's north-western tip and is about 110 sq km in area. The reefs around the small chain of islets along Kohinggo's northern shore teem with brightly coloured fish.

There's a wrecked US Sherman tank at **Tahitu**. It was lost in action when US marines overran a Japanese strongpoint in mid-September 1943. Just offshore is **Saikarasa Island**.

The Japanese mounted several guns at the western end of this island in WWII to close off the Blackett Strait to shipping. Most of them have now been removed.

Lola Island

The *Zipolo Habu Resort* (☎ & fax 61178, PO Box 165, Munda) on Lola Island is a very popular retreat. Joe and Lisa Entrikin rent leaf-house cottages, most with a kitchen, for S$94/121/154 a single/double/family. Bathroom facilities are separate. The island has palms, a white-coral beach, and excellent fishing – fishing and snorkelling gear is for rent. Bring your own food if you want to cook, otherwise the excellent meals package (mostly seafood) is S$99 per day. The 30-minute canoe ride from Munda is S$75 return, or free if you stay five nights.

A couple of km west is **Pakepake Island**, where there's a leaf-hut *rest house*. There are also white-sand beaches, fishing, snorkelling, and bushwalks to enjoy while you're here.

RENDOVA ISLAND

This 400-sq-km island lies due south of New Georgia's Roviana Lagoon. It's about 40 km long and home to 3000 people. Ren-

dovans regularly perform war dances at cultural festivals. Bamboo panpipe bands are also popular locally.

Rendova Peak (1063m) dominates the island. To the south are highland plateaus overshadowed by the 820m Mt Herohiru. There's a small network of lagoons along the northern coast.

In WWII, Rendova was liberated by US marines in June 1943. Although the Japanese had more than 20 large anti-aircraft guns at Rendova Harbour, the island was easily recovered. The Americans immediately began preparing to seize the Japanese airfield at Munda, 11 km away on New Georgia. Rendova Harbour became a US naval base housing 15 to 20 PT boats, including *PT 109*, a boat with John F Kennedy a crew member.

The Americans hid large guns on Pao and Kukurana islands and used them to bombard the Japanese at Munda. On the night of 1 August 1943, all the PT boats set out to intercept four Japanese destroyers which were ferrying 900 men to reinforce their base on southern Kolombangara. One of the destroyers, the *Amagiri*, ran down *PT 109* on its return journey. See the Sinking of *PT 109* aside earlier in this chapter.

Medical Services

Rendova's main clinic is at Ughele. Nurse aid posts are at Lokuru and Hopongo.

Things to See & Do

Most visitors only spend 15 to 20 minutes in **Ughele** when the *Iuminao* calls in. The market stalls by the jetty operate on days the ship visits. The harbour's clear water is ideal for swimming and snorkelling. There's also a lagoon with an attractive sand beach about two km along the coast to the north.

The small Ughele Falls is about two km up the Ughele River. It provides the village's water supply so it's not for swimming.

Rendova Peak, also called Mt Longguoreke, is often shrouded in clouds. Climbing it takes two days return, and

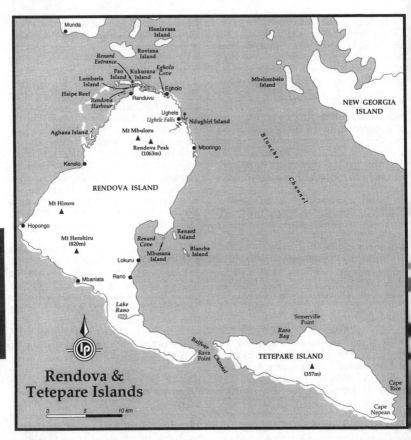

Rendova & Tetepare Islands

0   5   10 km

requires a guide. Initially the ascent is reasonably easy, but nearer the top the ridges become very steep and the going is tough. Ask at Ughele for both a guide and permission from the custom owners to climb it.

Egholo Cove is a large coastal inlet with plenty to explore by canoe. There's a rusting war wreck on the shore at its southern entrance beside the small settlement of Egholo. A sunken US two-seater warplane lies in about 10m of water near **Randuvu**. You can see it when snorkelling in the very clear water. Villagers will point it out.

Dancers at **Mbangopingo**, a small village by Lokuru, have performed at several international festivals. Their dances include the Heruo, which is about the seasonal ripening of ngali nuts in October, and a dog-imitation dance.

Places to Stay

There are no proper rest houses on Rendova, though larger villages have a basic leaf hut that visitors can use. A nominal fee will be charged. You would need to get advance permission from the local chief.

Getting There & Away

The *Iuminao* arrives at Ughele from Honiara Monday morning and Thursday afternoon en route to Munda and Gizo. It calls in again on Tuesday morning and Friday afternoon on its way back to the capital. Economy fares from Ughele are S$69 to Honiara, S$30 to Munda and S$39 to Gizo. To get elsewhere around the island, you'll need to take a canoe.

AROUND RENDOVA ISLAND
Lumbaria Island

Also spelled Lubaria, this pleasantly quiet islet resort is just off the north coast of Rendova Island and has plenty of nearby sandy beaches. You can snorkel around looking for sunken war remains, dive for shells, or watch large fish (including barracudas) swimming around the nearby Renard Entrance.

The **John F Kennedy museum** is beside where Kennedy lived in between naval actions. There's a not-too-impressive collection of WWII memorabilia, including US and Japanese machine guns and helmets. There's also an idol which was once worshipped, and several weapons from head-hunting days.

The *Lumbaria Island Resort* has two houses providing a total of 14 beds at about S$25 each, or S$90 with meals. Cooking facilities are available – bring your own food.

Make arrangements with Ketily Zonga, PO Box 27, Munda, or the Agnes Lodge in Munda can sometimes forward enquiries. Rides from Lumbaria to Munda cost about S$70 by chartered motor canoe. They leave early in the morning, as the sea gets quite choppy by midday.

TETEPARE ISLAND

Tetepare, also called Montgomerie Island, is 26 km long and seven km wide. It covers an area of 120 sq km, rising to 357m at its centre. The landscape is rugged, and the island has interesting flora and fauna, including plenty of mud crabs. People from Viru Harbour in New Georgia occasionally come over to Tetepare to hunt crocodiles.

The island's saltwater croc population mostly lives along Tetepare's north-eastern coast between Somerville Point and Cape Rice.

Terepare is likely to be the next big battleground between the loggers and advocates of low impact eco-tourism. The issue is complicated by the question of land ownership. It has been unpopulated for three generations, and 30 different villages have laid claim to it.

The only way to get to or around the island is by canoe. You might be able to get a ride from Lokuru on Rendova.

Marovo Lagoon

Marovo Lagoon, on New Georgia Island's eastern seaboard, is the world's largest island-enclosed lagoon and has been proposed for World Heritage listing. It skirts round Vangunu Island and ends at Nggatokae Island. In novelist James Michener's opinion, the Marovo Lagoon is the eighth wonder of the world.

This shallow lagoon, with abundant reefs and sandy cays, is protected along much of its north-eastern side by narrow barrier islands, five to 60m high. Many of these landforms have golden, sandy shores or slender sandbars. Marovo's best beaches are on the lagoon side, with those on the islands of Sanihulumu, Porepore, Matiu, Sambulo, Landoro and Lumalihe excelling. Only 20 of the lagoon's many islands are inhabited.

Tall mountains radiate outwards from their extinct breached volcanic rims near New Georgia's eastern shore. Narrow crests are separated by deeply incised valleys, particularly in the case of Mt Mahimba (821m) and Mt Hungu (605m). These high landmasses descend into large, mangrovefringed coastal swamps, especially near the Njai Passage. Many of these swamps have crocodiles.

The Marovo Lagoon has been overfished in the past, and protective measures

WESTERN

WESTERN

Marovo Lagoon

0   5   10 km

New Georgia Sound
(The Slot)

PLACES TO STAY
1 Uepi Island Resort
2 Vanua Rapita Lodge
3 Lagoon Lodge
4 Kajoro Sunset Lodge
5 Hideaway Lagoon
6 SDA house
7 SDA house
8 Seghe Rest House
9 Horena Lodge
10 Matikuri Lodge
11 Tibara Lodge
12 Tachoava Lodge
13 SDA Rest House
14 Ropiko Lodge
15 Lusina Lodge

To Kavachi Submarine
Volcano

have been introduced to allow stocks to replenish. If you intend game fishing in the lagoon, enquire about current regulations.

The landmass the lagoon partially surrounds is Vangunu Island. This 520-sq-km volcanic island has a very indented coastline and two distinct centres. Mt Vangunu's 1123m high crater dominates the south and is often shrouded by clouds. In the northeast is 520m Mt Reku, whose several isolated rocky pinnacles tower over the Mbareke Peninsula, where most of the island's 4000 people live, including many carvers. The swampy Nggevala River forms a division between the island's two parts.

Mendaña may have seen Vangunu in 1568 as he named an island in this area Ysla de Arrecifes, meaning 'Island of Reefs' (ie the Marovo Lagoon). Seventh Day Adventists are numerous in Vangunu, so it may be hard to organise anything on Saturday.

Information

Clinics are at Seghe on New Georgia, Chea and Mbatuna on Vangunu, and Penjuku on Nggatokae.

There are no telephones in this region, nor any electricity apart from private generators. Water generally comes from water tanks or communal outdoor taps and should be treated before drinking.

Accommodation & Food

The World Heritage Committee (a UNESCO organisation) has been instrumental in establishing a network of seven village-level eco-tourist lodges in the lagoon. They have been built in the traditional style using custom materials, yet tourist comforts are considered (eg they all have a sit-down toilet). The hosts are keen to show visitors cultural aspects of traditional village life. Bush walks, trips to tabu sites and other activities are offered.

World Heritage lodges are found at Horena, Matikuri, Mbili Passage, Tachoava, and Sombiro, with two at Telina. All have access to a radio, which should make advance bookings straightforward through the Visitors' Bureau in Honiara. The World Wide Fund for Nature (WWF) has also been active in the area, and helped to set up Vanua Rapita Lodge. Kitchen facilities are available in these places: bring your own food, as stores are few and far between. Apart from Matikuri, the lodges provide local-style meals. Kerosene lamps are used for lighting.

There are a few other rest houses and lodges dotted around, plus Uepi Island resort, a long-established tourist-class complex in a prime dive location. If you can't afford to stay there, stick to the eco-tourist lodges and visit Uepi on a day trip.

Getting There & Away

Air Three airfields are convenient for visiting the Marovo Lagoon. Seghi airfield on New Georgia Island receives only Solomon Airlines flights. Batuna airfield on Vangunu Island and Gatokae airfield on Nggatokae Island are serviced only by Western Pacific. You therefore may end up flying in with one airline and out with the other, taking ships or canoes in between.

Solomon Airlines flies into Seghe from Honiara (S$200) daily except Tuesday, with the flight continuing to Gizo (S$115) or Munda (S$80). Western Pacific has a flight on Tuesday and Thursday from Honiara to Gatokae (S$175) then Batuna (S$185), before returning the same way. Gatokae to Batuna costs S$65. Its multi-stop Honiara-Geva flight on Monday and Friday includes Batuna.

Sea The *Iuminao* and the *Ramos I* pass through Marovo Lagoon – see Getting There & Away at the start of this chapter. From Honiara, the Wings Shipping economy/1st class fare is S$55/86 to the Mbili Passage and S$59/89 to Patutiva. Economy fares from Patutiva are $21 to either Chea or Gasini in the lagoon; 1st class is S$36 extra, and is probably not worth it for such a short trip.

Anchorages include those at Chemoho, Mbatuna, Mbale (all on Vangunu Island), Matikuri Island, Mbili Passage, and at Penjuku and Kavolavata on Nggatokae Island.

Getting Around

There are no roads and few paths, so most people have a canoe or access to one. You'll probably have to pay for a charter. World Heritage is hoping to set up a water taxi to transport guests between its lodges.

SEGHE

Donald Kennedy's coastwatch base near Seghe was only 18 km south of the Japanese stronghold at Viru Harbour. Nonetheless, the Japanese never found it. Kennedy's group had a prisoner-of-war compound, and their own schooner with which to make surprise attacks on Japanese barges.

Allied successes depended heavily on the help provided by coastwatch islanders. Their reports of Japanese air and sea activity gave US forces vital minutes to prepare their counter strokes. Downed Allied aircrew and shipwrecked sailors often found refuge with Kennedy's people. A much-prized reward was a bag of rice for each person (friend or foe) that the islanders rescued.

Seghe, a subprovincial headquarters on New Georgia's south-east coast, has grown up around the airfield, which was built by US Seabees in 10½ days flat. There's an intact P-38 Lightning fighter at the end of the runway in six metres of water; scuba divers often sit in its cockpit to be photographed. The attractive seven-km-wide Nono Lagoon is just to the west.

Patutiva, about three km north-east of Seghe off Vangunu, has thatched houses built on stilts by the water. A market appears here magically when the passenger ships stop by.

Places to Stay & Eat

The *Seghe Rest House* is near Seghe airfield and costs S$35 per bed. It's under the same ownership as Matikuri Lodge (see the next section) and has a kitchen.

Horena Lodge is on a tiny islet near Mbareho Island in the Nono Lagoon, seven minutes by canoe from Seghe. Ten people can be accommodated for S$40 (S$30 each for couples). There's a kitchen, or food can be provided for S$25 a day (S$20 each for couples). The owners, Renter and Eddie Tivuru, are Seventh Day Adventist. Activities include night-time crocodile spotting.

MATIKURI ISLAND

Matikuri and the surrounding area have many attractive beaches, good fishing, excellent snorkelling, beautiful sunsets and several custom sites to visit.

The *Matikuri Lodge* has four leaf houses costing S$45 an adult and S$22.50 a child. Transfers from Seghe are S$20 per person each way. There are cooking facilities; bring your own food as meals aren't provided. Canoe hire costs S$30 to S$50 per day (plus fuel), and excursions include an overnight trip to Nggatokae.

VANUA RAPITA & AROUND

Vanua Rapita Lodge is situated on tiny Michi Island off Vangunu Island, and is run by the mainland village Michi. Opened in 1995, it can accommodate up to 12 people in three leaf huts. Beds cost S$38.50. Snorkelling gear and paddle canoes are free, as are tea/coffee-making facilities. Varied optional activities cost S$75 per day – possibilities include a village tour, tabu site visits, custom dances and nature walks. You get masses of food at breakfast (S$10), lunch (S$15) and dinner (S$25), or you can opt for self-catering. The friendly villagers are of the Tabakokoropa tribe and have set up a large conservation area which stretches up to Uepi Island. (Apparently their ancestors owned Uepi until they sold it for one kayak!) Tranfers from Seghe are S$25 each way. Bookings can be made through WWF in Gizo or GTS in Honiara.

About nine km north are the Mindeminde Islands, a group of 34 very beautiful islets with mangroves and sandy shores.

UEPI ISLAND

With the shallow waters of the Marovo Lagoon to the west and the deep waters of the New Georgia Sound to the east, Uepi (pronounced 'oo-py') is ideally placed to be a prime diving centre.

The three-km-long, one-sq-km islet has an extensive reef around it – perfect for **snorkelling**. You can lie in 30 cm of water at Uepi's jetty, and look down a 30m submarine wall.

There are several exceptional **dive sites**. These are at Uepi Point, Charoopana Island (a drift dive through teeming fish) and Landoro Island, with its drop-off and beautiful coral gardens. On most dives you're likely to see sharks – sometimes even hammerheads. Barracuda are also numerous. In addition there are also cave dives and enormous gorgonian fans. Like many nearby islands, Uepi has a small, resident coconut-crab population. Much more plentiful are the mangrove crabs regularly served for dinner.

The Uepi Island Resort has a fully equipped dive shop. Island-based dives cost S$110 each; more distant sites have a surcharge and some may have a custom fee to pay. Regulator/BCD rental cost S$10 each per dive and snorkelling gear is S$10 for the day. A resort course costs S$175, and full certification courses are available. **Fishing** is also good: boat and equipment hire costs S$65 per hour. Sailboards are free.

The resort offers a programme of excursions and activities throughout the lagoon, including river tours and visits to woodcarving villages. Day trippers, including yachties, to Uepi are welcome (no notice required), though a small charge is made for repeat visits.

The *Uepi Island Resort* offers a choice of lodges or bungalows, respectively going for S$162/258 and S$248/346 a single/double. That's pricey as only the bungalows have private shower and toilet, but all rooms do have generator electricity and tea/coffee-making facilities. The meals package is compulsory and costs S$125. The food is excellent, and plentiful in both choice and quantity; dinners are sociable affairs, usually preceded by a drink at the bar. Bookings must be made and paid for at least a week in advance, through Tropical Paradise Pty Ltd (☎ & fax 0061-77 75 1323), PO Box HP 84, Hermit Park, Townsville, QLD 4812, Australia. The Honiara Agent (☎ & fax 26076), Roco Ltd, PO Box 920, has an office in the NPF plaza.

The resort is a 40-minute motor-canoe ride from Seghe airfield. There's a transfer fee of S$36/18 each way per adult/child.

MAROVO ISLAND

Sasaghana on the island's western side has many woodcarvers. On its eastern shore is Chumbikopi, where villagers have a war canoe on display (S$10 custom fee), and do custom dances by prior arrangement. Also on this side is Chea, where the Honiara-Gizo boats stop. Villagers offer a good selection of carvings at decent prices, and there should be somewhere to stay.

TELINA ISLAND

Many stylish, modern, carving designs have spread from this friendly SDA island, and its woodwork is highly regarded.

Opposite the island, on Vangunu, is *Kajoro Sunset Lodge*, owned by John Wayne, who also carves. He will tell you his tribal history and take you on excursions, including to nearby snorkelling sites (own gear needed). Beds are S$30 each, and evening meals are S$10, though there are cooking facilities. About three km inland on the Laghemba River is the Laghemba Falls. Canoe transfers to/from Mbatuna are provided at a reasonable price.

Across the bay to the west is *Lagoon Lodge*, owned by Romulus Paoni. It's of similar standard and charges S$25 per bed (S$20 for couples) and S$15 for dinners. There's a kitchen, and various excursions are offered. Both owners have big ideas for the future and are currently building more rooms.

VANGUNU ISLAND

This 520-sq-km volcanic island has a very indented coastline and two distinct centres. Mt Vangunu's 1123m crater dominates the south and is often shrouded by clouds. In the north-east is Mt Reku (520m), whose several isolated rocky pinnacles tower over Mbareke Peninsula, where most of the island's inhabitants live, including many carvers. The swampy Nggevala River forms a natural division between the island's two parts.

Cheke

A couple of km west of Cheke village is Muven Kuve's *Hideaway Lagoon*. He has four rooms at S$30 per bed and simple cooking facilities. Local-style food (three meals) is provided for S$15 per day. Muven says he pioneered eco-tourism in the Marovo Lagoon but was bypassed when World Heritage was doling out grants to certain lodges. Consequently, he doesn't have modern facilities (eg the toilet is a plank over a sheltered inlet). But, to compensate, Muven is an experienced and interesting host who offers a range of excursions. Travellers have verified that he knows the best snorkelling spots. Transfers are available to/from Mbatuna or Gasini.

WESTERN

Chemoho

There are several islands near Chemoho with dazzling, sandy beaches. Matiu and Porepore are the closest. The best plan is to charter a motor canoe for the day and try to see Sanihulumu, Sambulo and Lumalihe islands.

Chemoho has an SDA house available for visitors, but people are rarely around to let you in.

Mbatuna

This village has a Western Pacific agency and several stores. There is an *SDA house* here which visitors may use for about S$10 a head. It's up the hill, about a four-minute walk from the agency, and has a kitchen, hot water and flush toilet. Batuna airfield is a few minutes' walk in the other direction – check-in first at the agency.

TACHOAVA ISLAND

This tiny island, east of Vangunu Island, is good for bird-watching and snorkelling. Monitor lizards can also be seen. *Tachoava Lodge*, run by Mirinda Choko, provides beds for S$30 and evening meals for S$10. A kitchen/communal area is being built, and a further accommodation house is planned. Canoe transfers cost S$30 to Mbatuna and S$20 to Sombiro.

NGGATOKAE ISLAND

Nggatokae, pronounced 'gat-oh-kye', is also spelt Gatukai and Gatokae. Captain Manning on the *Pitt* in 1792 made the first sighting by foreigners. Not realising it was a separate landmass from Vangunu, he named it Cape Traverse.

Nggatokae is formed from a large volcanic cone, reaching its peak at 887m on Mt Mariu's narrow crater rim. There's an area of raised reef near Peava in the east. Coastal areas on the Marovo Lagoon's northern side are swampy. In the past, war canoes from Nggatokae raided as far as Choiseul, nearly 200 km away. Many of its 1700 people are carvers.

Gatokae airfield is at **Sombiro**. There's an SDA building here which serves as a *rest house*. A 20-minute walk from the airfield is *Ropiko Lodge*, considered one of the best of the World Heritage lodges. It's run by Piko Riringi. He can undertake excursions to the nearby Japanese plane wreck from WWII, and other sites. The lodge has ocean views and a kitchen. Beds are S$30 and dinner is S$10.

A long arm of Nggatokae reaches up to **Mbili Passage**, the first stop in the Marovo Lagoon for ships from Honiara. Adjoining it is Mbili village, on a long, slender SDA island called Minjanga. It's noted for its carvers and wonderful sunsets. *Tibara Lodge* on Minjanga Island, next to Mbili village, can accommodate up to eight people; beds are S$30 and dinner is S$10. There's also a kitchen, and good snorkelling nearby. The owner, Luten Watts, is the local chief.

The people of **Mbiche** village, in the south, were avid head-hunters until they were shelled prior to WWI by an Australian warship acting for the British government. Paka, one of the last head-hunting chiefs in the Solomons, is buried at Mbiche, and his skull is still visible beside his grave. The village is also known for its stone bowls. There are plans for a rest house.

Penjuku is a very tidy SDA village. Many of its people are weavers or stone carvers. Nearly all visitors are met by a local elder who performs a welcoming dance at their arrival. A small fee will be charged. The village should be able to provide accommodation.

Getting Around

You can organise a motor-canoe ride from either Mbili Passage or Penjuku to make a trip through the lower parts of the Marovo Lagoon. There's also an enjoyable canoe trip from Penjuku along the base of the Marovo Lagoon to Sombiro, with a diversion up the Sombiro River if required.

A coastal footpath connects most places in Nggatokae. World Heritage has plans to set up walking tours round the south of the island, if the landrights issue can be settled.

MBULO ISLAND

Unused agriculturally, Mbulo's steep, craggy cliffs are formed from a raised reef which surrounds a 200m high volcanic core. Caves in its cliffs were used in former times as graves. There is also an ancient burial ground near the island's centre. You will need permission to visit Mbulo; the custom owners live beside Peava's sandy beach, four km away, on Nggatoke's east coast.

KINGGURU ISLAND

Mbaghole (pronounced 'bag-oh-ly') village is in a very picturesque setting, with palm fronds overhanging the beach. Ask the locals if saltwater crocodiles are a danger. *Lusina Lodge* provides simple accommodation and food.

KAVACHI SUBMARINE VOLCANO

Kavachi was above the sea's surface from late April to early June 1991. It rose about 15m high, spitting volcanic magma out constantly. The volcanic island grew to about a third of a hectare, before subsiding again below the waves. Sunsets all around the area were a spectacular blood red, their brilliant colours caused by volcanic dust.

Kavachi has erupted four times in the past 40 years, each time in a different position. In 1991, it appeared 19.5 km southwest of Nggatokae. In 1952 and 1972 its eruptions were much closer to Tetepare Island. On the latter occasion, it threw plumes of sea water and rock 60m into the air, though no island was formed. There was also activity in 1985 when it briefly caused surface water to boil.

MBOROKUA ISLAND

Called Murray's Island by Manning in 1792, Mborokua is 62 km south-east of Peava. It is four sq km in size and uninhabited, an isolated, dead volcano, breached on its western side. The sea surges into its half-moon bay, making a difficult mooring for any vessel attempting a visit.

The Shortland Islands

Only nine km from Bougainville in Papua New Guinea, the scattered islands of the Shortlands group lie at the Solomons' north-western tip. The main island is Shortland, or Alu, as it is often called. Its principal neighbour is Fauro. About 3500 people live in the group's 340 sq km. Copra production and logging are its main industries.

Shortlands people and their wantoks, the Treasury Islanders, are keen to keep their identity unaffected by outside influences. Many refuse to learn any Melanesian language other than their own. Consequently, they will reply to other islanders in English, even if spoken to in Pijin. This applies particularly to older islanders and traditionalists, though young people are less inclined to follow this rule.

Visitors should always ask permission to enter a village, and then see the chief. Otherwise you will be asked to leave. Melanesian chiefs in these islands have a status akin to Polynesian chiefs and bear considerably more authority than their counterparts elsewhere in the Solomons.

Shortlands people tend to be more direct in their manner than other Solomon islanders. If you do something wrong, you'll be told so, whereas in other parts of the country villagers will usually tactfully overlook your error.

Visitors to the Shortlands should always ask permission first before strolling through someone's vegetable patch or coconut plantation. The answer will almost invariably be

WESTERN

Bougainville Warning

The Bougainville situation means you should check with immigration before entering the region. Foreigners who do stay here need to register with the authorities on Shortland Island: either at the police field force in Lofung (opposite Faisi Island) or at immigration at Korovou. ∎

Shortland Islands

To Treasury Islands (25 km)

0   10   20 km

---

yes and, once given, that permission is yours for a lifetime. But if you don't ask, villagers may wonder if you are being deliberately secretive and are planning to steal some food.

History

Villages between 800 and 1000 AD were generally built on coastal sites close to a creek.

The modern age began when Captain John Shortland saw the group in 1788 from the *Alexander*. Outside contact was limited at first, with ancient customs continuing unaffected. On one occasion warriors from Mono captured Fauro and massacred most of its people.

In 1878 a local chief called Gorai began supplying blackbirders with labourers for overseas plantations in exchange for guns. These new weapons enabled him to rule over all the Shortlands.

The Shortlands were the first islands in the Solomons group to be occupied by the Japanese in WWII. However, when the nearby Treasury Islands were liberated by the Allies in late 1943, the Shortlands were bypassed. Until peace came in 1945 they were left as isolated prisons, unable to be resupplied or evacuated and of little value to their occupiers.

Arts
The Shortlands used to be a major centre for pot making, with the oldest remains so far discovered dating back to between 800 and 1000 AD. About 40 abandoned village sites have so far revealed pieces of broken pottery. The industry declined once trading vessels arrived with metal or enamel utensils for sale. No-one has made any pots in the Shortlands for over 20 years.

Information
There's a church-run hospital at Nila on Poporang Island. Clinics are at Harapa in Shortland Island and Kariki on Fauro Island. Korovou has an immigration office.

The only proper rest house in the region is on Faisi Island. Radio for permission well in advance if you want to stay elsewhere.

Gizo-based dive operators can organise diving/land packages to the Shortlands on request, notably to Nila and Ballalae.

Getting There & Away
Air Solomon Airlines' Gizo-Choiseul Bay flight goes via Ballalae on Wednesday, Thursday and Friday. The fare from Ballalae is S$140 to Gizo and S$80 to Taro.

Sea None of the major shipping companies has regular services to the Shortlands – from Honiara, you may have to hop on one of CEMA's boats. Some Gizo-based vessels, such as *Western Queen, Parama* and *Vele*, make infrequent trips to the Shortlands, depending on cargo.

Anchorages of varying quality are found at Korovou, Nuhu, Ghaomai, Harapa and Kamaleai Two on Shortland, and Kariki and Toumoa in Fauro. Faisi Island and Nila both have a jetty.

Papua New Guinea You used to be able to go to/from Papua New Guinea (PNG) by taking a motor-canoe ride across the Western Entrance. The route will remain closed until the Bougainville situation is resolved. The PNG government regards any foreigners who visit Bougainville as having entered PNG illegally. The Solomons government cooperates with this and refuses permission for anyone to leave the country this way.

Getting Around
There are plenty of motor canoes at Korovou and Nila, available for charter or (if you're lucky) for shared rides. Fuel costs S$2.40 per litre. To get to Ballalae airfield, you can get a ride for S$20 with the Solomon Airlines agent, who starts off from Maleai. If the police field force has to meet a plane, they might take you for free.

A network of logging tracks dissects the flat terrain in eastern Shortland Island.

SHORTLAND ISLAND
Shortland is about 22 km long by 16 km wide. Only Balo Hill in its centre rises as high as 185m.

Shortland's north-western side is dotted with reefs and islets and is good for fishing, swimming and diving. **Harapa** was the original Gilbertese settlement in the Shortlands and received its first newly arrived Micronesians in 1962. The village has grown in size since then, and other Micronesian settlements have sprung up at nearby Kamalei Point, Kamaleai Two and Laomana Island. There's plenty of bird life on the small islands in nearby Maliusai Bay. In the south-west is Ghaomai Island, where there are several fine beaches and an attractive reef. Many of the islands on the north-eastern side also have sandy beaches.

Korovou, the local subprovincial headquarters, is at the end of a narrow spit between Kulitana Bay and Shortland Harbour, and has a store. Several Japanese aircraft remain sunk at their moorings in the bay. Others lie submerged three km from Korovou at Shortland Harbour's western end, which was a WWII Japanese seaplane base.

Across the channel is **Poporang Island**, where Nila village has a store. Offshore, several Japanese seaplanes and barges lie in 10 to 15m of water, all sunk at their moorings. Hidden in the bush are more Japanese remains, including three large coastal batteries, parts of four seaplanes, and a command centre. A reef surrounds both Poporang and Pirumeri islands, which are low, flat and densely wooded.

Immediately south is Mangusaiai Island. Its large village of **Maleai** was the pottery centre for the whole Shortlands until the process died out recently. You can still see some remains, as long as you ask Maleai's chief first. Near Maleai, on a tiny island in Shortland Harbour, is a store (with beer) which doubles as the Solomon Airlines Agency.

FAISI ISLAND

Faisi was the first place in the Solomons to be seized by the Japanese, in April 1943, and was used by them as a wartime destroyer base. There are attractive reefs along the island's eastern side, as there are along its small neighbours, Orlofi and Onua islands.

The *Faisi Rest House* has two rooms where beds are S$25 each. There's a kitchen, a covered verandah, and a sometimes functioning electricity generator. It's near the southern tip of the island, and is run by the family who live 200m clockwise round the shore. They have a motorised dugout for hire.

BALLALAE ISLAND

Until recently, this small, unpopulated island, with its tiny grass airstrip, had the unlikely status of an international airport. For cost reasons it now only receives domestic flights.

Three fairly well-preserved Japanese Betty bombers can be seen in the thick bush beside the airfield, as can other wrecked ones nearby. They're hard to find without a guide; bring plenty of repellent to ward off biting mites. Unexploded bombs are scattered along the seashore, and some seaplane wrecks lie in the shallow waters surrounding the island.

Ballalae Island was the scene of great cruelty towards Allied civilian prisoners in WWII. About 470 were brought from Singapore and forced to build the airstrip. Many died in 1943 from dysentery or exhaustion, while others were shot for saying the Japanese wouldn't win. Some deliberately ran into the path of US bombs during air raids and were killed. The remainder were beheaded when the airbase was completed.

FAURO ISLAND

This 29-km-long, hilly island with steep volcanic ridges rises to 400m at two points. Lightly populated Fauro is 19 km from Shortland. It is surrounded by reefs, as are its many small neighbouring islands.

The northern part of the island is shaped like a long hooked arm, and is the remains of a drowned volcano. All along this narrow isthmus are dazzling, sandy **beaches**. Some of Fauro's adjacent islets are no more than sandbars, while others have a canopy of coconut trees. Fishing, swimming, snorkelling and diving are good all around, but especially along the island's southern coast.

At **Kavakava Bay** there's a sunken Japanese freighter. It's hard to spot from the surface and still leaks oil. **Flying Fox Lagoon** is close by. There have been no flying foxes here since a cyclone in 1972, but this small lagoon is a good place to find mud crabs and large oysters. Fishing is good, though there are plenty of stingrays in the area.

Fauro's largest neighbour, **Ovau Island**, used to contain many wild pigs, but their numbers are now greatly reduced. There's also good game fishing in the area. Anyone wishing to visit Ovau should first get permission from the chief of Kariki village on Fauro, or from the rival claimant to custom ownership, the chief of Samanagho Island.

Oema Island and Oema Atoll are well-stocked with clams. They're both treated as bird sanctuaries by local people.

The Treasury Islands

Mono and Stirling are the only substantial members of the Treasury Islands group. First seen by Americans Dale and Read in 1787, and given their name by Shortland one year later, the Treasuries are 29 km south-west of the Shortlands and have an area of 80 sq km.

MONO ISLAND

Although its people speak Alu, the language spoken in the Shortland Islands, Mono was originally settled by people who came from north-western Vella Lavella, who landed on Mono's northern side at Soanatalu.

Almost all the Treasury Islands' 1000 people live in Falamai. The ancestors of these friendly islanders killed 18 of the crew of the British whaler *Offley* in 1842, and 33 crew from the US vessel *Superior* 20 years later. Captain Simpson in HMS *Blanche* brought peace to the area while surveying it shortly afterwards.

Falamai has a clinic, a community library, a leaf-style rest house and a black-sand beach. All visitors should ask the chief's permission to see the area.

Getting There & Away

Air Mono airfield on Stirling Island receives only one Solomon Airlines flight per week: it leaves Gizo (S$140) for Mono at 9.45 am on Wednesday and returns there at 10.40 am.

Sea As with the Shortlands, your best chance of arriving by ship is on a Gizo-based vessel. Canoe traffic is light between Mono and Shortland, though there's often

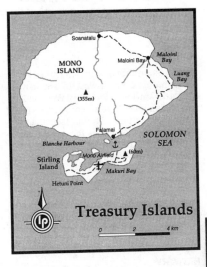

Treasury Islands

someone going to Korovou on Friday morning and returning Sunday. A shared canoe ride there costs about S$30. The Treasuries' usual anchorage is at Falamai.

STIRLING ISLAND

Unpopulated Stirling is on the opposite side of Blanche Harbour, and 1.5 km from Mono. You'll find an airfield, the remains of a large WWII Allied base, and a network of tracks on this narrow six-km-long raised coral platform.

At the end of WWII, a large number of US aircraft were abandoned here. There weren't enough pilots to fly them back home, so they were deliberately bent and then bulldozed into the bush to prevent further use. Although most have now been removed, there are still wrecked planes in the sea at the base of the island's cliffs.

WESTERN

Choiseul Province

Choiseul (pronounced 'choy-zul') split from Western Province in September 1991. Lying along a north-west to south-west axis, 161-km-long Choiseul Island and its neighbours total 3294 sq km in area. Only 200m from eastern Choiseul Island, across the Nggosele Passage, is the largely unoccupied Rob Roy Island, while eight km further east is Wagina Island, which has been a centre of Gilbertese resettlement since 1962.

Three-quarters of Choiseul Province's 16,600 Melanesian people live in the main island's western half, and there are a further 2000 Gilbertese living in Wagina.

HISTORY

Mendaña's 1567 expedition saw a large island north-west of Santa Isabel and called it San Marcos. This was probably Choiseul Island.

Louis de Bougainville, who arrived 200 years later, named the island after Choiseul, the then French foreign minister. In the 19th century, head-hunting and slave-raiding parties from the New Georgia group regularly attacked the island. In the 1870s Liliboe, a central Choiseul Island bigman, evened the score by leading raids westwards. He also made forays against neighbouring Wagina until it became totally uninhabited.

Joint negotiations between Britain and Germany granted Choiseul Province to Germany in 1886, and then to Britain in 1899. In 1916, there were ferocious tribal wars on Choiseul Island, though these were brought under control by a peace treaty in 1921.

The Japanese landed on Choiseul Island early in 1942, and some remained there till the end of WWII. The island's inhabitants suffered little from the occupation, though they were fearful that the occupiers would seize their crops and treat them badly. Con-

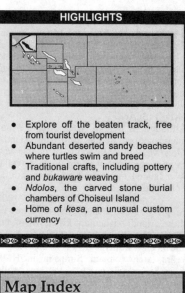

HIGHLIGHTS

- Explore off the beaten track, free from tourist development
- Abundant deserted sandy beaches where turtles swim and breed
- Traditional crafts, including pottery and *bukaware* weaving
- *Ndolos*, the carved stone burial chambers of Choiseul Island
- Home of *kesa*, an unusual custom currency

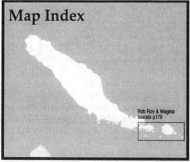

Map Index

Rob Roy & Wagina
Islands p179

sequently, chiefs organised constant patrols throughout the island.

Except for brief diversionary landings at Voza, Sanggighae and Choiseul Bay in late 1943, the only permanent Allied force on Choiseul Island consisted of 18 coastwatching islanders. This tiny force managed to kill 93 Japanese and only lost one man.

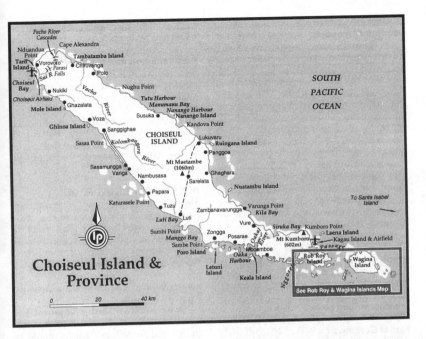

Choiseul Island & Province

0   20   40 km

CLIMATE

Choiseul Bay, in the north-western part of the province, receives 3559 mm of rain annually spread over an average 260 days. Temperatures range between 23°C and 31°C throughout the year. Morning humidity levels hover around 88%, reaching 90% for three months a year, while afternoon humidity averages 79% or less.

ARTS

Although it originated in Bougainville, *bukaware* is made by weavers in Choiseul Island in small quantities. A few potters are still active at Choiseul Bay and around Chirovanga. These are the last places in the Solomons where this traditional craft survives.

Today, small-sized kesa money is found in most parts of Choiseul Island. If you want to see some, just ask around. Larger examples are only seen in the Nuatambu area, the currency's original source.

Kesa Money

Kesa is an old form of shell currency that is still used in Choiseul Island. In the past it was used for bride price, compensation payments, land settlements, peacemaking and forming alliances.

Nine clam-shell cylinders make one kesa. A man's status depended on how much currency he owned. The history of each kesa, and all the transactions it had been through, were widely known. It's heavy and bulky – not the sort of money you could tuck away in a pocket.

Tradition has it that an entirely different people (possibly Polynesian) made this money. They collected huge numbers of clam shells from all over the island before settling on tiny Nuatambu. They then either disappeared or were first allowed to settle and trade their currency before being killed. ∎

SOCIETY & CONDUCT
Legendary People
Many Choiseul Islanders believe in a mythical tribe, the Voromangas. They have never been seen, but are believed to live at the source of the Kolombangara River, which flows out of Mt Maetambe. Villagers say Voromangas can occasionally be heard in the mountains blowing their panpipes and conch shells, especially inland from Sasamungga. Like the Kakamoras, they are said to be very strong.

According to another tradition there are also some monkey-like inhabitants – the Sinipi – in Choiseul Island's interior. These legendary people are said to resemble cave dwellers and use shells as knives to cut up mangoes, their favourite food.

Every village is said to have a *basana*. This is a spirit with two long front teeth and lengthy black hair. Basanas can trick people, or help them find food and track enemies. In head-hunting days, war canoes bore the dog-like face of a basana as a figurehead on their prows.

Burial Customs
The distinctive carved stone burial chambers of north-western Choiseul Island are called *ndolos*. They are about one metre high and 50 cm in diameter. In the centre is a hollow for the chief's bones. Pre-Christian Choiseul Islanders believed that once these bones were placed inside it, the ndolo became the sacred habitat of spirits.

INFORMATION
Taro, on tiny Taro Island in Choiseul Bay, is the provincial capital. Check the security situation before travelling to the region, as the airport has been closed in the past due to the Bougainville conflict. Gizo-based dive operators can organise diving/land packages to Choiseul on request.

Communications
Although there is a telephone connection to the Telekom office in Taro (☎ 0061-145 110 203), it is routed by satellite through Australia, and calls cost a hefty S$9.50 per minute. Each clinic has a radio, which you might be able to use.

Medical Services
Taro has a small hospital, plus there's a mission hospital in Sasamungga and a hospital on Mole Island run by the Eagon logging company.

There are clinics at Papara, Posarae, Panggoe, Susuka, Polo, Voza, Chirovanga (also spelled Sirovanga) and at Kukutin on Wagina Island. Nua-tambu and Burukuni have SDA clinics.

ACCOMMODATION & FOOD
The only proper rest houses are in Taro and Sasamungga. To stay anywhere else, it's a matter of contacting the local chief or mission priest – preferably well in advance using a service message – and asking if there's a leaf house you can use. If you are able to stay, the price will be modest, or you may even be able to trade accommodation for goods or food.

Bring plenty of food with you if you intend to stray off the beaten track. Some fresh bread from Taro's bakery would be appreciated by villagers.

GETTING THERE & AWAY
Air
Choiseul airfield is on Taro Island. Solomon Airlines flies daily, except Tuesday, from Honiara (S$375). Routes vary; Gizo is always included, Munda and Ballalae often are. Monday's flight takes 3½ hours as it's very indirect, with four stops and great scenery on the way. Western Pacific flies on Wednesday (via Gizo and Ringi Cove) and Friday (via Kagau and Gizo).

Kagau airfield is on a tiny island off Choiseul Island's east coast, a 15-km canoe ride from Wagina.

Sea
The only company that services Choiseul Province regularly is National Shipping. Every two weeks or so it goes from Honiara to Choiseul Bay (S$76), including stops at Wagina (S$58), Sasamungga (S$71) and

other ports. From Choiseul Bay it's S$9 to Sasamungga and S$49 to Wagina.

Gizo-based boats such as *Matari* and *Wataro* sometimes make the trip to Choiseul, but there's no regular schedule as it depends on cargo.

GETTING AROUND

There are only 25 km of road on Choiseul Island, with the longest section being between Vanga and Sanggighae.

Narrow footpaths connect most of the villages in the western end of Choiseul Island. Wagina Island has no roads, though a footpath connects villages on the south coast. Elsewhere in the province travel is by motor canoe – fuel costs S$2.80 per litre.

Choiseul Island & Around

Choiseul Island was traditionally called Lauru. Like the Shortland Islands, it is culturally closer to Bougainville in Papua New Guinea than to the Solomons.

Less than 35 km wide, Choiseul Island is a long, narrow, densely wooded island with an interior cut by steep, rugged ridges and deep gorges. Its highest point, near the centre, is Mt Maetambe, a volcanic cone rising to 1060m.

Much of Choiseul Island's shoreline consists of long, narrow beaches, some of them bordered by large, shallow freshwater marshes. Fens, occasionally the homes of saltwater crocodiles, are extensive along the coast and in some isolated inland areas. A swamp along the Oaka River in the island's south-east almost bisects Choiseul Island.

Although the island had a comparatively quiet time in WWII, there are several wrecked barges and aircraft in the shallows along Choiseul Island's western coast. Because of the island's limited facilities, few of these potential scuba sites have been explored yet.

TARO ISLAND

A site survey in 1972 recommended that Taro Island, off Choiseul Island's north-west coast, be considered unfit for human habitation because of its poor water supply and many mosquitoes. But a settlement sprang up anyway, fuelled by British aid. Taro is now the capital of the province, containing government buildings, a small hospital, a school, Telekom and Solomon Airlines offices, a post office, a bakery and several stores. Some people also live on the mainland.

Most of Taro Island's mosquitoes are on the west coast where there's an onshore reef of dead coral. The sandy beaches on the east side are relatively free of the insects. The newly built *Provincial Government Rest House* is by the football pitch and has six double rooms for S$35 per bed. There are overhead fans, communal showers and kitchen facilities. Electricity on the island is provided by a generator that's prone to breakdowns.

CHOISEUL BAY

The Parasi Falls, on the Sui River, are worth a visit. Go there by canoe, as it's a rather swampy area.

The attractive village of Vorovoro is six km north of Choiseul Bay. Two km beyond, at Nduandua Point, there's a plantation with a large collection of kesa money and ancient carvings. Also in the area are a number of archaeological and tabu sites.

CHIROVANGA

This is around the point, on the north-west coast. A few local women still make clay funerary urns and cooking ware. Once a pot is made, it's dried for a month, then decorated in between two firings. One km inland from Chirovanga are the Pacho River Cascades.

Chirovanga is close to the mouth of Vacho River, the longest Solomons waterway navigable by canoe. On both sides of the Vacho's upper reaches are attractive grass-covered hills interspersed with rocky outcrops and ravine-like valleys.

CHOISEUL

HOLGER LEUE

Islanders travel by canoe throughout the region's waterways

SASAMUNGGA

On the island's west coast, Sasamungga is the largest village on Choiseul Island and the United Church mission here has a *rest house*. Radio in advance if you want to stay.

Coconut plantations are almost continuous along this stretch of coast, but the largest concentration is at Sasamungga, by the village's sandy beach.

Canoes travel far up the Kolombangara River to the high grasslands at its headwaters. This is a popular area for hunting wild pigs with spears and bows and arrows.

NAMBUSASA

In 1936 a cargo cult developed here. Its followers believed a large steamship would arrive laden with all kinds of trade goods. Warehouses were erected to receive the expected cargo and bullyboys terrorised all non-believers. The movement collapsed, to most people's relief, in 1940.

MT MAETAMBE

Alluvial gold has been found on this mountain. There's a path up it from Luti Bay's sandy beach. The trail climbs to over 750m at Sarelata – Choiseul Province's only inland village. The path then descends to Lukuvaru on the island's eastern coast. It's a two-day hike and requires a guide.

MANGGO BAY

This bay has a number of caves and rock sites where early people used to live. They are at either end of the bay, at both Sumbi Point and Poro Island. A black-sand beach runs along much of the shore.

OAKA HARBOUR

A pleasant beach on this harbour separates the sea from a swamp. Islanders canoe four km up the nearby Oaka River and then take a marshy track across the island to Vure on the other side.

To the east, across from Mboemboe's

beach, are several small, sandy offshore islets. About 15 km west of the harbour, opposite the village of Zongga (pronounced 'john-ga'), are more small offshore islands. One of these islands is the tiny heart-shaped Letuni Island, surrounded by white, sandy beaches.

NUATAMBU ISLAND & AROUND
Off Choiseul Island's east coast, this is actually two small islands joined by a sandbar. The words *nua tambu* mean 'sacred island'. The large amount of broken clam shell found here indicates that Nuatambu was the principal manufacturing site for kesa currency. Ancient ceramics have also been collected here, suggesting that pots may have been made at Nuatambu as long ago as 1000 AD.

Nuatambu is slowly sinking, and the large amount of broken pottery and clam shell found at very low tides implies it may have been larger in the past. There's an ancient burial site on the hill nearest the mainland. It's surrounded by a tall coral and limestone wall.

The beaches from Nuatambu to Luku-varu in the north are a dark-olive colour because of the high proportion of minerals. In contrast, long stretches of white-sand beach extend from Nuatambu to Kumboro Point at Choiseul Island's south-eastern tip. A few exceptions are found at headlands, in the occasional deep black-sand bay, or where there are mangroves.

MT KUMBORO
There are fine views from the summit over southern Choiseul Island, Wagina and northern Isabel Province. It's a three-hour climb from the coast and you will need a guide to find the path.

Rob Roy & Wagina Islands

ROB ROY ISLAND
Also known as Vealaviru Island, Rob Roy, off Choiseul's south-eastern coast is owned by an expat and no-one else lives there. Vegetation is mainly coconut trees and rainforest, and the highest point is only 150m. Because of the small number of people using the area, there are still plenty of fish, dugongs and turtles.

WAGINA ISLAND
Also called Vaghena Island, this 78-sq-km landform was first observed by foreigners in 1769. The French explorer Jean de Surville, in the armed merchant ship *St Jean Baptiste*, called it Île de la Première Vue (the first island seen). In the late 19th century, the original Melanesian population fled after being decimated by disease and head-hunting Choiseul Islanders and New Georgians who were keen to secure the island's supply of turtle shell – a valuable commodity at the time.

CHOISEUL

Between 1963 and 1964, Gilbertese people moved here from the overcrowded Phoenix Islands in the eastern part of what is now Kiribati. Micronesians from all over the Solomons regularly take holidays on Wagina, as most have relatives on this island.

Wagina's 1000 inhabitants live in three beachside villages on its southern side. There's an ancient burial site on top of a cliff near Nikumaroro village, with a flat coral slab forming a chamber over human bones. Turtles swim and breed in local waters, and islanders hunt them for their meat and eggs.

Northern Wagina is unpopulated and is partly mangrove swamp. On the north coast is Lengambangara Cave, 35m inland at Lengambangara Point. It's currently used to house platforms where men rest while on fishing expeditions. Local legends tell of its use over many centuries.

Although Wagina is a slightly raised reef, its highest point is no more than 40m above sea level. Large deposits of bauxite have been found on Wagina. These have not yet been mined, as the minerals are in the cultivated part of the island, and there have been disputes over who owns the bauxite: the Gilbertese settlers or the original Melanesian land owners.

Offshore in the vicinity of the Hamilton Channel are several coconut-covered islands with sandy shores. One of these, Tema Volasi Island, houses an ancient Melanesian burial ground.

CHOISEUL

Isabel Province

Isabel Province is dominated by Santa Isabel, the longest island in the Solomons. Often simply called Isabel, the island is 200 km long and 30 km wide. Other islands within the province include San Jorge, many lesser islands in the Western and Arnarvon groups, and Ramos to the east.

Isabel Province has 16,500 people in an area of 4014 sq km. About 96% of its people are members of the Church of Melanesia (COM). Logging is a major activity.

Nickel, copper, manganese, zinc, chromium, silver and gold have all been found in the province, but none have yet been mined commercially. That is expected to change, with the province's estimated 45 million tonnes of nickel due to be mined soon. In addition to fishing and the farming of coconuts for copra, some villagers grow coffee and cocoa and run cattle, while others dive for trocchus shells and bêches-de-mer. The province receives few foreign visitors at present, but some eco-tourist projects have recently started.

HISTORY

Mendaña sighted Santa Isabel on 7 February 1568 and anchored the following day. He called the harbour Estrella (Star) Bay and the island Santa Isabel after the patron saint of his voyage.

Relationships between Spaniards and islanders were initially friendly. The visitors were impressed by the local chief Bilebanara, who wanted to learn Spanish and promised to supply food in return. When insufficient supplies came, the Spaniards seized hostages to trade for extra food. Violence ensued. This, together with the Spaniards' disgust at the islanders' cannibalism and worship of lizards, snakes and crocodiles, prompted them to depart after only two months.

Islanders say that during their stay the Spaniards penetrated deep inland in search of gold, reaching Santa Isabel's central

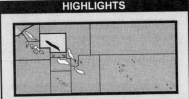

HIGHLIGHTS

- Explore Buala, the relaxed provincial capital surrounded by forests and coconut plantations
- Stay at eco-tourist villages near Buala, where you'll see traditional dances, go on guided bush walks and learn Pijin
- Visit Kia, the northern village guarding three inlets, where houses are built on stilts over the water
- Take a turtle-monitoring trip in the Arnarvon Islands, one of the largest nesting grounds for the endangered hawksbill turtle

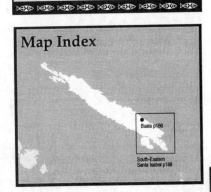

ridge. Others claim there was some fraternisation, resulting in a smattering of Spanish blood in today's population. It's true there are some light-skinned people along Santa Isabel's north-western coast, but it's more likely this is a consequence of past contacts with Polynesians.

ISABEL

181

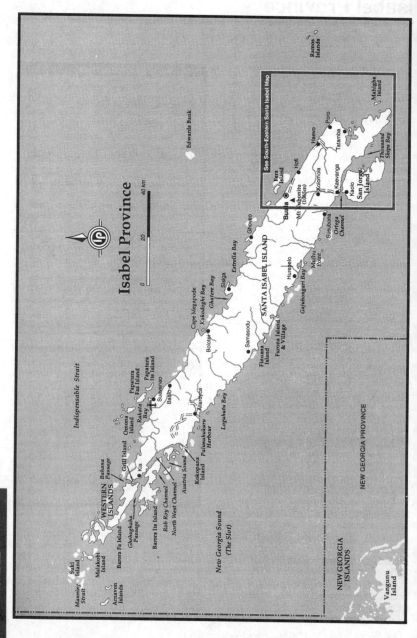

ISABEL

The next visitor was the French explorer Jean de Surville, in 1769. He captured a young islander from northern Santa Isabel called Lova Saragua and 'displayed' him in Paris.

Isabel Province was thereafter visited by few foreigners until 1845, when the French missionary Bishop Jean-Baptiste Epalle went ashore unarmed at Midoru in south-eastern Santa Isabel. When he refused to exchange his episcopal ring for two lemons (one partly eaten), he was mortally wounded. Although rescued, he died three days later.

In the mid-19th century, the people of Isabel Province suffered repeated head-hunting and slave raids, mainly by people from Simbo, New Georgia and Malaita. In addition, epidemics of influenza, dysentery, whooping cough and measles (all brought by European sailors) took a terrible toll.

The head-hunters stripped most of Santa Isabel's southern coast of people. Many fair-haired women were carried off as slaves, while most of those who survived fled to the eastern end of the island. Others sought refuge by building houses in trees. One such dwelling, 18m up, was equipped with piles of stones which were hurled down on enemies below.

The Church of Melanesia's prominence in the affairs of the province began in 1866. Bishop Patteson healed Chief Soga of Sepi, nephew of Santa Isabel's most famous head-hunting chief, Bera. Soga, who had been dying of malaria, showed his gratitude by converting to Christianity and making sure everyone else did likewise! He also helped bring head-hunting raids to an end by organising effective resistance to them in south-eastern Santa Isabel.

In 1886, Britain and Germany both proclaimed spheres of influence over the Solomons. Isabel, initially under German control, was transferred to Britain in 1899.

The missionaries and their local helpers, the catechists, were much more influential prior to WWII than was the remote British government. When village constables, later known as village headmen, were appointed

in 1923, inevitably the question was asked of government officials, 'Who is boss – king or archbishop?'. On Santa Isabel it was the Anglican archbishop.

In 1929, Richard Fallowes, a British missionary who supported the local people's right to autonomy, pressed for a Santa Isabel parliament. This popular call soon spread as far as Nggela. However, any European who advocated indigenous self-rule was considered to be a threat to imperial power, and Fallowes was deported in 1934.

He returned in 1939 to reorganise his campaign. Sometimes called the Chair & Rule Movement, it was named after the chair and wooden staff (or rule), the symbols of traditional Solomons authority. Despite support in Santa Isabel, Fallowes was expelled again in 1940, causing the movement to languish.

In 1942, Japanese forces occupied Santa Isabel and its neighbours, establishing a large seaplane and barge base at Suavanao in Rakata Bay. The Americans made frequent air attacks on the harbour, including two accidental bombings of friendly islanders at Baolo and Kia.

Santa Isabel's scouts were particularly active, winning a small skirmish at Mufhu Point in late 1942 and rescuing 28 downed Allied pilots. Rescued pilots were secretly passed down the coast at night and picked up by US seaplanes at Tatamba. The Japanese withdrew in late 1943.

FAUNA
The thinking rat is endemic to Isabel Province, although there is a related species in Guadalcanal. This friendly creature lives at the top of tall trees and eats nuts and fruit. Adults weigh about one kg and can be up to 75 cm long. How it got its name isn't certain, but may relate to its habit of using its jaws and feet to open nuts.

POPULATION & PEOPLE
The people of Isabel Province are Melanesian and 75% of them live in Santa Isabel's south-eastern corner.

ISABEL

ARTS

Tapa cloth is made locally from the bark of paper-mulberry trees and tinted a lightish blue using a dye made from crushed orchid leaves. Dolphins' teeth are used to make necklaces and sometimes as currency.

Traditional dances are regularly held at cultural festivals nationwide. The *bao*, or stick dance, is frequently performed. In the past it celebrated the launching of war canoes, the birth of a first-born child, or the successful end of a fishing or head-hunting trip.

SOCIETY & CONDUCT

Legendary People

Many local people insist there was once a pygmy tribe in the mountains called the Mongoes, who died out in WWII. Akin more to fairies or leprechauns than to humans, it is said they were too stupid to survive, and used to steal even when offered gifts freely.

Local Customs

Inheritance is matrilineal in Isabel Province, with ownership of land passed on through the mother. This developed in head-hunting days – women's lives were usually spared during raids, so matrilineality ensured the survival of *kastom* ownership.

Shell money is still purchased from Malaita Island to pay bride price and to settle custom-ownership disputes.

MEDICAL SERVICES

Buala, the provincial capital, has a 30-bed hospital. There are also clinics spread around the province at Nodana, Poro, Tatamba, Vulavu, Guguha, Kalenga, Kolomola, Kolotubi, Susubona, Samasodu, Kia, Bolotei and Baolo. Malaria is widespread, especially in Kia and Santa Isabel's southern coastal villages.

ACCOMMODATION & FOOD

Although they're not particularly used to tourists, people in this province are very hospitable. Many villages have a leaf house which visitors can use, but you'll need your own food and cooking gear. On arrival in a village, always ask the chief where you can stay. Often accommodation will be free of charge.

Buala has the only proper rest houses, though there are simple leaf-style visitors' houses at Kaevanga, Kolomola, Samasodu, Kia, Baolo, Buma, Tausese, Poro and Tatamba on Isabel, at Kaolo on San Jorge, and on the Arnarvon Islands.

Larger villages should have a basic store. Water supplies are good, with over 50% of the area's rural population receiving fresh, drinkable water.

GETTING THERE & AWAY

Air

Solomon Airlines flies to the province from Honiara on Monday and Friday. In the morning the flight is to Fera (S$135); in the afternoon it's to Suavanao (S$180). There is a Solomon Airlines agent (☎ 35015) in Buala. Western Pacific doesn't fly to Isabel.

Sea

The Isabel Development Corporation sends the *Ligomo IV* or *Ligomo V* to Isabel Province from Honiara every week. Fares range from S$38 (Sepi) to S$52 (Kia); to Buala it costs S$44.

The *Ocean Express* links Honiara to eastern Isabel. It departs on Tuesday at 8 pm and calls at various ports between Sepi (S$45, students S$35) and Buala (S$55, students S$45). It arrives at Buala around 2 pm, and commences the return journey from there at 7 am on Wednesday. Wings Shipping's *Compass Rose II* does a similar trip every third Friday; Honiara-Buala is S$48, Sepi-Buala is S$28.

Yacht There are wharves at Buala, Tatamba, Kaevanga, Allardyce and Kia. Santa Isabel also has anchorages at Cockatoo Island, Thousand Ships Bay, Susubona, Gajuhongari Bay, Furona, Finuana Island, Samasodu, Loguhutu Bay, Palunuhukuru Harbour, Kokopana Island, Suavanao and Kokodoghi and Estrella bays. In addition,

:here are anchorages at Astrolabe and Albatross bays on San Jorge.

Two channels in the province require
particular care. The Ortega Channel is
usually navigable to a minimum depth of
2.4m. The North West Channel between the
mainland and Barora Ite Island is exceptionally narrow – in places only 7.5m wide
– and can be extremely turbulent due to frequent tidal races accompanying routine
changes of tide. There are also concealed
rocks and overhanging branches to contend
with, making any passage through the
channel hazardous for yachts and canoes.

GETTING AROUND
The Airport
Fera airfield is on Fera Island, three km (10
minutes by canoe) from Buala. Get a ride
with the Solomon Airlines agent for S$5
each way.

Sea
Transport around the province is generally
easiest by motor canoe or ship. However,
Isabel's shores are very exposed to rough
weather, especially its south-eastern and
western coasts. Motor-canoe journeys are
usually wet and expensive. The cheapest
charter is via Buala's provincial fisheries
(☎ 35108). Per day, it charges S$20/30 for
a small/big canoe and S$18/30 for a 15/25-
horsepower engine. The COM headquarters
in Buala sometimes hires its canoe out for
S$30 per day. Fuel costs about S$2.45 a
litre.

Land
When people in Isabel Province talk of
roads, they mean anything from single-lane
cart or logging tracks down to what are no
more than very obscure, windy and slippery
footpaths barely half a metre wide. Always
ask how broad local roads are before setting
out.

There are 22 km of genuine tractor
routes in the province, 17 km of which
connect Kaevanga to Kolomola. In addition
to those around Buala, there's a short track
between Kamaosi and the sea at Kasera,

another between Buma and Visena, and
some logging roads around Allardyce.

There is an arduous walking trail across
the central bush of south-eastern Santa
Isabel connecting Hofi with Kolomola. The
route is across dense, scrub-covered valleys
and steep mountain ridges, and can only be
done with guides.

An easier route, albeit still strenuous and
often indistinct, is from Buala along the
coast to Putukora, and then on to Tatamba.
It begins behind the COM church at Jejevo
and you'll need guides for this route too.
The most difficult stretches are from Buala
to Nareabu and Ghurumei to Poro. Frankly,
ships or canoes are much easier.

Santa Isabel Island

Formerly known as Ysabel or Santa Ysabel,
and called Bugotu or Mbughotu in the local
language, this large, mainly volcanic landmass consists of steep and sheer-sided
mountain ranges dissected by narrow river
valleys. Mangrove and freshwater swamps
are common in the lowlands.

There are several long-established
inland villages in south-eastern Santa
Isabel. Some are on ridges as high as 500m
and were built there for defence during the
violent head-hunting days of the mid-19th
century.

About 75% of Santa Isabel's people live
in an area covering about 20% of the island
in the south-east, leaving most of the central
and northern parts uninhabited. Consequently, the average population density is
only five people per sq km.

Fishing is exceptional off Santa Isabel's
north-western tip. Fish race each other to
take any unbaited, unlured line being trolled
behind a yacht or motor canoe.

BUALA
About 2000 people live in Buala (pronounced 'bwar-luh'). This very quiet little
town is spread along 2.2 km of the attractive
10-km-long Maringe Lagoon between the

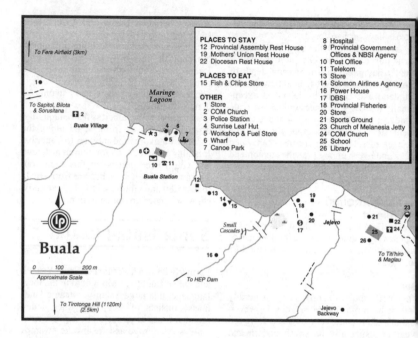

PLACES TO STAY
12 Provincial Assembly Rest House
19 Mothers' Union Rest House
22 Diocesan Rest House

PLACES TO EAT
15 Fish & Chips Store

OTHER
1 Store
2 COM Church
3 Police Station
4 Sunrise Leaf Hut
5 Workshop & Fuel Store
6 Wharf
7 Canoe Park
8 Hospital
9 Provincial Government
   Offices & NBSI Agency
10 Post Office
11 Telekom
13 Store
14 Solomon Airlines Agency
16 Power House
17 DBSI
18 Provincial Fisheries
20 Store
21 Sports Ground
23 Church of Melanesia Jetty
24 COM Church
25 School
26 Library

leaf-style village of Sapitol and the more modern settlement of Jejevo. Buala also includes the original Buala village, the government centre at Buala Station, and the rather oddly named Jejevo Backway.

Buala hugs a narrow littoral strip between the Maringe Lagoon and Tirotonga Hill's very steep sides. Forests and coconut plantations cling precariously to the rugged escarpment, which climbs to 800m over only 2.5 km.

Orientation & Information
Within the Buala Station area are the provincial government offices and workshop, the hospital (☎ 35016), the police station (☎ 35063), the post office, NBSI and Solomon Airlines agencies, a wharf, a canoe park and a Telekom office (☎ 35040, fax 35056). By the wharf is the sunrise leaf hut, where functions are held.

Jejevo has a DBSI branch, a sports

ground, a provincial library (behind the school), another jetty and the local COM headquarters. The COM churches in both Buala village and Jejevo have sections of altar panelling strikingly inlaid with fragments of pearl shell.

Places to Stay & Eat
The best place to stay is the *Provincial Assembly Rest House* (☎ 35031, ext 212) in Buala Station. It's clean and only charges S$15 for a bed in one of four double rooms with overhead fan. There is a kitchen and dining room, but only one shower.

The friendly *Mothers' Union Rest House* (☎ 35035) in Jejevo charges S$33 a night. It has seven rooms, communal washing and cooking facilities, and a card phone.

Near the COM headquarters is its *Diocesan Rest House* (☎ 35011), charging S$35 per bed. There's a kitchen block, and huge

ISABEL

toads leap around the garden at night. Another rest house is apparently being built next to the church in Buala village.

There are several stores in the Buala area. The blue store by the shore in Buala Station sells fish and kumara chips for S$2.50 at lunchtime most days – even on weekends. Nearby is the provincial fisheries, where fresh fish is sold. Buala Station has a small market most weekdays.

AROUND BUALA

Two province-owned tractors use the lagoon's black-sand beach to get to Bilota, two km to the north-west, and Sorusitana, the same distance further on. The only easy way beyond, or to the shoreside settlements south-east of Jejevo, is by motor canoe. Otherwise, there's a very narrow, overgrown and indistinct bush trail from Jejevo to Titi'hiro (pronounced 'ti-tee-ro') one km to the east, and beyond there to Maglau and Nareabu.

Maringe Lagoon

Five small islands face Buala, giving the usually calm waters of this lagoon a most picturesque aspect. The largest island is low-lying Fera, which has golden sand along much of its northern rim.

Fera is connected by a nine-km-long fringing reef to Vaghena and Juakau islands. There's more good underwater viewing between Juakau Island and Nareabu. Vaghena Island has four short stretches of golden sand on its western side, while Juakau has brown beaches on both sides of its northern tip.

Tirotonga Hill

A 25-minute walk uphill from the power station is a new dam, built in 1996 as part of a S$2.2 million project. Buala is the first provincial capital to get hydroelectric power. There are great views over the lagoon from here.

Tirotonga village is about two km southeast of Buala and about 400m up Tirotonga Hill, from where there are more panoramic views. You can reach it via Titi'hiro.

Eco-Tourist Villages

In 1997 three bush villages in the hills behind Buala opened up for eco-tourist visits. It's part of an EU project which also encompasses honey production and sustainable logging. The charge for visits is S$100 per day, which includes accommodation, meals, traditional dances, and activities such as guided bush walks and Pijin lessons. A five-day bushwalking itinerary can be constructed. Sleeping is on pillows and mats, unless you bring your own bedroll. For more information, contact William Feitei (☎ 35119, fax 35113) of the Isabel Sustainable Forest Management Project, PO Box 7, Buala Station. The project can also arrange visits further afield, such as to the Arnavon Turtle Sanctuary.

Mt Sasari & Mt Kubonitu

Four km inland from Buala is the province's highest mountain, Mt Sasari (1120m), with Mt Kubonitu (1065m) four km further south. You can see Malaita and the Nggela Islands from either peak. There are paths up both mountains which guides from Buala village will know.

Tafala

There are several abandoned villages south of Buala, some only a few km from the sea, others deep in the bush. High in the mountains beside Mt Kubonitu is Tafala, where there are some tabu stones. Although it's only seven km south-west of the town, it's 11 km on foot. You will need a guide.

SOUTH-EASTERN SANTA ISABEL ISLAND

There's a long, sandy beach at **Poro**, with surf sometimes up to two metres high.

Tatamba is the island's subprovincial headquarters. Nearby is Tanabuli Island, a WWII coastwatch site, and Lighara, which has a white-sand beach. Also close to Tatamba is tiny Tirahi Island, where there are plans to build a tourist resort.

The Lumasa Seseo Cave at **Lokiha** is about one km north-west of Mboko Point. It was used as a women's seclusion place

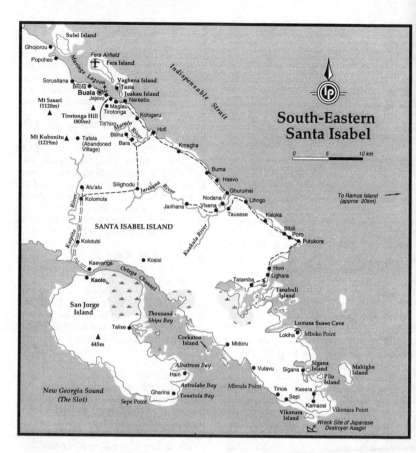

South-Eastern
Santa Isabel

during childbirth and has a face carved beside its entrance.

Mahighe Island, covered in coconut palms, has a white-sand beach on its western shore. Although Mahighe is unpopulated, nearby Pilo Island has a small settlement.

Sigana is partly on the mainland but mostly on small, sandy Sigana Island, 500m offshore. Seven km to the south-east is Vikenara Point – a place of very rough seas. The sunken Japanese destroyer *Asagiri* lies in deep water two km due south of **Vikenara Island**, which also has sandy beaches.

The chiefs Bera and Soga are both buried at **Sepi**. Bera's grave is a pile of stones, Soga's is a Christian one. Nearby are several skull houses, tall artificial mounds used as lookouts in head-hunting days, and Sepi's sandy shore. One km inland of **Tinoa** is a skull repository and a well-preserved 19th-century *toa*, or fortress, built of limestone rock. The remains of Bera's main fortress are only a short distance inland from **Mboula Point**. Its limestone walls held gun emplacements in head-hunting days.

Bishop Patteson used to camp on the sandy beach at **Cockatoo Island** in the 1860s. Patteson often had a pet cockatoo perched on his shoulder, hence the island's name.

The sheltered waterway of **Thousand Ships Bay** was a popular anchorage for 19th-century traders. It was also used by the Japanese fleet in 1942 to form up prior to its assault on Tulagi. There are several attractive coral gardens on its south-eastern side.

Kaevanga

As this is one of Santa Isabel's more fertile and populated areas, Kaevanga has stores and a market. A track runs up into the hills to Kolomola past an orange plantation at Kolotubi, where you can buy oranges direct from the villagers.

North of Kaevanga the coast is at first rocky, then mangrove-lined beyond Mufhu Point. Inland the landscape is high and ridged. Occasional small, sandy islets lie between one and two km offshore.

The people of Santa Isabel's central area suffered significantly from head-hunting. Although raids ceased over 80 years ago, the only major settlements between Kaevanga and Allardyce are Susubona and Samasodu. This scarcity of inhabitants extends across the island to the northern coast.

NORTH-WESTERN SANTA ISABEL ISLAND

The northern coastline is irregular, with many swampy bays and a few sandy beaches separated by rugged promontories and sheer cliffs. Close to one of these marshy inlets is **Cape Megapode**, named after the many incubator birds nesting there. Although Mendaña reported that this area was heavily populated, 19th-century head-hunting has left it with only six settlements north-west of the Maringe Lagoon.

Furona village occupies the whole of tiny Furona Island, one km from the mainland. About 12 km to the north-west is the shark-shaped and coral-surrounded **Finuana Island**.

Although islanders salvaged most of what the Japanese left behind in **Suavanao** when they hurriedly withdrew in late 1943, there are still several downed US aircraft hidden deep in the bush. Local people regularly visit Papatura Faa, Papatura Ite and Omona islands to tend their coconut trees, and scuba fans will find plenty of fish and colourful coral on the reefs around these low-lying offshore islands.

Kia

Over 1000 people live in Kia, a large village with stores, a fisheries centre and a police station. It was built in head-hunting days to command all three channels approaching it. These are the Bahana Passage, North West Channel and Ghehughaha Passage.

Many of Kia's houses are built on stilts over the water, forming a six-km line. Standing imposingly over them is an enormous, iron-clad COM church. There's good swimming off the nearby coral islets.

The oral traditions and language of Kia's people are similar to those practised in New Georgia's Roviana Lagoon. In the past, there was a trade network with Choiseul and other western areas. Because of these links, they were treated as westerners (people of Western Province), which usually protected them from the wrath of the head-hunters. Even now, canoe transport is sometimes available to southern Choiseul.

There's a small crocodile farm in Kia, and there are plenty of trocchus shells and bêches-de-mer in the area.

San Jorge Island

The province's second-largest island, named Ysla de Jorge by Mendaña's fellow Spaniards, was subsequently also called St George Island. Its inhabitants knew it as Moumolu-Naunitu.

Despite being 200 sq km, San Jorge Island has only 500 people. The largest of its four villages is Kaolo, the subprovincial

ISABEL

headquarters. The island is popularly considered to be the place where the spirits of dead Santa Isabel people reside. Consequently, you should ask permission wherever you go on San Jorge.

There is attractive coral growth and golden, sandy beaches at its eastern end, particularly in Astrolabe and Tanatola bays. A few hundred metres to the west of Sepe Point in the adjacent inlet is a wrecked Japanese barge. Small amounts of ammunition litter the nearby beach.

Much of north-eastern San Jorge is extremely swampy, with several shallow marshes inhabited by saltwater crocodiles. In the island's centre is a 445m hill allowing views of the Nggela and Russells groups.

Mudshells are a local delicacy on San Jorge. They're found in the mangroves and taste like scallops.

The Western & Arnarvon Islands

With more than 100 islands of varying sizes, the Western Islands, along with the tiny Arnarvon Islands, cover 432 sq km. Many of them scarcely protrude above sea level and none are permanently inhabited. Though some of these islands are swampy and unused, most have extensive reefs and sandbars. Fishing in the area is unsurpassed.

The Arnarvon Islands are one of the largest nesting grounds in the world for the endangered hawksbill turtle. A community-managed marine conservation area was established in 1995 to protect the local land and marine environment. Nature enthusiasts are welcome to accompany staff or turtle-monitoring trips. Staff can also arrange bookings at the local *rest house*. For more information, contact Michael Orr (☎ 20940, fax 21339, PO Box 556), the project manager in Honiara. It's possible to get to the Anarvons by canoe from Wagina Island (see the Choiseul Province chapter).

Gardens and coconut trees line the extremely narrow North West Channel which separates Barora Ite Island from the Santa Isabel mainland. Kia families canoe across the channel to tend their crops here.

There are very attractive lagoons throughout the Western Islands, notably Austria Sound and Rob Roy Channel. Gill Island, near Kia, has a particularly fine white-sand beach, as does Malakobi Island further to the north-west. Suki Island is excellent for scuba diving, with colourful coral gardens, turtles and sharks.

Ramos Island

In 1568 Mendaña gave the name Ramos to Malaita Island. However, In 1824 the Russian hydrographer Krustenstern misread his charts and instead bestowed the name on tiny present-day Ramos.

This slender 1.5-km-long island is accompanied by a smaller companion islet, plus nine low rocks which jut vertically from the sea. Together their area is less than one sq km. Uninhabited Ramos, locally called Onegou Island, is 39 km due east of Poro. It is a prime fishing spot. People say that the spirits of the dead come from nearby islands to make it their final resting place.

Rennell & Bellona Province

Traditionally known as Mu Nggava and Mu Ngiki respectively, Rennell and Bellona islands are Polynesian outliers sharing similar languages and cultures. Both are uplifted coral atolls and are extremely rocky. Rennell appears to have been raised five times in the remote past, as five separate stages can be clearly seen on its cliff face. Because of its unique and specialised ecology, East Rennell has been made a national wildlife park and nominated for World Heritage listing.

Rennell is 202 km south of Guadalcanal, about 80 km long, 14 km wide and 629 sq km in area. At its south-eastern end is Lake Te'Nggano, the South Pacific's largest expanse of fresh water. To the south of Rennell are the Indispensable Reefs, which extend over 123 km of sea.

Formerly part of Central Province, the islands became a province in their own right in January 1993, the same month that Cyclone Nina caused severe local damage. The capital is Tinggoa, on Rennell island.

HISTORY

Lapita people occupied Bellona briefly in about 1000 BC. Settlements on both islands followed in around 130 BC, with another major occupation in about 1000 AD. The present-day Polynesian inhabitants say their ancestors landed on Bellona around 26 generations ago in about 1400 AD. They apparently came from 'Ubea', assumed to be the modern-day Uvea, or Wallis, in the French-ruled Wallis and Futuna group. There were seven couples led by a chief called Kaitu'u; each couple produced a clan, but only Kaitu'u's descendants have survived.

The two islands were officially discovered in 1793 by Captain Benjamin Boyd in the merchant ship *Bellona*, after which the smaller island was named. There were only five fleeting visits by Europeans prior to Bishop Selwyn's short stay in July 1856.

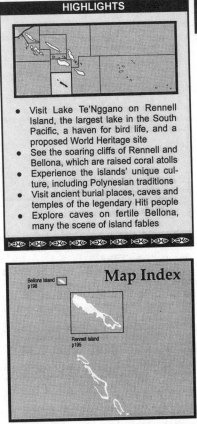

HIGHLIGHTS

- Visit Lake Te'Nggano on Rennell Island, the largest lake in the South Pacific, a haven for bird life, and a proposed World Heritage site
- See the soaring cliffs of Rennell and Bellona, which are raised coral atolls
- Experience the islands' unique culture, including Polynesian traditions
- Visit ancient burial places, caves and temples of the legendary Hiti people
- Explore caves on fertile Bellona, many the scene of island fables

Map Index

Bellona Island p198

Rennell Island p195

The two islands were always free of cannibalism, but had long periods of internecine war until well into this century.

The first missionaries came in 1910, and three stayed – all Melanesians. An epidemic followed, during which many people died, including a chief's mother, and the missionaries were blamed for the deaths. Because the pagan priests realised that

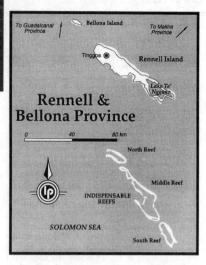

too. Because of this and the gods' failure to punish him, the Bellonese stopped fighting and converted to Christianity.

Even more dramatic events occurred on Rennell the following month during the so called Niupani Madness. Those who were undecided between Christianity and paganism were keen to find out which religion was the best. They therefore called on the believers to pray daily, either to God or, in the pagans' case, to Semoana. The Christians were advised to prepare themselves for the Day of Judgement by getting married, as only married people could go to heaven. So all the Christians were married – each adult, teenager and child – including suckling infants. When the Judgement Day failed to materialise, non-Christians began fighting Christians and vice versa. Several people were killed.

After three days the fervour subsided and the dead were buried. Then, at a church service a few days later, a picture of Jesus was seen to speak. This was widely reported around Rennell, convincing the vast majority to become Christian. Fighting between Christians and non-Christians ceased, and everyone moved into larger villages with newly built churches in the centre. Ancient rituals, gods and traditions were abandoned and replaced by fundamentalist Christianity.

Christianity represented a serious challenge to their traditional authority, the three missionaries were killed.

The Protectorate government closed both Rennell and Bellona to outsiders to avoid further casualties, and to protect the inhabitants from foreign diseases to which they had no immunity.

Isolation lasted until 1934, when three mission ships arrived to recruit a few villagers each for religious instruction elsewhere. The recruits came back in 1936, and for two years the people of both islands worshipped their ancient gods alongside Christianity.

In September 1938, a Christian Rennellese teacher, Moa, set out for Bellona during a storm which miraculously abated once he had prayed. Arriving in Bellona in the middle of a major clan skirmish, he destroyed the two ultra-sacred statue-gods which had been brought from Ubea by the original settlers.

Bellonese priests predicted he would be struck down immediately for this exceptional blasphemy, but he survived. Moa then healed a dying pagan priest and others

CLIMATE

Rennell and Bellona are much wetter than Honiara and several degrees cooler Rennell, being broader, is warmer than Bellona. It also has two distinct climates with West Rennell normally drier and less humid than East Rennell, which can be quite stormy.

Rennell's annual rainfall is about 4250 mm. January and March are the only months when it doesn't rain almost daily though long droughts sometimes occur Bellona is similar.

POPULATION & PEOPLE

Rennell is sparsely populated for its size with only 1500 inhabitants. Bellona is much smaller (9.75 km long and 2.5 km wide) but home to 1000 people.

Life on Rennell and Bellona is so different from that in the rest of the Solomons that you can easily feel you're in another country. Values are often dissimilar and life goes on regardless of events elsewhere in the nation.

Bellonese people sometimes talk as if the two islands are one. Consequently, just like the Rennellese, they speak of Lake Te'Nggano on Rennell as 'the lake', as well as saying 'east' and 'west' to mean east and west Rennell.

ARTS

The people are skilled and inventive woodworkers who carve and inlay nontraditional walking sticks, as well as strikingly fierce-looking masks. They also make model outrigger canoes, replica shark hooks from an unjointed bend of a branch or root, and, on Bellona, necklaces from the teeth of flying foxes.

More than a dozen different kinds of clubs were used in the two islands' fierce tribal wars over the limited garden land available. Modern replicas have stone heads, while miniature ceremonial ones are carved with multiple barbed points.

Several carvers from Rennell and Bellona live in White River village, just west of Honiara, and carve extremely vivid models of island life. Dramatic examples of these are on display in the capital's Central Bank.

Islanders also carve eagles, crocodiles, turtles and snakes, and weave shoulder bags. Traditionally the patterns on the bags were in black, using vine skin on Rennell and banana stems on Bellona. Recently red, blue, purple, yellow, orange and green tints have been introduced. The bags are woven in a check design and bordered with black geometric patterns. Mats are made in similar styles.

SOCIETY & CONDUCT

The Danish National Museum of Copenhagen specialises in recording the traditions of these two closely related islands. Since

1961, several of their anthropologists, especially Torben Monberg, a Dane, and Samuel Elbert, an American, have made detailed studies of the two islands' oral histories, traditional religions and languages. Their first book, *From the Two Canoes*, gets its name from the inhabitants' popular name for their islands.

Local Customs

The pre-Christian people of Rennell and Bellona wore tapa and were ornately tattooed. They also used to press their noses together as New Zealand Maoris do when greeting each other in a *hangi*, though this custom has now almost completely disappeared.

Great changes came with the islands' conversion to fundamentalist Christianity. Clothes have replaced tapa except during cultural festivals and wrestling.

Both SDA and SSEC people on Rennell and Bellona have renounced ancient activities such as traditional dancing, tika-dart throwing, shark fishing, eel netting, bird and flying-fox snaring, the harvesting of shellfish and coconut crabs, and searching for fat tree worms called longicorns. Though old tabus have gone, new ones have developed, including rulings against the eating of scaleless fish, flying foxes, grubs and crustaceans.

In pre-Christian Rennell and Bellona, no connection was noticed between intercourse and pregnancy, although illegitimate or unwanted children were treated as a sign of a god's displeasure. Premarital relationships among young adults and adolescents were – and still are – granted considerable licence.

Tattoos

Since the conversion to Christianity, there has been much less tattooing done on both islands, and the practice of near-total body decoration has died out. Few young people are tattooed at all nowadays, though there are plenty of middle-aged and elderly islanders, especially on Bellona, who have an ornate arrangement of tattoos.

Traditionally, special tattoos were reserved for priests and chiefs, symbolising a god's presence in a tattooed part of the body. This was a useful defence in battle: to attack a tattoo was to attack the god and to blaspheme.

Tattooing was so painful that men gained considerable prestige by being tattooed, and likewise forfeited it by refusing such bodily decorations. A heavily tattooed young man could be sure of plenty of female company and would draw attention to his tattoos in courtship.

Wrestling
Hetakai is a traditional form of wrestling on Rennell and Bellona islands which involves males of all ages. With two contestants competing at a time, the victor is the one who knocks down his opponent first, becoming champion by winning all his bouts. Hetakai wrestlers wear loin cloths made from tapa.

LANGUAGE
People in Rennell and Bellona speak similar Polynesian languages, both of which are closely related to Maori. Frequently, Rennellese and Bellonese have many words for something where English only has one. 'Break' has 88 Rennellese or Bellonese equivalents, 'cut' has 82, and 'carry', 31. There are 136 words for different tree varieties, 48 for yams and pana and 101 for types of fish.

INFORMATION
The Rennell and Bellona Provincial Office (☎ 24251, PO Box 1764) is in Honiara's Chinatown. Staff will help organise trips to the province, including booking accommodation by radio.

There are no telephones on the islands yet. Although you can make telephone contact with Telekom on Rennell (☎ 0061-145 11 272), it's an expensive international call routed through Australia via satellite.

Scobie's Walkabout Tours (see the Getting There & Away chapter) does trips around Rennell every January

GETTING THERE & AWAY
Air
From Honiara, Solomon Airlines flies into Rennell (S$185) on Sunday, Tuesday and Friday. There's a stopover at Bellona (S$170) on each occasion. The Bellona-Rennell sector costs S$60. Western Pacific flies to Rennell on Sunday and Thursday but does not currently land at Bellona.

Rennell airfield is known locally as Tinggoa. There have been plans for a while now to open an airfield in East Rennell at Lake Te'Nggano – it may happen one day

Sea
Boat services are very infrequent. National Shipping makes the 24-hour trip from Honiara once a month at best – often intervals are much longer. Universal Shipping and the Church of Melanesia visit very occasionally. The fare to either island is around S$60.

Rennell's only anchorage is at Lavanggu though ships also wait offshore at Tuhunganggo and Mangga Utu.

Vessels calling at Bellona moor about 200m offshore at Potuhenua. Smaller boats are used to convey passengers and cargo to and from the beach through a narrow channel blasted in the coral. This anchorage is usually too rough for yachts.

Rennell Island

Rennell's coast is almost totally comprised of 200m limestone cliffs which are covered by dense bush. A narrow fringing reef completely surrounds the island.

The northern coastline is generally straight, but the undulating southern coast has a deep inlet in its centre at Kanggava Bay. From the island's raised and rocky rim, the land surface gradually descends to just above sea level in Rennell's central basin.

Both the east-central and far-western parts of Rennell are uninhabited wilder

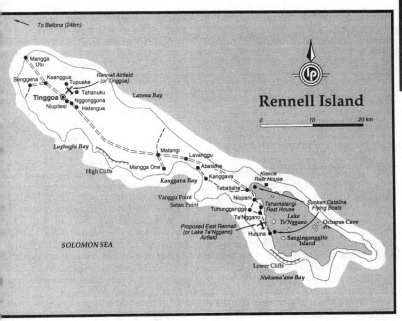

To Bellona (24km)

Rennell Island

0   10   20 km

Mangga Utu
Senggena Kaanggua
Tupuake Rennell Airfield (or Tinggoa)
Tinggoa Tahanuku
Niupilesi Nggonggona
Hatangua

Lavena Bay

Lughughi Bay

Matangi
Lavanggu
Mangga One Abataihe
High Cliffs Kanggava
Kanggava Bay Tebaitahe
Vanggu Point Niupani
Satan Point Tuhunggangggo
Te'Nggano
Proposed East Rennell Huluna
(or Lake Te'Nggano)
Airfield

Kiakoe Rest House

Tahamatangi Rest House
Lake Te'Nggano
Sunken Catalina Flying Boats
Octopus Cave
Sanginanggito Island

SOLOMON SEA

Lower Cliffs
Nukuma'anu Bay

...esses of towering trees. Between these two wastelands is the most fertile part of the island.

Scattered throughout the western end are shallow pockets of bauxite, with deposits totalling about 25 million tonnes. These pockets coincide with the island's cultivable land, and so although mining operations would leave the wild surrounding bush intact, no fertile ground would remain for the Rennellese to grow their crops on.

Flora & Fauna

Flora The endemic Rennellese orchid is particularly striking. It has multiple mauve veins on a white flower, with a pale-yellow undersurface. Despite the poor soil on most of the island, Rennell's coconut palms, known as Rennell talls, give very high early yields. Seed nuts are sent to plantations all around the country, especially those in the Russell Islands.

Birds A number of bird species are endemic to Rennell. They include the very tame Rennell fantail and Rennell white-eye, the Rennell shrikebill, which likes the undergrowth, the Rennell starling, the Woodford's white eye, and the now-rare Rennell white spoonbill. Finally, there is the very common Rennellese pygmy version of the white ibis, locally called *tagoa*, which is also found on Bellona.

Bird-watchers have identified at least eight subspecies on Rennell which have evolved distinctive features through confinement to this remote island. These include the pygmy parrot, which has red on its abdomen and yellow on its wings and chest. The little pied cormorant is smaller on Rennell than elsewhere and the black bittern is paler. Ornithologists suspect more endemic bird subspecies may yet be found. The plentiful fresh water in Lake Te'Nggano and the dense scrub in the west have enabled bird species to flourish. The lake attracts circling flocks of frigates, cormorants and boobies, especially at dawn and dusk.

Reptiles Living in Lake Te'Nggano's brackish waters are the black and white-banded sea krait, widespread but usually preferring the sea, and the endemic *tugi-hono*, a freshwater snake. The latter, found only in Lake Te'Nggano, is also venomous, but very docile. According to islanders it has never been known to bite anyone. Tugi-honos are striped, varying in colour from yellow, red and blue to greyish-brown and black, depending on the kind of vegetation they inhabit.

People

Around a quarter of Rennellese men and nearly a third of Rennellese women lack the fibularis tertius muscle in their legs. This is the highest proportion worldwide for any ethnic group.

Although the phenomenon has little effect on their health, studies of other Pacific Islanders who also lack the muscle may help identify more precisely where the Rennellese people originally came from.

Information

There are medical clinics at Tinggoa and Te'Nggano, and a first-aid post at Lavanggu. The island is malaria-free.

The only electricity on Rennell Island is provided by a few private generators. Modern toilets are rare. In some villages there are pit latrines with wooden boards for sitting on, but in other settlements there is simply a specific area of bush reserved for toilet use.

There are no rivers or streams on Rennell. Lake Te'Nggano is brackish, though villagers use its water for washing and cooking. Rainwater catchment tanks and occasional wells throughout the island provide drinking water, but only enough for most people's basic needs. There are a few stores on the island selling a limited range of foodstuffs.

Places to Stay

Saul & Linnet's Lodge, at the end of Tinggoa airfield, is clean, well run and has kitchen facilities. There are 10 beds at S$2 each. The custom-built *Airport Lodge* by the airfield has the same facilities, charges the same prices and sleeps six. There are also a couple of places to stay in the vicinity of Lavanggu – ask around locally.

The eastern end of Lake Te'Nggano already has two *rest houses*, and more may be built. *Tahamatangi Rest House* on the south-west shore has room for nine adults at S$35 a head. There are basic kitchen facilities, though the family will cook good lunches and dinners for S$20 each. Marti Tauniu, the owner, conducts lake excursions. Canoe transfer from the road terminus at Tebaitahe costs S$40. A little isolated on the north shore is the similarly priced *Kiakoe Rest House*. There is a kitchen, or lunch and dinner are S$15 each and breakfast is S$7; canoe transfers are S$10 per person.

Getting Around

Transport around Rennell is limited and subject to delays. There's a 32-km tractor trail between Tinggoa, west Rennell's administrative centre, and Lavanggu. This has recently been extended for 18 km through the island's very rocky central isthmus to Lake Te'Nggano.

To reach the lake it used to be necessary to hire a canoe from Lavanggu to Tuhunganggo (one hour, often through rough seas), then climb a steep and slippery path up the cliff and walk for 40 minutes. Even with the new road, getting there's no picnic. The only land-based transport is three tractors and trailers; one always (hopefully) meets the aeroplane and boat. The bumpy, uncomfortable ride through dense rainforest from Tinggoa airfield to the lake takes at least four hours, including a stop at Lavanggu. Add an hour or so if it's heavily loaded and the weather's bad. The return trip from the lake to meet the morning plane usually commences in the middle of the night, though it should be possible to instead get a daytime tractor and spend the night by the airfield.

The tractors are also available for charter at $20 per hour, but you'll need to pay for the round trip even if you only travel one way. Anyone can get aboard the tractor and travel anywhere on its route by paying the charterer or the driver S$1.

LAVANGGU

The cliffs are lower here and access is easy for ships. Lavanggu, on Rennell's south central coast, has a small white-sand beach and an attractive fringing coral reef providing good snorkelling. There are similar beaches across the bay at Abataihe and Kanggava. Rennell is only three km wide at Lavanggu.

LAKE TE'NGGANO

The eastern end of the island is essentially a sea-level lake surrounded by lofty cliffs. The 130-sq-km lake is 27 km long and up to nine km wide, with brackish waters.

Lake Te'Nggano's western end is dotted with about 200 coral islets, and there are small swamps where taro grows in profusion. Four large villages hug the shore: Te'Nggano, which is the local subprovincial headquarters, Tebaitahe, Niupani and Hutuna.

The lake is noted for its brilliant sunrises, with houses on stilts over the water in the foreground and coral limestone hills in the distance. Bird life is abundant. Cormorants and teals seem to be everywhere, constantly diving into the water. Marine life includes the recently introduced *tilapia*, freshwater prawns and giant eels, while its reed-lined shores provide cover for plenty of monitor lizards.

The US had a Catalina seaplane base by the lake in WWII, and eight planes were sunk in a surprise Japanese raid. Some of these wrecks are within range of snorkellers: one is four metres down about a km east of Tebaitahe, another is three metres down and only 10m offshore at Hutuna.

Motor-canoe charters for lake trips are pricey at around S$200 per day including fuel, while guided rainforest walks cost S$10 per person per hour. Octopus Cave on the north shore is a popular excursion.

Bellona Island

Bellona (pronounced 'bell-oh-na' and sometimes spelt Bellon) is densely populated and has an extremely fertile interior. It's 180 km south of Guadalcanal, 15 sq km in size and surrounded by sheer, forest-covered cliffs ranging in height from 30m to 70m.

Bellona's cliffs are often easy to climb, unlike Rennell's, which are impossible in all but a few places. The cliffs descend quite abruptly into a depression in the island's centre, reaching right down to sea level in places.

Bellona's people often call the island Te Baka, meaning 'the Canoe'. With a bit of imagination you can see why – the shape of the island, the ubiquitous sound of the crashing surf and the inland ground rising to the water's edge makes you feel you're in a giant canoe.

A 10-million-tonne phosphate deposit has been found on the island, but the project is on indefinite hold. The villagers are aware of the environmental devastation that has happened on other Pacific islands where minerals have been extracted.

Since the late 1970s, there has been a reaction against the dominance fundamentalist religion has over Bellonese life. Many people, especially the young, are sorry that so many of the old traditions have been lost since the introduction of Christianity and so many cultural artefacts destroyed. Consequently, many Bellonese people have deserted the large church-dominated villages and returned to their traditional lands in small one or two-family settlements that are strung along the island's central road.

Bellona is pock-marked with caves, many of them the scene of island fables. There are also sites from the legendary Hiti

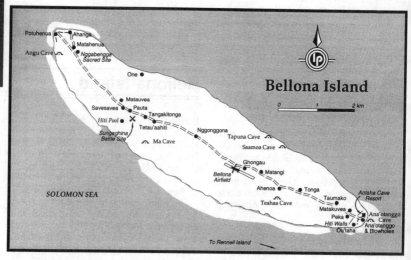

Wars, though most of these, like the ancient burial places and temples, are now overgrown. You will need the help of an informed islander to identify them.

Tika-dart throwing was a favourite pastime in pre-Christian Bellona. This ancient sport has been abandoned in favour of rugby and soccer though there are still old throwing tracks, obscured by long grass, at Pauta and Ghongau. There are beaches at Ahanga and One.

Fauna
Bellona is home to an orange-coloured wasp. You'll also see plenty of swifts flying low over the ground, hunting for insects on the wing.

Population & People
Many young Bellonese are extremely articulate. They often regard their *wantoks* on Rennell as rather conservative and distinctly quieter people than themselves. The people of Bellona have a particularly tense relationship with Malaitans, regularly getting into strife with them in Honiara and on plantations around the country.

Information
Bellona's only clinic is at Pauta, and there's no malaria. As on Rennell, drinking water is always scarce. There are freshwater springs, but as they flow only intermittently, most islanders depend on rainwater catchments for their supplies.

Places to Stay
The friendly *Suani Rest House* at Tangakitonga charges from S$27 per person. Meals are S$8 each, or you can use the kitchen. The rest house also offers a laundry service, bike hire (S$10), and bushwalking/snorkelling trips with lunch (S$30). The new, beautifully situated *Aotaha Cave Resort* on the eastern coast enjoys cool sea breezes. Beds are S$36 and they also offer cave tours and bike hire. Excellent local-style meals are S$10, and there's a kitchen.

Getting Around
A tractor trail runs from Potuhenua in the north-west, Bellona's only anchorage, and continues to the south-eastern tip at Ana'otanggo. Along it is a sequence of vil-

ages, gardens and coconut plantations. Transport is on foot or by the one tractor on the island, which meets every flight and ship. The fare, payable to the driver, is S$1, irrespective of distance travelled.

The central road is the island's main meeting place. People will stop and talk to you wherever they meet you along it. Islanders claim this route was in use before the ancestors of the present-day Bellonese arrived.

WESTERN BELLONA ISLAND

Bellona's most sacred ancient rituals took place at the Nggabengga site in **Matahenua**, where there were the two sacred 'godstones' Guatupu'a and Tepoutu'uigganggi. These were brought by Kaitu'u and his companions when they first arrived from mythical Ubea.

The gods of these stones were believed to be human-eaters. Great courage was required to invoke them, as the slightest error in the ritual meant certain death. Moa destroyed the stones in September 1938 without suffering any harm and the gods' failure to react caused the islanders to abandon their old religion.

Around here is a network of caves where early Bellonese settlers used to live. These were occupied right up to the 1930s. Angu Cave is about 450m to Matahenua's southeast. During one of ancient Bellona's long civil wars, a family, sole survivors of an annihilated tribe, hid in this cave for many years before they were discovered. By then, peace had returned and they were allowed to survive.

Bellona's last pagan priest was buried at Matauvea in 1956. Nearby is Pauta, the subprovincial headquarters, locally called the area council.

According to island tradition, Kaitu'u fought an epic battle at **Sungaghina** against the Hiti, and killed 100 of them by a ruse. There's also a Hiti pool nearby.

Islanders will point out a place close by the road at Tangakitonga called **Tetau'aahiti**. This is where the Hiti wounded Kaitu'u. About 600m further south is the Ma Cave, where they hid afterwards.

Nggonggona, popularly known as Nggo or No, is where Bellonese men play rugby most afternoons. Women also sometimes play volleyball here.

EASTERN BELLONA ISLAND

One km to the north of Matangi are Tapuna and Saamoa caves. Tradition says the Hiti lived in stone buildings inside them. Some stone remains can still be seen in **Tapuna Cave**, where Kaitu'u trapped and killed most of the Hiti. One survivor escaped to Saamoa but was tracked down there by Kaitu'u.

About 300m south of the road at Ahenoa

The Legendary Hiti

According to legend, the Polynesian arrivals in 1400 found a people called the Hiti on both Rennell and Bellona. They lived in caves or in the depths of forests and had strange customs. Their skin was as furry as a flying fox's and their hair reached to their waists or their feet.

The Hiti were seldom dangerous, but played tricks on the newcomers, including making off with their women and disappearing at will. They had beautiful gardens, could easily find water on porous Rennell, and taught the Polynesians how to cook certain plants.

Over the years the Polynesians steadily eliminated them all in what the Bellonese call the Hiti Wars. Nevertheless, there are still occasional reports of Hiti being seen on Bellona. Some Rennellese claim they've actually been taken to Hiti villages but inexplicably can't find their way back once they've escaped. Many dismiss these claims as either dreams or sheer fantasy. ■

is the **Teahaa Cave**, the site of another of Kaitu'u's victories over the unfortunate Hiti.

On the northern side of the road at Taumako is a now-overgrown burial ground where many past chiefs of Bellona were interred. A little further east is **Matakuvea**, where stone plates were found in a cave. They were subsequently lost, but islanders expect other similar artefacts lie hidden in the surrounding area.

The two ancient graves at Peka are those of Kaitu'u and his successor, Mu'akitanggata. Kaitu'u's is the one to the east.

The Hiti Walls at **Ou'taha** are a line of tall, weathered coral rocks. A close look suggests they are the remains of a coral reef which, by chance, resemble human-made walls. Island tradition says these huge coral structures were built by the Hiti before Kaitu'u and the first Bellonese arrived. Some people make similar claims for large coral blocks at Potuhenua at the island's western end, though these look even less artificial than those at Ou'taha.

There are very fine views towards Rennell from the cliff tops at **Ana'otanggo**. Below is a cave with a large gallery and throne-like platform inside. At the base of the cliff are small blowholes.

Malaita Province

Of the province's 96,000 people, all but 2000 are Melanesian. The remainder are Polynesian and live on the two atolls of Ontong Java and Sikaiana.

Malaita Island and its immediate neighbour, Maramasike, occupy about 98% of the 4243-sq-km province. Together they are 191 km long and 47 km wide. Transport is fairly limited, making enjoyment of the province's varied attractions difficult and time consuming.

Malaita Island

Malaita Island has an elongated interior, with narrow coastal plains often merging into small swamps. The inland highlands, which have been eroded by deep valleys and sharp ridges, rise to a 1303m peak at Mt Kolovrat.

The island's many fast-flowing rivers act as natural barriers to cross-island movement. The geographical divisions that contributed to the constant inter-tribal fighting up until the 1920s have since ensured the survival of many different dialects and languages.

Malaita is pronounced 'mal-eye-ta' by northerners and 'mal-a-ta' by southerners. Over the years, the island has had several other names. Don Alvaro de Mendaña, who saw it on Palm Sunday, called it Ramos, meaning 'palm fronds' in Spanish. In 1767, Philip Cartaret modestly named the island after himself, while at other times it's been called Maiden Land, Maleita, Malayette and Malanta. Malaitans often call it Mala, which is really the name for the island's northern part only.

Malaita Island has a large bush population of about 15,000 people. Some Malaitans from the central and south-eastern parts of the island still worship ancestral spirits

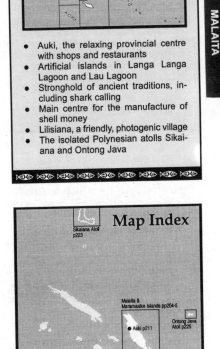

HIGHLIGHTS

- Auki, the relaxing provincial centre with shops and restaurants
- Artificial islands in Langa Langa Lagoon and Lau Lagoon
- Stronghold of ancient traditions, including shark calling
- Main centre for the manufacture of shell money
- Lilisiana, a friendly, photogenic village
- The isolated Polynesian atolls Sikaiana and Ontong Java

Map Index

Sikaiana Atoll p223

Malaita & Maramasike Islands pp204-5

Auki p211

Ontong Java Atoll p225

and live almost entirely by shifting cultivation and barter.

The artificial islands in the Langa Langa and Lau lagoons are a distinctive feature of Malaitan life. These have been built in the shallows with coral boulders taken from the nearby reef. On these islands the tradition of shark worship still lingers in parts.

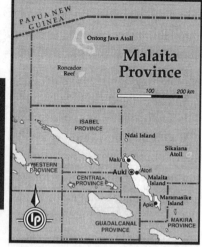

History

The Kwaio (pronounced 'kwoy-oh' or 'koy-oh') people, from Malaita Island's east-central mountains, cite genealogies going back 150 generations to about 1400 BC, although there is as yet no scientific evidence to support these claims. The oldest archaeological remains found so far come from certain Kwara'ae villages and date back to 440 AD.

In the early 19th century, a foreigner could count his life expectancy in minutes rather than years if separated from his ship in Malaita Island waters because of the ferocity of the local people. Life was also dangerous for the islanders themselves. Villages were fortified against the head-hunting raids that occurred regularly; some of these raiders were locals, while others came from Santa Isabel.

By the 1870s, despite this dangerous environment, Malaita Island had become a favourite recruiting place for blackbirders. Malaita's population was larger than that of other islands and there were many landless men prepared to volunteer for overseas work, particularly in north-eastern Australia's sugar-cane plantations. Between 1871 and 1903, about 9000 Malaita and Maramasike islanders were recruited. While they were often said to be the South Pacific's best workers, they also earned a reputation for being the most volatile and pugnacious. Many had returned by 1906, bringing back with them trappings of the white people's world, such as calico and Snyder rifles.

Yet labourers were often kidnapped by blackbirders rather than recruited, and islanders were frequently killed. Soon Malaita Islanders learned to distrust all white people, regularly murdering them to avenge earlier atrocities committed by other Europeans. This was particularly so among the Kwaio – the most fierce, traditional and independent of the islanders.

The British Protectorate government retaliated and tit-for-tat fighting erupted sporadically during the years 1880 to 1911. In 1909, a district office was opened in Auki, a sign that government by punitive raid was coming to an end. Despite this, intertribal skirmishing persisted. When asked in 1920 by the League of Nations about Malaita and Maramasike islands, the British government admitted, 'There is incessant warfare'. At this time, although Malaita Island men rarely wore clothes, no man ventured far without his bow and arrows.

The Kwaio Rebellion On 4 October 1927, District Officer William Bell and his cadet Lillies were at Kwaiambe in Kwaio territory to collect tax. With them were 14 north Malaitan special constables. The two officials each sat at a table, waiting to receive the Kwaio bush people's head-taxes of five shillings a person, and the surrender of their beloved Snyder rifles, the possession of which had recently been made illegal.

Some tribespeople paid the tax, but Basiana – the local *ramo*, or contract assassin – tricked Bell and crashed his rifle down onto the official's skull, splitting it open. In the ensuing melee, Lillies and 13 of the 14 police were also killed.

The reaction in Tulagi, the Solomons'

capital at the time, was excessive. A force was raised of European volunteers, and the Australian cruiser HMAS *Adelaide* sailed from Sydney. The cruiser shelled all the villages it could find. The inept European volunteers, more concerned with drinking their whisky than carrying out their peacekeeping duties, spitefully sprayed the Kwaio's taro gardens with weedkiller, destroying them almost permanently.

The government's 40 northern Malaitan police proved totally relentless. Of the 200 Kwaio arrested, six were hanged the following year at Tulagi (including Basiana), while 30 died of dysentery or despair in jail. The authorities acknowledged 60 to 65 were killed by the local police, and about 100 more died of starvation in the bush after their gardens were destroyed. The Kwaio claim 1246 were killed and that 59 villages, 538 shrines and 1066 gardens were destroyed.

The police force's main sport, other than hunting people, was to desecrate Kwaio shrines. Consecrated ritual objects, ancestral relics, slit drums and sacrificial stones were defiled or destroyed. This ruthless policy subdued the Kwaio but left a long legacy of ill feeling towards all aspects of government.

There were many reasons for the Kwaio Rebellion. The confiscation of rifles had removed a potent symbol of early 20th century Malaita Island manhood. In addition, tribespeople objected to a head-tax which subjected them to foreign rule. And in order to pay the tax, many people had to enlist on labour ships.

At the same time, the Kwaio felt their ancestral gods would not provide good yam and taro crops if Christianity was not firmly resisted. The Kwaio also disliked the newly created village headmen who were appointed by the Protectorate authorities. These villagers were often accused of misusing power and of making false charges against innocent fellow Malaita Islanders.

Marching Rule By 1939, Malaita Islanders were refusing to work on any plantations where expatriate managers and overseers used whips and dogs. Despite the careless bombing by US planes of two Malaita Island settlements, including Laulasi, in August 1942, many Malaita and Maramasike islanders went to Guadalcanal to work at the huge US base there. They found the US forces a complete contrast to their prewar colonial masters, and extremely generous. Furthermore, black Americans wore the same clothing as whites, ate the same food and used the same equipment. Many islanders hoped the Americans would stay to rule the Solomons after the war, but the unpopular British officials remained at their posts.

By late 1945, a mass movement called Marching Rule, or Maasina Rulu, or Ruru (an 'Are'Are expression for 'brotherhood rule'), had emerged to unite Malaita and Maramasike islanders. The movement's aim was for Malaitans to manage their island themselves – independently of the churches and the colonial authorities – to receive better pay and work conditions on plantations, and to earn a better return on any taxes they paid.

Malaita and Maramasike islanders resented the way island customs were treated lightly by the government. For example, adultery was punishable by death in traditional Melanesia, but to the British it was a matter of little concern.

So the Marching Rule Movement set up its own courts to deal with breaches of customary law and the movement's rules, including failure to pay its taxes. Offenders were fined by Marching Rule courts or imprisoned in their own jails, though serious matters such as murder, rape and assault were handed over to the colonial authorities.

Whole villages moved to the coast. New villages were built like US army camps, complete with three-metre-high stockades and tall watchtowers with sentries to guard the gates at all times. Meeting halls were built and Marching Rule flags displayed.

Marching Rule was nationalistic and anti-British, yet it was also cargo-cultist.

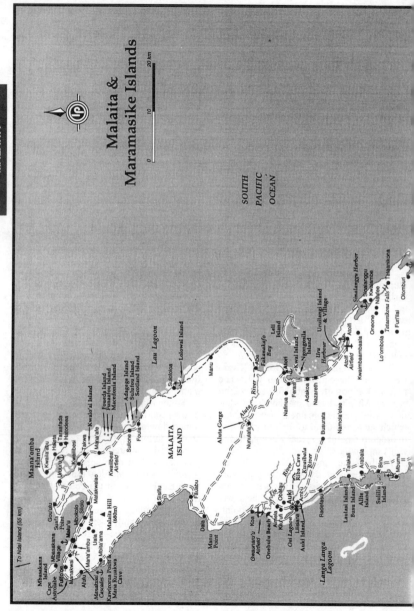

Malaita &
Maramasike Islands

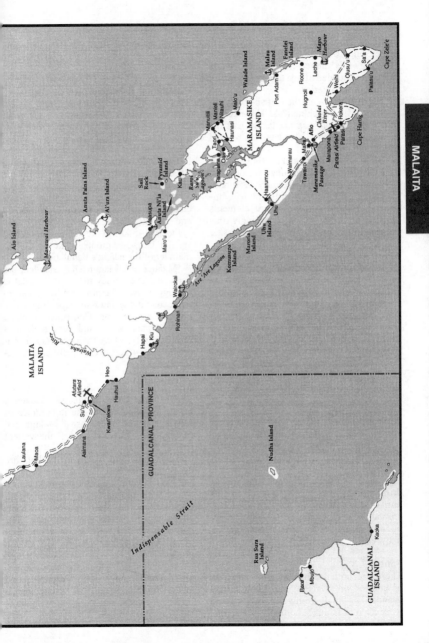

Huts were erected to house the many gifts expected from the USA. Lookouts were posted daily to spot the ships believed to be bringing this hoped-for bounty, while rumours abounded of mysterious US planes landing in the interior.

For over two years the British warily co-operated with Marching Rule. However, by mid-1947, action was needed to halt the persecution of those islanders who refused to join the movement.

Mass arrests began and in 1949 as many as 2000 people were detained for refusing to demolish their stockades. By 1950 relationships with the government had improved, though some die-hard elements resisted until 1955. Not surprisingly, this episode left many Malaita and Maramasike islanders with a deep distrust of Britain.

Post-Independence Since Independence in 1978, fears have been expressed (mainly in the western Solomons) of possible Malaita and Maramasike islander domination. Although among the last to benefit from the spread of schools and churches during the colonial period, Malaita and Maramasike islanders, who make up about 25% of the country's population, now occupy top positions in all walks of national life, including politics.

Climate

Auki has approximately 236 rain days a year, with an average total annual rainfall of 3271 mm. The wettest period is from January to March, averaging over 350 mm a month; if you plan to travel then, pack a raincoat or umbrella. May and June are the driest months, each receiving less than 200 mm of rain. Morning humidity reaches around 90% six months a year, while afternoons average 77%. Temperatures range between 23°C and 30°C.

Fauna

There are both freshwater and saltwater crocodiles on Malaita and Maramasike islands. The small freshwater species lives in some of Malaita's northern rivers; the larger, seawater variant lives in the south's muddy, mangrove-lined estuaries, including the 'Are'Are and Raroi Su'u lagoons and Maramasike Passage.

Population & People

There are 15 tribal language and dialect groups, of which the largest is made up of 21,500 Kwara'ae from north-central Malaita Island. 'Are'Are speakers in southern Malaita number 12,500. Another large tribe is the 11,000-strong ancestor-worshipping Kwaio, who live in the mountains along the east-central coast.

Around 12,000 Lau people live in artificial islands off north-eastern Malaita Island and along Maramasike's south-eastern seaboard 145 km to the south. Another 10 smaller language groups make up the remainder of the island's population.

Malaita and Maramasike islanders are perceived even today to be rather volatile and aggressive. The province has a restrictive economy, where only copra and cocoa produce any income. Consequently many of its people now live and work in all parts of the country, where their presence as migrants and workers occasionally inspires resentment.

Arts

Small bride dolls, made of blackened kerosene wood, reflect the importance of marriage in the traditions of Malaita and Maramasike. War clubs recall the violent past.

Loya cane and *bukaware* baskets are decorated with black and brown designs, and red and yellow-painted combs are completed with spokes made of palm wood. Caneware is very strongly woven and includes trays, coasters and table mats. The baskets made by Kwara'ae women are used by them to carry washing or garden produce.

Small, simple figures, frequently representing birds and people, are carved and inlaid with shell. In northern Malaita, dance sticks are usually painted black, with hornbill designs on top.

Model 25-cm-long tuna canoes are carved from wood. Forehead discs are fashioned out of clam and turtle shell and worn by custom dancers. Locally produced oyster-shell pendants often carry a frigate-bird motif, and some ear decorations are made of flying-fox teeth.

Musical Instruments Bamboo panpipes, played in groups of four, eight, 10 and even 16 or more tubes, are common on the island. The pipes are often arranged in double rows.

Slit drums are made from hollowed-out logs, cut with a narrow central gash. Laid on their side, they are beaten with sticks and emit a deep, resounding boom.

Rattles made from hollow nuts are attached to dance sticks and to the legs or wrists of dancers in many parts of the island. Conch shells are often used to summon people or to send messages, and at times are used for musical accompaniment.

Society & Conduct
Local Customs Descent is patrilineal on Malaita and Maramasike, unlike in the western Solomons. In the bush, married men and women still sleep separately in houses confined to one sex only, and in many parts of Malaita and Maramasike adolescent love affairs are ruled over by custom.

In the more traditional areas, it is forbidden for a man to have sex with an unmarried girl. Such an activity could cause the girl's father first to sue for damages and, if these were not forthcoming, to seek revenge. Shell money and pigs would be expected from the offender – or the equivalent in cash from a foreigner.

Malaita and Maramasike islanders cling more tenaciously to their customs than other Solomon Islanders. Their varied cultural life has fascinated anthropologists since WG Ivens wrote about the Lau Lagoon in *Island Builders of the South Pacific* in 1930. Roger Keesing spent much of the 1970s in east-central Malaita studying the life of a Kwaio chieftain. (He also

collaborated with Peter Corris to write *Lightning Meets the West Wind*, about the 1927 Kwaio uprising.)

Shell Money The island's traditional currency, shell money, is used only for bride price, payment of certain ceremonial debts, compensation for insults and injuries, the purchase of land, pigs or canoes, and as personal adornment when worn around the neck at ceremonies.

Shell money is made of small pierced discs, usually taken from the shell of the pink-lipped *spondylus*, or spiny rock oyster. It can also be made from mussels, pearl shell, the chambered nautilus, or from the lips of a conch, but these have less value. Colour counts towards value too – pink shell money is worth twice as much as the red type. Then, in descending order of value, come orange, brown, white and black.

A large piece of shell is smashed up into tiny rounded fragments, each of which has a hole pierced in it. Next, the pieces of shell are heated on stones to produce orange and brown hues. After this, they are all strung with a length of plant, or nowadays, nylon twine. The shell pieces are then polished. The traditional method of vigorous rubbing on a grinding stone lubricated with water and black sand has largely been replaced by the use of soapy water.

A typical string of shells, is called a *tafuliae* and contains many hundreds of discs on its 10 legs, or strands. These are one fathom long (almost two metres), and each is divided by turtle-shell plates. These tafuliaes are worth up to S$400. If need be, lengths may be broken off into shorter amounts to buy smaller items. In northern Malaita Island, the cost of a bride was once 50 strings of shell money, whereas in some southern parts of the island only one spear was required to buy a wife.

In the past a young man often put himself and his family into lifelong debt to buy a wife. Even today in isolated bush villages people may still pay 30 to 40 fathoms of shell money for bride price, though the

MALAITA

Artificial Islands

A distinctive feature of Malaita Island is the large number of artificial islands, particularly in the Langa Langa and Lau lagoons. These have been built on sandbars or exposed reefs by heaping boulders up until a permanent landmass remains.

Although new artificial islands are being built even now, a few go back many generations to the 1550s. The biggest are more than one sq km in size and some of these larger artificial islands are surrounded by a coral wall, giving the appearance of a coastal fortress. However, the majority are very small and consist of nothing more formidable than a few houses on stilts.

At first sight the houses may look flimsy, but in fact they are usually sturdily built of bamboo, palm and pandanus leaves. Although the cookhouses are usually on the ground, the sleeping area is raised on stilts to permit air to circulate underneath, and to provide room for tidal surges during cyclones.

If a young married couple decides to build an island, they will initially make it big enough for one or two houses and then add to it as the family expands. They first scour the floor of the lagoon for large, smooth stones, ferrying them by canoe to the proposed site. Once the mound of rocks has risen to a height of between two and three metres above sea level, the island builders fill in the holes between the stones with sand. Houses are then built and coconuts palms planted.

Typically, islands take over a year to build and require regular help from friends and relatives. A few palm trees may eventually take root, but most food comes from mainland gardens, or through fishing. The islands' only supply of fresh water is rain; all other drinking needs have to be met by carrying water over from the mainland.

The islands were originally built as an escape from the endemic warfare plaguing Malaita Island, especially in the 19th century. As all land was already owned, there was none for an expanding population. By constructing an island only a short distance from shore, a cool, mosquito-free environment could be secured. Most island builders maintained gardens onshore by agreement with mainlanders, tending their crops by day and returning home at dusk. Others were fisherfolk – such as those from Lau Lagoon – who exchanged their catch for crops from mainlanders. ∎

church has had an impact on lowering the price paid along the coast, concerned by the debt young men face and the social problems that arise as a result. Mission villages have set a maximum price of five strings of shell money (worth S$2000) for each bride.

Other Custom Currencies Malaita Islanders also make shell currency armbands, forehead discs, necklaces, pendants and earrings. Some types of shell jewellery, particularly headbands, have porpoises' or dolphins' teeth in them. Flying-foxes' teeth are also used in some parts as bride price.

Pigs are another form of custom currency. Pig-exchange ceremonies, also involving shell money or dolphins' teeth, were plentiful on Malaita and Maramasike, and still are in the Kwaio area. They're fairly low key compared to those in parts of Papua New Guinea and Vanuatu.

Tattoos Although some older Malaita Island men have tattoos by their eye creases, younger men nowadays prefer facial engravings on their cheeks. Facial engravings are small circular lines or crisscross designs drawn on the face, arms or back – but without colouring. It is done with a bone or wooden instrument to mark out the pattern and to cut away the flesh. The operation is repeated several times over a period of days. Coconut water and lime juice are applied to prevent bleeding and to aid the formation of scars.

Ramos In precolonial times a ramo, or *lamo*, was a Malaitan warrior-leader who operated as a paid assassin. Such people still exist, but ritual contract killing no longer occurs. To be a ramo, a man had to kill at least one other person and then intimidate or terrorise all who objected to his action. A Malaitan who wanted revenge would pay for a ramo with pigs and shell money.

Shark Worship Sharks were often worshipped and a few Malaita Islanders still believe human spirits reside in them. A shark-caller could summon a shark and send it to sink an enemy's canoe. The shark would either kill the person there and then, or bring the victim back to be ritually killed later.

Dolphin Drives These are elaborate affairs, with villagers clashing stones together underwater to create a resonating effect which attracts dolphins into shallow inlets. They are then slaughtered for their meat and teeth.

Information
Charges & Custom Fees Some Malaitans are resentful of outsiders and indifferent to the possible earnings offered by tourism. Such people often quote ludicrously high amounts for things like canoe rides and shell money demonstrations, and won't negotiate as they really don't care if you accept or not. Other Malaitans *are* tempted by what they see as easy pickings provided by tourists. The result? Again, high prices.

Recently fraudulent claims for custom fees have become a problem. A local might falsely state he is the landowner and demand a fee he has no right to. This is a tricky situation for the tourist, who has no way of knowing who owns what. If you refuse to pay a genuine claimant, you could end up having to pay compensation too. Try to politely and tactfully confirm whom one should pay. Or commission the claimant to be your guide, to ensure they won't disappear and leave you to face the genuine landowner alone (or other bogus claimants!). Another possibility is to agree to pay, showing the money, but not handing it over till you've seen the sight and are about to leave. Perhaps the best option is to acquire a local guide right at the outset, before anyone asks for money.

Medical Services Malaita Island has a hospital at Kilu'ufi (near Auki) and at Atoifi. The island's dentist is based at Kilu'ufi.

On the western side of the island there are medical clinics at Malu'u, Mbita'ama,

MALAITA

Fauabu, Auki, Talakali, Hauhui, Rohinari and Afio. Along the eastern side they are at Kwailibesi (SDA-run), Takwa, Gwaunotolo, Sulofoloa, Nafinua, Olomburi, Manawai Harbour, Tarapaina, Taramata, Tawa'aro and Sa'a. There are also various nurse-aid posts scattered around, including in the bush.

Accommodation

Auki has plenty of places to stay, but elsewhere on Malaita the options are limited. There are rest houses at Malu'u, Atoifi, Foula, Maoa and on Kwai and Ngongosila islands. In other villages you'll need to ask the local chief. The larger villages such as Kwari'ekwa, Heo, Hauhui, Hapai, Kiu, Waimarau and Tawairoi probably have a simple visitors' house available.

Solomon Village Stay (see Accommodation in the Facts for the Visitor chapter) has a couple places on Malaita Island: one in the north and another south of Auki.

Getting There & Away

Air All flights into Malaita come from Honiara. Solomon Airlines flies at least twice daily to Auki (S$105), and on Thursday morning there's one direct flight to Parasi (S$135) on Maramasike Island.

There's a Solomon Airlines office (☎ 40163) in Auki.

Western Pacific Air Services flies into Afutara (S$95) on Monday and Thursday morning and into Kwailibesi (S$125) on Monday morning. It may also have flights between the different Malaitan airports.

Sea From Honiara, National Shipping runs a boat to Auki that continues up the coast and on to Ontong Java Atoll; another goes to Su'u, then down the coast and on to the Stewart Islands (Sikaiana Atoll). These boats depart once a month, at best. Universal Shipping occasionally goes to Ontong Java.

Malaita Shipping's MV *Ramos I* leaves Honiara at 6 pm on Tuesday and Friday, arriving at Auki at 11.30 pm (S$30) and returning the next day at 9 am. Every second

Sunday at 8 pm it departs Honiara for Malaita's north-eastern ports – to Atoifi costs from S$68. Every second Wednesday it sets off for south Malaita, calling at ports between Su'u (S$54) and Manawai (S$64); Su'u to Manawai costs S$24.

Wings Shipping sends the *Compass Rose II* on a return trip to Auki every Wednesday (fare from S$29), and to northern Malaita ports as far as Olomburi each Friday. In either case departure is from Honiara at 6 pm.

The *Ocean Express* leaves Honiara at 7 am every Monday, arriving at Auki at around noon (S$35, students S$25). It returns the same day.

Tavuilo Shipping usually sails the MV *Faalia* from Honiara to Auki on Monday, Thursday and Saturday night. The deck-class fare is S$20; S$45 includes a cabin.

Getting Around

The Airport Gwaunaru'u airfield is 10 km from Auki and an S$10 ride in the Solomon Airlines bus on a smooth, newly paved road.

Sea Although you can use the scheduled shipping service to hop around the island, most travel will be by motor canoe. Charter prices are higher here than anywhere else in the Solomons, with S$150 or more per day (excluding fuel) often being demanded in the Auki/Langa Langa Lagoon area. In Auki, the best place to try is the Fisheries Development Centre (☎ 40161), which charges S$80 to S$100, depending on canoe/motor size. This rate is good until 4.30 pm, after which you'll have to pay the driver overtime.

There are wharves at Auki and Fouia. Anchorages include Mbita'ama, Malu'u, Haleta (on Maana'omba Island), Kwalo'ai and Scotland islands, Sulofoloa, Atori, Uru and Sinalanggu harbours, Olomburi, Manawai Harbour, Ai'ura Island, Maasupa, Maka, Wairokai, Rohinari, Waisisi Harbour, Kiu, Mbuma and Laulasi. In addition, yachts often moor beside Aio and Anuta Paina islands' sandy beaches.

Land There is about 325 km of road on Malaita Island. Roads run north from Auki to Fouia, across the island to Atori and Atoifi, and southwards to Asimana. There's also a track from Su'u to Hauhui, and another between Haarumou and Maka. These comprise the longest stretches of road in the Solomons, but they are almost completely unsealed. Road surfaces are regularly eroded, and many routes are prone to flash flooding – especially the road to Atori.

Trucks can be infrequent. The best time and place to get a ride in Auki is at the wharf or nearby market when a ship calls in,

or from 1 to 2 pm on other weekdays. The return journey from the country to Auki usually requires an early start. Trucks are slow and uncomfortable, but reasonably priced; from Auki to Malu'u, three hours away on the north coast, it's S$10.

Another option, only in Auki, is to charter a taxi; try phoning tel 40034. The Solomon Airlines minibus is also for hire (when it doesn't have to meet flights).

AUKI

The small township of Auki (pronounced 'ow-ky'), has been Malaita Island's capital

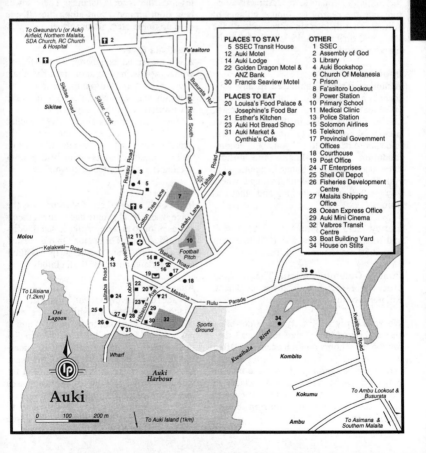

PLACES TO STAY
5 SSEC Transit House
12 Auki Motel
14 Auki Lodge
22 Golden Dragon Motel & ANZ Bank
30 Francis Seaview Motel

PLACES TO EAT
20 Louisa's Food Palace & Josephine's Food Bar
21 Esther's Kitchen
23 Auki Hot Bread Shop
31 Auki Market & Cynthia's Cafe

OTHER
1 SSEC
2 Assembly of God
3 Library
4 Auki Bookshop
6 Church Of Melanesia
7 Prison
8 Fa'asitoro Lookout
9 Power Station
10 Primary School
11 Medical Clinic
13 Police Station
15 Solomon Airlines
16 Telekom
17 Provincial Government Offices
18 Courthouse
19 Post Office
24 JT Enterprises
25 Shell Oil Depot
26 Fisheries Development Centre
27 Malaita Shipping Office
28 Ocean Express Office
29 Auki Mini Cinema
32 Valbros Transit Centre
33 Boat Building Yard
34 House on Stilts

since 1909. In the 1920s, the town had a perimeter fence, and Europeans who ventured beyond it always took an armed escort due to the danger of ambush.

Nowadays, a town of about 4000 people, Auki has shops, hotels, restaurants, provincial government buildings, churches and a boat-building yard within its borders, plus a hospital close by. Valbros Transit Centre is a new development east of the wharf. In due course it should feature a public garden, food outlets and a hotel. Auki's two main streets are Loboi and Hibiscus Aves.

Auki is one of the most photogenic of the Solomons' main towns. Attractive features are the nearby leaf-house villages of Ambu and Lilisiana on either side of the inlet, and artificial Auki Island across the harbour mouth.

Information

Although it's not publicised in any way, there is a Secretary for Culture & Tourism (☎ 40059). His name is Henry Torapasi, and he has an office in the upper row of provincial government offices by Telekom, and should be able to tell you about accommodation around Malaita and custom demonstrations in the Langa Langa Lagoon. Ask him about Anonakinaki village, where you can see custom cooking and other traditions.

Money Auki has branches of ANZ bank and NBSI. They're open Monday to Friday from 8.30 am to noon and from 1 to 3 pm.

Post & Communications The Telekom office (☎ 40152, fax 40220) is on Batabu Rd, north of the post office.

Water Supply Auki only has water pressure at three or four designated times a day, for about 1½ hours on each occasion. Often there's no water from mid-afternoon until early the next morning. It's wise to treat or boil all drinking water in Auki. Places to stay generally have supplementary water tanks, but it's worth enquiring before checking in.

Medical & Emergency Services Auki's hospital is at Kilu'ufi (☎ 40272), 3.5 km north of town. In the centre, there's a clinic off Loboi Ave, and close by is the police station (☎ 40132).

Lookouts

There are good views over Auki and its harbour from a high point at the southern edge of Fa'asitoro, about 200m behind the prison. Even better are those from the steep hillside road to Busurata, just to the east of Ambu. This road offers very fine views over Auki Harbour, Osi Lagoon and towards the Nggela Islands. The view is best from around 700m along the hillside road up to the crest 500m further on.

Kwaibala River

Along the Ambu road there's a pump house, with a good swimming spot in the Kwaibala River nearby. At the pump house ask for Jack Sibisoa, who can guide you up to the cave waterfall nearby.

Just before the Kwaibala River reaches Auki Harbour, there's a private house built over the water on two concrete stilts, with a rather rickety coconut-palm bridge connecting it to the mainland at Kombito.

Fa'asitoro

In the early colonial era, Fa'asitoro was the place where local people had to dress themselves prior to entering Auki to see the district officer's staff or doctor. On their return to Fa'asitoro, they would strip off their town gear and don their bush clothes.

Auki Island

At one time everyone on this artificial island was a shark worshipper. The 80m wide island is one km from the town and is home to two families. Each has its own distinct walled-off custom area where ancestral skulls can be seen. Men can enter these sites with permission, but they're tabu for women. There's a childbirth seclusion area that only women can enter.

Auki Island people have been known to ask visitors to pay a S$50 landing fee to see their island and then to charge extra for each site visited. It's simply not worth that sort of money, and the problem is, you won't know what they'll charge till you get out there. In any case, they weren't letting anyone on the island in late 1996 due to a local dispute. Fines have been imposed in the past for taking unauthorised photos of tabu sites, so ask first. The same applies before you touch anything.

There's a small islet just to the north of Auki Island. Extending southwards from them both is a five-km-long stretch of colourful coral growth.

Getting There & Away Plenty of canoes go to or past the island from the Auki wharf, Lilisiana and Ambu. You may be able to hitch a free lift, but if you charter a canoe you'll probably pay S$10 each way.

Lilisiana

This very friendly, welcoming village is a 1.2-km walk from the wharf. It has several houses raised on stilts over the shore.

Women make shell money and necklaces here, polishing them on special work benches. If nobody is working when you visit, just ask someone and people will soon get their wares out for you. Purchase prices are lower than in souvenir shops.

Lilisiana's very peaceful beach is a narrow, long, golden sand spit beside coral shallows. It's immediately to the north of the village and is the closest one to Auki. You should ask the villagers for permission to swim or sunbathe there. They will usually agree, but there is a rule barring revealing swimsuits.

Beside the beach is the Osi Lagoon. Its trees teem with colourful parrots, and sea birds are plentiful at its northern end.

Places to Stay

There are a couple of other cheap rest houses in town, but they don't match the places mentioned below.

The best deal for those on the lowest budgets is *Francis Seaview Motel* (☎ 40282, PO Box 83). It's on the 1st floor,

above the shop with the murals, and has seven double rooms with desk fan. Shower facilities are basic, but there's a kitchen, it's central, and it only charges S$20 per bed. Check-in at Francis & Sons store which is one block west (confusingly, the sign above the store says WT Co Ltd) and open Monday to Saturday from 6 am to 6 pm.

The *SSEC Transit House* (☎ 40173, PO Box 141) is very clean and quiet, and popular with visitors. It has three rooms with a total of eight beds and charges S$30 a person. The kitchen is communal, and there are shared showers and toilets.

Auki Motel (☎ 40014, PO Box 153) is also good. It's on the 1st floor above shops, and has three beds per room. The cost is S$35 per bed or S$70 as a single/double. Unfortunately there are no kitchen facilities. Instead, hot meals are available: breakfast is around S$7 and lunch about S$10. If you want dinner, book by 4 pm.

The *Golden Dragon Motel* (☎ 40113, PO Box 16) is above the ANZ bank. Smallish four-bed rooms are S$38.50, and standard doubles are S$132 with private shower/WC, or S$99 without. There's a kitchen and a lobby area. If no-one is around when you arrive, enquire at the Auki Store opposite. Reception stays open for passengers arriving on the late evening boat.

The most expensive place is the *Auki Lodge* (☎ 40131, PO Box 171), and it's rarely full for that reason. There are eight rooms with private shower/toilet, extensive grounds, a bar and lounge with satellite TV. Singles/doubles start at S$93.50/126.50 with fan, or S$165/198 with air-con. The rooms with air-con have tea/coffee-making facilities. Tours to Langa Langa Lagoon can sometimes be arranged here. The restaurant serves pricey but tasty food: breakfast is S$16.50 and lunch and dinner are S$22 and S$27.50 respectively.

Places to Eat

The *Auki Hot Bread Shop* is open daily from 6 am to 8 pm. The store under the Auki Motel is open 24 hours.

MALAITA

There are several snack-type places to eat at in the market. The best is *Cynthia's Cafe*, with simple meals for under S$10. It closes at 8.30 pm on Friday, otherwise it's 5 pm on weekdays and noon on Saturday. *Esther's Kitchen* on Hibiscus Ave is similarly priced but slightly better. It is open weekdays for breakfast and lunch, and has a pleasant 1st-floor dining area.

Opposite is *Josephine's Food Bar* serving good fish and chips for S$3. *Louisa's Food Palace* next door has the same owners. Renovated in 1996, it now has an air-con room and a leaf-style extension. All three meals are available (except on Sunday when it's open for dinner only) and the food is local, Chinese or western. It should be licensed soon.

Auki Market operates Monday to Saturday and sells fruit, vegetables, meat and fresh fish. Bluefin tuna is usually on offer; a whole one costs around S$18, or it's also sold by the slice.

See also Auki Motel and Auki Lodge under Places to Stay – you don't have to be a guest to eat in either place.

Entertainment

The Auki Mini Cinema in Hibiscus Ave has three daytime sessions: Monday to Friday at 8.30 am, 11.30 am and 2.30 pm; Saturday 7.30 am, 10.30 am and 1.30; closed Sunday. Entry costs S$4.

AROUND AUKI

A tough one-hour walk north-east of Auki is Dukwasi and the **Riba Cave**. The custom fee often starts around S$20, but you should be able to reduce this if you protest vigorously. You will need a guide.

The cave is very slippery and covered with the excreta of hundreds of swallows. There are stalagmites, a sink hole, several large subterranean chambers and an underground river. Come with a powerful torch (flashlight) and in old clothes.

The best beach in the Auki area is the two-km-long **Onebulu Beach**. It's at the mouth of the Fiu River, 9 km north of Auki. Another one km north is the sandy beach that fringes Gwaunaru'u airfield. It continues as far as the large village of Koa three km beyond, where there's a good reef for snorkelling.

At the north-west end of the airport runway is **Aukwaria**, a cultural centre that puts on feasts and traditional dances. Enquire at Auki's Solomon Airlines office on Batabu road.

SOUTH-WESTERN MALAITA ISLAND

All distances given are from Auki wharf by vehicle along the road. Additional distances are given for canoe.

Langa Langa Lagoon

Extending from seven to 32 km south of Auki, this lagoon is famous for its artificial islands, particularly Laulasi and Alite. Tours of the lagoon can be arranged by various people in Auki – ask at hotels or see the Secretary for Culture and Tourism. JT Enterprises (☎ 40197), Hibiscus Ave, Auki, can take up to five people for a visit to Laulasi, Busu or Alite for a total of S$150. This includes the canoe, motor, fuel and driver, but not custom fees. Many people charge much more than that.

Radefasu

- 7 km

From the sea, Radefasu resembles an artificial island, as it's built out into the water on a coral platform. Shell money is made locally and most households have some to sell.

Laulasi & Busu Islands

- 16 km & 2 km by canoe

Laulasi is an artificial island built in the early 1600s. Busu is a larger island immediately to the south-west. Ancient traditions are zealously preserved by the people, who can put on an impressive show for tourists at their cultural centre.

Separated from public areas are spirit houses where the skulls of ancestors and dead enemies are housed. Only males may enter these sections of the island. Likewise, the female seclusion area is reserved for women.

Shark Calling on Laulasi Island

The former animists on Laulasi traditionally worshipped sharks as their totem. In dramatic ceremonies, held until the 1970s, sharks were actually fed by hand after villagers had summoned them by rhythmically beating together stones underwater.

During the ceremony, the village priest calls out the name of a particular shark. In response, the shark swims to a boy standing on a rock in about 30 cm of water, who feeds it a piece of pork. The younger, smaller sharks are fed first, until finally the oldest and largest shark receives the biggest piece from the boy, who then climbs on its back. The shark swims around the lagoon, carrying the boy, before returning to the submerged rock for him to disembark.

The Laulasi people explain this incredible phenomenon by saying a shark ancestor in the past had promised not to attack the islanders as long as they fed it and its descendants pork. In return, people would be left unharmed and the sharks would ensure that a plentiful supply of tuna remained in the area.

Because of these traditions, predominately red or black clothing is absolutely tabu on Laulasi. Black is the colour of local pigs, the usual sacrifice to the sharks, while red could be mistaken for blood, and thereby arouse the sharks and ancestors believed to be residing in them. Even today, you will not be allowed to wear these colours while visiting. ∎

Cultural displays include dances, custom singing, and demonstrations of traditional building methods and shell-money manufacture. If you go as part of a tour, there may be a welcoming ritual involving a challenge by mud warriors who will be pacified by an offering of shell money.

Visits used to centre on Laulasi, but recent local disputes have meant that the focus has shifted to Busu. As on Auki Island, islanders charge an unrealistically large amount as a landing fee, and further sums for each site visited or each demonstration staged. You won't be sure in advance what they'll charge, so it's questionable whether it's worth the hassle and expense of going there. I heard of one couple who ended up paying S$550 in various fees, plus S$250 for transport.

Getting There & Away To visit Laulasi independently involves a S$4 truck ride to Talakali, an SDA village 16 km from Auki. As long as you avoid Saturdays, you should be able to arrange a return trip by dugout or motor canoe, but you'll have to bargain for an acceptable price.

Alite Island
- 20 km & 3 km by canoe

There are in fact two Alite islands, the larger being natural and unpopulated. Villagers live on the much smaller, artificial island about 300m away. As on Laulasi, they continue the tradition of shell-money making but shark worship is no longer practised. The larger island has a sandy beach on its western side. There's coral to view and seashells to collect. You can get a canoe to the islands from Arabala, an attractive village on the Malaita Island mainland which is built on stilts out over the water.

Sililiu Island
- 26 km & 2 km by canoe

This island has sand beaches all around it. The closest place to find a canoe to get you there is two km away at Bina.

Su'u Harbour
- 56 km

A new central government-funded *rest house* with three rooms has opened in **Maoa**, 12 km north of Asimana. It's owned by Jonathan Kuka. Two km south-east of scenic Su'u village is Afutara airfield. The coastal road continues as a track to Hauhui.

To carry on further south is only possible by boat. Ships call in at the larger centres in the 'Are'Are Lagoon, and at Maka beside the entrance to the Maramasike Passage.

Kiu

Marching Rule began here in 1944. An old timber-hulled vessel is wrecked near the inlet's mouth, one km to the north-west of Kiu.

'Are'Are Lagoon

The lagoon begins 27 km south of Su'u and is 29 km long by one km wide, stretching southwards from Rohinari to Uhu. A 15-km track connects Haarumou with Waimarau and Maka.

The lagoon's islands, which are covered with coconut palms, are long, slim and low, with continuous white beaches on their ocean sides (especially Uhu, Maroria and Komusupa islands). Mangroves fringe their inland lagoon sides. On the mainland shore, the land rises from swamps to thickly forested highlands.

Western 'Are'Are people make single strands of shell money, which are still used for bride price.

Haarumou

At the Haarumou People's Centre shell money is produced and carvers make pan-pipes, and you can also pay local pipe bands to perform. From Haarumou there's a footpath over the mountains to the Raroi Su'u Lagoon.

Five km south along an unsealed road is **Waimarau**. There's a custom house, carved with images of men, women and fish, where ancestral bones are stored. Women may not enter, but they can peer in through the doorway.

NORTHERN MALAITA ISLAND

The northern road from Auki to the Lau Lagoon follows the coast from Sisifiu to Silolo, providing sea views. Long stretches of white-sand beach line the shore. Distances are from Auki wharf.

Sisifiu
● 44 km

There's a custom house here containing many ancient artefacts. Local carvers make reproductions for sale.

Mbita'ama
● 65 km

A marine cave called Mana Ruuakwa at nearby Kwaiorua Point penetrates inland, terminating in a deep hole in the ground, with blue water clearly visible from above. Whenever the hole has been filled in, the sea has flushed it out. Islanders say that sharks come in here to sleep.

Newly made shell money is often available for sale in Mbita'ama. There are also a few relics around from WWII.

Afufu
● 68 km

This small fishing village is a centre for traditional dancing. The dances focus on everyday activities such as fishing and ngali-nut collecting. One of these dances is about girls collecting seashells to decorate themselves for festivals.

The only major Allied action occurring in WWII on Malaita was the destruction of a Japanese radio station here by US marines in November 1942. It was the sole Japanese outpost on the island.

Mbasakana Island
● 75 km

Beautiful Mbasanka Island (pronounced 'mbathakana') is just over two km long by one km wide. Surrounded by a fringing reef and attractive white-sand beaches, this flat landmass is about 1.5 km across the water from Fulifo'oe on Malaita's northern coast.

People from Mbasakana village, where half the island's 250 inhabitants live, will point out an interesting cave if asked. Villagers here are very welcoming and may be able to find you somewhere to stay, as long as it's only for one night. Both motor canoes and paddle canoes make the trip from the mainland.

Mana'ambu

- 81 km

Several tree houses (called *biu* and pronounced 'bee-you') are used by young men in Mana'ambu. There are usually four occupants between the ages of 11 and 20, two at either end of the age range. Boys who have recently been initiated live in the houses because they are now considered to have matured beyond the need for maternal care.

Two km west at **Manakwai** there's a river where you can swim and some small cascades.

Malu'u

- 82 km

This small subprovincial headquarters is a good halfway stop between Auki and the Lau Lagoon. The beach is rather limited, but does have a monument to Malaita's first missionary who arrived in 1894. There's some lively surf to ride, along with good snorkelling off the reef. There's also a wrecked Japanese plane, accessible by dugout or motor canoe. The town has some small stores, a market on Wednesday and Saturday mornings, and electricity and piped water supplies.

Malu'u Lodge (there's no phone – make advance bookings by radio) has recently opened above Tang's store. There are seven rooms and the charge is S$44/66 a single/double. There is no kitchen for self-catering but meals are available. Staff can arrange snorkelling and canoe trips and panpipes and custom dancing performances. Also in the village is a five-room *rest house*, with a kitchen, charging S$30/40 a single/double. In the nearby village of Keru, the local church has two cheap rooms available.

A'ama

- 82 km & 4-km walk

A trail to the hilltop behind Malu'u leads to A'ama, where there's another biu. You will need a guide. A further one km, a slow trek through thick bush, is **Uala**, where there's a skull house.

Mbokolo

- 87 km

A sandy beach extends to Silolo. The best part is at Mbokolo.

In the vicinity of **Matakwalao**, five km east, are several traditional sites and Malaita Hill (680m). To explore these you'll need a guide – ask around Matakwalao market on Wednesday or Saturday.

Maana'omba Island

- 106 km & 3 km by canoe

This pleasantly flat island has white-sand beaches on its western side. Its 700 people live at either end of the island, many of them at Taraafada, Hatodeea or Kwaila'abu. The sea is only 1.5m deep for most of the three km between Maana'omba and Uruuru on the mainland. From Uruuru, beaches stretch west to Suafa Point. There's good snorkelling all through this area, especially at Gou'ulu.

Lau Lagoon

The lagoon is about 35 km long and contains more than 60 artificial islands. It stretches from the shallows between Uruuru and Maana'omba, where there are several artificial islands, down to Lolowai – the most southerly artificial landform. Over half have been built in the last 60 years. The ever-present fresh sea breezes make these offshore villages much more pleasant and cool than the often-humid mainland.

On some of the Lau islands, Christianity is practised in tandem with old beliefs

Lau Childbirth

Traditional childbirth rituals are still followed by some animists. After giving birth, women cut the umbilical cord themselves, wrap their babies in pandanus leaves and paddle themselves back on small rafts to their island villages, escorted by other women in canoes. For 30 days they are confined to the *bisi*, or women's seclusion house. ∎

MALAITA

and traditions. Some people are still animist or pagan, and there's a strong history of shark worshipping, especially on Funaafou Island.

A few of the islands have rather unexpected names, such as Macedonia and Scotland. The latter was built by a family who worked for a Scot in Western Province, and they named the island after him.

If you want to visit an artificial island, ask onshore whether it's all right to do so. Then, on arrival there, ask for the chief and repeat your request.

Takwa & Around
- 108 km

Several of the islands are within easy reach by canoe from Takwa's shore. There's a market every Saturday, where shell money and porpoises' teeth are sometimes used as currency instead of cash.

Three km south at **Mana'afe**, a cultural centre allows foreigners to take part in Lau village life. Another seven km brings you to **Sulione**. It has a market every Monday and Thursday that attracts traders from the nearby artificial islands. They may have canoe space to take you back with them.

Foueda & Funaafou Islands
- 116 km

These two artificial islands are still very traditional, with chiefs being buried in their canoes in the men's club houses. Visitors may not enter these, though you may be allowed to peer in from outside. Both islands also have non-Christian altars and cemeteries, as well as skull houses.

Funaafou is large for an artificial island – about half a km in size – and has about 400 residents. Shark-calling rituals still occur occasionally, the most recent were in 1985 and 1988. Another shark-calling ritual is planned for 1997.

Fouia
- 120 km

Nathan Wate has a *rest house* here, and he can also arrange local tours and activities, such as visits to Sulufou Island. The road

Shark Calling on Funaafou Island

Traditionally sharks were called when the chief priest suspected they would begin to attack people unless they were fed freshly killed pork. After having been fed pork a young boy would ride around the island on the back of a shark. As long as this occurred satisfactorily, the priest could expect that at his death his spirit would enter sharks at will, moving between the smaller reef varieties and the larger pelagic species as required.

However, if the boy was attacked or killed, the priest had to compensate the family for their child. He was also barred from repeating the ceremony, so his spirit lost the chance at his demise of entering sharks.

Unlike in Laulasi, shark calling rituals are still occasionally performed at Funaafou. A few animists still live on the island, but the ritual is now performed more as a celebration of traditional culture rather than being motivated by belief. ■

finishes at the wharf but a footpath continues about 35 km southwards to **Abe**. You may be able to get a motor canoe from there to Atori, to connect you up with the cross-island road back to Dala.

Adagege Island
- 120.5 km

This large artificial island is especially custom-oriented. Women are restricted from entering those areas of the village where there are animist temples and where skulls are kept. There's another walled-off section which is a women's seclusion zone. You'll recognise the priest by the dolphin-teeth necklace he wears.

Sulufou Island
- 121 km

Sulufou, the oldest and largest of the artificial islands in the Lau group, is a strikingly picturesque village on stilts. About half a km offshore, this one-sq-km circular island has a most dramatic aspect from the sea.

There are four main families on the island, each with its own anchorage. In front of the COM church is a stone where refugees from northern Malaita Island used to sit, pleading for sanctuary.

Sulufou Island is very densely populated, with about 1000 permanent residents and up to 2000 visitors at Christmas. From 1868 to 1875, the island was the home of the young Scottish castaway John Renton. There's no organised accommodation, but if you want to stay, the chief may be able to organise something for one or two nights only. A dugout-canoe ride from the mainland should cost a couple of dollars each way.

CENTRAL & EASTERN MALAITA ISLAND

The road across the mountainous interior to the east coast around Atori and Atoifi is regularly washed out during the midyear wet season. Beginning near Dala, the route's most scenic spot is at Nunulafa, where it crosses over the Auluta Gorge 20m below.

Atori, 61 km east of Auki, is a sub-provincial headquarters, and has a cultural centre. There are several surfing beaches and bays north of Atori, including **Fakanakafo Bay**. A footpath goes from here along the coast up to Fouia. On the way it passes another surfing beach at Manu, 14 km north of Fakanakafo Bay.

Three km to the south-east of Atori is **Kwai Island**, a beautiful but overcrowded islet with a surrounding beach. Canoe prices from the mainland are often high, though you might get a better deal if you can share the ride with a local. The *Kwai Island Rest House* is welcoming.

There's a narrow sandbar that you can use at low tide to reach **Ngongosila Island**. This sand-surrounded island is where Bell and Lillies were buried after their murder in 1927 at the hands of Kwaio tribespeople. Ngongosila is even more

crowded than Kwai, and also has a small *rest house*.

It's six km from Atori to **Leli Island**, and a 20-minute motor-canoe trip. The beaches on this sand-surrounded, unoccupied coral atoll are the best in the area. Most visitors come here for the fishing and snorkelling. Ownership of the island was under dispute in 1996; an issue which will have to be resolved before tourist visits can resume. In the 1880s, several ships were looted here.

The road stops at **Atoifi**, the main centre for Kwaio people who have left the bush. There are several traditional villages nearby, such as **Kwaimbaambaala**, which tourists may visit providing prior arrangements have been made with the chief. Atoifi has a cheap, simple *rest house*.

Sinalanggu Harbour & Around

Villagers here used to call whales into the harbour in a similar manner to the shark callers. In the bush behind the inlet are many *labu* and shrines from earlier generations of Kwaio people. Labu are hilltop settlements built near ridges and fortified with walls where necessary.

Inside a labu are ancestral shrines and a men's meeting house; dwelling places are usually outside. Those within 10 km of Sinalanggu Harbour are at Oneone, Lo'ombola and Furi'ilai. You will need a guide to

---

Visits to the Kwaio

East-central Malaita Island's mountainous interior is only very seldom visited by Westerners, and you should think very carefully before going there. As government officials themselves require escorts here, they discourage foreigners from contacting the Kwaio. Nonetheless, trips inland are possible for those who can afford to pay penalty rates for guides, and are prepared for the possibility of an angry, perhaps even violent, rejection by the Kwaio once they find them. The Kwaio may also demand huge compensation. ∎

The Kwaio: A People Apart

About 1000 of the 11,000 Kwaio people live in the mountains of east-central Malaita Island. They have rejected the modern world in favour of the traditional life and religion of their ancestors. Their stronghold is the isolated mountainous interior between Uru Harbour and Olomburi.

These Kwaio believe the ancestral spirits are omnipresent, watching over both the living and the dead. According to the Kwaio, every event is caused by an ancestor. The task of the living is to enquire through magic which spirits are causing any perceived misfortune and what is required to placate them – usually the sacrifice of pigs. Mortuary and marriage feasts are held – pigs and shell money are the currency, not cash.

Magic is regularly used, especially for revenge and healing. Among the Kwaio the distinction between sorcery and religion is blurred. Sorcery is sometimes employed for personal gain, yet it's also routinely performed by the whole clan as a ritual.

Villagers are traditionally dressed; unmarried girls and women go naked and smoke pipes, while married women wear minute T-pieces. Traditional staffs demonstrate authority, and bows and arrows, clubs and spears are always present when Kwaio bush people gather for feasts and law making. Sporadic violence still occurs, caused by acts of seduction or adultery, insults against a person or their ancestors, and pig or taro theft.

Villages are built along the traditional pattern – men's houses above, domestic dwellings in the centre and menstrual huts below. These small, scattered bamboo houses, built flush to the ground, are shifted every few years.

In defiance of the national and provincial governments, the bush Kwaio refuse to pay taxes and have their own judgements for dealing with serious criminal cases. They have declined to take part in provincial and national activities until they are paid compensation for their people who died during the 1927 rebellion, and for the desecration of ancestral sites at the time. Since the mid-1980s, they have been seeking S$294.6 billion to compensate for all the dead Kwaio, desecrated shrines and destroyed villages. Naturally, the Solomons government is not keen to encourage this claim. In fact, little has been heard of it since the late 1980s, when Christian Kwaios began explaining to their bush wantoks that this sort of money just doesn't exist to be paid. ■

---

get to these settlements, but admission to the shrines is only granted to local men who have passed certain rituals.

Two British officials and 13 north-Malaita police were killed in **Kwaiambe** in 1927 by Kwaio who refused to pay head-tax and surrender their rifles. A three-hour climb up a cliff face is **Tataanikona**, a beautiful spot with a waterfall and pool.

Very traditional Kwaio bush people live in **Naufee**, three km south-west of Sina-langgu Harbour. Food is cooked in ground ovens using preheated river stones.

Manawai Harbour & Around

The eastern coast between Manawai Harbour and Maramasike Passage is good

for wild-pig hunting. There are also plenty of swordfish to be caught at sea.

Aio, Anuta Paina and Ai'ura islands all have attractive sandy beaches. The hill on Anuta Paina offers a view along Malaita Island's eastern coast as far as the Maramasike Passage.

Anuta Ni'ia Island

Also called Windmill Island, this sandy islet in Raroi Su'u Lagoon has megapode birds which lay their eggs in the island's warm sand (see Flora & Fauna in the Facts about the Country chapter). To see the megapodes, you must first get permission from the custom owners at Maro'u in Takataka Bay.

Ndai Island

Ndai, 55 km north of Malaita Island, is a semi-oval-shaped, slightly raised coral structure with a surrounding reef. It's seven km long and 3.25 km across. Ndai has six small, brackish lakes and is covered with forest and scrub. Its highest point is only 20m above sea level.

The island's sole village is Bethlehem, where the Melanesian inhabitants speak a language with some Polynesian features. Ndai is the abandoned remains of a settlement in the south.

It's traditionally believed that the spirits of dead Malaita Islanders go to Ndai. In another legend, the maximum number of people living on the island at any one time can only be 100. If a baby is born, or an extra person comes to stay, someone else will die. Consequently, unless numbers are down, the chief will only allow you a very short visit.

Getting There & Away
A one-day chartered canoe ride from Malu'u in northern Malaita Island, allowing a few hours on the island, will cost about S$150 plus fuel.

Maramasike Island

Small Malaita, as Maramasike is often called, is separated from Malaita Island proper by the 20-km-long Maramasike Passage, a narrow, snake-like waterway. In places it's less than 400m wide and occasionally only four metres deep. Despite this, there is plenty of coastal shipping travelling through.

This 700-sq-km island has a population of approximately 7000. It's distinguished by low hills separated by long, high limestone ridges, and an indented shoreline. For Maramasike, refer to the Malaita & Maramasike Islands map earlier in this chapter.

Medical Services
Maramasike's four medical clinics are at Afio, Sa'a, Tarapaina and Taramata.

Accommodation
There's a simple village-style *visitors' house* at Haunasi, and the school at Rokera has a well-equipped rest house. Elsewhere, you have to rely on the hospitality of locals.

Getting There & Away
Malaita Shipping, National Shipping and Wings Shipping all have boats that call at Maramasike ports. National Shipping's fare from Honiara to Sa'a/Port Adam is S$45/48.

There are anchorages at Port Adam, Mapo Harbour and Oau. Temporary havens for passing yachts can be found in a number of small bays around the island, as well as in Raroi Su'u Lagoon and the Maramasike Passage.

See the Getting There & Away section in the chapter introduction for more information.

Getting Around
There's an unsealed road from Afio to Olusu'u via Rokera, though it was damaged by a tidal wave in 1993. A footpath goes from Rokera, via Cape Hartig and Palasu'u, to Sa'a and Olusu'u. Manuitili, Nitauhi and Taori are connected by paths to Haunasi.

SOUTHERN MARAMASIKE ISLAND
The large archaeological site at **Hugnoli** has many burial stones and shows some similarities to Polynesian sites further east in the Pacific. You will have to get permission to visit the area from the custom owners at Weihii.

Dancers from **Palasu'u** decorate themselves with streaks of white paste made from ashes and then dance while playing bamboo panpipes. Six km to the north at **Olusu'u** are sand beaches.

NORTHERN MARAMASIKE ISLAND
Fanalei Island, like its small neighbour, Malau Island, is surrounded by sand. As

Green turtles can weigh up to 140 kg

Fanalei is only one metre above sea level some of its houses are built on stilts out over the water.

Walade Island is a picturesque artificial island inhabited by Lau speakers. It's only 200m from the mainland and highly populated, with some of its leaf houses built with two storeys. The coast to the north of Walade (pronounced 'walande') is very rugged and prone to rough seas.

Custom rules are observed in Walade and nearby Fanalei. Large numbers of fish, turtles and dolphins inhabit the area. The latter are hunted for their teeth for use as bride price. The standard fee is 1000 dolphins' or porpoises' teeth and five fathoms of single-strand shell money from Laulasi. The name of **Raroi Su'u Lagoon** means 'middle passage'. Its calm, protected, mangrove-fringed waters are full of clams and shells. At its northern tip is the appropriately named Pyramid Island.

Haunasi has a cultural centre where traditional arts and customs are preserved. Islanders work here making handicrafts and recording genealogies, legends and traditional music.

The shells from **Tarapaina** are transported to northern Malaita Island to be made into shell money, as they are considered the province's best. It's a two-km canoe ride from here to O'orou Island, an extinct volcano.

The remains of a US WWII aircraft wreck are exposed at low tide on the shore at **Kau**. Five km to the north-west is Sail Rock, used for target practice by US aircraft in WWII.

Sikaiana Atoll

The triangular atoll of Sikaiana (pronounced 'sik-eye-arna') lies 212 km to the north-east of Malaita Island. The atoll's lagoon has three small, raised islets on its western side, and Sikaiana Island, built up from an extinct 45m high volcano, to the east. The atoll's total land area is less than two sq km, and it has a population of under 300. People live on Sikaiana, Matuiloto and Matuavi. There are also two small artificial islands: Te Palena is a mere 50m by 30m in size; Hakatai'atata is currently abandoned. The islands are also known collectively as the Stewart Islands.

The whole atoll is just over 10 km from east to west, and over six km at its widest point. In its centre are the deep waters of the Te Moana Lagoon, with a number of sandbars and coral heads close to the main island.

The surrounding reef descends steeply, with tremendous depths only a few metres out. Lack of anchorages and a heavy swell make access to the island extremely difficult. Small inter-island vessels visit regularly to collect copra and bêches-de-mer. Access is by canoe across the treacherous reef.

Sikaiana's volcanic soil is extremely fertile. Freshwater swamps on the main island have been artificially deepened to sea level to provide taro beds. Fertility is preserved by regular mulching with vegetable matter from beyond the swamp.

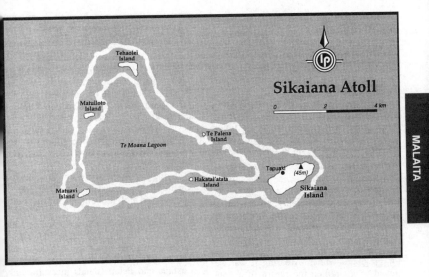

Sikaiana Atoll

Although the average annual rainfall is about 2500 mm, there are no creeks. Drinking water is scarce and comes from shallow wells and rainwater catchment tanks.

History

According to tradition, the discoverer of Sikaiana was Tehuiatahu, who came with a number of companions from an unknown Pacific island called Luahatu. In due course, his followers split into three clans which were ruled alternately by kings from two of these three groups.

Over time, drifters from other Polynesian islands arrived, creating a fourth tribe. Meanwhile, land ownership remained in the hands of the two original ruling clans. There was constant dissension until the land issue was resolved in a just way by a king called Mono.

This island group was first reported to the outside world in 1606, when Luka, a Sikaianan prisoner of war, was found by Quiros in the Duff Islands. He described his home island to the Spaniards, who recorded it as Chicayana. He told them of several two-way journeys between it and the Duffs,

as well as Samoan visits and devastating Tongan raids.

Captain Hunter of the *Waaksamheyd* saw Sikaiana and its neighbours in 1791, naming them the Stewart Islands. In the following years whalers and vessels seeking turtle shells and bêches-de-mer occasionally visited, some using Matuavi as a shore base for melting down whale blubber.

In 1844, Captain Cheyne of the *Naiad* found two English beachcombers here, and in 1859, the crew of the Austrian warship *Novara* made a detailed description of island life.

In 1861 the whaler *Two Brothers* rescued 43 Micronesians from Kiribati who were adrift in two canoes. They were put ashore in Sikaiana where 36 of them stayed, thereby increasing the population by 20%.

Sikaiana suffered heavily in the 1986 Cyclone Namu, losing most of its coconut palms. The atoll has not fully recovered and consequently is still rather economically depressed.

Population & People

The inhabitants of Sikaiana are Polynesian,

and probably originate from many sources, but especially Tuvalu and Tonga. Their very mixed language has both Maori features and Tongan expressions. Because of the similarity of their language to that of the people of Ontong Java, they treat the latter as their *wantoks*.

A Tongan form of filarial mosquito is present in Sikaiana. This is the only place other than Tonga where it can be found, which suggests it was brought by a Tongan migration or raid at some time in the unrecorded past.

Society & Conduct

Loincloths are occasionally still woven on hand-looms from banana fibre that has been soaked in the sea to make it slightly shiny. It's then dyed with a checked pattern. An especially long cloth was traditionally made for pregnant women. Wearing it was believed to guarantee the return of a good figure after pregnancy and childbirth. Some Sikaianan women dress in this material even now.

Getting There & Away

Although crossing the reef by yacht is exceedingly hazardous, especially at night, the lagoon is usually calm. Islanders can advise you where to anchor.

See the Getting There & Away section in the introduction to this chapter for boat schedules.

SIKAIANA ISLAND

There is a medical clinic close to Tapuaki, which is the atoll's main centre. Between it and the four small villages on the south-east coast are the remains of a stone boundary line placed by Tehuiatahu to restrict a rival group of settlers, the Hetuna, whom he later killed.

An alcoholic beverage of fermented coconut juice is the island's speciality, as locals learnt how to make it from early 19th century whalers. It's called palm toddy or white beer because it goes milky when it's ready to drink.

Ontong Java Atoll

The country's northernmost point is Ontong Java. Equally well known as Lord Howe Atoll, it should not be confused with the three Lord Howe Islands scattered around the South Pacific. Many of its 1700 Polynesian inhabitants call it Luaniua (which is variously pronounced 'loo-an-ee-wa' and 'loo-an-new-wa' and also spelt Luanguia and Leuaneua).

Lying just south of the Equator and 258 km north of Santa Isabel, this attractive boot-shaped atoll is about 50 km from north to south and 57 km wide. It's the largest lagoon in the Solomon Sea, exceeding 1400 sq km, and contains 122 islands. However, the total land area is only a minute 12 sq km. The widest piece of dry ground on both Luaniua and Pelau islands measures only one km, while the average breadth of many of its islands is only a third of this.

Except for three isolated rocks, no land is higher than 13m above sea level. Most islets are barely two to three metres high, making the whole atoll vulnerable to rising sea levels generated by the greenhouse effect. These small, long, low and narrow landforms are composed entirely of coral debris.

Tiny islands rise from the reef, mainly in the south-east. The only two with sizeable populations, and a lagoon-side village each, are Luaniua with 1300 people and Pelau with 400. A few other islets have temporary shelters where a small number of people – about 50 in all – are now living almost permanently. These are Ke Ila, Avaha and Kapai.

There are fine beaches, good coral, and plenty of fish throughout the lagoon, and excellent fishing along Keku Lau and Kea'auloa reefs, and at Ke Ila. Local fisherfolk will show you where to cast your line.

On the two populated islands, freshwater swamps occur where natural depressions have been artificially deepened to sea

A: Tabu shrine, Vangunu Island, Western Province
B: Santa Ana fishing floats, Santa Ana Island, Makira/Ulawa Province
C: Bowl from Western Province
D: Makira Custom House at the Cultural Centre, Honiara, Guadalcanal Island
E: Making Shell Money, Busu Island, Langa Langa Lagoon, Malaita Province

MARK HONAN

SIMON FOALE

SIMON FOALE

MARK HONAN

HOLGER LEUE

SIMON FOALE

SIMON FOALE

SIMON FOALE

Top Left: Spearfisher, Sikaiana Island, Malaita Province
Top Right: Marovo Lagoon, Western Province
Bottom: Kangava Bay, Rennell Island, Rennell & Bellona Province

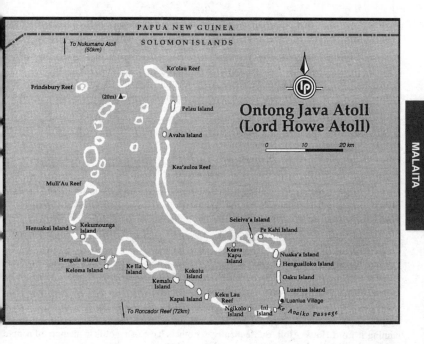

level for use as mulching pits for swamp taro. The coastal areas consist of narrow strips of coconut palms and scrub, mainly on the ocean side. In any one year, it's estimated 600,000 coconuts are consumed – almost one per person each day.

The people of Ontong Java often pay in copra for goods at the atoll's two small stores on Luaniua and Pelau. They also collect bêches-de-mer for the Hong Kong market, and trocchus shells for processing overseas into 'pearl' buttons and ornaments.

Houses here are still built flush to the ground. A network of poles form the frame, while the roof is a thatch of pandanus leaves. The kitchen is part of the main building, with smoke rising through a hole in the roof. Islanders call this traditionally designed dwelling a custom house.

As coconut palms are too precious to be felled and there are few trees of any other sort, paddle canoes are usually made from driftwood washed ashore after a storm. The *makua*, or chief, makes the first incision with a chisel to drive off evil spirits before the log is hollowed out. Seaweed is rubbed over the hull to seal any cracks, booms are attached and an outrigger fitted.

History

Pottery dating back 2000 years has been found on the atoll. Studies into the atoll's language, Luanuian, suggest it is related to both the Samoan and Tongan tongues. It's believed to have separated from its mother language in about 300 AD, passing first through Tokelau or Tuvalu to the east before reaching the atoll from there.

The present inhabitants trace their ancestry back 36 generations to about 1200 AD. According to legend, the first coloniser was one Marou, who floated ashore from the north to be met by two couples already there. They had just finished making Luaniua village. The couples accepted his leadership once he built them a *haleiku* – a traditional house of worship. Akapu, a descendant of Marou's made several 1400-km canoe journeys to Tikopia to bring back turmeric, landing on Malaita Island and Santa Cruz en route.

Islanders claim their original homeland is Tokelau. Oral histories tell of several attacks over the centuries by Tokelauans attempting to impose their authority over refugees from Tokelau who had settled on Ontong Java.

The Dutch adventurers Le Maire and Schouten may have sighted Pelau and its adjacent islets in 1616. But it was Abel Tasman who, on 22 March 1643, was the first to definitely see the atoll. He called the group Onthong Java, as he believed this sighting was the precursor of good fortune. *Untung* means 'luck' in Malay, and 'Java luck' was a 17th century Dutch expression for 'good fortune'.

In 1791, John Hunter was the first European to step onto Ontong Java's soil, renaming it Lord Howe Atoll. Subsequently, whalers and bêche-de-mer traders visited; they were followed in the 1870s by blackbirders.

Germany annexed the atoll in 1893 but ceded it to Britain in 1899. Meanwhile, in 1895, employees of 'Queen Emma' of Rabaul in Papua New Guinea (who was part-American, part-Samoan) established a trading post at Luaniua. As happened so often, new contacts brought new diseases – malaria, tuberculosis and the 1919 worldwide flu epidemic. The population of 2000 soon plummeted to below 600. Numbers rose again once the area was closed to foreigners in 1939.

Fauna

There are sea birds everywhere in Ontong Java. Some islanders, like those on Anuta, keep frigate birds as free-flying pets. Also plentiful is the black-naped tern, which is believed to breed only on this atoll. This medium-sized nearly all-white sea bird has a black line running from its eyes to the nape of its neck.

There are plenty of megapode birds, usually in pairs. They lay their eggs in mounds of mulch they've built themselves. The birds flourish, as most people won't eat them or their eggs because of their traditional association with the atoll's legendary hero Akapu.

Arts

Gaunt, geometrically shaped female deity figures were a distinctive feature of the atoll's statue art. The lower part of the face was portrayed as an inverted triangle with straight lines to represent the eyebrows and nose. Some of these still survive.

Graveposts, which are called *ke ava* in the Ontong Java language, are made from both wood and coral rock, and are decorated with stylised human faces. These posts are a distinctive feature of the atoll's cemeteries and are carved with adzes and clamshell scrapers. Some wooden graveposts have birds carved in relief on them, while others have fish motifs in memory of people lost at sea.

Pearl shell is shaped to make fish-hooks, necklaces and nasal pendants. On ceremonial occasions, some men wear an ornamental nasal pendant designed in the stylised shape of the human form.

Women in Ontong Java use a back-loom for weaving banana fibre. Loincloths made on a loom are then dyed yellow with turmeric. Locally crafted, basketwork fans are beaten against the hand as an accompaniment to women's songs. In the *momo'sanga* dance, the dancers' bodies and clothes are stained with turmeric.

Society & Conduct

Islanders from Ontong Java observe traditional customs in relation to marriage and property. The male line owns the coconut groves and does the fishing, while the female side maintains the taro plots and is prominent domestically. Postmarital residence is in the woman's house.

Makuas & Pohoulus The two main islands each have a chief priest called a makua. In the position of authority above them is the *pohoulu*, who is like a king. In the past, he had the power of life and death over his subjects. If an islander angered him, the pohoulu would pronounce a sentence of death, and within a few days the victim would just waste away and die – as if by magic – having lost the will to live.

Tattoos In Ontong Java, many men and women are tattooed. The forehead is decorated with marine or geometrical designs in childhood. Later, the tattoos are extended to other parts of the body. Some islanders have tattoos in the shape of the hook used to catch a local delicacy, the oil fish.

Medical Services
Luaniua and Pelau both have clinics.

Accommodation
If you want to stay on either Luaniua or Pelau, you should contact the village chief in advance. If he agrees to your visit, he'll find you somewhere to sleep. Bring plenty of food. If instead you're on a one-day visit by ship, ask someone to show you around. This will ensure your presence is readily accepted.

Food & Drinks
Although rainfall is moderate, with 2550 mm on average each year, finding fresh water has been a chronic problem in the atoll. However, the multitude of coconuts provide the islanders with ample coconut water, which is sometimes fermented to make an alcoholic toddy. Dried clam meat is plentiful and turmeric is always available to flavour food.

Getting There & Away
There's no airfield as yet, though one is planned for Pelau. Universal Shipping charges S$80 for the two-day, one-night trip from Honiara.

Yachts and ships can use 23 passages through the reef. Ke Avaiko Passage to the south of Ini Island brings you to the main anchorage at Luaniua. Some yachts have exited the Solomons from Ontong Java. This is acceptable as long as you inform immigration in Honiara in advance, and also the island police officer or local chief when you depart. Entry protocol is, naturally, the reverse of this process.

See the Getting There & Away section in the introduction to this chapter for boat schedules.

LUANIUA ISLAND
There's plenty to see, including haleikus and *maraes* (Polynesian sacred places) in Luaniua village. The main *haleiku*, called Som'aru House, is in the *malae*, or village centre, beside a large stone which was once worshipped as a god. Nearby is a cemetery with traditionally carved headstones. On the reef is the WWII wreck of a US Aircobra aircraft.

PELAU ISLAND
This island's name is derived from the Malay word *'pulau'*, meaning island. Ko'olau cemetery is 100m in from its north-western beach. It's the burial place of the Ko'olau people, who are believed to have arrived from the north in the distant past and settled in Pelau.

Their gravestones are cleanly cut coral monoliths varying from one metre to three metres high.

RONCADOR REEF
Islanders call the reef Ke Uopua and consider it a good fishing ground, though being 72 km due south of the atoll across open sea it's only visited infrequently. In 1568, two of Mendaña's ships were caught in a cyclone and narrowly avoided being swept onto a reef believed to have been Roncador Reef.

NUKUMANU ATOLL
About 50 km due north of Ontong Java is Nukumanu, or Tasman, Atoll in Papua New Guinea. Despite the colonial-era boundary separating the two island groups, the people

MALAITA

of both are pure Polynesians and regard each other as wantoks.

Motor canoes ply between Nukumanu and Pelau on a monthly basis, even though seas are often rough. The 350 people of

Nukumanu collect bêches-de-mer and sell it to Pelau for resale to Honiara's Chinese.

Check with immigration in Honiara before contemplating visiting Nukumanu or exiting the country there.

Makira/Ulawa Province

Makira, Ulawa and their seven small neighbours are sometimes called the Eastern Solomons, even though Temotu Province is further east. Makira, the main island, has 3043 sq km of the province's 3188 sq km, and is 139 km long by 40 km wide. The other islands are within 32 km of its shores, except for Ulawa, 75 km distant.

The province has about 28,000 people and is well known for its preservation of ancient traditions. Traditional dancers in Star Harbour, and Santa Ana, Santa Catalina and Ulawa islands are particularly skilled. Carvings are best in Santa Catalina.

HISTORY

Makira/Ulawa Province's first inhabitants, the Lapita, settled at Pono'ohey on Makira Island, where pottery from about 1400 BC has been found.

Although much of Makira/Ulawa Province's past was violent, there were also long periods of peace. During such times, ceramics were made, trade flourished between Makira and Ulawa, and large canoes came annually from Temotu Province.

At other times, there was fighting between coastal and bush people. Men from Santa Ana would hire themselves out as mercenaries and attack the Makiran coast. For safety, many people lived deep inland. Professional murderers were active until early this century. One, called Sam, proudly boasted he had 64 killings to his tally!

The first-born child was often buried alive by its father. Captives were either burnt or trampled to death, and their skulls stored as trophies for posterity.

Ancestor worship was practised all over the island. When a chief died, his body was placed on a platform up to 10m high and ritually washed daily until only the skeleton remained. Human flesh was considered essential for any feast. Sometimes guests invited to a ceremony were captured and eaten.

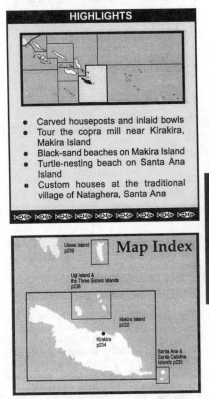

HIGHLIGHTS

- Carved houseposts and inlaid bowls
- Tour the copra mill near Kirakira, Makira Island
- Black-sand beaches on Makira Island
- Turtle-nesting beach on Santa Ana Island
- Custom houses at the traditional village of Nataghera, Santa Ana

Map Index

Ulawa Island
p239

Ugi Island &
the Three Sisters Islands
p238

Makira Island
p232

Kirakira
p234

Santa Ana &
Santa Catalina
Islands p235

MAKIRA & ULAWA

Hernando Henriques, one of Mendaña's expedition leaders, sighted Makira Island in May 1568. The Spaniards' policy of seizing hostages in order to exchange them for food provoked many angry responses – three lines of canoes attacked the expedition members at Ulawa, while another 93 individual canoes attacked them at Waiae Bay.

On Mendaña's return in 1595, one of his four vessels was lost during a volcanic eruption on Tinakula in Temotu Province. Remains found at Pamua on Makira

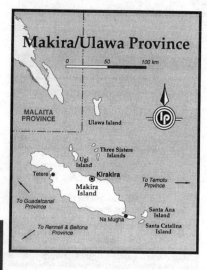

Makira/Ulawa Province

MALAITA PROVINCE

Ulawa Island

Three Sisters Islands

Ugi Island

Tetere

Kirakira

To Temotu Province

Makira Island

To Guadalcanal Province

Na Mugha

Santa Ana Island

To Rennell & Bellona Province

Santa Catalina Island

Island's northern coast suggest the survivors landed and built a fort there, though their subsequent fate is not known.

Jean de Surville found the province again in 1769, relabelling several islands with French names. Other explorers followed, including John Shortland in 1788 and Alexander Ball two years later. But it was 19th century whalers who made the first lasting contacts, trading regularly at Makira Harbour by 1849. Those who careened their ships there soon gave the name Makira to the whole island. Meanwhile, a number of European traders settled on Ugi and Santa Ana islands.

Despite the favourable reception whalers were receiving at Makira Harbour, life elsewhere in the province remained dangerous for foreigners until the early 1900s. A small band of Marist missionaries who had arrived in 1846 were particularly unlucky. By the following year, three of them had been killed and eaten, another had died of malaria and the remainder had prudently withdrawn.

Makira Island was ravaged by epidemics in the early 20th century. Nearly every year

dysentery, whooping cough and chest infections swept through the island. One epidemic in 1910 wiped out five small villages near Pamua. None of the 200 inhabitants survived. In 1920, there were three deaths to every birth on Makira Island.

To make conversion to Christianity easier, the missions encouraged people to move to the coast. This quasi-migration, well underway by WWII, speeded up when the Marching Rule Movement from Malaita and Maramasike islands briefly took hold in the mid-1940s. Consequently, the province's population is now almost exclusively coastal.

FAUNA
Birds
The Makiran mountain rail lives only on the main island, in highlands above 650m. It's a 25-cm-long flightless bird with a bright-scarlet bill and legs, and practically no tail. The body is mostly brownish-black, but dark slate-blue from head to breast.

There are three other subspecies endemic to the province. The red-throated fruit dove on Ugi and Makira islands has a snow-white head and chin. There's a lowland relative of the pink-spotted fruit dove in Ugi and Santa Ana islands, and a mini-version of the glossy swiftlet on Makira Island.

Crocodiles
There are more saltwater crocodiles in this province than in any other part of the country, leading to occasional fatalities. Most bays and rivers on the southern coast of Makira Island, from Oneibia to the Weraha River near Mwaniwowo, and especially Maro'u Bay, have sizeable colonies of the reptile. There are also large concentrations in the Three Sisters group.

Turtles
The small and very rare olive, or Pacific Ridley, turtle nests occasionally in a few places around Makira Island's coast; this is the only part of the Solomons it's known to visit.

Carved housepost combining human figure and fishes

ARTS

Houseposts of between two and four metres depict designs of naked human figures, or figures that are half human and half fish or bird. Carvings of naked human figures up to 1.5m tall are made on Santa Ana and Santa Catalina islands.

Light-coloured wood is carved, then blackened and inlaid with mother-of-pearl. Turtle-shell or pearl-shell ornaments are also made, sometimes incorporating dogs' teeth as currency.

Makira Island

Makira Island was initially called Santiago by the Spaniards, but was renamed San Cristobal by Mendaña, a name still used today. Others have called Makira Island either Arosi, after the language of the island's western end, or Bauro, the vernacular of the Kirakira area.

Two-thirds of Makira Island's 22,500 people live on the northern coast. Much of the southern shore is sparsely populated, especially between Makira Harbour and Mwaniwowo. The inhabitants are pure Melanesian, except for a number of resettled Tikopians at Nukukasi.

Makira Island's mountains run like a spine down its centre, reaching 1040m and falling steeply to the sea along its southern shore. A large number of rivers penetrate the island in roughly parallel lines every two to five km.

Makira has more inland swamps than any other island in the country. Some are as high as 80m above sea level, while one, stretching east from the Northern Wairaha River towards Maro'u Bay on the island's south-western coast, is over 17 km long.

Climate

Makira Island's weather station at Kirakira records 235 days of rain and an average rainfall of 3601 mm a year. Mwaniwowo gets about 6000 mm each year, mostly from June to September.

MAKIRA & ULAWA

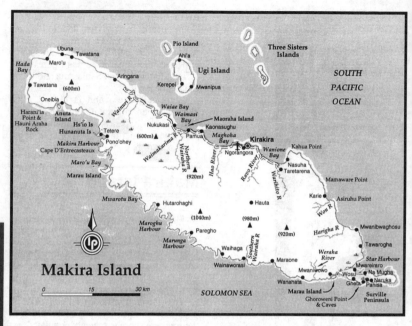

Makira Island

MAKIRA & ULAWA

Morning humidity levels reach a very muggy 95% in February, averaging 93.3% for the six months between January and June. September to November has the lowest figure – 86%. Afternoons are more pleasant as humidity levels remain close to an average 76% throughout the year. Temperatures range between 31°C and 20°C, with the coolest month usually being August.

Society & Conduct

Pre-Christian religious and ceremonial life in Makira Island was closely bound up with fishing. As the islanders' gods were mainly associated with the ocean, sharks, tuna and frigate birds appear on many carvings, and a number of traditional dances are based on a shark theme or legend.

In the past, it was widely believed that the spirits of dead people resided in sharks. In certain parts of the province, some males were thought to be closely related to sharks from birth. If the shark was injured, the man would be too.

It was also believed a child could swim and play with a shark which had the same name as the youngster. Sacrifices were often made to sharks, and at death a man's bones might be put inside a carved shark-shaped wooden casket.

Kakamora legends abound. It is claimed that a Kakamora child was caught in 1969 on Makira Island, but it escaped once it grew up.

Information

Kirakira, the provincial capital, has an 80-bed hospital, and there are 13 clinics around the island. Proceeding anticlockwise from Kirakira, these are at Nukukasi, Aringana, Ubuna, Tawaraha, Oneibia, Tetere, Maroghu Harbour, Paregho, Waihaga, Na Mugha, Mwanibwaghosu, Karie and

Nasuha. There's also a nurse aid post in the bush at Hauta. Malaria and water-borne illnesses are the principal health problems.

Rural water supplies have improved, but seek local advice before drinking it. In Kirakira the tap water needs to be boiled first. Sanitary toilets are the exception rather than the rule outside Kirakira.

Accommodation
Few tourists come here and there's only one official rest house in Kirakira on Makira Island. Ask in the provincial offices there if other places have opened up around the island. Otherwise, the larger villages should be able to accommodate visitors on an informal basis, so ask to see the chief on arrival. If all else fails, clinics may let you stay in their staff accommodation.

Getting There & Away
Air Kirakira's airfield at Ngorangora is served only by Solomon Airlines. Three mornings a week a return flight leaves Honiara for Kirakira, continuing on Monday to Santa Ana Island and on Wednesday and Saturday to Santa Cruz. From Kirakira it costs S$85 to Santa Ana and S$305 to Santa Cruz.

Sea Several shipping companies service Makira Island, but only some call at the other islands in the province. The fastest boat is the *Ocean Express*, which leaves Honiara every Thursday at 8 am and arrives at Kirakira at 6 pm. At 6 am the next morning it embarks on the return trip. Wings Shipping sends the *Compass Rose II* from Honiara to Santa Ana every two or three weeks, calling at all Makira's northern ports en route. From Honiara to Kirakira/Santa Ana costs S$60/68 in economy class, S$72/80 in 1st class and S$95/103 with a cabin; Kirakira to Santa Ana is S$25 in economy. National Shipping does the same trip, but calls at all the south coast ports; Honiara-Santa Catalina is S$59. The Isabel Development Corporation vessels sometimes make the trip from Honiara to Tetere and Kirakira. Universal Shipping's service

from Honiara to the province stops at Ulawa and Ugi islands, as well as Tawatana and Kirakira on Makira Island; the fare is S$60 irrespective.

There's a small jetty at Na Mugha, and anchorages at Kirakira, Maoraha Island, Waimasi and Hada bays, Makira and Marunga Harbours and Mwaniwowo.

Getting Around
The Airport The four-km ride from Ngorangora Airfield into Kirakira in the Solomon Airlines vehicle costs S$2.

Sea & Land There's a 48-km unsealed road along the northern coast between the Waimakarima and Warihito rivers. A 27-km track continues westwards from Nukukasi to the Wainuri River. A forestry road running near the Wairaha River connects the north and south coast. Travel anywhere else on the island is by motor canoe. Shared rides are possible if you ask around the canoe departure points: the 64 km from Kirakira to Na Mugha and the 119 km to Makira Harbour should cost around S$35 and S$70 respectively. One-day canoe charters from the provincial fisheries in Kirakira cost S$40 or S$50 with a 15 or 25 horsepower engine. Fuel, at around S$2.30 per litre, is extra.

KIRAKIRA
A government station was established at Kirakira in 1918. Since then it has become Makira/Ulawa's provincial centre and the home of 3200 people. It is pleasantly shaded by a dense and colourful canopy of trees. The name is often written as Kira Kira.

Information
Kirakira has a hospital, a post office, a police station, a library, branches of Solomon Airlines, Telekom and NBSI, plus provincial government offices.

Things to See & Do
The large, dilapidated old building up the main street used to be the district officer's

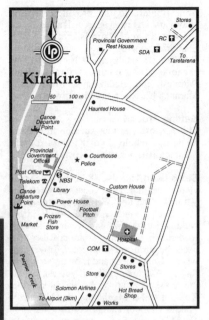

Kirakira

0   50   100 m

Stores

*Provincial Government
Rest House* RC

SDA

*To
Taretarena*

Haunted House

*Canoe
Departure
Point*

*Provincial
Government
Offices*

★ *Courthouse
Police*

Post Office
Telekom ☎
NBSI
Library
*Canoe
Departure
Point*
Power House
Custom House

*Football
Pitch*

*Frozen
Fish
Store*
Market

Hospital

COM

Store
Stores

Solomon Airlines
*Hot Bread
Shop*
To Airport (3km)
Works

Puepue Creek

10.30 pm Monday to Friday and they are happy for people to look around. See the five-stage process by which copra is transformed into oil. The oil is then used for making soap.

Places to Stay & Eat
The *Provincial Government Rest House* has eight double rooms with communal kitchen and washing facilities. The charge is S$20 per person, payable to Owen, the friendly, helpful caretaker who lives in room No 9, or to the accounts department in the provincial offices, which also deals with advance bookings.

Kirakira has no restaurants, but there is a *Hot Bread Shop* and several other stores. The two stores near the Roman Catholic church are open till 8 pm daily. A couple of places in the stores opposite the hospital sell beer – the easternmost one is cheapest. There's a small *market* by Puepue Creek; the adjoining store sells fresh, albeit frozen, fish for S$6 per kg.

NORTH-WESTERN MAKIRA ISLAND
The north-western coast of Makira Island is rugged and sparsely inhabited. Thickly wooded hills frequently reach right down to the water-line. These timber-clad uplands, and the island's mountainous spine, are often cloud covered.

Elsewhere, northern Makira Island has long black-sand **beaches**, such as at Wanione, Maghoha and Waimasi bays. At Maro'u a long black-sand beach stretches along the shore to Tawatana; outrigger canoes are still built here.

The passengers and crew of the Spanish galleon *Santa Isabel* are believed to have landed near the headland 750m east of **Pamua** in 1595, after becoming separated from Mendaña's second expedition. Remains of a hilltop fortress have been discovered there, together with pottery that has been positively identified as 16th-century Spanish. However, there's nothing left to see nowadays.

At **Harani'ia Point** is Hauni Araha Rock. Dead people were brought here as it

residence in colonial times and is supposed to be a **haunted house**. A girl hanged herself from the entrance after an unhappy love affair with a former district officer. Her ghost is said to be very beautiful, and if you meet her she'll be very friendly at first but then turn nasty! The **custom house** by the football field has murals, a leaf roof and carved houseposts.

It's rather stony for **swimming** at the tiny jetty, but there's a sandy beach about one km to the east of the town. The leaf-house village of Ngorangora is the same distance to the west.

Ngorangora airfield, where aircraft land only a few metres from the sea, is four km west of Kirakira. The coral shore at the airfield's eastern end has a number of small blowholes. A further two km west is a small **copra mill** operated by Makira Coconut Production Ltd. It's just off the main road by the sea. Shiftwork is from 6.30 am to was believed their spirits would then leap from the rock into the sea and swim to paradise – thought to be around 80 km away off Guadalcanal's Marau Sound.

The Solomons' most protected anchorage, **Makira Harbour** was a favourite spot for whalers. It's characterised by a narrow inlet and a wide, sheltered lagoon. Its black-sand beach is interspersed with rocky shores and mangrove swamps. The fishing is excellent, and tuna is especially plentiful.

Tetere, the main village near the harbour, is a subprovincial headquarters.

SOUTH-EASTERN MAKIRA ISLAND

Maroghu and Marunga harbours both have black-sand beaches interspersed with mangrove swamps. All through this area are the remains of many abandoned villages.

About 20 km south of Kirakira is **Hauta**, which receives occasional eco-tourist visitors who walk along the river from the north coast. It's a good area for bird-watching but visits must be pre-arranged. Contact Soltrust in Honiara.

On the east coast is **Tawarogha**, where surfers have found some good waves between May and July.

Surville Peninsula

There's a custom house with impressive carvings at Wosu. Several villages on the two-km-wide peninsula's southern side contain the grass-covered remains of rectangular, coral-walled burial enclosures, locally called *hera*. The largest concentrations are at Naruka and Panisa, which have two and three hera respectively. There's another on the peninsula's northern coast at Mwareiraro.

There are two caves at **Ghoroweni Point**, one a burial site containing a large number of skulls, the other a sea cave with white lime pictographs both inside and out.

Na Mugha is frequently called Star Harbour after the nearby inlet. It's a subprovincial headquarters and was formerly a centre for woodcarvers. Offshore are two small sand-surrounded islands, each with an extensive and colourful reef.

Santa Ana Island

This friendly island of 1600 people is 7.5 km from Makira's eastern tip, and 77 km from Kirakira. Formerly called Owa Rafa or Owa Raha, the island is a raised coral atoll. From certain positions Santa Ana can look like a peaked cap. Mt Faraina, a 143m plateau in the centre, dominates the whole island.

Santa Ana is very fertile and contains low levels of phosphates. Taro and bananas grow well in the island's north, while kumara flourishes to the west. Walled enclosures have been built to fence off gardens from foraging pigs.

The island has two beaches on its western side. Turtles lay their eggs on the one to the north of Mary Bay. Seas are too rough for this to occur on the island's eastern shore.

History

The sea caves at Rate and Feru are believed to have been the first places occupied in

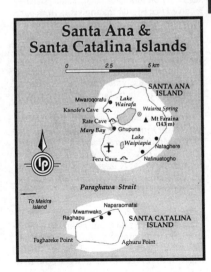

Santa Ana & Santa Catalina Islands

0   2.5   5 km

SANTA ANA ISLAND
Mwaroqorafu   Lake Wairafa
Kanofe's Cave   Waiarea Spring
Rate Cave   ▲ Mt Faraina (143m)
Mary Bay   Ghupuna
Lake Waipiapia   Nataghere
Feru Cave   Nafinuatogho

Paraghawa Strait

To Makira Island   Naparaomafai
Mwamwako
Raghapu   SANTA CATALINA ISLAND
Faghareke Point   Aghuru Point

Santa Ana, in about 1280 BC. However, the island's first village was established on Mt Faraina around 30 BC. Once the inhabitants moved permanently down to the seashore in the 14th century AD, the principal settlement moved to Mwaroqorafu.

Gallego, in Mendaña's first expedition in 1568, named and visited both Santa Ana and its smaller neighbour Santa Catalina. Hostage-taking by the Spanish at Mary Bay led to a dawn attack by the Santa Ana Islanders. In reprisal the Spaniards burnt the nearby village. Thwarted by islander resistance and their failure to find gold or make mass conversions, the Spanish sailed back to Peru, taking with them three Solomon Islanders as proof of their discoveries.

In 1769, Jean de Surville spied Santa Ana and Santa Catalina and called them the Îles de la Délivrance, as they were the first inhabited places he reached after his vessel was becalmed.

Santa Ana's people traded and raided as far as eastern Guadalcanal. They also engaged in regular commerce with the people of Santa Catalina Island and the Star Harbour area of Makira Island, as they all shared a common language. Santa Ana also received occasional trading visits from parts of Temotu Province. From 1877 onwards, it had one or more resident European traders.

Until WWII, young men's initiations on the island required participation in a huge tuna hunt. Though these only occurred every few years, young males were barred from marrying until they had taken part in one.

Traditionally, Santa Ana's leaf houses were built flush to the ground. Until the 1970s, slightly more than half were still constructed this way. Nowadays only a few remain, mostly at Nataghera. The others are almost entirely built on stilts but with the kitchen sections on the ground.

Arts

Santa Ana and Santa Catalina are renowned for their small, ornately crafted ceremonial food bowls, dance sticks and fishing floats. These are carved from a light-coloured

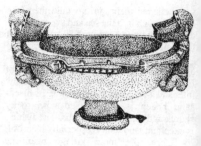

Carved inlaid bowl with spirit figures

softish wood which is then blackened with charcoal and inlaid. The floats are weighted with a stone and their tops decorated with frigate bird, shark and dolphin designs.

Wooden bowls are usually shaped like sharks or large fish. Those incorporating a half-human, half-shark figure called Okro are particular favourites. Other common designs portray birds, pigs or dogs. Shark-like caskets are made to hold the bones of dead heroes.

In the now-rare *mako mako* dance, members of one party of villagers decorate themselves with red mud, face paint and masks, and shuffle around apparently aimlessly. Then a conch shell sounds, heralding the arrival in canoes of another, darker-skinned group. They inspect the first group, who represent less-sophisticated tree dwellers, then capture some and drive the rest off. This dance portrays coastal people from the western Solomons overwhelming local bush people, probably in some long-ago head-hunting raid made against this area.

Society & Conduct

Santa Ana has a mixture of Melanesian and Polynesian traditions. Although the islanders physically resemble Melanesians, their property-ownership customs are similar to those of the Polynesians, whose ancestral lands belong to families rather than clans.

Medical Services
There's a clinic at Ghupuna on the west coast.

Things to See & Do
At **Ghupuna** there are commercialised carvers who try to monopolise the few tourists arriving on the boat. Take the ancient Polynesian track over the hill to **Nataghera**. Here are two traditionally designed custom houses where 500 years worth of ancestral skulls, bones and war canoes are kept. Females may not enter, and photographs mustn't be taken without permission.

The custom houses' most striking exhibits are houseposts with human designs. These dramatic sculptures represent spirits who were believed to combine human abilities with those of birds, fish or other animals. Many small caskets and bowls with spirit figures carved on them are also stored inside. Several are shark-shaped and hold ancestors' bones.

After a devastating epidemic in the 19th century, **Mwaroqorafu** village was permanently abandoned. Nowadays, only ruined walls, mounds and well sites remain. There's a small rockshelter nearby called Kanofe's Cave, which was first occupied in about 140 AD.

The waters of Lakes Wairafa and Waipiapia are too brackish to drink from, but are fine for swimming, fishing or canoeing.

Places to Stay
Ghupuna has a leaf-style *rest house*. There's no telephone.

Getting There & Around
The island's only anchorage is at Mary Bay, also called Port Mary. By canoe to Kirakira would take 2½ to four hours depending on the weather and engine size, and use 18 to 23 litres of fuel.

Footpaths connect the island's three villages, and there are trails up Mt Faraina from both Ghupuna and Nataghera. See Makira Island's Getting There & Away section for more details.

Santa Catalina Island

Santa Catalina is about three km south of Santa Ana. Also called Owa Riki, Santa Catalina is a low, raised coral platform. There is very little surface water, even though Santa Catalina is in a high-rainfall area.

About 300 people live in the island's three main villages, which are concealed by trees and spread along Santa Catalina's sandy northern shore. Subsistence gardening and copra production are the main activities. The standard of traditional carving is said to be better here than on Santa Ana.

Medical Services
The island's Aoriji clinic is by Mwamwako.

Special Events
The island's major annual event is a festival called Wogasia which lasts for a week in May or June. The feature is a spear fight, followed by a marriage partnership ritual.

Annual yam harvest ceremonies occur over two or three days in March, soon after the crop has been harvested.

Accommodation
There are no rest houses on the island, but if you ask the chief well before your visit, he may be able to find you somewhere to stay.

Getting There & Away
For a shared canoe ride, expect to pay around S$5 for the three km to Santa Ana and S$50 for the 80 km from Kirakira.

Ugi Island & Around

Alternatively known as Uki Ni Masi, Ugi is 11 km north of Makira Island. The island, about 10.5 km by 6.5 km, has about 1000 people, most of whom live along Selwyn Bay's golden, sandy shore.

MAKIRA & ULAWA

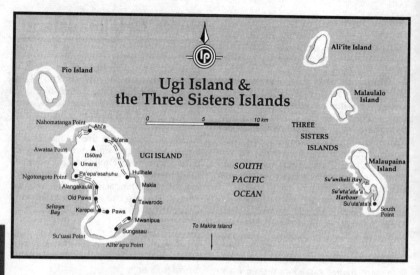

Ugi is a raised coral reef reaching up to 160m at its highest point. Much of this land is covered with scrub, though coconut groves and food gardens flourish near Pawa. Ugi has a pleasant climate and receives about 3000 mm of rain a year. There is an onshore reef reaching from the island's south-western tip to the middle of Selwyn Bay.

The best beaches are at Ugi's north-western and south-western points, where there are also coral gardens.

Ugi has its own language. Although the small number of people who live in the Three Sisters group use the same words, their pronunciation is slightly different.

Black wooden bowls inlaid with pearl shell are made locally.

Medical Services
There's a clinic at Kerepei on the south-west coast.

Accommodation
There's no organised accommodation in Ugi, despite the island's attractive beaches. Officials often stay at Pawa's large school,

though you'll need to radio the headmaster before you consider this option.

Matthias Ramoni is planning to build a rest house near Alangakaula, and eventually a resort, too. Radio the church beforehand to find out if anything's been done about this.

Things to See & Do
An archaeological site at **Su'ena** has revealed continuous occupation of the island since about 1470 AD. Many ornaments were found, including trocchus-shell arm rings. The remains of two ancient forts are about two km inland from **Makia**, and about one km apart. There's also a traditional shrine at Sungasau.

Northern Ugi was strongly influenced in the mid-1940s by the Malaitan Marching Rule Movement. Consequently, **Ahi'a** village was built according to the layout of a US Army camp, with a large central square and houses in straight lines.

Getting There & Away
A shared motor canoe ride between Kira-kira and Selwyn Bay would be about S$20.

There's an anchorage at Pa'epa'esahuhu. See Makira Island's Getting There & Away section for more details.

PIO ISLAND
This small, unoccupied island is sometimes called Bio. About 5.5 km north-west of Ugi, it has an extensive beach on its western side. There's also a long sand spit to its east. You can reach the island by canoe from Ugi.

THE THREE SISTERS ISLANDS
Also known as the Olu Malau group, the Three Sisters lie about 20 km east of Ugi. All of these are low-lying raised coral atolls. Because of their lack of fresh water, there's only the one village, at Su'uta'ata'a on the south-west coast of Malaupaina Island.

About 100 people live there, plus a number of now-wild cattle left behind when a plantation closed down. Ali'ite, largely unused by humans, is the home of large crocodiles, monitor lizards and flying foxes.

There are several good swimming, diving and fishing spots, but beware of the many hungry crocodiles throughout the area. They're the main reason for the lack of people!

Getting There & Away
You'd be very lucky to find a shared ride in a motor canoe – chartering one from Ugi or Kirakira would probably be necessary.

Ulawa Island

Although geographically, linguistically and culturally closer to southern Malaita, Ulawa is administered jointly with Makira Island. It's a 17-km by five-km elongated island of about 65 sq km, with around 2600 inhabitants.

The island's thickly forested interior is cut by ravines. The western coast is mainly lined by low coral-limestone cliffs, while the eastern seaboard is generally coral sand.

There are some beaches along Ulawa's southern shores.

Ulawa's local administration is at Hadja. Most of the island's people live in a belt of coastal villages close by, especially between Lenga and Rongomawa. The design of Su'uomoli, on the north coast, was strongly influenced by Malaita's Marching Rule Movement; the village is built around a large central square.

History
Ulawa was first settled in about 750 AD. Prior to the 20th century, Ulawans traded throughout the Makira/Ulawa Province area, and with Maramasike and south-eastern Guadalcanal. Internal conflict revolved around clan feuds, interrupted by the occasional inter-island raid.

Mendaña's first expedition named Ulawa La Trequeda, or Truce, Island in 1568, though the islanders made a surprise attack soon afterwards. De Surville in 1769 called it Contrariété, meaning 'annoyance', because his ship was becalmed, though it was known as Ulawa by the late 19th century.

MAKIRA & ULAWA

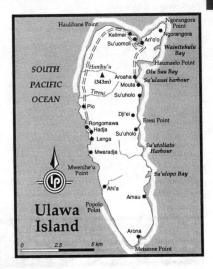

Arts

The *weto* dance originated in Ulawa, although it's now performed throughout the province. It is performed by women on special occasions only, such as mortuary feasts, the instalment of chiefs, and sometimes weddings. As much as four fathoms of Malaitan shell money is paid to the dancers for their performance. Men occasionally dance the weto also. When they do, they use dance sticks curved like birds, fish and snakes instead of the hand movements used by women.

In Ulawa many roof decorations are of snakes representing a winged serpent deity. Canoe houses are often ornamented with carvings of a local sea spirit called Tararamanu.

Island craftspeople make dance sticks and ceremonial bowls. Their fishing floats are very similar to those of Santa Ana, and have frigate birds, sharks and dolphins carved on them. Each group of Ulawan villages has a custom house where older examples of these artefacts are kept, together with other important traditional objects. Every clan in the area contributes houseposts for the custom house, including some depicting a dog's head.

Medical Services

Taheramo Clinic, just west of Su'uomoli, is newly opened; Hadja has the island's only other clinic.

Places to Stay

Hadja has a very simple *leaf house* where visitors can stay.

Getting There & Away

A shared motor canoe ride for the 84 km between Hadja and Kirakira costs about S$50 and would only be safe in the calmest weather. The same applies to Walade Island, 59 km away off the east coast of Maramasike Island (Malaita Province). The shared fare to or from there would be about S$35. There are anchorages at Su'uomoli and Su'ulopo Bay. See Makira Island's Getting There & Away section for more details.

Getting Around

A 15-km unsealed road connects the main settlement of Hadja with Aroaha in the north-east.

Temotu Province

Formerly called the Eastern Outer Islands, Temotu Province lies at the Solomons' most easterly point. This widely dispersed archipelago is separated from the main mass of the country by the 6000m-deep Torres Trench.

The province is made up of three island groups. First there are the four volcanically derived Santa Cruz Islands: Santa Cruz (sometimes called Nendo), Tinakula, Utupua and Vanikoro. Contrasting with these are the low coral terraces and sandy atolls of the nearby Reef Islands. Finally, there are the isolated extinct volcanoes of the Duff Islands, Tikopia, Anuta and uninhabited Fatutaka – lonely rocks in an otherwise empty sea.

The islands of Temotu have a total land surface of only 926 sq km, yet they are scattered over a huge 150,000 sq km of ocean. Their nearest neighbours are the Torres and Banks groups at the northern tip of Vanuatu, 173 km to the south-west. In contrast, Makira/Ulawa and the main bulk of the Solomons are some 400 km due west.

Temotu's population of 19,620 is predominantly Melanesian and most people (or inhabitants) are confined to the larger islands. Most Polynesians live on small coral cays or on isolated volcanic islands.

FAUNA

The docile Pacific tree boa, whose habitat spreads eastwards from Temotu to the Samoas, is very common in the Reefs. The very rare Santa Cruz ground pigeon is found in only three places in the world: Tinakula, Utupua and Espiritu Santo, Vanuatu's largest island. This brownish-black pigeon has a reddish-purple gloss.

SOCIETY & CONDUCT

The people of the Santa Cruz Islands and the majority of the Reef Islands are non-Austronesian Papuan-speaking Melanesians like most of the people of Papua New

HIGHLIGHTS

- Travelling by boat – the only way to get around this isolated province
- Visiting distant Tikopia and Anuta, both virtually unaffected by modern life
- Red-feather money, one of the world's most unusual currencies
- Tinakula, the most active volcano in the Solomons
- Snorkelling in Santa Cruz's West Passage
- Tapa cloth, which is made locally from tree bark

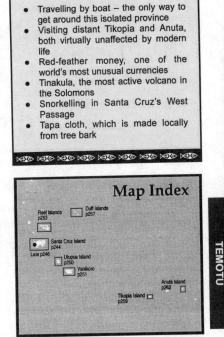

Map Index

Reef Islands p253
Duff Islands p257
Santa Cruz Island p244
Laia p246
Utupua Island p250
Vanikoro p251
Tikopia Island p259
Anuta Island p262

TEMOTU

Guinea. Linguistically, they differ from most other Solomon Islanders, except for those in the Russells, Savo, Vella Lavella and much of Rendova.

Traditionally there were extensive trade networks throughout the province. Santa Cruz exported food, pigs and crafts in every

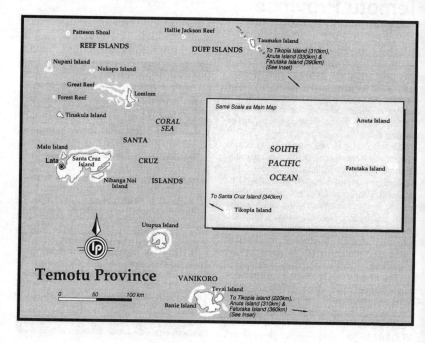

direction, and red-feather money to the Reefs and Duffs. Both Santa Cruz and the Reefs exported shell discs and fabric to Utupua and Vanikoro. In return, Santa Cruz received wives, sailing canoes and crews from the Reefs and Duffs, and food and weapons from Utupua and Vanikoro. Tikopia exported sennit, tapa, turmeric and mats to Anuta and Vanikoro, receiving in return birds' eggs from Anuta and food from Vanikoro.

HEALTH

Ringworm is widespread among young children, tuberculosis is prevalent in outlying areas, and there's the local insect-borne malady, Santa Cruz fever, to contend with. Fortunately, none of these presents a significant hazard to travellers. Although some islands are malaria-free, the province as a whole averages around 170 new malaria

cases per month, so bring sufficient medical supplies with you in case the local clinic has run dry.

ACCOMMODATION

Accommodation is limited in Temotu. Lata, the provincial capital in Santa Cruz, has some places to stay. There's also a small resort in the Reefs. For lodgings elsewhere, you should send a service message to local churches or chiefs, giving them enough time to see if there's a family who will accommodate you. It's best to do this from Lata or Honiara. Making contact by tele-radio may also be possible.

Islanders often find it hard to say no to a hungry foreigner, despite their own poverty. So bring plenty of food for yourself and your hosts, as well as items to give away or trade, such as fish hooks and lines, betel nuts and tobacco.

FOOD

On the smaller outlying islands of the province, such as the Reefs, the Duffs, Tikopia and Anuta, villagers eat the Polynesian rat as well as fish, turtles, pigs and chickens.

GETTING THERE & AWAY

Lata, on Santa Cruz Island, is the gateway to Temotu. It has the province's only airfield, called Santa Cruz, which receives a Solomon Airlines flight from Honiara (S$455) on Wednesday and Saturday mornings. The trip takes three hours, including a stopoff in Kirakira. Western Pacific's flight on Tuesday morning goes direct to/from Honiara (S$455) and takes two hours.

Boat services to Lata from the rest of the Solomons are patchy at best. National Shipping tries to maintain a twice-weekly service from Honiara, charging S$84 to Lata and S$94 to the Reefs. Universal Shipping sometimes makes the trip; its fare is S$80 to either place. The ship is generally crowded at Honiara, so make bookings well in advance. Travel time from the capital is two days, including a stop in Kirakira.

GETTING AROUND

The only way around this far-flung province is by boat, and delays getting back to Lata from the outer islands are commonplace. Boats that make it to Lata from the rest of the province usually continue to the Reef Islands, but the full loop of Temotu's islands is only undertaken once every month or two, and even then islands may be missed out because of rough seas. National Shipping's deck fares around the province from Lata are S$31 to the Reef Islands, S$26 to Utupua, S$28 to Vanikoro, S$36 to Tikopia, S$47 to Anuta and S$51 to the Duffs. Completing the full loop takes at least seven days.

Yacht crews arriving in the eastern Solomons should report to immigration at Lata. However, boats heading north from Vanuatu sometimes call in at outer islands like Tikopia without detouring to Lata to clear customs. This is generally no problem as far as the local chiefs are concerned, provided a few gifts are offered.

Santa Cruz Island

Santa Cruz wins the prize for the island with the most names. Although officially called Nendo Island, Santa Cruz is currently more commonly used. It was previously known as Ndeni, Nitendi, Indemi, Nambakena, Ndende, New Guernsey and Lord Egmont's Island. Including its small neighbours, Santa Cruz is about 660 sq km in size (44 km long and 25 km wide) and has a population of 10,300.

Santa Cruz's western end is composed of a fertile 180m-high coral plateau. The rest of Santa Cruz has few people and is largely undeveloped. It's volcanic, reaching up to a 517m high point in the east and providing views of the Torres Islands of Vanuatu. The northern coast is mainly rocky, but it does have some narrow, attractive beaches similar to those on the western shore. Mangroves are plentiful in the lagoons of the southern and eastern coasts. Inland the island is densely wooded; there are even a few isolated remnant stands of kauri near Nanggu and Luesalo.

History

Settlement of Santa Cruz first took place around 1500 to 1400 BC at Nanggu on the island's southern coast. The inhabitants probably migrated from mainland Papua New Guinea.

The first European contact was made by Mendaña. He sailed too far south on his return to the Solomons in 1595, and on 7 September found and named Santa Cruz. Despite several skirmishes, the Spanish made friends with a local chief called Malope and began to build a camp at Pala at the south-western end of Graciosa Bay. However, relationships with the local people deteriorated when the Spanish took the islanders' pigs without paying for them.

TEMOTU

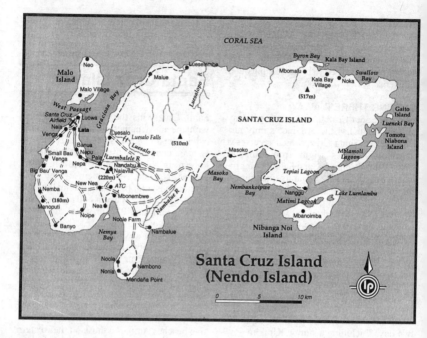

Santa Cruz Island
(Nendo Island)

After a month, some of the Spanish mutinied and Malope, the friendly chief, was killed. On 18 November 1595, the Spanish abandoned their ill-fated colony because of local hostility. Nearly 50 of the settlers had perished, some at the hands of the islanders, some from malaria (including Mendaña).

In 1606, Quiros tried to rediscover Santa Cruz but found the Duff Islands instead. It was left to Philip Cartaret in the HMS *Swallow* to chance upon the fabled Santa Cruz in August 1767. Believing he had discovered new territory, he called Santa Cruz and the Reef Islands the Queen Charlotte Islands. Violent resistance from the islanders drove him away after only a few days.

In between sporadic European visits, the islanders routinely fought among themselves. For their defence, villages were fortified with coral walls, some of which can still be seen. But the greatest threat was foreign diseases. In 1827, Santa Cruz was as heavily populated inland as along the coast. By 1897, the interior was deserted. Then, in fifteen devastating years from 1906, malaria and tuberculosis took a terrible toll, reducing the population from 3000 to only 500.

A major sea action, the Battle of Santa Cruz, was fought offshore in October 1942. The battle was considered to be a draw; the Japanese were driven off, but the USA took slightly heavier losses, including the aircraft carrier USS *Hornet*. A wrecked aircraft carrier lies in the depths just north of Santa Cruz, her aircraft still ranged along her flight deck. Some people contend this is the *Hornet*, though it's probably the USS *Wasp*, lost in the same area a month earlier.

Climate

Santa Cruz gets plenty of rain – occasionally up to 5800 mm a year, though the annual average is 4325 mm. There's rain most days, especially in February and March. Consequently vegetation is lush.

Temperatures range between 32°C from December to February and 22.5°C in August. Humidity ranges from 90% (mornings in March and April) to 78% (November afternoons).

Flora & Fauna

The fertile coral plateau supports large garden areas and coconut groves, with many betel-nut, breadfruit and cut-nut trees. Similar flora is found on nearby Malo Island.

Bird life is plentiful, as are large and attractive butterflies. Two bird species are endemic to Santa Cruz: the Santa Cruz white-eye is a small olive-coloured bird which is commonly seen; Sanford's white-eye is a medium-sized brown species with a slightly curved yellow bill.

Feral pigs roam the bush around Graciosa Bay. They are the only living reminder of the abortive Mendaña expedition of 1595.

Arts

Nelo dances occur near a full moon and continue from the afternoon until dawn – perhaps even longer. The eight to 20 performers lead their fellow villagers around a crowded dancing circle accompanied by much feet stamping and chanting, followed by lavish feasting. Some performers wear an elaborate nose pendant, also called a nelo, during the dance. These ornaments are made of turtle or clam shell and are treated as family heirlooms.

Ask around Lata to see if a traditional Nelo dance is planned.

Information

Lata has a 46-bed hospital. There are also clinics around Santa Cruz at Nanggu, Lueselembe, and Kala Bay.

Despite heavy regular rainfall, there are sometimes water shortages in Santa Cruz, including in Lata. Some villages have droughts lasting several weeks; at these times coconut water is the only potable fluid readily available.

Things to Buy

A few Santa Cruz women still use backlooms to produce very finely woven bags made of hard-wearing, fawn-coloured banana fibre. This material is also used to produce loincloths, baskets and table mats. Ask around Lata market or in nearby villages.

Red-feather sticks are worn as hair decoration during traditional dances. These 35-cm-long sticks are decorated with an exterior of mainly red feathers, and banded with five white and black stripes. They are sometimes for sale.

Getting There & Away

See the chapter introduction for information on scheduled air and sea services.

There's a wharf at Lata. The jetty at Nanggu is awaiting repair from cyclone damage. There are anchorages at Kala Bay, Big Bau'Venga, Nea, Mbonembwe, Lueneki Bay, Byron Bay, Lueselembe, Nepa and the Luembalele River mouth. Boats can berth right by the shore at Luesalo (also called Shaw Point).

You can take a shared motor canoe the 78 km to Lomlom in the Reefs for S$50, but the four-hour trip there is frequently dangerous due to rough seas.

Getting Around

Sea National Shipping's fare from Lata to either Kala Bay, Gaito or Nanggu is S$20. Lata to Gaito takes three hours, and seas are often heavy along the east coast.

If you're looking for a shared canoe ride it's a matter of asking around and trusting to luck. For a canoe charter, the provincial fisheries in Lata probably gives the best rates per day: S$35 for the canoe with driver and S$35 for the engine. Mixed fuel in Santa Cruz costs around $3.30 a litre.

Land All motorable roads and tracks, including new coral-built roads funded by the EU, are in the south-west corner of the

TEMOTU

island. These run south from Lata, though there are also a couple of Forestry roads looping north-east from Noipe.

Movement on land around Santa Cruz is often on foot. Flag down tractors and 4WD vehicles that come by, but ask how much a ride will cost before you get aboard.

LATA

About 1500 people live in Lata, while another 4000 live along Graciosa Bay's western shore. In the distance you can see volcanic Tinakula.

Up the hill and about 200m from the wharf is a large, grassy park surrounded by modern buildings. Local people call the whole area Lata Station. In 1970, the Protectorate opened a district substation here. Soon a hospital (☎ 53045), government offices and modern houses had sprung up. Within the government offices is the Temotu Development Authority (☎ 53145,

fax 53036), which runs the provincial farm, fisheries and rest house.

Lata Station also has an NBSI bank, a post office, a Telekom branch (☎ 53034, fax 53036), SIBC Radio Temotu (☎ 53047), and an immigration office (☎ 53061).

The Provincial Assembly sits one week in every six in the open-sided courthouse beside the library. Debates are always lively and you can stand outside and watch. North of the wharf is a custom house. Inside is a collection of feather money, which you may be able to see if you ask, and round the back is a dancing circle. Sport is a major community activity in the early evenings and at weekends in the park. Soccer, volleyball and basketball are all popular.

PLACES TO STAY
5   Paul Brown's Rest House
10 Luelta Resort
28 Provincial Government Rest House

PLACES TO EAT
19 Dairy Shop & Snack Bar

OTHER
1   Airfield Terminal
2   Santa Cruz Airfield
3   Solomon Airlines
4   Custom House
6   Market & Fisheries
7   Store
8   Store
9   Store
11 Store
12 Hospital
13 Government Offices & TDA
14 Immigration Office
15 Telekom
16 Post Office
17 Police
18 Government Vehicle Workshop
20 NBSI
21 Com Church House
22 Power House
23 Mango Tree Market
24 Government Offices
25 Provincial Assembly/Courthouse
26 Library
27 SIBC Radio Temotu
29 Water Tank
30 Radio Towers

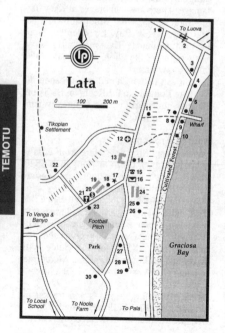

Lata

Places to Stay & Eat

The *Provincial Government Rest House* (☎ 53145) is behind the SIBC Radio Temotu building; it has five double rooms plus communal kitchen and washing facilities. It charges S$20 a night, but it's always full during the Provincial Assembly sessions held every six weeks. It's pretty basic and it could be cleaner. Read the amusing comments in the guest book. Just beyond the jetty at Freshpoint is *Paul Brown's Rest House*, charging S$20 a night. It's of a similar standard, but with simpler cooking facilities and no fridge.

The best accommodation is at *Luelta Resort* (☎ 53144, fax 53115), near the wharf to the south. There are 12 double rooms at S$30 per person. They're small but have a fan and new fittings, and you can sit on the covered verandah. Unfortunately, showers are in a different block. In the absence of a kitchen, excellent filling meals are offered: a cooked breakfast is S$12.50 and lunch and dinner are S$16 each. Non-guests can eat here, but book in advance.

The only other place to sit down and eat is the *PLGP snack shop*, within the row of stores. It offers drinks, a couple of rice dishes (S$8) which aren't always available, and fish and chips (S$3). The latter is cheaper at the place facing the bank. Amid the row of stores back from the street is a *dairy* and a *bread shop*.

Market traders congregate under the mango tree in the park any time of day. At the wharf, the *market* is held daily, except Sunday, from 6 am to sometime in the afternoon, and the adjoining fisheries sells off the day's catch cheaply.

GRACIOSA BAY

You can occasionally see small sailing canoes crossing the bay in the distance, tacking back and forth to catch the eddying breeze. Most come from Luesalo on the opposite shore, where Santa Cruz's kauri logs are exported from. Stiff breezes make Graciosa Bay ideal for windsurfing.

Luowa, a village 15 minutes' walk north of Lata and beyond Santa Cruz airfield, has a dancing circle surrounded by smooth coral slabs. Beyond is a pleasant beach with a colourful coral garden and a good view of Malo Island. The water is extremely clear for snorkelling, but the tide through the West Passage can be strong.

The road southwards from Freshpoint along Graciosa Bay passes first through what amounts to a cultivated rainforest. A coconut plantation grows among many other trees, including cut-nuts, pawpaws, betel nuts, breadfruit and *sumai* trees. There are also plenty of bananas and cassava.

About two km further on, the road reaches the first dwellings within a four-km sequence of uninterrupted leaf-house villages, starting at Banua, where there's a dancing circle, and concluding at Pala. Some village homes are on stilts and have an open verandah, others sit on a low pad of coral rocks, while a third group have a small, hut-like annexe which is the cook house. Occasionally there are copra driers made of leaf, instead of the metal ones you see elsewhere in the country. There are a few basic village stores.

Some of the huts on stilts are young men's houses. Once a boy has reached adolescence, he leaves his parents' house to live in one of these until he marries.

The chief's house at **Nepu**, two km south of Banua, is raised on coral stones up on the hillside, indicating his high status. By the shore is a dancing circle. About 500m beyond **Pala** is a long, sandy beach. Just inland from here is the pumping station, or water source, as it is often called, for the whole area. Fresh water bubbles out from the porous coral rock into a clear, blue pool. You may swim in the creek below, but not in the pool itself. Mendaña's Graciosa Bay settlement was about 10m west of the track to the pumping station.

About 200m beyond the pumping station turn-off is **Luembalele River**. There's no bridge and it is only easy to cross at low tide. The coastal path continues another 17 km to Lueselembe on Santa Cruz's northern coast. There's a waterfall close to Luesalo.

TEMOTU

THE NEMYA BAY TRAIL

The route to Nemya Bay is very indistinct, windy and undulating, so you will need a guide. The path begins at Pala's pumping station, and immediately leads up the hillside on to the western coastal plateau.

Nandabu and **Naiavila** are abandoned villages on a large 220m-high knoll about 1.5 km south-east of Pala. They are surrounded by bush and separated by a 70m stretch of undergrowth. In some parts the villages are bordered by a wall which surrounds six sq km of remains. These include ovens, houses, a temple, three men's houses, fireplaces, walls and a dancing circle. Ask around in Pala for guides if you want to see these sites. A short-lived cargo cult emerged at Nandabu in the early 1930s, with followers praying to wooden images for European goods, including guns. A police officer drove the cultists out.

WESTERN COASTAL TRACK TO BANYO

This coral road along Santa Cruz's western coast passes many coral walls and several friendly villages. There are wonderful sunset views from the beach at Nela, one km south of the western end of Santa Cruz airfield. The beach just north of the western end is also scenically curved and golden, but it's not so good for swimming.

One km south of Nela is **Venga** (pronounced 'veng-ay'), a large, neat village with two dancing circles. At low tide, villagers beachcomb in the shallows. **Small Bau'Venga** is four km further south. The delightfully sheltered white, sandy cove is protected from the sea by two reefs. Its name means 'Venga's smaller beach', and the water here is clear and blue. Less than one km further on is its twin, Big Bau'Venga. Both beaches are popular picnic spots for Lata weekenders. The coral outcrops and the clear, white sand make for good, safe snorkelling. Some villagers fish here with bows and arrows.

The track continues for another 12 km past Nemba and Manoputi, ending at Banyo. Along this stretch are several freshwater springs close by the high-tide line. At Banyo a footpath climbs up the plateau and joins a track after a further 1.5 km. It's another two km to Noipe and a further three km to meet the road connecting Lata with Noole Farm.

NOOLE FARM ROUTE

This track begins beside the twin radio towers in Lata. It leads southwards across Santa Cruz's western plateau before turning east. At New Nea, 10 km south of Lata, a footpath leaves the track and heads southwards to one of the island's prettiest shoreside settings at **Nea**. It is on Nemya Bay, where there's good snorkelling and surfing, with three-metre-high waves. Nea is experimenting with eco-tourism: villagers give tapa-making tours and it may be possible to stay overnight. Enquire in Lata at Luelta Resort or at the Temotu Development Authority before setting out.

East of New Nea is the Agricultural Training Centre, and a few km further on is **Noole Farm**, where there's a market every Wednesday afternoon. The footpath eastwards to Nanggu requires a guide. A coral road goes southwards towards Mendaña Point and splits, but both branches revert to a footpath before reaching the coastal villages.

MALO ISLAND

This three-km by 5.5-km island, also called Neo Island, has several stretches of sandy beach on its western side. Walking is good on the eastern side, and snorkelling is excellent on the southern coast. It's 2.25 km from Lata and has an interior of high raised coral with thick bush, including some kauri. Malo village and Neo, which has good views of Tinakula, are the island's only large settlements. People frequently go to/from Lata market, so it should be easy to arrange a canoe ride for a few dollars.

EASTERN SANTA CRUZ ISLAND

Along Santa Cruz's northern shore are plenty of long, thin, sandy beaches. These average only 100m in length, often merging

TEMOTU

with alluvial flood plains. Access to the eastern part of the island is only by canoe or ship.

Byron Bay and its village of Mbomalu have a surf beach, and there are coral gardens which are good for snorkelling. Towering 517m above and three km behind the bay is Santa Cruz's highest point. From here you can see Vanuatu's most northerly isles.

Kala Bay, also called Carlisle Bay, is a protected inlet with consistent surf at its entrance. It has two settlements – one on a small island in the bay. At low tide, lava-lava clad islanders from the island village walk the 100m through the shallows to the mainland village.

At the entrance to the harbour there's a decrepit memorial to Commodore Goodenough and his two crew, who were killed here in 1875.

South-eastern Santa Cruz's main village is **Nanggu**, at the entrance to the five-km-long Tepiai Lagoon. It has a store, and there's a dancing circle onshore.

The lagoon's mangrove swamps have saltwater crocodiles in them. The Mblamoli Lagoon, seven km away, is similar. Inland from Nanggu are kauri forests.

Tinakula Island

This active volcano, also called Temami, Mami, Tenakula, Volcan and Volcano Island, is 42 km north of Santa Cruz. The eight-sq-km Tinakula rises 850m in a near-perfect cone. Its circular shape was marred in the 1950s by a massive landslide on its western side, where a 50m-wide lava river occasionally flows. Tinakula's forest-covered lower slopes are the home of the extremely rare Santa Cruz ground pigeon.

History

Tinakula throws out pumice and ash in periodic bursts every one to two hours. The first recorded sighting of this was in 1595 during Mendaña's second expedition. In 1767, Cartaret reported eruptions of ash and rock. Later visitors told how the volcano spewed huge red-hot boulders down into the sea, producing deep, resounding hisses.

In the 1950s, during a period of apparent quiet, a small village called Temateneni grew up on the volcano's south-eastern shore, with about 100 Polynesian people from Nupani and Nukapu living there. When Tinakula erupted in 1971, a mass evacuation occurred. Eyewitnesses told of flames rising as high as 300m from the summit, and five tidal waves lashed nearby Malo and Santa Cruz. A couple of families eventually returned, but nobody lives on Tinakula currently.

Getting There & Away

Tinakula's main landing spot is a small beach near Temateneni. Getting ashore across slippery rocks is dangerous in calm seas and impossible in bad weather. The black-sand beach by the landslide area is another possible access point.

The 42-km journey from Lata by chartered motor canoe takes about 2½ hours in good weather – the trip is not recommended when it's rough. If a storm comes up when you are ashore, your boat driver may have to leave you there for several days until the seas are calm again.

Utupua Island

Utupua lies about 70 km south-east of Santa Cruz and 43 km north-west of Vanikoro. Cartaret stumbled upon it in 1767, calling it Lord Edgecombe's Island or New Sark. The island is about 11 km across, with an area of 69 sq km. It is completely surrounded by a fringing reef two km offshore. Utupua has a deeply indented circular coastline of mangrove inlets with small, narrow black-sand beaches at their mouths.

Mt Rautahnimba at 365m is Utupua's highest peak. The island is densely wooded, with agricultural land and coconut trees limited to its coastal fringes.

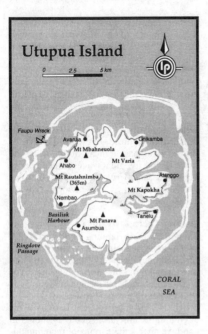

Utupua Island

0   2.5   5 km

Faupu Wreck

Avarua ● ●Gnikamba
Mt Mbahneuola ▲
Ahabo ▲ Mt Varia
Mt Rautahnimba ▲
(365m) ▲Atanggo
Nembao● ▲ Mt Kapokha
Basilisk
Harbour ▲ Tanelu
● Mt Panava
Asumbua
Ringdove
Passage

CORAL
SEA

The mainly Melanesian population of around 740 is served by a single clinic, at **Nembao**. In this village, Utupua's largest, are a small number of ellipse-shaped leaf dwellings constructed in the style of traditional custom houses. Nembao is at the mouth of Basilisk Harbour. Named after a 19th-century British exploration vessel, the harbour is bordered on three sides by kauri-clad mountains, giving it a fjord-like aspect.

Along the coast to the north is **Ahabo**. People from this Tikopian settlement regularly scour the onshore reef at low tide for seafood. The nearby offshore reef claimed the mission boat *Faupu* in 1971.

Getting There & Around
The National Shipping fare from Utupua to Vanikoro (3½ hours) is S$22 and to Lata (seven hours) it's S$26. Inter-island travel by motor canoe is rarely safe as the seas are too stormy. However, the sea within

Utupua's encircling reef is fine for canoes and they are the normal means of transport around the island.

There's a wharf at Nembao, and anchorages at the eastern end of Basilisk Harbour.

Vanikoro

Banie Island and its small neighbour Tevai (also called Te Anu and Lord Amherst's Island) are known jointly as Vanikoro or Vanikolo. The two islands are 190 sq km in area. Rainfall is heavy, with an annual average of over 5100 mm.

A crater rim forms the main island's tallest peak, Mt Banie (923m). The other three mountains beside it are all subsidiary volcanoes, with traces of lava flow still recognisable. An extensive reef surrounds most of the coastline, both onshore and offshore.

Much of the coast is covered by mangroves. Inland are huge kauri trees. The island's thick bush, according to some, conceals the dwarf-like Kakamoras. Vanikoro's population is around 800.

Vanikoro's rivers are home to many crocodiles, and flying foxes populate the trees. The slaty flycatcher, a small grey bird, is endemic to Vanikoro.

History
According to oral tradition, the two islands were first settled around 200 AD by Melanesians. In the early 18th century, Tive (a warrior chief from Tikopia) led a Polynesian war party to Vanikoro. Apparently he occupied Tevai Island and killed all the Melanesians there. Later in the same century, Banie Islanders forced the Tikopians to withdraw. A Tongan canoe party which arrived in 1788, was mistaken for Tikopians and all were killed.

In 1826, Peter Dillon (see the Disaster on the Reef aside) estimated Vanikoro's population to be about 1000 – all Melanesians. By 1932, because of devastating shipborne epidemics, this number had fallen

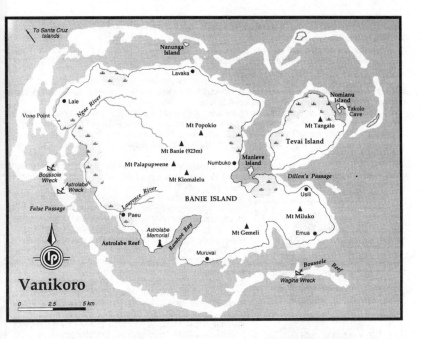

Vanikoro

TEMOTU

to 62. In 1923, the Protectorate government established a station at Paeu, as Vanikoro was more 'peaceful' than Santa Cruz, mainly because of its small population. In WWII, Dillon's Passage was used by US and New Zealand forces as a seaplane base.

Vanikoro once had the largest quantity of kauri in the Solomons, but by 1964, when logging ceased, only a few trees remained. Since then, copra has been the main product. There are plans to log the newly grown kauris, and airlift the logs out.

Arts

Vanikoro is renowned for its Temate devil dances. The performers are completely covered in leaves and their outfits represent gods or goddesses and their children. Hollow masks with V-shaped eyes are also worn. These are tilted in various directions for comic effect. Temate are believed to have come from Veluko, a mythical – or since vanished – island between Vanikoro and Tikopia.

Getting There & Around

The National Shipping fare from Vanikoro is S$22 to both Tikopia (13 hours) and Utupua (four hours). There's a jetty at Emua and anchorages at Numbuko and Paeu.

All transport around the island is by canoe. Motor-canoe charters should cost S$50 per day plus fuel. Ask around to arrange a shared ride.

BANIE ISLAND

Banie Island's main centre is **Emua** and has Vanikoro's only clinic. There are traditionally designed, ellipse-shaped houses, a sandy beach and coral gardens.

Outrigger canoes are plentiful at **Muruvai**, a new Tikopian settlement. Six km away on the Boussole Reef is the spot

Disaster on the Reef

A French expedition, led by the explorer Le Comte de La Pérouse, was wrecked at Vanikoro during a violent cyclone in 1788. Both French frigates, the *Boussole* and the *Astrolabe*, were lost on the island's treacherous reefs.

La Pérouse's ship, the *Boussole*, was driven backwards onto the reef near Vono Point and sank so quickly that very few escaped. Most of those who did reach land were killed, their skulls preserved in the local spirit house.

The *Astrolabe*, which apparently went through a false passage in its attempt to rescue the first ship, fared slightly better. Most of the crew got ashore safely at Paeu. They then built a two-mast vessel from material salvaged from their wreck. Eventually all but two, presumably unprepared to risk their lives at sea again, sailed away into blue oblivion. Their fate is not known.

Tantalisingly, several ships could have rescued the two surviving French sailors and heard their tale of the disaster. Captain William Bligh, after the mutiny on the *Bounty* in 1789, reached Vanikoro after he was cast adrift in an open boat with 18 loyal crew members. Maybe the Frenchmen wouldn't have accepted a hazardous ride in an open, crowded boat, but in any case the opportunity didn't arise. Bligh decided against landing, fearing a hostile reception from the natives. He and his crew pressed on, eventually reaching Timor and safety. Edwards in 1791 and D'Entrecasteaux in 1793 sailed past Vanikoro in rather more substantial vessels, but also didn't land.

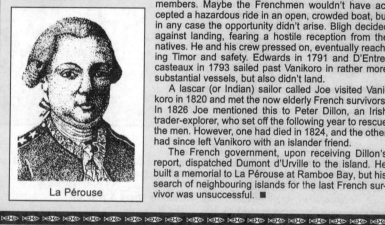

A lascar (or Indian) sailor called Joe visited Vanikoro in 1820 and met the now elderly French survivors. In 1826 Joe mentioned this to Peter Dillon, an Irish trader-explorer, who set off the following year to rescue the men. However, one had died in 1824, and the other had since left Vanikoro with an islander friend.

The French government, upon receiving Dillon's report, dispatched Dumont d'Urville to the island. He built a memorial to La Pérouse at Ramboe Bay, but his search of neighbouring islands for the last French survivor was unsuccessful. ■

La Pérouse

where the *Wagina* was wrecked in a cyclone in 1985.

In **Paeu**, close to the Laurence River, is the spot where La Pérouse's survivors built their doomed getaway vessel. A museum has been built but there's nothing in it yet. It will eventually house the relics recovered from the two sunken French vessels. Along the coast is **Ramboe Bay**. The Astrolabe memorial to La Pérouse and his crew is on this inlet's northern side.

TEVAI ISLAND

Tevai means 'water' in Polynesian, though only Melanesians live here now. Tiny **Nomianu Island** was separated from Tevai by a tidal wave in the 1930s. It's slowly rejoining its much larger neighbour as silt accumulates in the narrow channel between the two. At the top of Nomianu is Takolo Cave, where the Temate first hid on their arrival in Vanikoro.

DILLON'S PASSAGE

This very narrow channel separating Vanikoro's two main islands is the grave of several ships. Dugong, shark and barracuda can all be found here.

The Reef Islands

The Reefs, also known as the Swallow, Keppel and Matema Islands, lie 78 km north of Santa Cruz. These 16 small landforms total only 78 sq km, yet they are spread over 4000 sq km of ocean.

The Reef Islands can be split into two groups – the Outer Reefs and the Main Reefs. The Outer Reefs consists of five very small, low-lying, sandy islets only a few metres above sea level. They feature coral-debris beaches, scrub and coconut vegetation, and surrounding reefs. The population is Polynesian. The most distant islets are Nupani and Nalongo, about 71 km northwest of the main group. Closer, but still 28 km away, is Nukapu. Makalom and Pileni are only 10 and five km respectively from the northern edge of the Main Reefs.

The principal islands are in the Main Reefs group. These are Nifiloli, Fenualoa, Ngalo, Ngawa, Nanianimbuli, Gnimbanga Temoa, Gnimbanga Nende, Nola, Ngatendo, Pigeon and Matema. The largest islands are only 15m to 31m above sea level.

True to their name, the Reef Islands have considerable onshore, and in some cases offshore, shoals. A line of four reefs stretches westwards for 21 km from Lomlom, while the Great Reef extends 25 km in the same direction from Nifiloli.

The Reefs lie in a high rainfall area that averages about 4200 mm a year, with October being the wettest month. Tidal surges occur during some cyclones, occasionally inundating low-lying villages.

History

Fragments of Lapita pottery and obsidian dating back to 985 BC have been found at Nenumbo on Ngawa Island.

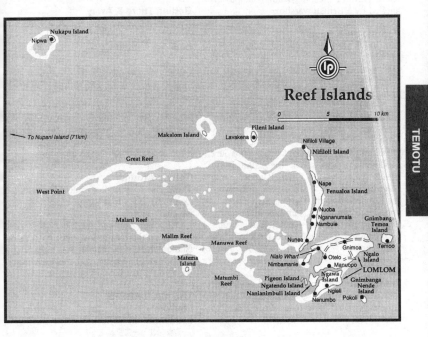

In 1595 Mendaña called the Reefs the Yslas Ilena de Muchas Palmas, meaning 'islands covered with many palms', but it wasn't until the visit of the French explorer De Tromelin, aboard the *Baionaise* in 1828, that nine of the 11 islands in the Main Reefs group were identified.

Bishop Patteson visited Nukapu in the mission ship *Southern Cross* in 1871. This was shortly after Australian blackbirders had been in the area, kidnapping five young islanders and shooting others. Apparently they had dressed themselves up as missionaries to deceive the locals. While sleeping ashore, Patteson and two of his shipmates were battered to death. One of the assailants was the son of a man shot by the blackbirders.

The bishop's violent death produced an outcry in Britain and Australia, including demands for effective controls over the blackbirders. Nevertheless, as punishment for its part in Patteson's death, Nukapu was shelled by a British warship.

Population & People

The Reefs are home to about 6000 people, of whom 1000 are Polynesian. A further 500, mainly Melanesians, have moved to Santa Cruz and Makira because of overcrowding.

The people of the Main Reefs are Melanesian except for those of Nifiloli, who are Polynesian. Fenualoa is very mixed, while Matema's people, though physically akin to Melanesians, are not pure Melanesians and speak the same Polynesian dialect as the Pileni Islanders. The other Melanesians speak 'Reefs' or Gnivo – the Lomlom dialect. There is also a noticeably large number of albinos in the area. Some Reef Islander women have cruciform-shaped tattoos on the back of their thighs.

Society & Conduct

Trading Canoes In precolonial days Reef Islanders were daring navigators. Routine annual voyages were made from Pileni to Santa Ana, 460 km away, and very occasionally even to Rennell, 775 km distant. These journeys were in outrigger trading canoes called *te puke*.

Although trading canoes were mainly made at Taumako in the Duffs, some were also built at Pileni. Unlike Duff Islands canoes, the Reef Islands version had no deckhouse. These nine-metre-long craft had a central crosspiece supported by an outrigger, which carried a raised platform where the sailor could rest. The canoe was powered by a large, claw-shaped sail and was sturdy enough to cross open seas.

Two-person dugout canoes are still common around Lomlom. These craft use palm leaves as sails, which canoeists discard when paddling against the wind.

Medical Services

There are clinics at Manuopo on Ngalo Island and at Nuoba on Fenualoa. The Reefs are free of malaria.

Getting There & Away

By ship it's about four hours to Lata and seven hours to the Duffs. Normal access to Lomlom is through the Forrest Passage. Lata can be reached by canoe, but the sea can be very rough around the Reefs, with occasional fatalities, so don't tie yourself to a tight schedule.

The Reefs' main anchorage is at Mohawk Bay, and there's a wharf at Nialo, on Ngalo Island. Several of the outlying islands have sandy shores, though there's often an encircling reef to cross first.

Getting Around

There is a four-km tractor route on Lomlom, but it is only usable in dry weather.

Although you can walk between some islands on the reef at low tide, most inter-island travel is by canoe. Ask around for shared rides and be prepared to wait, otherwise you'll just have to charter one.

THE MAIN REEFS
Lomlom

Lomlom is the collective name for Ngalo

(or Ngambelipa), Ngawa and Nanianimbuli islands. Lomlom (pronounced 'lumlum') is the main centre for the Reefs, with 3800 people. Its principal village is Manuopo. Wilson Nimepo provides accommodation near the police station in Mohawk Bay.

There are coral cliffs with several small marine caves, which are only accessible by canoe, at Ngalo's northern tip. Nearby Nola Island is similar, but it lacks Ngalo's beaches because of its raised coral structure.

Nifiloli & Fenualoa Islands

Despite ethnically mixed marriages and many centuries of close proximity, only recently has regular social contact become commonplace between Nifiloli's 200 Polynesians and their nearby Melanesian neighbours.

Nifiloli Island has several stretches of sandy beach at its northern end. The remainder is raised coral, thickly covered with coconut palms.

Stretching westwards from Nifiloli village is the 25-km-long Great Reef. Dazzling coral and colourful fish make this a favourite dive site.

At low tide you can walk from Nifiloli to Fenualoa Island. The northern side of Fenualoa (also called Ngasinue) has no beaches, only coral cliffs densely covered with coconut palms. Its 1200 people are spread along its western shore.

Matema Island

Matema, or Nodua, is a beautiful island surrounded by golden sand and inhabited by 150 friendly Polynesian-speaking people. Both scuba diving and fishing are ideal here.

Gnimbanga Temoa & Gnimbanga Nende Islands

These two small islands, sometimes called Pangini and Pokoli respectively, both lie to the east of Lomlom and have only 200 people between them. Temoa has a number of caverns with pools fed by freshwater springs.

Pigeon Island

Despite the name, there are no pigeons – just lots of parrots – on this tiny raised-coral islet opposite Ngatendo in Mohawk Bay. Accommodation is at the family-run *Ngarando Resort*. In addition to a small store, the island has two houses, each with shower, toilet, kitchen facilities and satellite TV. Prices in Australian dollars are A$66/99 for singles/doubles, though some newly built rooms go for A$44/77. To make a booking, contact the resort by teleradio from Honiara or Lata. If required, breakfast is A$8, lunch is A$13 and dinner is A$24.

The resort organises boat and fishing trips, and provides free snorkelling gear. Single scuba dives are A$50, including equipment. Underwater visibility is usually good to at least 30m.

Pigeon Island is far enough from Ngatendo to be free of mosquitoes, but close enough that you can walk over to it at low tide. The resort organises transfers for guests to/from Lata for S$100 or less per person each way, depending on the number of passengers.

THE OUTER REEFS

Nupani Island

Isolated Nupani, also called Nimba, is entirely given over to subsistence crops and coconuts. Both it and its smaller, uninhabited sister, Nalongo (or Naloko) Island, occupy a large lagoon five km by six km wide. Some of Nupani's 100 people tend gardens on volcanic Tinakula.

Nukapu Island

Another large lagoon surrounds Nukapu, also called Nipwa and Tromelin Island. About 150 people live here, cultivating edible fruits and nuts in Nukapu's centre. In Nipwa there's a memorial to Bishop Patteson's violent death.

Pileni Island

Over 200 people live on Pileni, also known as Nimibile. This sandy, palm-covered island, with several good swimming places, is the main centre of Polynesian language

TEMOTU

and culture in the Reefs. In the past, it was the starting point for many epic sea voyages.

Pileni people probably came from Tuvalu. They have the same deities as islanders on Sikaiana and Ontong Java, and are culturally closer to them than to Temotu's Polynesians.

Historically, Pileni's people were allies of the Sikaianans. On one occasion, a Tongan war party, returning from a battle with the Sikaianans, came ashore at Pileni and were immediately wiped out by continuous volleys of Pileni arrows.

Makalom Island

Also known as Makolobu, or Booby, Island, uninhabited Makalom is a bird sanctuary for hundreds of boobies. There's excellent swimming and diving off its reef.

The Duff Islands

The Duffs are a scattered line of eleven small rocks and islands, about 150 km north-east of Santa Cruz. This 28-km-long group, sometimes known as the Wilson Islands, occupies an area of only 14 sq km. Taumako is the largest of the islands, with a high point of 280m, yet it's under six km long.

History

Lapita settlement occurred in the Duffs in about 900 BC. This was followed in the first millennium AD by Melanesian occupation. The Melanesians were in turn superseded, probably in the mid-15th century, by newly arrived Polynesians – the forebears of the present-day islanders.

European discovery took place on 7 April 1606 by Quiros, the leader of the third Spanish expedition. He was searching both for Santa Cruz, where he had been with Mendaña in 1595, and for the fabled Terra Australis, believed to be close by.

In 1797, Captain Wilson in the missionary ship *Duff* came to the islands and named them after his vessel. The missionaries hoped to convert the local chief but they found a very stratified society. The chief's double canoe ran down any commoner's craft which got in its way in its haste to reach the mission ship first. The church

---

Red-Feather Money

Temotu is the home of one of the world's most unusual currencies – Santa Cruz red-feather money, or *touau*. Although none has been made for several years, existing coils of this currency are still sometimes used for bride price.

Brown pigeon feathers are bound together in plaits to form the basis of a long coil, which is covered with the red head and breast feathers of the scarlet, or cardinal, honeyeater. This 10 to 13-cm-long bird is found only in Temotu and has a long curved bill. For each red-feather coil, about 600 of these birds are trapped, plucked of a few feathers and then released alive.

Bride price is normally between five and 24 coils, plus some modern bank notes. Despite the large amount of money involved, the girl has the right to veto applicants. After the currency exchange ceremony is over, the father of the newly wed daughter announces he has red-feather coils for sale, usually for about S$300 to S$400 each, to any young men with marriage on their mind.

This custom, formerly widespread throughout the province, is now only sometimes seen on the Duff Islands. Bride price is still often paid elsewhere, but modern currency and commodities are used. If you have a chance to see a red-feather money ceremony, don't miss it. Simply ask the family's permission to watch and then be as unobtrusive as possible. ∎

HOLGER LEUE

MARK HONAN

HOLGER LEUE

Top: Market in Auki town, Malaita Province
Middle: Shopfront in Auki, Malaita Province
Bottom: Auki, Malaita Province `

Top Right: Canoes at Nembao village, Utupua Island, Temotu Province
Top Left   Panpipe band leader in Kirakira, Makira Island, Makira/Ulawa Province
Bottom Right: Woman with facial tattoos from Tikopia Island, Temotu Province
Bottom Left: Cedric, the Arika Tafua or No 2 Chief of Tikopia Island, Temotu Province

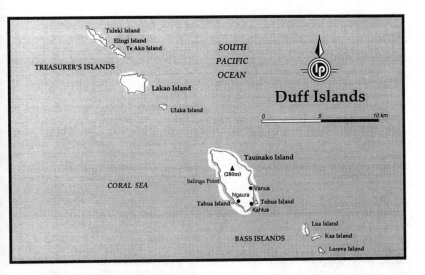

people called Taumako 'Disappointment Island' because no-one there listened to their teachings. Other than these visitors, only the occasional sailing ship came by until the regular shipping services of this century.

Population & People
About 400 Polynesian-speaking people live in the Duffs, maintaining close links with their Reef Islands neighbours. Despite their language's origin – the word *taumako* means 'potato yam' in Polynesian – physically and culturally they resemble Melanesians, the result of intermingling over many generations.

Society & Conduct
The Duff Islands are still ruled by hereditary chiefs. Although keen followers of the Church of Melanesia, some islanders also believe in ancestral spirits and consult witch doctors. Duff Islanders still sometimes use Santa Cruz red-feather money for bride price.

Duff Islanders used to trade around Temotu on ocean-going canoes. In Quiros'

time, these outrigger craft were large enough to carry up to 50 people, but by the early 1800s they could only carry 10. Each one had a wooden deckhouse covered with palm leaves so the sailors could rest out of the sun. Although small souvenirs are now made, full-sized trading canoes are only built these days for major international cultural events and consequently are very rare.

Medical Services
There is a clinic at Ngaura.

Getting There & Away
The fare for the seven-hour, 110-km boat trip from the Duffs to the Reefs is S$22. Vessels anchor along the coast near Salinga Point or by Tahua Island. Outrigger canoes paddle or punt their way through the reeds and reef between there and villages round the coast.

TAUMAKO ISLAND
The island is tall, wooded and craggy, with many sheer drops to the sea. The 200 inhabitants mainly live opposite tiny Tahua Island, or beside a beautiful sandy beach at

TEMOTU

Ngaura. You can walk across to Tahua at low tide.

TAHUA ISLAND

In contrast to the ample space on Taumako, 200 people are packed tightly together on this minute, human-made and mosquito-free island, which Quiros called Venecia. Well before his arrival, coral stones had been placed on a sandbar until the resulting landform was large enough to support a village. There are now more than 30 leaf houses, plus palm trees and paths marked with coral stones.

LAKAO ISLAND

Lakao, also called Temelfua or Treasurer's Island, is home to a single family. Other islanders go there to visit their gardens or to collect sea-birds' eggs. The remaining eight islands in the group are all uninhabited.

Tikopia Island

Tikopia is just over five sq km in size, with white-sand beaches along its south-western shore. It's two km wide, 3.5 km long and about 380 km south-east of Santa Cruz. Its population and culture are distinctly Polynesian.

The island is an extinct single-cone volcano, Mt Reani (380m), from which you can see the Banks Islands in Vanuatu on a clear day. Below its summit is a crater lake, Te Roto, which is ideal for swimming, fishing and trapping wild duck.

Tikopia is a very lush island, mostly hilly except for the south-west corner. It's extensively cultivated, with almost all the available ground used to grow crops, including turmeric. Gardens and coconut groves extend high up Mt Reani's slopes.

Marshy areas around the inner lake shore and on the western edge of the island are given over to swamp taro. Plenty of fish are caught off the reef, and turtles are caught in the open seas.

Tikopia has significant rainfall, averaging 4000 mm a year; rain is heaviest from October to March. Cyclones occasionally strike with savage ferocity, as occurred in 1952 and 1953. Year-round temperatures average from 25°C to 29°C.

History

Early History Tikopia erupted from the sea about 80,000 years ago. Permanent human settlement took place about 1000 BC, when a great quantity of Lapita pottery was made locally. Around 100 BC, local ceramics production ceased and supplies were imported from various sources in Vanuatu up to about 800 AD.

Western Polynesians began arriving on the island around 1200. The subsequent period was one of gradual elimination of the pre-existing population. According to Tikopians, these were the Fiti-kai-kere, or Fire Eaters of the Earth, who built the island's stone fences prior to the current inhabitants' arrival. The last of these were eaten by Tongans during one of their periodic raids.

Arriving early in the 16th century, Te Atafu, a member of the Tongan ruling line, came to Tikopia to dominate it. He ruled over similar adventurers from Uvea (present-day Wallis Island), Rotuma (now part of Fiji), Niue and possibly Ontong Java. Around 1600, the descendants of drift-voyagers from Uvea finally emerged supreme, however, by marrying into Te Atafu's line.

Tensions between different groups, each wanting the best land, produced several tribal wars. In about 1700, a pale-skinned clan called the Nga Ravenga were wiped out during a night attack by one of the other clans. There was some cannibalism of the victims – the last time this occurred on Tikopia.

Another tribe, the Nga Faea, chose ritual suicide around 1725. The whole clan, numbering over 100, took to the sea, again because of land shortage, knowing they faced certain death. As a silent tribute to these two lost tribes, the north-western side of Tikopia is called Faea and the south-west is known as Ravenga.

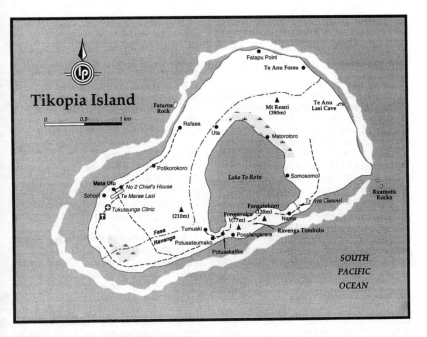

In the early 18th century, a Tikopian chief called Tive (pronounced 'tea-vy') took his forces to Vanikoro, 240 km to the north-west. They slaughtered all the Melanesians on Tevai Island. Later in the same century, a Melanesian resurgence drove these Tikopian colonists out.

European Contact Although there had been previous sightings, the first substantive contact with Europeans was in 1813, when the Irish explorer Peter Dillon stopped by in his ship the *Hunter*. He landed three passengers at their request – a Prussian doctor called Buckhardt and his Fijian wife, and a lascar sailor called Joe. He returned in 1826 to pick them up.

The lascar showed Dillon a sword scabbard and other European articles he had found when he had visited Vanikoro in 1820 – apparently remnants of the lost La Pérouse expedition. Buckhardt confirmed that French-made glass and pottery were being used on Tikopia when he arrived in 1813.

When the French explorer Dumont d'Urville visited in 1828 to check this out, he estimated Tikopia's population to be between 400 and 500. Following this visit, 115 people died, probably of influenza or gastroenteritis. The Tikopians' initially high mortality rate when exposed to foreign foods and sicknesses meant that very few were kidnapped during the blackbirding era.

In 1852, a small group of Roman Catholic missionaries came ashore. When the relief ship called by the next year, they had all disappeared. No-one on the island could say where! Most likely, they had been killed for challenging the islanders' ancient traditions too directly.

In July 1928, Professor Raymond Firth began his year-long anthropological studies on the island, which led to the publication of his famous book *We, the Tikopia* in 1936. Even today, it is a great source of pride to the inhabitants.

Population & People

Tikopians are light-brown skinned and physically akin to the people of Samoa and French-ruled Wallis Island. Because of the island's small size, strict population control used to be imposed, though recent missionary activity has discouraged this. The 1929 population of 1285 people grew by 36% to 1750 in 1952. Such overcrowding has forced many younger Tikopians to leave.

By 1970, 40% of the population had departed, settling variously on Nukufero in the Russells, Nukukasi on Makira, Muruvai on Vanikoro, Ahabo on Utupua and in White River village, Honiara. Consequently, the island's population has dropped to around 1000.

Society & Conduct

Each of the four Tikopian chiefs traces his descent from his tribe's legendary ancestor. The *ariki kafika*, or No 1 chief, traces his descent from Uvea; the *ariki tafua*, or No 2 chief, from Niue; the *ariki taumako*, or No 3 chief, from Tonga; and the *ariki fangarere*, or No 4 chief, from mixed western Polynesian sources, including Anuta, Ontong Java, the Duffs and Mota Lava in Vanuatu's Banks Islands. However, only 5% of Tikopia's people are members of the latter tribe. These four chiefs represent the island's main divisions and in the past were often political rivals.

The authority of the chief is felt throughout his clan. Everyone knows who the chiefs are and to which group they belong. This system of authority has been left undisturbed, both by the former colonial regime and the post-Independence government. Both knew that while the chiefs were loyal, so would their people be.

Tikopian houses, which are ellipse-shaped, flush to the ground and made of leaves, are entered by crawling through a small one-metre-high opening. To exit you must crawl out backwards, facing inwards unless you are the last person out, as it's considered rude to turn your back on someone, especially a chief. Similarly, people will sit down in front of a chief to avoid standing above him and therefore being disrespectful.

Traditionally, Tikopian girls would bow when walking past a man. This no longer happens, but women still tend to defer to men, and stand well aside when men pass them on a path. So far, there has not been a female chief. In 1993, when the No 1 chief died in his 40s, his fellow chiefs declined to recognise his adult daughter as chief. Instead, her great-uncle has assumed power until her young brother is old enough to fulfil the role.

Kava ceremonies are no longer part of Tikopia's tradition, but the practice of betel-nut chewing is widespread. Some elderly men still wear a wrapping of plain, undyed tapa made from the inner bark of paper-mulberry trees. Most men now prefer lava-lavas, which children wear like a loincloth. However, tapa is still usually worn for special ceremonies, for which many people will paint their skin with turmeric.

Tapa is made by soaking and beating the inner bark of paper-mulberry trees

Inter-Island Voyaging In the past, there was frequent trade between Tikopia and the Banks Islands, 204 km to the south-west. This gradually diminished then halted due to the high level of losses at sea.

Anuta is Tikopia's closest neighbour, 150 km to the north-east. The two islands are close enough for the people of both to regard each other as *wantoks*, with each family having kinsfolk on the other island. Regular canoe visits used to be made to Anuta, with Tikopian canoeists sometimes diverting to desolate Fatutaka Island for sea-birds' eggs. Another classic trade route was to Vanikoro, where Tikopian mats were traded for Vanikoran arrows. On very rare occasions, voyagers went as far as Rennell, over 1000 km away.

Medical Services
The only clinic is at Tukutaunga, near Mata Utu. There are plenty of flies and mosquitoes, but no malaria.

Accommodation & Food
If you want to stay, send a radio message in advance asking the chiefs for permission. Alternatively, ask the chiefs on arrival, but be prepared to catch the same ship out again if they say no. There's no rest house, but it may be possible to sleep in the clinic for a while. If you get permission to stay on Tikopia, another ship may not come around to take you back for a couple of months, so bring lots of food. There are no stores on the island.

Things to Buy
The islanders produce finely woven sleeping mats which are avidly sought by people from other islands, particularly Vanikoro. Other locally produced items that might make good souvenirs include tapa, wooden headrests, scale-model canoes complete with outriggers, and shark hooks made from pearl shells.

Getting There & Away
The boat service from Tikopia takes around 11 hours to Anuta and 13 hours to Vani-

koro; the fare to either place is S$20 and departures are only every one or two months. Ships stop at Tikopia for between four and eight hours, so check with the captain before you set off exploring. Boats usually anchor offshore between Mata Utu and Potikorokoro.

Getting Around
Many small paths wind between gardens and villages, with few places in the island's densely inhabited western half more than five minutes apart. To make the most of your short visit, ask to see one of the chiefs, who will appoint someone to be your guide. Alternatively, children are usually happy to show you around – you'll probably pick up an entourage of curious kids anyway!

MATA UTU
Close to the No 2 chief's house is the **Te Marae Lasi**. This broad path doubles as a 200m-long tika-dart pitch where interditrict contests are held every Wednesday. Small stones (called 'memory stones') at either end indicate personal bests. The island record corresponds to the roof post in a hut at the north-east end. There's also a dancing circle nearby.

About 100m further south is **Takarito**, where there's the overgrown sacred burial place of the Nga Faea tribe and a sacred stone. In pre-Christian times, it was believed the island would have plenty of fish as long as the stone was ritually washed and worshipped.

LAKE TE ROTO & AROUND
Tumuaki, a raised ledge, provides very good views of the southern part of the island and **Lake Te Roto**. This beautiful, brackish, freshwater lake is surrounded by swampy land. Te Roto is no more than one or two metres deep along the narrow Ravenga shore, but in its drowned crater centre it drops to 80m. Islanders fish with seine nets for the indigenous pink, salmon-like *kiokio* fish, grey mullet and the recently introduced *tilapia*.

The lake was not always closed to the

sea. In 1606, the Spanish recorded it as an open bay. By 1828, Dumont d'Urville noted the Ravenga Tombolo spit was in place along three-quarters of its present length.

Namo village is the site of **Te Ava**, a channel intermittently opened to allow excess lake water to flow to the sea. It's usually opened after January rains have filled the lake. As the waters flow out to the sea, islanders trap fish with long-handled nets. **Potusataumako**, the next village west, is the domain and home of the No 3 chief. Some relics of the Taumako clan are here. Nearby, at Potusakafika, is a stone fish trap.

The massive volcanic pinnacles of **Fonganuku** and **Fongatekoro** rise steeply from Lake Te Roto's southern shore. On Fongatekoro's summit is the burial place of Pu Lasi, one of the principal ancestors of the Tikopian No 1 chief's line, and traditional founder of Anuta. The tomb is marked by a small rectangular platform and can only be approached by a precipitous trail.

All members of this chief's tribe must, at least once in their lifetime, clamber up here and pay homage to the clan's dead ancestor by placing a basketful of clean sand on the grave. Fongatekoro, meaning 'Fortress Hill', served as a natural strong point during several Tongan raids in the 17th century.

Traditional festivals were held in Somosomo in pre-Christian times. There are also some ancient stone slabs at Matorotoro, one km northwards along the lake's shore, where similar ceremonies took place. Across Te Roto is the sacred district of **Uta**. In pre-Christian times, annual religious rites were held in the dancing circle and ancient burial grounds.

EASTERN COAST

Just beyond Fatapu Point are some blowholes. About one km eastwards along the rocky northern shore is the small natural arch of Te Ana Forau.

Te Ana Lasi Cave is a large rockshelter – its name means 'Great Cave' in the local

language. Archaeological evidence suggests the cave was inhabited as early as 1800 BC. Immediately below is another natural arch.

Anuta Island & Around

Diminutive Anuta, also called Anudha or Cherry, lies 450 km due east of Santa Cruz. Its nearest populated neighbour is Tikopia, with which it retains close traditional ties. Some 55 km south-eastwards is lonely, uninhabited Fatutaka.

Anuta is only 400 sq metres in area. It's a small volcanic island with a fringing onshore reef. Anuta's highest point is Te Maunga, a 65m-high hill which is used for intensive agriculture. There's a relatively

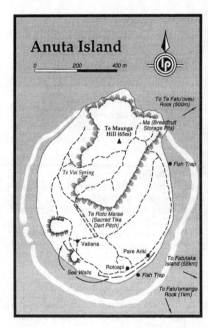

Anuta Island

large, flat coastal plain below it on the island's southern side, as well as two cliff promontories. Two large rocks rise up out of the sea to the east – Te Fatu'oveu and Fatu'omango. The beaches are of sparkling white sand.

Seas are often very rough between Anuta and its distant neighbours the Duffs and Tikopia, but there's a 23m to 36m-deep submarine plateau extending 6.5 km northwest which provides the island with excellent fishing.

High winds occur locally, particularly in December. Annual rainfall averages 3000 to 3500 mm. Storms and droughts devastate the island alternately; particularly bad cyclones occurred in 1916, 1970 and 1972.

Anuta's few visitors comment on the neatness of its gardens. Hillsides are terraced to the summit and plants are mulched and carefully tended. Although the spring at Te Vai is the island's only source of freshwater, Anuta is extremely fertile because of the soil's high phosphate level. There are two fish traps, one beside Rotoapi, the other on the island's north-eastern shore below Te Maunga.

History

A small group of Lapita people first occupied the island from around 965 to 650 BC. They were followed in about 350 BC by an unknown people, probably Austronesians, who used plain pottery and appear to have remained until between 500 and 700 AD. Anuta was probably then deserted until around 1100 AD when a community the Anutans refer to as the Afukere, or Earth-Sprung, appeared.

In about 1580, the ancestor of the modern Anuta, Pu Lasi, arrived from Tonga and found the Afukere in residence. Finding the weather hostile he withdrew to Tikopia, after which time it seems that all the Afukere died. On his return, Pu Lasi found instead a motley crew of Uveans, Samoans and other Tongans, and became their overlord. His rule is the probable reason Tongan expressions are used by present-day Anutans.

Anuta's subsequent history was characterised by raids by outsiders – particularly Tongans – and internecine strife. One of these civil wars, in about 1790, left only four male survivors – three of them brothers. Once peace returned, Tikopian influence predominated, producing considerable intermarriage between the people of the two islands.

Captain Markham visited Anuta in HMS *Rosario* in 1871. He noticed the Anutans were Polynesians, chewed betel nut, had large holes in their ears and resembled Samoans. The islanders knew some simple European words and had a taste for tobacco, which suggested that there had been some unrecorded visits by European sailors previously.

The proclamation of the British Protectorate in 1893 left the authority of the Anutan chiefs undisturbed. However, at Independence Anuta at first refused to join the rest of Temotu in the new Provincial Assembly, fearing it would lose its traditional autonomy. Although Anutans now vote in both national and provincial elections, they still see themselves as inhabitants of an autonomous microstate, independent in mind if not in fact.

Population & People

Anuta's population has remained constant at around 200 for over 100 years, though recent migrations have reduced that figure somewhat. Anutan society has been studied by various anthropologists and archaeologists over the years, notably by Dr DE Yen and Janet Gordon of the Bernice Bishop Museum, Honolulu, in 1971 and the US anthropologist Richard Feinberg in 1972 to 1973.

Society & Conduct

Tattoos indicate status; consequently, the island's two chiefs are strikingly decorated. Tapa is made locally from breadfruit trees and it's still worn by many people, especially the two chiefs and their wives. Frigate birds are often kept as free-flying pets, a habit shared with Ontong Javans.

TEMOTU

As in Tikopia, women usually defer to men. Anutan girls weave mats to pay their own bride price, and ceremonial clubs and fishing spears are also produced. Clamshell adzes are made for carving, and digging sticks are produced for gardening.

Anutan Chiefs The No 1 chief is the *tui* Anuta, or king of Anuta, and what he says is law. He rules in consultation with his *maru*, or weekly council of elders, and the No 2 chief. The day after the maru, the *pono* – a general assembly of all the island's adults – is held to pass the maru's decisions on to the people.

The two chiefs hold their positions as direct descendants of the settlers of the 1580s. The tui Anuta is descended from Pu Lasi, while the No 2 chief's ancestors were Uveans who arrived slightly later.

Medical Services

Anutans have traditionally considered that major illnesses come from breaches of communally acceptable behaviour rather than from germs and the lack of hygiene. Some islanders believe disrespect towards others, particularly chiefs and priests, will lead to sickness. Recovery only comes when offenders acknowledge their guilt and are forgiven by the injured parties. Perhaps this explains why Anutans have declined offers to set up a medical aid post – medics only visit for a few hours when the ship stops. At least there's no malaria on Anuta.

Accommodation

If you want to stay on Anuta, get permission from the two chiefs by radio. It could be several months before you can leave again, so get immigration to extend your visa to cover possible delays, and bring plenty of gifts and food.

Things to See & Do

The island's main village, **Rotoapi**, is protected by a line of five coral sea walls. Its houses are low, ellipse-shaped and thatched with sago or coconut-palm leaves. The island's principal marae, Pare Ariki, is 100m to the north-east and contains four god stones and 19 graves of pre-Christian chiefs. **Vatiana** is a smaller village, protected by another sea wall. Behind is the Te Roto marae, also called Te Marae Tika, a 180m-long tika-dart pitch.

Anuta has always had adequate food supplies, despite its high population density, because of the many *ma*, or breadfruit storage pits, at the north-eastern end of **Te Maunga**. *Masi*, or preserved breadfruit paste, is stored underground for several years and remains perfectly edible, protected by regular replacement of its covering leaves. After a devastating cyclone in 1970, Anuta declined outside help because there was ample breadfruit in store.

Getting There & Away

Ships make it to Anuta even less frequently than they do to Tikopia. Rough seas sometimes force vessels to abandon attempts to reach the island, even though Anutan passengers are aboard. Access for ships' dinghies is difficult, with surf constantly breaking directly onto the reef along its entire length.

Dinghies occasionally capsize while crossing the two breaks in the coral near Vatiana, so take dry clothing and cameras in a plastic bag if you want to visit the island.

As long as sea conditions permit, ships anchor for between four and eight hours. That's ample time to look around.

FATUTAKA ISLAND

Uninhabited Fatutaka – also known as Mitre, Fataka and Fatu (the Polynesian word for 'rock') – lies in the domain of Anuta. It's a 1.6-sq-km seasonal hunting ground to which islanders come for sea birds and eggs. Medium-sized sailing canoes are still built in Anuta for the journey to Fatutaka.

Although Anutans once tended gardens on Fatutaka island in the distant past, Tikopians periodically felled its coconut palms to prevent marauding Tongans from using it as a base. The island is now rocky and infertile.

Glossary

Afukere – a legendary race of people from Anuta Island

amtrack – amphibious, tank-sized, tracked vehicle used to carry assault troops ashore or across marshes

AOG – Assembly of God church

atoll – low-lying island built up from successive deposits of coral on a submarine volcano peak and surrounding a central, often circular lagoon; because atolls are low lying, they lack soil depth and fresh water, usually offering only a marginal base for human habitation

back-loom – loom consisting of a few loose sticks and a hand-tied string needle; tension is provided by tying one stick to a tree or a wall and another to a loop around the weaver's waist; loincloths and bags are the most common products

bêche-de-mer – sea cucumber also known as trepang or seaslug; processing to remove toxins involves gutting, boiling for 1½ hours, washing and drying; bêches-de-mer are highly prized by Chinese cooks

bonito – blue-fin tuna

booby – gull-sized sea bird with a brown or blackish body and white head; usually lives in large colonies on tall, sea-girthed rocks

breadfruit – large, starchy fruit with a prickly green skin; it can be boiled, mashed, or fried like potato chips and is a popular food among Polynesians; the tree sap is used to treat sprains and bruises

bush knife – machete used for a range of tasks, such as building houses, cutting grass and opening coconuts

careen – to keel a ship over to one side so that barnacles can be removed from its hull

cargo cult – religious movement whose followers hope for the imminent and magical delivery of vast quantities of modern wealth and goods (ie cargo) through the generosity of supernatural forces or the inhabitants of faraway countries

cassava – edible, starch-yielding root; its young foliage is consumed as a green vegetable, though poison in the root, indicated by a bitter taste, has to be leached out first by cooking

cay – tiny coral island, or large sandbar, on which vegetation has begun to sprout

CEMA – Commodities Export Marketing Authority

CFC – Christian Fellowship Church

COM – Church of Melanesia, formerly known as the DOM (Diocese of Melanesia); belongs to the worldwide Anglican Church

copra – dried coconut kernels which are processed to make oil for margarine and soap

coral – rock-like structure composed of the dead, calcified remains of many generations of tiny sea creatures called coral polyps which live in huge colonies on top of existing submarine formations; the polyps cannot survive in cold or fresh water, or in murky or dark conditions

custom house – building where sacred art objects are stored; also refers to traditionally designed leaf houses built flush to the ground, as opposed to the more modern ones that are raised on stilts

custom ownership – traditionally acknowledged ownership of land, objects or reef, whether owned by individuals, families, clans or tribes; custom owners can refuse access to their property if they wish, and they expect to be asked permission before anyone crosses their land or uses anything considered by tradition to be theirs

cut-nut – common Solomons name for the Tahiti chestnut, a large relative of the *ngali* nut with a hard, brown outer shell and a firm, crisp-tasting, greyish-brown chestnut inside which is often eaten raw

DBSI – Development Bank of the Solomon Islands

district officer – title held by British Protectorate officials who were in charge of an area of the Solomons equivalent to a present-day province

edible fern – a fern-shaped vegetable which tastes like a mild form of spinach and is often flavoured with coconut cream; also called *kasume* or fern cabbage

expat – short for 'expatriate' and used to describe a foreigner (usually white) who is resident in the Solomons

fumarole – small volcanic or thermal fissure in the ground from which rise columns of steam, smoke or gas, or where naturally heated water bubbles up

GTS – Guadalcanal Travel Service

Hiti – a legendary race of small people from Rennell and Bellona islands who are believed to have skin as furry as a flying fox and hair that grows to the ground; they liked to play tricks and could disappear at will

HMAS – His (or Her) Majesty's Australian Ship; the term identifying a ship as an Australian warship

HMS – His (or Her) Majesty's Ship; the term identifying a ship as a British warship

IDC – Isabel Development Corporation

ISIC – International Student Identity Card

Kakamora – legendary race of small-statured, immensely strong people

kasume – see *edible fern*

kava – mud-coloured, mildly intoxicating drink made from the roots of the *Piper methysticum* plant; although drunk in nearby Vanuatu, it's no longer imbibed in the Solomons, except on rare ceremonial occasions on Tikopia and Anuta islands

kumara – another name for the sweet potato, which is eaten as a staple in the Solomons; although it filtered across the Pacific from South America to New Zealand and New Guinea prior to European

settlement, it was not grown in the Solomons until it was introduced by New Zealand missionaries in the 1860s

lagoon – area of water sealed off from the open ocean by a network of reefs or sand-bars

lava-lava – length of material that is wrapped around the waist; it's often worn by men in the outlying islands, especially where Polynesian influence is strongest

leaf house – standard village dwelling with a bamboo frame thatched with sago palm; nowadays most are raised up to a metre above ground, though traditional ones were most often flush to the ground; inside there are usually a number of raised platforms to sit and sleep on

legendary people – races such as the Kakamoras, Sinipi, Afukere, Hiti and Mongoes are traditionally believed to have lived in different parts of the Solomons; they are attributed with special powers such as exceptional strength

mangou – thin, dark-reddish-green vegetable shaped like a long pen and peeled before cooking

manioc – another name for *cassava*

marae – meeting place sacred to Polynesians, with temples, graveyards and ceremonial pitches for *tika-dart* throwing

matrilineal – relating to descent and/or inheritance through the female line

Mongoes – legendary race of people from Isabel Island who are more akin to fairies or leprechauns than to humans

MV – motor vessel

NBSI – National Bank of the Solomon Islands

NFD – National Fisheries Developments Ltd

ngali nut – bush almonds that are eaten raw as a snack or cooked in puddings

NGO – Non-Governmental Organization; organisations such as the Peace Corps, Voluntary Service Overseas (VSO) and the Red Cross

Nissen hut – British equivalent of a *Quonset hut*

NPF – National Provident Fund

pana – prickly form of *yam*

pandanus – palm-like plant with coiled, slender stems that grows mainly in marshy ground; the dried leaves are woven into very strong floor mats; also called screw pine

patrilineal – relating to descent and/or inheritance through the male line

pawpaw – tropical fruit with orange pulp and black seeds; also known as papaya

pelagic – living in the upper waters of the open sea

pole-and-line fishing – fishing method where large numbers of tuna are caught on feathered, hookless lures hanging by a short line from a pole held over the side of a trawler; the tuna are driven into a frenzy when live bait is thrown among them, and will strike at anything, including the 15 to 20 pole-and-line lures

Polynesian outliers – islands on the extreme fringes of the Solomons that are inhabited by Polynesians; they include small atolls and the largish uplifted coral landforms of Rennell and Bellona islands

pontoon – temporary floating jetty or bridge

PT boat – patrol torpedo boat (usually American) used in WWII

purse-seining – fishing with a large net which is draped around a school of fish and then closed like a purse around them

Quonset hut – military storage shed made from corrugated iron

reef – ridge of coral, rock or sand lying just below the sea's surface; called an onshore, or fringing, reef when it adjoins the shore, and an offshore reef when there is a stretch of open water between it and the land

RIPEL – Russell Islands Plantation Estates Ltd

roti – soft, unleavened bread, usually filled with curried fish, meat or vegetables

sago palm – A three to four-metre-high tree topped with stiff, glossy fronds which yields sago (a starchy cereal) from its trunk

SDA – Seventh Day Adventist church; members worship on Saturday and seldom do any work or conduct any business then

seabees – members of the US Construction Brigade (CB) in WWII

sennit – rope made from the fibrous husks, or outer casings, of mature coconuts

SIBC – Solomon Islands Broadcasting Corporation

Sinipi – a legendary race from Choiseul Island who are thought to live in caves and use shells as knives

slippery cabbage – spinach-like green vegetable with reddish streaks through it

SSEC – South Seas Evangelical Church

SSEM – South Seas Evangelical Mission; the *SSEC*'s predecessor

stamping drums – tall, hollow drums made of bamboo which are held in a vertical position while they are rhythmically and repeatedly beaten on the ground

tapa – cloth made from the bark of ebony, paper-mulberry or *breadfruit* trees; mainly worn by Polynesians, but also used by the people of a few Melanesian islands on ceremonial occasions; the bark is peeled off, beaten with wooden or stone mallets until white, and dried in the sun; it's often decorated with various traditional designs

taro – plant cultivated as a staple food all over the Pacific; young taro leaves are edible after cooking and taste like spinach, but old leaves, or any from a purple-stemmed plant, should not be eaten; the edible root of the swamp taro is grey and dull tasting, while the dry version is purplish and more pleasant, especially with coconut cream; called *dalo* (or *ndalo*) in Fiji and Papua New Guinea

tika dart – javelin-like bamboo dart with a narrow, ellipse-shaped tip made from heavy wood; tika-dart throwing is part of traditional Polynesian ceremonies on Tikopia

T-piece – small piece of cloth that covers the groin, leaving the abdomen exposed

trocchus – snail-like tropical sea creature whose shell is polished to make elegant ivory-coloured ornaments; until the emergence of plastic, most so-called pearl buttons were made of trocchus; sometimes called turban shell because of its 'wound-around' shape

USP – University of the South Pacific; its main campus is in Suva, Fiji, though there are annexes elsewhere, including one in the Kukum area of Honiara

USS – United States Ship; the term identifying a ship as a US warship

WWF – Worldwide Fund for Nature

yam – starchy tuber which is a Melanesian staple food; it ranges in length from 20 cm to over a metre and weighs up to 45 kg; can be pole-shaped (regarded as male by islanders) or have twin legs (ie female) and texture can vary from tender to crisp, depending on the species

Index

LONELY PLANET PHRASEBOOKS

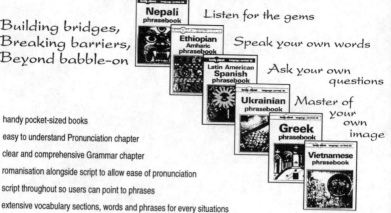

Building bridges,
Breaking barriers,
Beyond babble-on

Listen for the gems

Speak your own words

Ask your own questions

Master of your own image

- handy pocket-sized books
- easy to understand Pronunciation chapter
- clear and comprehensive Grammar chapter
- romanisation alongside script to allow ease of pronunciation
- script throughout so users can point to phrases
- extensive vocabulary sections, words and phrases for every situations
- full of cultural information and tips for the traveller

'...vital for a real DIY spirit and attitude in language learning' – Backpacker

'the phrasebooks have good cultural backgrounders and offer solid advice for challenging situations in remote locations' – San Francisco Examiner

'...they are unbeatable for their coverage of the world's more obscure languages' – The Geographical Magazine

---

Arabic (Egyptian)
Arabic (Moroccan)
Australia
  Australian English, Aboriginal and Torres Strait languages
Baltic States
  Estonian, Latvian, Lithuanian
Bengali
Burmese
Brazilian
Cantonese
Central Europe
  Czech, French, German, Hungarian, Italian and Slovak
Eastern Europe
  Bulgarian, Czech, Hungarian, Polish, Romanian and Slovak
Egyptian Arabic
Ethiopian (Amharic)
Fijian
Greek
Hindi/Urdu

Indonesian
Japanese
Korean
Lao
Latin American Spanish
Malay
Mandarin
Mediterranean Europe
  Albanian, Croatian, Greek, Italian, Macedonian, Maltese, Serbian, Slovene
Mongolian
Moroccan Arabic
Nepali
Papua New Guinea
Pilipino (Tagalog)
Quechua
Russian
Scandinavian Europe
  Danish, Finnish, Icelandic, Norwegian and Swedish

South-East Asia
  Burmese, Indonesian, Khmer, Lao, Malay, Tagalog (Pilipino), Thai and Vietnamese
Sri Lanka
Swahili
Thai
Thai Hill Tribes
Tibetan
Turkish
Ukrainian
USA
  US English, Vernacular Talk, Native American languages and Hawaiian
Vietnamese
Western Europe
  Basque, Catalan, Dutch, French, German, Irish, Italian, Portuguese, Scottish Gaelic, Spanish (Castilian) and Welsh

---

LONELY PLANET JOURNEYS

JOURNEYS is a unique collection of travel writing – published by the company that understands travel better than anyone else. It is a series for anyone who has ever experienced – or dreamed of – the magical moment when they encountered a strange culture or saw a place for the first time. They are tales to read while you're planning a trip, while you're on the road or while you're in an armchair, in front of a fire.

JOURNEYS books catch the spirit of a place, illuminate a culture, recount a crazy adventure, or introduce a fascinating way of life. They always entertain, and always enrich the experience of travel.

ISLANDS IN THE CLOUDS
Travels in the Highlands of New Guinea
Isabella Tree

Isabella Tree's remarkable journey takes us to the heart of the remote and beautiful Highlands of Papua New Guinea and Irian Jaya – one of the most extraordinary and dangerous regions on earth. Funny and tragic by turns, *Islands in the Clouds* is her moving story of the Highland people and the changes transforming their world.

Isabella Tree, who lives in England, has worked as a freelance journalist on a variety of newspapers and magazines, including a stint as senior travel correspondent for the *Evening Standard*. A fellow of the Royal Geographical Society, she has also written a biography of the Victorian ornithologist John Gould.

'One of the most accomplished travel writers to appear on the horizon for many years . . . the dialogue is brilliant' – Eric Newby

---

SEAN & DAVID'S LONG DRIVE
Sean Condon

Sean Condon is young, urban and a connoisseur of hair wax. He can't drive, and he doesn't really travel well. So when Sean and his friend David set out to explore Australia in a 1966 Ford Falcon, the result is a decidedly offbeat look at life on the road. Over 14,000 death-defying kilometres, our heroes check out the re-runs on tv, get fabulously drunk, listen to Neil Young cassettes and wonder why they ever left home.

Sean Condon lives in Melbourne. He played drums in several mediocre bands until he found his way into advertising and an above-average band called Boilersuit. *Sean & David's Long Drive* is his first book.

'Funny, pithy, kitsch and surreal . . . This book will do for Australia what Chernobyl did for Kiev, but hey you'll laugh as the stereotypes go boom'
– Time Out

LONELY PLANET TRAVEL ATLASES

Lonely Planet has long been famous for the number and quality of its guidebook maps. Now we've gone one step further and in conjunction with Steinhart Katzir Publishers produced a handy companion series: Lonely Planet travel atlases – maps of a country produced in book form.

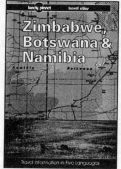

Unlike other maps, which look good but lead travellers astray, our travel atlases have been researched on the road by Lonely Planet's experienced team of writers. All details are carefully checked to ensure the atlas corresponds with the equivalent Lonely Planet guidebook.

The handy atlas format means no holes, wrinkles, torn sections or constant folding and unfolding. These atlases can survive long periods on the road, unlike cumbersome fold-out maps. The comprehensive index ensures easy reference.

- full-colour throughout
- maps researched and checked by Lonely Planet authors
- place names correspond with Lonely Planet guidebooks
  – no confusing spelling differences
- legend and travelling information in English, French, German, Japanese and Spanish
- size: 230 x 160 mm

Available now:
Chile & Easter Island • Egypt • India & Bangladesh • Israel & the Palestinian Territories •Jordan, Syria & Lebanon • Kenya • Laos • Portugal • South Africa, Lesotho & Swaziland • Thailand • Vietnam • Zimbabwe, Botswana & Namibia

---

LONELY PLANET TV SERIES & VIDEOS

Lonely Planet travel guides have been brought to life on television screens around the world. Like our guides, the programmes are based on the joy of independent travel, and look honestly at some of the most exciting, picturesque and frustrating places in the world. Each show is presented by one of three travellers from Australia, England or the USA and combines an innovative mixture of video, Super-8 film, atmospheric soundscapes and original music.

Videos of each episode – containing additional footage not shown on television – are available from good book and video shops, but the availability of individual videos varies with regional screening schedules.

Video destinations include: Alaska • American Rockies • Australia – The South-East • Baja California & the Copper Canyon • Brazil • Central Asia • Chile & Easter Island • Corsica, Sicily & Sardinia – The Mediterranean Islands • East Africa (Tanzania & Zanzibar) • Ecuador & the Galapagos Islands • Greenland & Iceland • Indonesia • Israel & the Sinai Desert • Jamaica • Japan • La Ruta Maya • Morocco • New York • North India • Pacific Islands (Fiji, Solomon Islands & Vanuatu) • South India • South West China • Turkey • Vietnam • West Africa • Zimbabwe, Botswana & Namibia

The Lonely Planet TV series is produced by:
Pilot Productions
The Old Studio
18 Middle Row
London W10 5AT UK

For video availability and ordering information contact your nearest Lonely Planet office.

Music from the TV series is available on CD & cassette.

PLANET TALK

Lonely Planet's FREE quarterly newsletter

We love hearing from you and think you'd like to hear from us.

When...is the right time to see reindeer in Finland?
Where...can you hear the best palm-wine music in Ghana?
How...do you get from Asunción to Areguá by steam train?
What...is the best way to see India?

For the answer to these and many other questions read PLANET TALK.

Every issue is packed with up-to-date travel news and advice including:

* a letter from Lonely Planet co-founders Tony and Maureen Wheeler
* go behind the scenes on the road with a Lonely Planet author
* feature article on an important and topical travel issue
* a selection of recent letters from travellers
* details on forthcoming Lonely Planet promotions
* complete list of Lonely Planet products

To join our mailing list contact any Lonely Planet office.

Also available: Lonely Planet T-shirts. 100% heavyweight cotton.

LONELY PLANET ONLINE

Get the latest travel information before you leave or while you're on the road

Whether you've just begun planning your next trip, or you're chasing down specific info on currency regulations or visa requirements, check out Lonely Planet Online for up-to-the minute travel information.

As well as travel profiles of your favourite destinations (including maps and photos), you'll find current reports from our researchers and other travellers, updates on health and visas, travel advisories, and discussion of the ecological and political issues you need to be aware of as you travel.

There's also an online travellers' forum where you can share your experience of life on the road, meet travel companions and ask other travellers for their recommendations and advice. We also have plenty of links to other online sites useful to independent travellers.

And of course we have a complete and up-to-date list of all Lonely Planet travel products including guides, phrasebooks, atlases, Journeys and videos and a simple online ordering facility if you can't find the book you want elsewhere.

www.lonelyplanet.com
or
AOL keyword: lp

LONELY PLANET PRODUCTS

Lonely Planet is known worldwide for publishing practical, reliable and no-nonsense travel information in our guides and on our web site. The Lonely Planet list covers just about every accessible part of the world. Currently there are eight series: *travel guides, shoestring guides, walking guides, city guides, phrasebooks, audio packs, travel atlases* and *Journeys* – a unique collection of travel writing.

EUROPE

Amsterdam • Austria • Baltic States & Kaliningrad • Baltic States phrasebook • Britain • Central Europe on a shoestring • Central Europe phrasebook • Czech & Slovak Republics • Denmark • Dublin • Eastern Europe on a shoestring • Eastern Europe phrasebook • Finland • France • Greece • Greek phrasebook • Hungary • Iceland, Greenland & the Faroe Islands • Ireland • Italy • Mediterranean Europe on a shoestring • Mediterranean Europe phrasebook • Paris • Poland • Portugal • Portugal travel atlas • Prague • Russia, Ukraine & Belarus • Russian phrasebook • Scandinavian & Baltic Europe on a shoestring • Scandinavian Europe phrasebook • Slovenia • Spain • St Petersburg • Switzerland • Trekking in Greece • Trekking in Spain • Ukrainian phrasebook • Vienna • Walking in Britain • Walking in Switzerland • Western Europe on a shoestring • Western Europe phrasebook

NORTH AMERICA

Alaska • Backpacking in Alaska • Baja California • California & Nevada • Canada • Florida • Hawaii • Honolulu • Los Angeles • Mexico • Miami • New England • New Orleans • New York, New Jersey & Pennsylvania • Pacific Northwest USA • Rocky Mountain States • San Francisco • Southwest USA • USA phrasebook • Washington, DC & the Capital Region

CENTRAL AMERICA & THE CARIBBEAN

Bermuda • Central America on a shoestring • Costa Rica • Cuba • Eastern Caribbean • Guatemala, Belize & Yucatán: La Ruta Maya • Jamaica

SOUTH AMERICA

Argentina, Uruguay & Paraguay • Bolivia • Brazil • Brazilian phrasebook • Buenos Aires • Chile & Easter Island • Chile & Easter Island travel atlas • Colombia • Ecuador & the Galápagos Islands • Latin American Spanish phrasebook • Peru • Quechua phrasebook • Rio de Janeiro • South America on a shoestring • Trekking in the Patagonian Andes • Venezuela

Travel Literature: Full Circle: A South American Journey

ANTARCTICA

Antarctica

ISLANDS OF THE INDIAN OCEAN

Madagascar & Comoros • Maldives & Islands of the East Indian Ocean • Mauritius, Réunion & Seychelles

AFRICA

Arabic (Moroccan) phrasebook • Africa on a shoestring • Cape Town • Central Africa • East Africa • Egypt • Egypt travel atlas • Ethiopian (Amharic) phrasebook • Kenya • Kenya travel atlas • Malawi, Mozambique & Zambia • Morocco • North Africa • South Africa, Lesotho & Swaziland • South Africa, Lesotho & Swaziland travel atlas • Swahili phrasebook • Trekking in East Africa • West Africa • Zimbabwe, Botswana & Namibia • Zimbabwe, Botswana & Namibia travel atlas

Travel Literature: The Rainbird: A Central African Journey • Songs to an African Sunset: A Zimbabwean Story

MAIL ORDER

Lonely Planet products are distributed worldwide. They are also available by mail order from Lonely Planet, so if you have difficulty finding a title please write to us. North American and South American residents should write to Embarcadero West, 155 Filbert St, Suite 251, Oakland CA 94607, USA; European and African residents should write to 10 Barley Mow Passage, Chiswick, London W4 4PH; and residents of other countries to PO Box 617, Hawthorn, Victoria 3122, Australia.

NORTH-EAST ASIA

Beijing • Cantonese phrasebook • China • Hong Kong, Macau & Guangzhou • Hong Kong • Japan • Japanese phrasebook • Japanese audio pack • Korea • Korean phrasebook • Mandarin phrasebook • Mongolia • Mongolian phrasebook • North-East Asia on a shoestring • Seoul • Taiwan • Tibet • Tibet phrasebook • Tokyo

Travel Literature: Lost Japan

MIDDLE EAST & CENTRAL ASIA

Arab Gulf States • Arabic (Egyptian) phrasebook • Central Asia • Iran • Israel & the Palestinian Territories • Israel & the Palestinian Territories travel atlas • Istanbul • Jerusalem • Jordan & Syria • Jordan, Syria & Lebanon travel atlas • Middle East • Turkey • Turkish phrasebook • Yemen

Travel Literature: The Gates of Damascus • Kingdom of the Film Stars: Journey into Jordan

ALSO AVAILABLE:

Travel with Children • Traveller's Tales

INDIAN SUBCONTINENT

Bangladesh • Bengali phrasebook • Delhi • Hindi/Urdu phrasebook • India • India & Bangladesh travel atlas • Indian Himalaya • Karakoram Highway • Nepal • Nepali phrasebook • Pakistan • Rajasthan • Sri Lanka • Sri Lanka phrasebook • Trekking in the Indian Himalaya • Trekking in the Karakoram & Hindukush • Trekking in the Nepal Himalaya

Travel Literature: In Rajasthan • Shopping for Buddhas

SOUTH-EAST ASIA

Bali & Lombok • Bangkok • Burmese phrasebook • Cambodia • Ho Chi Minh City • Indonesia • Indonesian phrasebook • Indonesian audio pack • Jakarta • Java • Laos • Lao phrasebook • Laos travel atlas • Malay phrasebook • Malaysia, Singapore & Brunei • Myanmar (Burma) • Philippines • Pilipino phrasebook • Singapore • South-East Asia on a shoestring • South-East Asia phrasebook • Thailand • Thailand travel atlas • Thai phrasebook • Thai audio pack • Thai Hill Tribes phrasebook • Vietnam • Vietnamese phrasebook • Vietnam travel atlas

AUSTRALIA & THE PACIFIC

Australia • Australian phrasebook • Bushwalking in Australia • Bushwalking in Papua New Guinea • Fiji • Fijian phrasebook • Islands of Australia's Great Barrier Reef • Melbourne • Micronesia • New Caledonia • New South Wales & the ACT • New Zealand • Northern Territory • Outback Australia • Papua New Guinea • Papua New Guinea phrasebook • Queensland • Rarotonga & the Cook Islands • Samoa • Solomon Islands • South Australia • Sydney • Tahiti & French Polynesia • Tasmania • Tonga • Tramping in New Zealand • Vanuatu • Victoria • Western Australia

Travel Literature: Islands in the Clouds • Sean & David's Long Drive

THE LONELY PLANET STORY

Lonely Planet published its first book in 1973 in response to the numerous 'How did you do it?' questions Maureen and Tony Wheeler were asked after driving, bussing, hitching, sailing and railing their way from England to Australia.

Written at a kitchen table and hand collated, trimmed and stapled, *Across Asia on the Cheap* became an instant local bestseller, inspiring thoughts of another book.

Eighteen months in South-East Asia resulted in their second guide, *South-East Asia on a shoestring*, which they put together in a backstreet Chinese hotel in Singapore in 1975. The 'yellow bible', as it quickly became known to backpackers around the world, soon became *the* guide to the region. It has sold well over half a million copies and is now in its 9th edition, still retaining its familiar yellow cover.

Today there are over 240 titles, including travel guides, walking guides, language kits & phrasebooks, travel atlases and travel literature. The company is the largest independent travel publisher in the world. Although Lonely Planet initially specialised in guides to Asia, today there are few corners of the globe that have not been covered.

The emphasis continues to be on travel for independent travellers. Tony and Maureen still travel for several months of each year and play an active part in the writing, updating and quality control of Lonely Planet's guides.

They have been joined by over 70 authors and 170 staff at our offices in Melbourne (Australia), Oakland (USA), London (UK) and Paris (France). Travellers themselves also make a valuable contribution to the guides through the feedback we receive in thousands of letters each year and on our web site.

The people at Lonely Planet strongly believe that travellers can make a positive contribution to the countries they visit, both through their appreciation of the countries' culture, wildlife and natural features, and through the money they spend. In addition, the company makes a direct contribution to the countries and regions it covers. Since 1986 a percentage of the income from each book has been donated to ventures such as famine relief in Africa; aid projects in India; agricultural projects in Central America; Greenpeace's efforts to halt French nuclear testing in the Pacific; and Amnesty International.

'I hope we send people out with the right attitude about travel. You realise when you travel that there are so many different perspectives about the world, so we hope these books will make people more interested in what they see. Guidebooks can't really guide people. All you can do is point them in the right direction.'

– Tony Wheeler

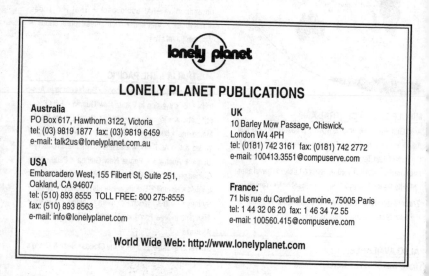

LONELY PLANET PUBLICATIONS

Australia
PO Box 617, Hawthorn 3122, Victoria
tel: (03) 9819 1877 fax: (03) 9819 6459
e-mail: talk2us@lonelyplanet.com.au

USA
Embarcadero West, 155 Filbert St, Suite 251,
Oakland, CA 94607
tel: (510) 893 8555 TOLL FREE: 800 275-8555
fax: (510) 893 8563
e-mail: info@lonelyplanet.com

UK
10 Barley Mow Passage, Chiswick,
London W4 4PH
tel: (0181) 742 3161 fax: (0181) 742 2772
e-mail: 100413.3551@compuserve.com

France:
71 bis rue du Cardinal Lemoine, 75005 Paris
tel: 1 44 32 06 20 fax: 1 46 34 72 55
e-mail: 100560.415@compuserve.com

World Wide Web: http://www.lonelyplanet.com